CW01370778

Queen
AS IT BEGAN

Queen
AS IT BEGAN

AUTHORISED AND REVISED EDITION
JACKY SMITH & JIM JENKINS

OMNIBUS PRESS
London / New York / Paris / Sydney / Copenhagen / Berlin / Madrid / Tokyo

Original edition © 1992 Jacky Gunn and Jim Jenkins
This edition © 2022 Omnibus Press
(A division of the Wise Music Group
14–15 Berners Street, London, W1T 3LJ)

Cover designed by Ruth Keating
Picture research by the authors, with thanks to the Queen Photographic Archive

ISBN 978-1-913172-63-3

Jacky Smith and Jim Jenkins hereby assert their right to
be identified as the authors of this work in accordance with
Sections 77 to 78 of the Copyright, Designs and Patents Act 1988.

All rights reserved. No part of this book may be reproduced in any form
or by any electronic or mechanical means, including information storage or
retrieval systems, without permission in writing from the publisher,
except by a reviewer who may quote brief passages.

Every effort has been made to trace the copyright holders of the
photographs in this book but one or two were unreachable. We would
be grateful if the photographers concerned would contact us.

A catalogue record for this book is available from the British Library.

Typeset in Bembo by Palimpsest Book Production Ltd, Falkirk, Stirlingshire

Printed in the Czech Republic

www.omnibuspress.com

This book is dedicated to Queen fans everywhere, and FM . . . wherever you may be.

CONTENTS

FOREWORD by Brian May   ix

CHAPTER 1 Dr Brian Harold May CBE, PhD, FRAS   1

CHAPTER 2 Roger Meddows Taylor OBE, BSc (Hons)   16

CHAPTER 3 The Smile Era   26

CHAPTER 4 Freddie Mercury Dip. A.D.   37

CHAPTER 5 As It Began   55

CHAPTER 6 John Richard Deacon BSc (Hons)(1st Class)   65

CHAPTER 7 The Trident Years   72

CHAPTER 8 Conquering Japan   124

CHAPTER 9 The John Reid Epoch   128

CHAPTER 10 Financial Independence   152

CHAPTER 11 Crazy Ideas   169

CHAPTER 12 Triumph Over America   179

CHAPTER 13 South America Bites the Dust   185

CHAPTER 14 A Change of Direction   194

CHAPTER 15 A Classic Collection   201

CHAPTER 16 Going Solo   215

CHAPTER 17 Back into Action   222

CHAPTER 18 Controversy Reigns   235

CHAPTER 19 From Rio to History   243

CHAPTER 20 Live Aid   251

CHAPTER 21 A Magic Year   259

CHAPTER 22 Barcelona or Bust   277

CHAPTER 23 A Different Perspective   287

CHAPTER 24 Personal Turmoil   293

CHAPTER 25 The Miracle   304

CHAPTER 26 Twenty-first Celebrations   319

CHAPTER 27 So Sad It Ends   330

CHAPTER 28 Tribute   336

CHAPTER 29 Moving On   352

CHAPTER 30 Made in Heaven   360

CHAPTER 31 Onwards   371

ACKNOWLEDGEMENTS   379

INDEX   381

FOREWORD

BY
BRIAN MAY

THIS BOOK IS A UNIQUE DOCUMENT. *QUEEN: AS IT BEGAN* IS A PROJECT started many years ago by two people who have been well able to observe in some detail, though from two slightly different viewpoints, the inner workings of the band over much of our history.

Jacky Smith has now, amazingly, presided over the Queen Fan Club for over thirty years. Since the first publication of this book, Jacky has led the fan club into autonomy and provided Queen fans all over the world with a unique channel of contact with us, the band members. The Queen Fan Club has actually broken all records for fan clubs worldwide, and continues to be strong to this day. Jim Jenkins is an 'independent', perhaps archetypal, 'superfan'. Jim has accumulated a huge body of information about the band's activities from the very beginning and continues to be recognised amongst fans as a leading authority on the Queen catalogue. Many of his articles have been published in collectors' magazines.

The book is an independent view of a sequence of events, many of which, even to us, are now becoming a blur, as everything happened so fast. This is the first serious attempt to log the developments, internal and external, which over twenty years took us from Kensington Market to Wembley Stadium and beyond. We, the band, have not attempted to control or censor what is written in these pages, but have responded to the authors' questions alongside the many other contributors whom Jacky and Jim have interviewed.

Current activity for Queen as it has become in the 21st century is very strong. So even this, it seems, is not the end of the story. But this new substantially updated version will be a source of much pleasure to anyone who has an interest in the inside story of the making of that unusual phenomenon known as Queen.

Brian May
September 2021

CHAPTER 1

DR BRIAN HAROLD MAY

CBE, PHD, FRAS

BRIAN HAROLD MAY WAS BORN ON SATURDAY 19 JULY 1947 AT THE Gloucester House Nursing Home, Hampton, Middlesex, to Harold and Ruth May. Harold May was an electronics engineer and worked as a senior draughtsman for the Ministry of Aviation. He was a practical man, who enjoyed making things – from furniture to toys and models – and was also a capable musician, proficient on piano and ukulele.

At the age of five Brian graduated from Cardinal Road Infants' School to Hanworth Road Primary School in Feltham, Middlesex. He liked music, often singing and dancing to the radio, so his parents booked him piano lessons. Brian hated those lessons – he had to practise on Saturdays when he would rather have been out playing.

Brian took after his father in his dexterity, always making models and toys. He was also an avid collector, as Ruth May recalls, 'He collected anything! He had collections of Eagle comics, cheese labels, puzzles and matchbox tops – among other things.'

When Brian was six, Harold decided his son was old enough to learn to play the ukulele. Brian showed amazing aptitude and soon wanted a guitar. So, for his seventh birthday, his parents bought him a small Spanish acoustic. From the chords he had learned on the ukulele he began to teach himself to play the guitar but found that the Spanish was too big for him to handle easily, and that its strings were too high off the fingerboard. He also wanted an 'electric' sound, so set about altering the instrument. Like his father, Brian was good with his hands and with Harold's help, he began by carving down its wooden bridge. This meant the strings were closer to the fingerboard and therefore easier to play. Then, to improve the sound, he made a pickup by winding copper wire around three small button magnets; it worked well. He fixed the pickups onto the guitar and had an acoustic Spanish guitar that sounded electric. He plugged it into the amplifier of the family 'wireless', which Harold had made.

When he was eight Brian began to play other instruments, such as the Jew's harp and tin whistle. He also showed an early interest in astronomy and photography; his father was a keen photographer, always involving his son in the developing and printing of his pictures, and Brian was given a camera of his own. He and his father also built a small telescope, which Brian even took on holiday. He spent many evenings in Sidmouth studying the stars – the clear air and lack of streetlights made them easier to see than on the outskirts of London.

Like most children, Brian had a vivid imagination. As a child he was frightened by a wooden chair in his bedroom: he told his mother it had a face and arms and was watching him. Not surprisingly, as he grew older one of his favourite books featured walking, talking trees, wizards, wraiths and little men with hairy feet: Tolkien's *The Lord of the Rings*. 'But this wasn't my absolute favourite,' says Brian. 'The best was *Out of the Silent Planet* by C. S. Lewis.'

In his free time Brian listened to records constantly: Lonnie Donegan, Johnny Duncan, Tommy Steele, The Everly Brothers and

Buddy Holly. He recalls: 'The first time I ever heard The Crickets, I was hooked. Their harmonies, just the sheer atmosphere they created. I wanted desperately to be able to make music like that.' He also had crushes on Connie Francis and Brenda Lee, whose records featured prominently on his playlist.

Brian stored his records in special boxes, filed and indexed. (As he was an only child, he didn't have the problem of meddling brothers or sisters playing with his precious collection – a collection, in pristine condition, that he still treasures.) He played along to them, gradually moving on from chords to single notes and then short, improvised solos. The music of the late fifties was very guitar-oriented, and Brian gained abundant inspiration from it. 'I would listen to the songs and want to know everything – how the harmonies worked, why they worked, what made one harmony affect you in a certain way.' He dissected each song as if it were a 'key chain' puzzle. These came in a number of shapes and the challenge was to take them apart and then reassemble them. Brian had several of these games and would time himself at putting them together after they had all been mixed up in a pile.

Although he hated his piano lessons, he persevered with them and by the age of nine he had progressed to Grade IV, passing both the theory and the practical exams. Then he gave up. His parents had an upright piano at home, and now that he was no longer being told to practise, he found he enjoyed playing. He even composed odd ditties and tunes, occasionally accompanied by his father on ukulele. Once, asked to write a tune for a school project, he wrote down one of his favourites, 'Happy Birthday To You' – played backwards. 'I wondered if the music master would notice,' he said. He didn't! At family parties he was usually called upon to play something on guitar or piano; being shy it was a task he tried, in vain, to wriggle out of.

In 1958, aged eleven, Brian passed the scholarship exam to attend Hampton Grammar School, in Hampton, Middlesex. This was in keeping with the family tradition, as his father had also gone there (and some years later, Brian's own son was to become a pupil). Brian's keen interest in music endured, although he didn't study it formally. He continued to look ahead to a career in astronomy and followed subjects that would help him towards this goal.

He played his guitar as much as he could in his free time and was often found sitting amid a circle of admiring school friends, playing songs such as Guy Mitchell's 'Singing The Blues'. A number of other guitarists were at Hampton, and they all met up at lunchtimes to swap ideas and play together. Classmate Dave Dilloway wanted to learn how to play guitar and asked Brian to teach him, to which Brian readily agreed.

'Those lessons took place at the back of our German class,' Dave remembered. 'I used to tape a paper fingerboard to my wrist, to simulate a guitar neck. Needless to say, Brian went on to pass his German O-level, I didn't!'

Brian was fast finding that his own acoustic guitar was inadequate for the music he was listening to and trying to emulate. Money was short at the time and wouldn't stretch to the new electric guitars such as Gibsons and Stratocasters that some of his school friends had, or to the Colorama belonging to his friend John Garnham, which Brian coveted. But, ever resourceful, he and his father hit upon the perfect solution: they would build a guitar to Brian's own specifications. Brian had played his friends' guitars and had a definite idea of what he was looking for and the sound he wanted to achieve. A small bedroom in the family house in Feltham was converted into a workshop and in August 1963 work began.

The first problem was the wood for the neck. This was solved by a family friend, who happened to be throwing out a solid mahogany fireplace and Brian began the laborious job of carving it into shape by hand; the wood was old and featured several woodworm holes. The body was made from a piece of oak, which was as hard as steel, blockboard and other odds and ends of wood that he and his father found. At one point, during work on the body, the chisel slipped and gouged a chunk out of it – Brian got so frustrated he threw the whole thing out of the window and started again. The tools they were using were also handmade, with the addition of penknives and a sanding block. When the neck was finally carved to Brian's satisfaction it was fitted into the body and bolted and screwed into place; a strong 'truss rod' was incorporated to keep the neck straight.

Brian went through his mother's button box for old pearl buttons to use as the fret markers but bought the fret wire, as he couldn't find a suitable substitute; he used a specially made jig to cut the wire down to the low profile he wanted. Once the body was complete, there was then the problem of the pickups and the tremolo arm – both essential parts of the instrument. The pickups Brian wound himself, with wire and magnets, as he had done for his first guitar, but the result was less than satisfactory so he resorted to buying a set of Burns pickups at three guineas each. He adapted them by filling them with epoxy resin to stop them being microphonic. The tremolo arm was made from a piece of mild steel, hand carved, rocking on the blade of a case-hardened steel knife edge, and the pull of the strings was balanced against two motorbike valve springs.

Before it was finished Brian took the guitar to school. He remembers being apprehensive as it didn't look as good as the commercially available models. But he was determined to complete it, and when it was finished, smoothed and varnished, it looked professional, and Brian was rightly proud of it. When he took it to school again his friends were impressed; one even offered to swap his own shop-bought electric guitar for it. Brian declined the offer – his unique instrument had taken him eighteen months' hard work and cost just £8 to make (plus £9-9s for the pickups). He wasn't swapping it for anything in the world! The guitar became known as the Red Special, or, less respectfully, The Fireplace, and fifteen years later Brian's bodyguard Tunbridge called it simply The Chap.

When Brian began to learn the intricacies of playing his unusual guitar, he was looking for a certain sound. He tried no end of plectrums – hard, soft, rounded, oval – but nothing gave him the sound he wanted. Then he tried coins and, after much experimenting he found the best was an ordinary sixpenny piece: it was small enough to hold easily, and he could use it in different ways. If he played it straight against the strings he achieved a hard but clean sound; if he hit the strings using the serrated edge, he got a harsh, grating sound. Now Brian began to concentrate on improving his playing technique.

Schoolwork and study came easily to Brian, and he worked hard. He was a well-respected and popular character with pupils and masters alike. He still loathed most sport, but liked swimming, and even swam once for the school – though he didn't win. He was an active member of the debating team and won a local Debating Society competition. Public speaking wasn't something he found easy – he was rather reserved – and he joined the debating team to try to gain confidence in himself, which he felt would be an asset in the future.

But he always made ample time for his music. Dave Dilloway says: 'We used to set up two tape recorders – I would play lead guitar, not too well I might add, into one, and Brian would play the chords. Then we would play back those two tracks, and over them Brian would play my cheap and nasty homemade bass guitar, and I would hit anything within reach – hat boxes and the like – as drums. Sometimes Brian would even add some vocals.'

It was crude and amateur, but they had fun. As Brian taught Dave more sophisticated chords, they were able to experiment further with Brian playing fast lead guitar, demonstrating his skill. A great spur at school was Pete 'Woolly' Hammerton. Says Brian, 'Woolly had a wonderful technique, even in those early days, and the fierce competition between us brought us on very fast. He later played with the local school group, The Others.'

During the summer of 1964, seventeen-year-old Brian attempted various jobs to fill time and earn money. One of those jobs was stamping out windscreen wiper blades ('mind crippling', he said) and another was booking out wages in a fire extinguisher factory.

Brian and Dave were regularly attending The Others' concerts around Hampton, which prompted them to form their own band. It started out with Brian on lead guitar, Dave on bass, Bill Richards on lead vocals and another classmate, John Sanger, on piano. The piano was useful when the band rehearsed songs such as 'Go Now', which The Moody Blues had just released. But Bill was playing with a rather cheap guitar – and Brian was the one who had to tell him, tactfully, that if he didn't get a better guitar he would have to leave. He couldn't – so he left! Bill commented, 'to be honest, I think Brian was even more tactful by underplaying the problem with the vocals, which weren't right at the time – although he was kind enough to say much later that I'd sorted it out.'

The band were then joined by their friend Malcolm Childs on guitar. They played together once or twice, but Malcolm proved unreliable and his place was taken by another school friend, John Garnham. John was allowed into the band partly because he had his own guitar, amplifier, microphone stands and microphones, but he was also the only member with previous live experience.

But none of them knew a drummer. An advertisement was placed in the window of the local music shop – Albert's in Twickenham. The first (and only) applicant was one Richard Thompson, so they took him on. One night the band were at a local dance at the Murray Park Hall in Whitton, watching the group Chris and The Whirlwinds. At the back of the hall stood a chap from Hampton School, playing harmonica and singing along – Tim Staffell. They introduced themselves and asked him to join the band. Tim at that time was a member of The Railroaders, but decided to leave and became the band's vocalist and harmonica player. Brian and Tim found they also shared an interest in the *Eagle* comic's hero, Dan Dare, or more specifically illustrator Frank Hampson.

The group wondered what to call this new venture, and almost settled on Bod Chappy and The Beetles, derived from words used by a teacher at the school to refer to people (bods), to address his pupils (chappy), and to describe a style of walking (beetling). 'We also considered The Mind Boggles,' says Brian, but finally settled on 1984. They had all read George Orwell's dystopian novel and were interested in science fiction and the name had, at the time, a futuristic ring.

The band started to rehearse regularly in Chase Bridge Primary School hall, next door to Twickenham Rugby Ground. It was close enough to Dave Dilloway's house for him to cycle there. He had a small trailer, which he attached to the back of his bike, loaded with his bass guitar and a massive amp. John Garnham, who was slightly older, had a bubble-car and would arrive at rehearsals with the microphone stands sticking out of the roof. They used the hall by courtesy of the local council. In a moment of inspiration, the council had decided that the local kids needed encouragement in their musical endeavours (it kept what they liked to call the 'yobbos' off the streets) and provided local halls and rooms free of charge for rehearsals.

Once, the band were told that the rugby club next door was playing host to a huge delegation of Jehovah's Witnesses, and were asked to keep the noise down. Could they ever! They opened all the windows in the school hall, turned up all the instruments and amps as loud as possible, and waited for the Jehovah's Witnesses to go quiet, signalling prayer. They then let loose their full sound . . .

During these rehearsals they got to know each other better as musicians and became closer as a band, and on 28 October 1964 they played their first gig in public, at St Mary's Church Hall in Twickenham. 'We all wore stuff that looked like army uniforms – we wanted a regimented look for some reason,' said Tim Staffell. 'It was such a small gig too, but we were so confident. We went down pretty well.'

Their second gig was a few weeks later, at Richmond County School for Girls. John Garnham, Brian and Tim all had girlfriends there, which is how they got to play it. That second gig was the last for John Sanger, as he was leaving to go to Leeds University.

At Hampton School, Brian was an active member of the amateur dramatics society, taking part in several of their productions. As it was a boys' school, the pupils had to take the male and female parts, and Brian's first female role was as Lydia Languish in Richard Brinsley Sheridan's *The Rivals*. He must have been good at female impersonation because he was subsequently asked to play the Lady Mary Lasenby in J. M. Barrie's *The Admirable Crichton*. The school also had a choir, of which Brian became a member.

He left school in 1965 at the age of eighteen, with ten O-levels – English Literature, English Language, French, German, Latin, Maths, Further Maths, Physics, Chemistry and Use of English, and four A-levels in Pure Maths, Applied Maths, Additional Maths and Physics. He applied to study at Imperial College, London.

As for music, Brian and 1984 went in one direction – rock'n'pop – while Bill Richards started writing songs and went in quite another, namely folk rock. He formed The Left-Handed Marriage in the summer of 1965, not with Hampton Grammar students, but with friends he had known since primary school

> *MIDDX. CHRON. 19.2.65*
> ## Scholarship awards
> Two Hampton Grammar schoolboys have been awarded open scholarships.
>
> Keith Taylor, aged 17, of 31 New Road, Bedfont, has been awarded a scholarship in mathematics of £100 per annum at the London School of Economics.
>
> Brian May, also 17, of 6 Walsham Road, Feltham, has been awarded a scholarship in physics of £75 per annum at the Imperial College of Science and Technology.
>
> In addition to his high standard in science, Brian has also done well in the school dramatic society taking a principal part in school productions. He is at present secretary of the Schools' Debating Society.

– namely Jenny Hill and Henry Deval on vocals, Peter Trout on drums, John Frankel on bass and piano and Terry Goulds on flute and vocals.

Brian entered Imperial in the autumn of 1965 to study physics and infrared astronomy, with a view to becoming an astronomer. His studies were based on interferometry, which involved looking at dust in the solar system. The only way of finding out about the dust was to look at light reflecting off it. This meant that, using a spectrometer, it was possible to see how fast the dust was moving and what it was actually made of. Although he was in London and Dave Dilloway was at Southampton University, 1984 continued to play small gigs, such as the Putney Boat Club, the Feltham R&B Club and the Molesey Boat Club. They rehearsed as much as possible between performances, when college work permitted. Gigs were infrequent during their first year, mainly because of the pressures of studying, but at the end of 1965, Dave Dilloway failed his exams at Southampton, enrolled at a local technical college to complete his degree and was able to devote more time to the band.

At some gigs they were requested to play from 7 p.m. until 1 a.m., covering as many as fifty songs. At one in Henley, they told the audience not to applaud but to throw money. They did, and the band collected another much needed £2. 'All our gear broke down one night,' recalls drummer Richard Thompson. 'The audience were getting restless, so I played a non-stop, half-hour drum solo to fill the gap until the equipment was fixed. I earned an extra ten bob for that!'

Brian's parents were keen to follow his progress and regularly attended 1984's bookings. Harold May used to transport the band and their equipment to many of the gigs in his Javelin car, as John's bubble-car was far too small to carry it all.

'The Happy Hendricks Polka', a minor hit at that time for Scandinavian band The Spotniks, included a very fast guitar passage, which Brian played during a gig at the Molesey Boat Club – much to the audience's amazement. An intrigued member of the crowd was heard to comment, 'Wow, his fingers look blurred they're going so fast!' It was only later that Brian found out that the guitar solo on the record had been played much more slowly and speeded up during the mixing.

In January 1967, Bill Richards and The Left-Handed Marriage made their debut album *On The Right Side Of Left-Handed Marriage*. A music publisher began to show interest in some of the songs, and an employee of the company, Brian Henderson (who was also a member of the 'original' Nirvana, an English pop rock band formed in 1965), persuaded them to consider recording several of their songs to offer to bands or singers looking for material. They signed a twelve-month contract, but Bill thought the sounds would be too 'thin' to interest other artists. He contacted Brian, who was living at that time in Belmont Grove, Chiswick, and sent him a tape of the songs.

Brian replied to Bill in March 1967, to say he liked the tape and hoped he would be favoured with 'connubial bliss'! Brian tried to persuade 1984 to cover a couple of Bill's songs, including the track 'A Little Less'. It never happened, but Brian did agree to help them on their next project, with the understanding it didn't interfere with his commitment to 1984.

On 4 April 1967, Brian and The Left-Handed Marriage went into AMC Studios in Manor Road, Twickenham, a small studio which was run by someone who had worked for EMI. They recorded 'Give Me Time' (the title was later changed to 'I Need Time' because someone else had released a song with the original title), 'She Was Once My Friend', 'Sugar Lump Girl' and 'Yours Sincerely'.

Brian and Dave Dilloway again joined The Left-Handed Marriage, this time at Abbey Road Studios, on 28 June 1967. They all, of course, walked over the famous zebra crossing – backwards and forwards. They were greeted by the studio A&R man who simply said 'Hello,

> **R & B WITH THE**
>
> **' 1984 '**
>
> at ALL SAINTS CHURCH HALL
>
> CAMPBELL ROAD
>
> (off STAINES ROAD)
>
> ON
> SATURDAY 9th JULY 1966
>
> from 8 pm - 11 pm
>
> TICKETS 5/-   REFRESHMENTS AVAILABLE

I'm a bastard'! This proved to be an accurate statement, as he showed no appreciation of Brian's skill or his sensitivity to lead guitar tone. They recorded 'I Need Time' and 'She Was Once My Friend'. It was the first time Brian had experienced working in a major studio.

Brian's final recordings with The Left-Handed Marriage took place on 31 July 1967 at Regentsound Studios. He played on three songs – the two previously recorded at Abbey Road (although Brian persuaded Bill to include a piano riff on 'I Need Time'), and a new song – 'Appointment'. He also provided backing vocals. During recording Brian was having problems with 'clicking' sounds coming from the Red Special. LHM's flautist Terry Goulds suggested fitting a capacitor to the guitar – problem solved! All involved were pleased with the final recordings.

Some of the places that 1984 were asked to play weren't too salubrious. During a concert arranged by ex-Hampton School pupil Pete Edmunds at the White Hart in Southall, a fight broke out among the crowd. Says Pete: 'It was like a scene out of a Wild West movie. There were bottles flying and chairs being smashed over people's heads. But the band played on. Well, for about ten minutes, anyway, when they all downed tools and fled. This one single policeman walked in – and the whole place emptied so fast!'

1984 also did gigs as support to other bands or acts – and once supported a snake dancer. They arrived at the gig and walked into the dressing room to find a large, half-naked woman with a huge snake draped around her neck. They were all taken aback, but she just told them to come right in. They played the gig but spent the entire time on stage transfixed by the gyrating rear-end of the dancer!

One of the band's most memorable support gigs was at Imperial College on 13 May 1967, supporting the soon-to-become legendary Jimi Hendrix. After their stint, 1984 wanted to get 'out front' to watch Jimi in action, and to do so without having to pay they had to sneak through the back and over the edge of the stage, ending up in the front row. As they tried to walk quietly past Jimi's dressing room, he came out. His unforgettable comment was: 'Which way's the stage, man?'

In September 1967, the band felt they were now good enough to enter a competition at the Top Rank Club in Croydon. Brian, Dave and Richard first went on stage to back singer Liza Perez, and then went on again with Tim Staffell as 1984; whether Tim's navy blue shirt with bright pink polka dots on it had anything to do with it or not, they won. It brought them brief recognition – 'And I won a Barbra Streisand album!' says Brian.

Some days later, at a gig at the London School of Medicine, 1984 were approached by a promoter who had arranged an all-night, star-studded event at Olympia. He needed a band to fill a spot, loved 1984 and told them he wanted to make them stars. Next day he took them to London's trendy Carnaby Street to buy new clothes, and they rehearsed a special half-hour set of cover songs. The event was billed as 'Christmas On Earth' and was due to take place on 23

December 1967 – with a line-up featuring Jimi Hendrix, Traffic, Pink Floyd, Herd, Tyrannosaurus Rex and many others. The band arrived at 3 p.m., having been told they would appear around midnight. They eventually went on at about 5 a.m. on Christmas Eve, and on leaving an hour or so later discovered that not only had money been stolen from their dressing room, but their vans and cars had been towed away. All they got out of that gig was the experience.

It wasn't long afterwards that 1984 finally called it a day. There were musical differences, and Brian's having to devote much of his time to study also became a bone of contention. They all felt that although 1984 was a good, popular local band, they didn't have the necessary spark to carry on and become a great one.

Brian threw himself wholeheartedly into his work and, as part of his studies, organised and supervised the building of a hut in Switzerland on Testa Grigia, a small mountain just below the Matterhorn. The equipment housed in the hut was apparatus for the study of zodiacal light. He also designed and built his own spectrometer and spent some time at the hut recording observations. But the climate was unpredictable and several times he and his companions had to dig the pathway from the door clear of snow while drifts would pile up to the roof.

After a while it was decided that the weather was detrimental to their studies, and they moved the hut and its contents to the sunnier climes of Tenerife. Brian and his supervisor set up the hut in Izaña, on the slopes of Mount Teide, the extinct volcano that dominates Tenerife. They enjoyed studying in such a warm climate, and between them wrote two papers based on their research and its results, which were published in *Monthly Notices of the Royal Astronomical Society*.

Before going to Tenerife, Brian had been approached by Professor Sir Bernard Lovell to join his research laboratory at Jodrell Bank in Cheshire after graduation. It was a great honour, and Brian seriously considered the offer, but he decided that his involvement in music was more important to him and that he had to be in London to develop it. Reluctantly he turned Professor Lovell down.

Brian and Tim Staffell were still in contact – Tim was at the Ealing College of Art – and they were discussing forming another band. Both realised how much they missed playing and being part of a group. They posted an advertisement on the Imperial College noticeboard asking for a 'Mitch Mitchell/Ginger Baker type drummer' to join a new band. They had quite a few replies and began to audition applicants for their new venture, one of whom was a medical student, Roger Meddows Taylor . . .

CHAPTER 2

ROGER MEDDOWS TAYLOR

OBE, BSC (HONS)

ROGER MEDDOWS TAYLOR WAS BORN ON TUESDAY 26 JULY 1949 AT THE West Norfolk and King's Lynn Hospital in King's Lynn, Norfolk, to Winifred and Michael Taylor. Michael was an inspector for the Potato Marketing Board. 'Meddows' was a family name that had been passed down successive Taylor generations, and it was subsequently passed on to Roger as a middle name. Roger's background wasn't particularly musical, although his mother had played the piano accordion as a teenager – an instrument she had to give up as it was considered 'unladylike'.

Roger had attended his first school, Roseberry Avenue Infants, in King's Lynn, for a year, then went on to Gaywood Primary, also in King's Lynn, for another two years. Then the family, now including sister Clare, born in 1953, decided to make the major move down to Truro, Cornwall, on 3 March 1957, where Roger was enrolled at Bosvigo School the following day.

ROGER MEDDOWS TAYLOR

In 1957, aged eight, Roger was watching his cousin play simple tunes on his guitar and decided then and there he wanted a guitar too. At first, he made do with a ukulele, on which he taught himself basic chords. It was enough to persuade him, even at that age, that he should form a band – there might be money to be made here. He commandeered the garage for practice but first he begged as many egg cartons as he could and stuck them all over the walls and ceilings – a primitive and inexpensive form of soundproofing.

The band were called the Bubblingover Boys and played skiffle music. Roger played, or tried to play, the ukulele, someone else had a tea-chest bass, and a couple of other lads had guitars. Roger remembers: 'None of us could actually play. We just stood there and strummed and twanged tuneless chords, it was dreadful! But we invited the neighbours and some friends along, and we charged them to get in!'

The band's first live gig was in Falmouth Road, Truro, on 23 July 1957.

The Bubblingover Boys played just once more, at the Bosvigo school dance. It was a short-lived venture, one reason being that none of them were very good at it, and another that in September 1959, Roger was awarded a choral scholarship at the Truro Cathedral School, and left behind his fellow band members. The scholarship involved joining the cathedral choir, but he was an unwilling member of that elite fellowship, as it involved singing three times every Sunday and at special services such as weddings and midnight mass at Christmas. Although the experience was invaluable, Roger never considered himself the choirboy type.

By now, Roger had saved enough money to buy himself a cheap, basic acoustic guitar. He taped popular songs from the radio and taught himself to play the basic guitar chords. He had managed to 'acquire' a copy of Bill Haley & His Comets' *Rock Around The Clock* on 'permanent loan' from a friend, but listened to anything and everything, trying to take it all in.

Roger was passionate about music, and he felt that his niche in life was somehow to be connected with it. His mother recalls: 'Roger was so ambitious, and his confidence in himself was immense. He just knew that one day he would make a name for himself and be living in London. I knew it too in my heart.'

In September 1960, Roger won a place at Truro School. This public boarding school was academically the best in the area, and Roger was the only pupil from the cathedral school to be awarded a free place there. As he lived nearby, he went as a day boy.

The joys of playing guitar were already beginning to fade for Roger, and he found himself more and more drawn to percussion. He started off by bashing upturned saucepans with his mother's knitting needles, using the lids as cymbals. He found a snare drum one day while out playing with friends and was given a hi-hat cymbal for Christmas 1961. His father presented him with a bass drum and a tom-tom – he had picked up both for £12 and had mended and polished them. Although it was a mismatched kit, Roger was exceedingly proud of it. He went out after Christmas and bought himself a brand new Zildjian crash cymbal for eight shillings – his first proper cymbal – and eventually another tom-tom as well.

Roger was a bright, intelligent schoolboy. He particularly liked English and Biology and, although music was his main love, he prudently looked ahead to an alternative career, should his confidence in his own abilities prove unfounded. Academia was not, however, his strongest point. He comments, 'I was a lazy scholar, I hated studying and I was certainly given no privileges.' He was, though, the only pupil in the school with hair below his collar. The boarders had to abide by the strict school codes, but as a 'day boy', Roger flouted them.

During 1963, he and some school friends, including Dave Dowding, formed a band. They called themselves The Cousin Jacks and rehearsed in a barn at Little Canaan Farm, Dave's home near Truro. Roger was initially their rhythm guitarist, but he didn't enjoy it, and subsequently took over on drums, where he felt far more comfortable. Their first gig was at Roger's home in Hurland Road – Roger gathered his friends together, even charging them to watch. They also played a couple of concerts for the local Liberal Party, and one or two other events, once changing their name for a brief period to the Falcons. After about twelve months the venture fell apart but some years later The Cousin Jacks re-formed with Roger on drums; he even designed his own bass drum logo using the band's name. Michael Dudley joined the band later, and Roger changed the band's name to Beat Unlimited – and designed another logo for his drums. They played their first gig on 8 August 1964, in St Mawes. However, Dave lost interest in the group at the beginning of 1965 and left – so the band decided to split up.

At that time the way of life in Truro was easy, relaxed and fun. Being blond, slim and handsome had its advantages with the local ladies: on more than one occasion he would be 'entertaining' one girl in the living room while another waited patiently in the garage. Schoolwork wasn't a problem for Roger, even though he was a self-confessed 'lazy scholar', but he and his mother were often at loggerheads over homework; Roger insisted he worked better with music blaring while his mother felt he would do better without it. He admits that he only passed his exams through intense revision the week before he sat them.

Roger was adamant that London was the place to be if he were to make music his career, but he also realised that, without help, getting there wasn't going to be easy. He decided to apply to colleges in the city but couldn't decide what subject. Biology still interested him, so he thought he might study something connected with that, but exactly what was another matter, and one that didn't occupy his mind too much at this stage.

Roger's parents then separated, so it was a time of personal turmoil for him and his young sister, Clare. His mother continued to be supportive, even if he didn't always take her advice: all she wanted for her son was that he be happy and eventually find a profession. His music was fine as a hobby, she thought, but a real career was infinitely more important.

In 1965, Oscar Carveth, a friend from Truro Cathedral School, introduced Roger to local band Johnny Quale (aka singer Johnny Grose) and The Reaction. The Reaction were a band founded in 1964 by Truro school sixth formers Jim Craven and John Snell. They needed a drummer and approached Roger after seeing him with Beat Unlimited. Roger agreed to join, but insisted on bringing Mike Dudley with him, which was agreed. The band rehearsed in the village of Malpas, near Falmouth – bass player Jim Craven's family summer home.

On 15 March, after rehearsing together for a couple of weeks, they considered themselves competent to enter the Rock and Rhythm Championship, an annual event that began in 1960 and continued for another ten years. Run by the Round Table in Truro City Hall, the competition attracted bands from all over Devon and Cornwall. Winners were judged on originality, musicianship, presentation, professionalism and potentiality, with the top group taking away a silver trophy. Johnny Quale and The Reaction came fourth – Roger also won a prize for best musician of the evening, and Johnny won best vocalist. It served to start them off on the Cornish music circuit, which was significant in those days, attracting many of the bigger London-based groups.

At the contest, the band had been introduced to Jack Pascoe, and Roger Brokenshire – a 'local legend' who was known as 'Sandy', as he'd been a professional singer going by the name of 'Sandy Shore' and had performed with many local bands. The two were well-known dance promoters and showed an interest in helping the band to get gigs around Cornwall.

ROGER MEDDOWS TAYLOR

With help from Pascoe/Brokenshire the band became well established by playing such venues as the Blue Lagoon in Newquay, the St Just Village Hall, the Gardens in Penzance, the Princess Pavilion in Falmouth and many other town and village halls. Johnny had been having problems with his voice, so in November 1965 he decided it was more important to go and watch the latest Elvis film than it was to turn up to the gig booked for that evening. As the booking was for Pascoe/Brokenshire, Sandy decided to come out of semi-retirement for the show. It worked, and the audience were treated to a roof-raising gig. The band asked him to become a full time member of the group. They dropped Johnny's name – The Reactions were born.

On 7 March 1966, The Reactions entered the Rock and Rhythm Championship again, this time with Roger Brokenshire on lead vocals. They all wore black polo neck jumpers and dark brown trousers – Sandy sported a sheepskin jacket dyed orange, blue and silver. The hard work and endless gigging over the past year paid off; they wowed the crowd and the judges, claiming top spot. They were awarded an engraved silver trophy, which Roger took home with him, and proudly displayed on his fireplace. Finally, they were asked to appear the following year as the 'special guests'.

1966 was another year of gigs: the band played three or four times a week around Cornwall and had accumulated a large following, although, Roger recalls, they often changed personnel. Lead guitarist for most of the band's existence was Geoff Daniel, with Jim Craven on bass, Mike Dudley on keyboards (including a Vox Continental organ!) and sax player John 'Acker' Snell. Mike Grose, Johnny's brother, another bass player, would occasionally appear with them. They were originally a soul band, playing lots of James Brown and Otis Redding covers, but in 1966 they all got hooked on Jimi Hendrix, and the band went psychedelic.

In the summer of 1966, the band were contacted by their old

singer – Johnny Grose (Quale) who asked if they'd like to record several demos with him; he would pay all the recording costs. They certainly weren't going to turn that opportunity down. So on 26 June 1966, Roger and the rest of The Reactions, bar Sandy, found themselves at Wadebridge Sound Studios, located in the local cinema. The band recorded four songs with Johnny on lead vocals, and Roger on backing vocals – the ballad 'What's On Your Mind', a Reaction song 'I'll Go Crazy', another ballad 'Buona Sera' and a rocker called 'Just A Little Bit'. Johnny was happy with each of the tracks by the time his session came to an end. But there was still a little time left on the booking, so Sound Studios asked if The Reactions would like to record on their own – for an additional small fee (about £20). After a quick discussion, the band decided to go ahead, but as there was no Sandy, Roger agreed to sing *and* drum – on the basis that as the backing singer, he knew all the words. So, with no preparation, they recorded the Wilson Pickett song 'In The Midnight Hour' and James Brown's 'I Got You (I Feel Good)'. A limited number of singles were pressed, and any left after the band took their copies sold in Truro's Riverside Cafe.

The Reactions had by now been given regular slots at both the Truro club PJ's, co-owned by Mike Grose and Pete Bawden, and the Blue Lagoon in Newquay, a venue that attracted a number of the well-established London bands. They supported such notables as Tyrannosaurus Rex, Slade (then known as The N'Betweens) and Ritchie Blackmore in his pre-Deep Purple days.

At the beginning of September 1966, Ricky Penrose, who had been in the original band in 1965, joined them again. Sandy decided that he wanted to take a break from singing, and left, so Roger volunteered to become full-time vocalist and drummer.

The previous October Roger had attended The Who's gig in Camborne. It had had a major effect on him, and he now decided The Reactions needed to change their musical direction. He ripped up the family piano, painted it in psychedelic colours, and he and the other band members would somehow manage to manhandle the frame into the back of the Transit van. When they arrived at the gig, Roger would tape a microphone to it, hit it with a sledge hammer and throw paint at it during what they referred to as their 'freak out' section. He loved the sound of it, but the rest of the band got fed up with having to heave it into and out of the van and it was eventually left behind.

On New Year's Eve 1966, the band were booked to support Screaming Lord Sutch at the Blue Lagoon in Newquay. Roger played a drum solo during the band's now legendary cover of 'Land Of A Thousand Dances', made famous by Wilson Pickett, which was declared the highlight of the gig.

That night Sutch's backing group were resplendent dressed as Roman Legionnaires, and after the show their organist, Matthew Fisher, approached Roger to join a new, London-based band he was forming. Roger was about to start an A-level course, so told Fisher that although he was interested, he couldn't commit at that time. The band were Procol Harum.

In May, The Reactions decided on yet another name change – dropping the word 'The' and the last 's' to become simply Reaction. Roger painted a Reaction logo on the group's Bedford van, to help promote the band on their travels through Devon and Cornwall.

Reaction played cover versions of songs by Dylan and Cream, plus a strange cross-section of music that was a bit ahead of its time in Cornwall. *The* household name then was Geno Washington, and their audiences would listen for a while, before launching into chants of 'Geno, Geno'. They had to play at least one of his songs, which themselves were usually covers of Sam Cooke, Sam & Dave or James Brown numbers.

Reaction continued to play many gigs – enough to cover the costs of a new Ford Thames van and their friend Neil Battersby to drive it. Neil also became their roadie, along with another friend, Peter Gill Carey.

Even though he was busy with the band, Roger's schoolwork didn't suffer, and he left Truro School in the summer of 1967 with seven O-levels – in English Language, English Literature, Biology, Physics, Chemistry, French and Maths. He also had three A-levels in Biology, Chemistry and Physics. By this time he had heeded the advice of his teachers, decided on a career in dentistry and been accepted to the London Hospital Medical School.

During the summer of 1968, Roger and Rik Evans, a friend with his own marquee company, were discussing ways of making money. They hit on the idea of erecting a marquee on the beach at Perranporth and Reaction playing in it. Roger would travel around the area in his minivan, sticking up fly posters for the events, and they would charge an entry fee. They called it the 'Summer Coast Sound Experience'; they used a homemade psychedelic light show, and got two or three hundred people in, paying five shillings each. Not surprisingly, the local authorities soon forced them to shut down. But Reaction played in the marquee a few times first, notably on 7 July 1968 for a dance to celebrate the finals of the Ladies Surf Championships. The band finally foundered after Roger left again for London that autumn: he had been the driving force behind them, and without him they drifted apart.

Roger played his final gig with Reaction at Trevallas Porth Beach on 21 September 1968. He began his degree course in October 1968, moving into digs in Shepherd's Bush with friend Les Brown, who was studying at Imperial College, and Geoff Daniel. Roger knew in the back of his mind that he didn't want to be a dentist for the rest of his life; music was much too important to him. But, as a means to an end, the course enabled him to live in London at someone else's expense.

At university, Roger was intent on joining another band. His appetite for fame and fortune was keen and he read the music press regularly, looking for an opportunity. In the early autumn, Les noticed a postcard pinned to the Imperial College noticeboard asking for a 'Ginger Baker/Mitch Mitchell type drummer' for a new band. He passed on the information to Roger, who, intrigued, contacted the name on the card the following day. Brian May sent Roger a lengthy, detailed letter stating exactly what type of drummer they were looking for. They arranged to meet, Roger inviting Brian and Tim Staffell over to Shepherd's Bush, where he had a set of bongos (his drums were still at home in Truro).

Brian and Tim arrived equipped with a couple of acoustic guitars and the three played a few tunes together. The pair were amazed by Roger's ability. 'I remember the first time I saw Roger on drums. His flamboyance just blew me away,' says Tim. Brian was convinced he was the right man when he saw Roger tuning his drum, something he thought looked incredibly professional. Roger was equally impressed by Tim's and Brian's playing, even though at that point they only had acoustic guitars.

The three met again in the Jazz Club room at Imperial College, plugged in and played for real. It clicked instantly and they became firm friends. They all had strong ideas about music, and even though their knowledge of the music business was scant, they felt that together they had the wit and intelligence to find their way through it.

CHAPTER 3

THE SMILE ERA

THE NEWLY FORMED TRIO CHRISTENED THEIR NEW BAND SMILE. IT was short and snappy – and the only name on which they could all agree. Tim put his artistic talents to good use and designed the logo – a huge grinning mouth, with bright red lips and dazzling white teeth. Later, The Rolling Stones settled on a surprisingly similar design.

Smile spent the autumn of 1968 rehearsing and perfecting their music. They played some cover numbers, but Tim and Brian also began to write songs together. Smile needed a van and recruited the services of Pete Edmunds, an old school friend of Brian and Tim, who had a beautiful MG sports car. He was persuaded to part with it in exchange for a bottle-green Thames van and became the band's first roadie.

Brian still found time to see other bands and travelled to Hyde Park in late June to see Pink Floyd and Jethro Tull. It was an immense concert, by far the biggest he had ever been to. Hyde Park was a prestigious place to play – a gig there meant you had made it to superstar status.

1968 was also the year that Brian finished his degree, and on 24 October he and his parents attended the Royal Albert Hall where he collected his Bachelor of Science (BSc) certificate from Her Majesty Queen Elizabeth the Queen Mother. Ruth May says: 'We were so proud of him. We knew that his music was so very important to him, but we secretly hoped he would continue studying, and finish his thesis. He'd done so much work towards it. But we were prepared to stand by him whatever he chose. We knew that whatever it was, he would do it well.'

Brian didn't desert Imperial altogether: after he had received his degree he continued to go to the college and give tutorials, also using the time there to continue work on his Ph.D. thesis.

Smile's first public appearance – in support of Pink Floyd at Imperial College on 26 October 1968 – was nerve-racking, if reasonably well received for a bunch of unknowns. Their style of music was rather wild and undisciplined; they would play a cover version of a popular song, using every change in tempo they could fit in. Often songs lasted as long as twenty minutes. They described themselves as a 'progressive rock band' and were all determined that this band would be more than just another hobby. They wanted desperately to make it work.

It was at around this time that Brian met Christine Mullen, a student from the Maria Assumpta Teacher Training College in Kensington. She and some college friends had attended a gig Smile had played there – the introduction came via Roger's girlfriend, Jo, who shared a flat with Chrissy. Brian and Chrissy became friends and fell in love. One of Chrissy's fellow students, Pat McConnell, and her sister, Helen, had met Smile in their local pub and they introduced Brian, Tim and Roger to a friend of theirs, John Harris. John was a keen music fan and a dab hand with electronics, too. He got on well with the band and agreed to become their sound engineer and roadie, alongside Pete.

Many of Smile's early gigs were played in Cornwall, Roger's home territory, where he was quite well known from his Reaction days.

The band were billed as the 'tremendous London band' and played such venues as PJ's in Truro and the Flamingo Ballroom in Redruth. They would stay with Roger's mother, sleeping on the front-room floor. She would regularly get up in the morning to find strange bodies sprawled everywhere.

At this point Roger made the decision to put a halt on his dentistry studies. It was becoming more and more obvious to him that he wasn't cut out for that life. He finished the first part of the course and was awarded the first half of his dental degree in August 1969. He decided to take a year off from study to concentrate on his music.

Smile played many gigs at Imperial College – so many, in fact, that they became known as the Imperial College Band. The college circuit during the mid-sixties was significant and far-reaching; many of the bands who made a name for themselves then did so by playing the universities and colleges up and down Britain. There was a smaller, less well-trodden 'pub' circuit too, but the colleges had the backing of their student unions and could afford to pay quite substantial sums to the bands they booked. Smile supported several popular bands, such as Tyrannosaurus Rex and Family. After the gig on 26 January, a friend of Brian's, Mary Davies, introduced the band to a friend of hers called Terry Yeadon. Terry was working at Pye Studios, just off Marble Arch in London's West End. Terry asked them if they would like to record a couple of tracks at the studio – but it would have to be 'out of hours'. The band said yes, and kept in touch with Terry.

On 31 January 1969, Tim Staffell brought Freddie Bulsara, a friend from art college, to a Smile gig at Imperial College. Freddie loved the Smile sound, got on well with both Brian and Roger, and became a regular at Smile gigs. He had many flamboyant and extravagant ideas about how Smile should look, act and play – and no qualms about telling them in detail.

THE SMILE ERA

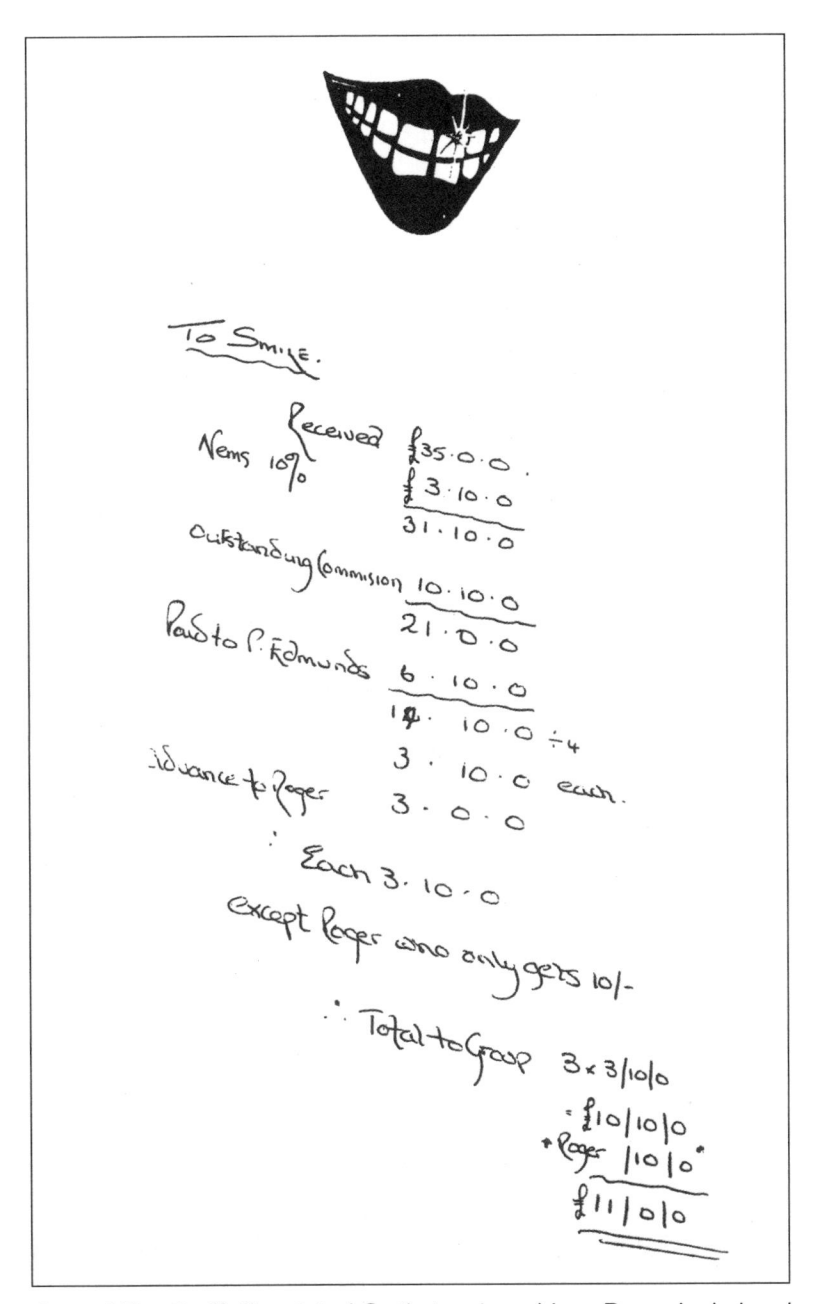

One of Tim Staffell's original Smile invoices. Note Roger had already borrowed £3!

Smile found room in the van for the ebullient Freddie when they travelled to their gigs near and far, and everyone recalls that whenever they arrived at those gigs, be they nearby or a couple of hours away, Freddie would emerge looking spotless and uncrumpled, his trousers – usually white satin – immaculate.

Some journeys caused a few problems for Smile and their entourage, notably one planned for a venue in Cornwall. They were on their way from London in the van when it broke down, in Andover, Hampshire. They had to hire a van from a local company, transfer all the gear into it and continue on, leaving their own behind, waiting for a friend to come out from London to repair it. Finally, they arrived in Truro and unloaded. The driver (hired along with his vehicle) had to head straight back to Andover, so they played the gig and left the gear at the hall overnight. Next day Brian, Tim, John and Freddie had to get back to London; Roger was staying in Truro. They begged help from several of Roger's friends to get the equipment from the venue to Truro railway station and proceeded to load it onto the London-bound train, which drew the attention of the guard, who informed them in no uncertain terms that they shouldn't be putting all that equipment on his train. But Roger's uncle just happened to be an area manager for British Rail and was visiting Truro. He saw the altercation taking place (by this time the train was late) and, after a quiet word with the guard, he walked off, saying nothing to his nephew. The guard helped them to load the rest of the gear without further comment, and the train pulled out of the station, leaving Roger crying with laughter on the platform wondering how on earth they were going to get it off at the other end. That problem was solved by Brian's good friend (and ex-1984 drummer) Richard Thompson, who collected them in London.

In February 1969 Smile were offered their second major gig, in support of Yes at a small clubhouse at the Richmond Athletic Club.

THE SMILE ERA

On 27 February a concert in aid of the National Council for the Unmarried Mother and Her Child, organised by Imperial College, took place at the Royal Albert Hall. The organisers had booked a great line-up and asked Smile if they would play – an offer they certainly couldn't refuse. Smile had been rehearsing for a short time with keyboard player Chris Smith, who had a huge shocking-pink Vox Continental organ on chrome legs, but the other band members felt they hadn't played enough with him, and they wanted the Albert Hall gig to be very strong. They decided they would have to get rid of him but fretted about who would be the one to tell him. Tim drew the short straw, and in the van on the way to that gig Chris was unceremoniously fired.

Smile thought they would have been bottom of such a prestigious bill, but found themselves billed above Free, featuring Paul Kossoff and Paul Rodgers. Then came Joe Cocker, Spooky Tooth and headliners the Bonzo Dog Doo-Dah Band. The event was compered by DJ John Peel. It was Smile's first exposure to a big audience, and not an auspicious start – Brian and Tim ran onto the stage, but as Tim was only equipped with a 30-foot guitar lead and the stage was 50 feet across, when he hit the first all-important chord nothing came out as he'd ripped the lead from the socket. (And as he was wearing socks and no shoes, he also collected a lot of splinters during the set.) Despite the slip up, Smile got their first-ever review after that gig: a journalist referred to them as 'the loudest group in the western world' but gave them no name check!

Smile went along to Pye Studio 2 one day in March, at midnight, as arranged by Terry Yeadon, although he hadn't actually told his employers that the band were recording. They recorded two songs – 'Polar Bear', a Brian penned song about . . . a polar bear. And a Brian and Tim song called 'Step On Me'. Acetates of the recordings were pressed by studio engineer Geoff Calvar, and given to them, and a copy of the actual taped recordings.

Smile were keen to adopt the trappings of a proper band, and around this time a friend of Roger's from dental college, Pete Abbey, became the band's manager. Although, Tim recalls, 'It was only a casual arrangement.' Pete was given a copy of the Smile tape, and he took it to John Anthony, a guy Pete remembered from some of the early Smile gigs in and around Cornwall, and had kept in touch with. John was now a record producer for Mercury Records, an American company with a London office. Lou Reizner, head of Mercury Records' European division, listened to the tape with John, and they liked what they heard.

On 19 April, Smile were playing at the Revolution Club in London, where they were introduced to Lou Reizner and John Anthony, who, after enjoying the tape, decided to go and see the band play live. Both Lou and John were suitably impressed and obviously thought the group had potential. Lou asked them to consider signing with Mercury. Being young and inexperienced, they saw the offer as their first real break, accepted and signed on 1 May 1969.

In June 1969, Mercury booked time at Trident Studios in London's Soho for their new signing. The band recorded three tracks: 'Earth', 'Step On Me' and 'Doin' Alright'. They were produced by John Anthony and engineered by Peter Kelsey, who became friends with the band, eventually moving into a shared house with them.

Mercury Records released two of the songs recorded by Smile earlier in the year – 'Earth', written by Tim as the A-side, and 'Step On Me', by Tim and Brian as the B-side. 'Step On Me' had originally started life as a 1984 song. The single was released in August 1969, but only in the USA, and it wasn't the success that Mercury, and Smile, were hoping for. Said Tim Staffell: 'The record company wasn't willing to commit themselves to it. I don't recall the single being much of a big deal. None of us were over the moon about it, because there was no money in it. Had there been, I think we'd have thought that we'd cracked it.'

THE SMILE ERA

Following another round of gigs, Mercury decided they wanted Smile to record more tracks, with a view to producing an album. They booked into De Lane Lea studios in Wembley in September and set them to work with producer Fritz Fryer. Brian and Tim had written quite a lot of songs together by this point and were pleased to be able to spend time recording them properly with some of the latest equipment. They recorded Blag and Polar Bear. They were also persuaded to record a song they had *not* written, a track called 'April Lady', with Brian singing. The band were happy with the results of their labours – but perhaps Mercury were not, since they never released the material.

At the end of 1969 the band played at the Marquee Club on London's Wardour Street, at a 'showcase' gig arranged by Mercury, in support of Kippington Lodge, featuring Nick Lowe (the band later changed their name to Brinsley Schwarz.) Smile played for just thirty minutes, to a small, largely unappreciative audience.

The band finished 1969 feeling despondent and depressed. Their dreams of stardom had so far failed to materialise. But all three of them were intrinsic optimists and remained confident, seeing in 1970 and the new decade with the belief that it could be their year.

Brian and Roger were ambitious and had tried hard to keep it all going – they knew the way to bigger and better things was through sheer hard work. Tim, however, had decided he'd had enough of slogging round the clubs and the college circuit; he wanted something more – and quickly.

Smile played at the College of Estates Management Hall on 6 March 1970; Freddie and Mary were in attendance as it was Mary's birthday. After the gig, Tim and the band discussed his leaving, and it seemed that Smile had reached the end of the road. They had two gigs planned in Truro PJ's for 7 and 8 March, and would have honoured them, but Pete Edmonds refused to drive them, so they had to cancel.

There were other gigs planned that Tim agreed to play as he tried to work out what he would do next. The first was Hertford Balls Park College on 21 March. The band went down really well, and most of the audience ended up on stage with them at the end of the show. But the thought of Tim leaving and the demise of Smile was a real blow to Roger, and he travelled back to Cornwall a couple of days later feeling down and disappointed.

Once he was back in his hometown, Roger arranged some dates for Freddie and his latest band, Sour Milk Sea, at PJ's on 17 and 18 April. He also played a couple of gigs at the club himself with two local bands: Third Ear on 3 April and Mighty Baby on 10 April.

Sour Milk Sea split up at the end of March, and so Roger faced having to cancel their PJ's gigs, but he didn't want to let the venue down. He asked his Smile bandmates, including Tim, if they would play the gigs instead. They all agreed, and on 16 April, Brian and Tim, along with newly band-less Freddie, took the train to Cornwall.

Smile played on Saturday 17 April, but on Sunday, Tim decided he really HAD had enough and took the train back to London. Pete Bawden called his PJ's co-owner Mike Grose to see if he would step in for the gig; he knew the Smile set list pretty well. He agreed, and on 18 April Smile, with Mike Grose, played their final gig at PJ's. For the encore the band decided to play 'Jailhouse Rock', and Freddie jumped up on stage and joined in – only the second time Brian, Roger and Freddie had been on a stage together. Freddie was elated he had finally got to sing with Smile; it had been a dream for some time.

Freddie and Brian took the train back to London the following day, but Roger decided to stay on in Truro, and caught the ferry to Falmouth with Mike, where they had a jam session with friends. Roger caught the train back to London a couple of days later – and obviously pondered Smile on the journey, as he called Mike as soon as he got back and asked if he'd like to play some gigs with Smile, which he agreed to do.

THE SMILE ERA

Smile were booked to play the Derby New Penny Club on 22 April 1970; Tim agreed to play the show, but it was his final appearance with the band. Two nights later they were booked to play Twickenham Eel Pie Island, and Mike Grose made the journey up from Cornwall for the gig, staying for the duration with Jo Morris, Roger's girlfriend at the time.

Smile were supporting the Climax Blues Band, and Freddie went along, perhaps hoping he would get onstage with them again, but sadly that didn't happen. The next day, Mike had to return to Cornwall; Roger followed him a couple of days later, as Smile were due to play at Torquay College, although they later cancelled the gig as Brian didn't want to travel all the way down there.

After Tim had finally left Smile, he auditioned for the band Humpy Bong. He was offered the job, and on 29 April 1970, he accepted. Humpy Bong were fronted by ex-Bee Gees drummer Colin Petersen, and their name was inspired by the school that Petersen and the Gibb brothers attended in Queensland, Australia. The band released one single, 'Don't You Believe It', and made one appearance on *Top Of The Pops* with it. It was a short-lived venture, and Tim moved on to play guitar for Jonathan Kelly. He finally decided to quit the music business in favour of model-making and special effects work, going on to make the models used in the popular TV series *Thomas The Tank Engine*.

After Tim's departure, Mercury Records dropped Smile – the original contract had been for just one single and the band was now non-existent. Mike Grose, along with friends Pat and Sue Johnstone, travelled back up to London for the very last Smile gig, at Imperial College on 9 May 1970. They supported T.Rex, Wishbone Ash, Mike Chapman, Taste and Kevin Ayres.

It was the end of the Smile era. Mike left to go back to Cornwall, while Pat and Sue stayed on in London.

But Brian and Roger were more determined than ever to make

their name in music, although Brian was still spending much of his spare time working on his astronomy thesis. They had long conversations about what to do next, soon bringing their close friend, Freddie, into the discussions.

CHAPTER 4

FREDDIE MERCURY

DIP. A.D.

FARROKH BULSARA WAS BORN OF PERSIAN PARENTS, BOMI AND JER Bulsara, on Thursday 5 September 1946 at the Government Hospital on the small spice island of Zanzibar, off the coast of Tanzania. His father, Bomi, was a civil servant, working as a High Court cashier for the British Government. At just a year old, Freddie had his first taste of fame when the local photographer took his picture and displayed it in his shop window – to be awarded first prize in a baby contest. At the age of five he started to attend the Zanzibar Missionary School, which was run by British nuns.

Freddie's sister, Kashmira, was born in 1952. Mr Bulsara's work meant he had to travel all over India, taking up different posts for short or long terms, so in 1954, at the tender age of eight, Freddie was shipped off from the quiet tranquillity of life in Zanzibar to St Peter's English boarding school in Panchgani, about fifty miles outside Bombay. It was there that friends began to call him Freddie, a name that the family also adopted.

Freddie's holidays were occasionally spent at school, but mostly with his grandparents and his Aunt Sheroo, who lived nearby, and sometimes with his parents in Zanzibar. It was during one such holiday, said Mrs Bulsara, that she acquired a new ornament. She remembers: 'In Zanzibar, at that time, the native people would make and sell handicrafts, ornaments and lots of handmade things. Freddie was strolling in the park one day when a local boy passed with his wares, and Freddie fell in love with a little ornament of a deer and her fawn. He bartered with the boy for it, but even though he did get the price lower, he still could not afford it – it was two shillings and fifty cents in African money, and he only had the fifty cents. So he said to the boy that if he came home with him he would get the money, as he really wanted that little thing for me. So he brought this young lad home, with all his goods, and asked me if he could borrow the money to buy the deer. At first I said no, but Freddie felt so sorry for the boy, after having brought him all that way, that in the end I relented and gave him the money to buy my present!'

As St Peter's was an English school, the sports played there were typically cricket, rugby, football, gymnastics and various other energetic pastimes.

'I *loathed* cricket, and long-distance running, I was completely useless at both,' recalled Freddie. 'But I could sprint, I was good at hockey, and I was just brilliant in the boxing ring, believe it or not!' His forte, though, was table tennis, and he became the school champion at the age of ten. Recalls Mrs Bulsara: 'Freddie was excellent at all sports, but when I heard about the boxing, I wrote to him from Zanzibar, where we were living, and told him to stop that, I didn't like the idea, it was too violent.'

Freddie was not only a good sportsman, but he was also very bright academically, and his artistic skills were incomparable. At twelve he was awarded the school trophy as Junior All-rounder. He loved art and was always sketching for friends or relatives. His maternal aunt,

Sheroo, was also quite artistic and would regularly ask the young Freddie to draw or paint for her: he was always quick to begin a new picture, but often side-tracked by other pastimes that meant he never found time to complete it. His aunt would sit him down and make him finish.

He was also music mad and played records on the family's old record player, stacking the singles to play constantly. The music he was able to get hold of was mostly Indian, but some Western music was available. He would sing along to either and preferred music to schoolwork.

The principal headmaster of St Peter's had noticed Freddie's musical talent and wrote to Mr and Mrs Bulsara, suggesting that they might wish to pay a little extra on Freddie's school fees to enable him to study music properly. They agreed, and Freddie began learning the piano. He also became a member of the school choir and took part regularly in school theatrical productions. He loved his piano lessons and applied himself to them with determination and skill, finally achieving Grade IV both in practical and theory.

During his time at St Peter's he formed his first band, The Hectics, with Derrick Branche on guitar, Farrang Irani on bass, Victory Rana on drums and Bruce Murray on lead vocals – Freddie was the pianist. They rehearsed in the school art room and played their first gig on 1 April 1961. They performed songs by Cliff Richard, Elvis Presley, Little Richard and Fats Domino, among others. The Hectics played only within the school, at fetes, parties and school dances. They were not allowed to venture outside for bookings, although the girls from nearby Kimmons School were allowed to attend. Freddie's choirboy training was useful and, even then, his inherent sense of theatrics was very much in evidence – he performed with flair and originality.

Freddie's early life in India and at boarding school was uneventful. He recalled that the family house in Bombay had servants, as did most prosperous Indian households at that time. The regime of school life was hard and he learned quite quickly to fend for himself, but when he was home from school his childhood was easy. There was always someone to prepare his meals, lay out his clothes for the day and take care of his needs. It was an impressionable time for him, and those early years meant he was ill-prepared for the realities of life outside that sheltered world. He presumed everyone had domestic employees.

In 1962, at the age of sixteen, Freddie failed his final exams at St Peter's, to his and his family's great disappointment. On 25 February 1963, he left India and travelled back to Zanzibar, with no academic achievements. He went to join his parents in their flat in Stone Town. He eventually secured his own apartment and in April began attending St Joseph's Convent School to start studying for his O-levels.

Freddie spent his time with friends in and around the markets, parks and beaches. He enjoyed sports, especially cricket and hockey. He cycled all over the island and often went to Fumba Beach to go swimming. He also loved climbing the coconut trees; he was a very fit and active young man. On his 17th birthday he was given a tape recorder, which he was totally delighted with. And by the end of that year he had achieved O-level passes in Art, History and English Language.

Zanzibar was then a British colony, but had a population of mainly Africans with Arabs and Indians in the minority. In late 1963, an election was held to hand over control of the island, in which the Arab people came to power. The Africans were in uproar and disputed the decision vociferously, forming their own political party, known as the Afro-Shirazi Party, to fight another election. In fact, two more were held, both of which the Arabs won. Zanzibar became an independent state on 10 December 1963, and the British finally handed over rule of the island to the Arab Sultan on 12 January 1964. In early 1964, the African population instigated a full-scale revolution.

Much of the British and Indian populations, although not under forcible pressure, fled their homes for their own safety, and among those driven out were the Bulsaras. They left with a couple of suitcases and little else, heading for England.

The Bulsara's arrived on UK shores on 4 May 1964. They lived initially with relatives in Feltham, Middlesex, first with Jer's sister at 19 Hamilton Close, then a couple of months later they moved just around the corner to 122 Hamilton Road, while waiting for their new home to become available. Mr Bulsara took a permanent job as an accountant for the Forte catering company.

Freddie was seventeen, and had decided he wanted to go to art college, but he needed at least one A-level to ensure he could get in. In September 1964 he enrolled at the nearby Isleworth Polytechnic School to study for an A-level in Art.

The Bulsara's finally managed to move into their new home – a small, terraced house at 22 Gladstone Avenue, Feltham, on 29 October 1964.

During the holidays, Freddie took a variety of jobs; one was in the catering department at Heathrow Airport, a stone's throw from home, and the other was on the Feltham trading estate, where he had a job in a warehouse lifting and stacking heavy crates and boxes. His fellow workers commented on his 'delicate' hands, certainly not suited for such work, and asked him what he did. He told them he was a musician just 'filling in time', and such was his charm that those co-workers were soon doing the lion's share of his work.

His mother persuaded him to save most of the money he earned, and he put it in a post office account, with Mrs Bulsara taking care of the book. He had accumulated, perhaps, £70 when he came to her and asked for his book. 'I asked him why,' she recalls, 'and he said he needed to lend a friend some money, as he was being thrown out of his flat and desperately needed it. I thought it would be ten pounds or so. He asked for fifty pounds! I asked if he was going to get it back, and he shrugged and said it didn't matter. That was his way; always generous, always thoughtful of others.'

Freddie studied hard, although he preferred the aesthetic side of school life to the more mundane academic side, and easily achieved his Art A-level, leaving Isleworth in the spring of 1966. His grade 'A' pass and his natural skill ensured that he was readily accepted by Ealing College of Art and, in September 1966, Freddie began a graphic illustration course there.

After Jimi Hendrix exploded onto the scene in 1967, and Freddie became an ardent fan, he spent time sketching and drawing his hero, drawings he would frame and use to decorate the walls of his rented flat in Kensington, where he'd moved from the family home in Feltham. At that time, Kensington was the place to be seen if you were a creative – it was the base of the world-famous Biba boutique and home to Kensington Market, a regular haunt of the 'in' crowd.

A fellow student at Ealing College was bass player Tim Staffell, with whom Freddie became good friends. Freddie, Tim and another art student, Nigel Foster, spent a lot of their spare time together as they all shared an interest in music. With the help of a couple of second-hand guitars and Freddie's voice, they managed to entertain themselves; Freddie was good at impersonations of Jimi Hendrix and would mime outrageously to his songs, using a ruler as a guitar. He and his two friends practised three-part harmonies, perfecting the technique rather well in the college lavatories.

As Tim and Freddie became close friends, Tim took him along to Smile's rehearsals. Freddie got on famously with Brian and Roger and loved the sound that Smile had achieved; he also had immense admiration and respect for Brian's guitar playing. Watching and listening to them made Freddie realise that he desperately wanted to be in a band himself; that early schoolboy exposure with The Hectics, however amateur, had given him a taste of the thrill of being on stage.

The thought of being in a band was now foremost in his mind, and he began to formulate a plan of action. Freddie never jumped in feet first; he always made time to test the water beforehand. He knew that before he could launch himself in that direction, he must complete his studies. He applied himself to that and, in 1969, left Ealing College with a diploma in Graphic Art and Design, the equivalent of a degree. Also that year he bought himself a cheap second-hand electric guitar, which Tim re-fretted to try to improve the sound, and he set about learning to play it. He had neither the time nor the money for lessons, so with the aid of a few books he taught himself the rudiments of playing. He only needed to learn enough to enable him to write songs, a skill which he found came anything but easily. He drew inspiration for lyrics from daily life, his own feelings and experiences. The resulting songs were, at times, intensely personal.

In the summer of 1969, Freddie was introduced to Liverpool band Ibex, who had come to London to try to make a name for themselves. Ibex were a three-piece, with guitarist Mike Bersin, John 'Tupp' Taylor on bass and Mick 'Miffer' Smith on drums. They also brought with them their apprentice manager, roadie and general dogsbody Ken Testi; part-time bass player Geoff Higgins used to travel down for occasional gigs, too. Geoff would play bass when Tupp, a big Jethro Tull fan, wanted to play flute.

'Ibex were going nowhere fast,' says Ken Testi. 'They had so much talent though, and it didn't go unnoticed by Freddie. He was a kind, penniless, outrageous guy, and he loved Ibex. He would come along and help Mike on vocals.'

Mick 'Miffer' Smith recalls: 'We auditioned Freddie to take over lead vocals from Mike. It was at Imperial College. We were all competent players, we could handle our instruments, but none of us was particularly good at singing. Freddie had a great voice, with a terrific range, but he didn't really know how to use it. Once we had Freddie, we were a little rough and ready, but we showed a lot of potential.'

During that summer Freddie asked Roger if he was interested in acquiring a stall in Kensington Market. Although Freddie was now with Ibex and playing a few gigs, they were earning very little, and the stall would be a way to supplement his income. Roger and Smile were low on funds too, so he agreed. The stall they took on was in an avenue of the market the traders called 'Death Row' as it sold mainly antiques. Freddie's Ealing College friends were more than happy to supply them with paintings and drawings to sell and Freddie also sold some of his own artwork. However, the stall wasn't exactly a success. After a rethink, the pair turned to selling clothes. They had a lot of contacts, and managed to get hold of some beautiful old Victorian clothes and scarves, fur coats, jackets and stoles. They even had several items made, out of fashionable velvet, lace and beading. The clothes sold quite well, and made a small but welcome profit. However, always with an eye on a bigger profit, one day Roger sold Freddie's own jacket, which a customer had spotted hanging up at the back, for £20. Freddie was furious and chased after the customer, demanding his jacket back. He returned the customer's money and ran back to Roger, threatening violence. Roger adamantly stood his ground, insisting he had only sold it so that they

Mick 'Miffer' Smith drawn by Freddie, signed 'Ponce'.

could get something to eat and pay the taxi fare home; even then Freddie hated the idea of using public transport.

Those were times of great friendship, but scarcity, for Ibex and Smile. Everyone knew everyone else and flats were always shared, at one time up to five people sharing two single beds pushed together, everyone sleeping sideways. Helen and Pat McConnell had a flat in Sinclair Road, near Earls Court in London, and everyone would regularly visit and sleep there. Helen remembers, 'On one occasion they were all there, all the bands, and they were playing so loudly. It was way past midnight. The next day we were thrown out, evicted! But it was such a fun time, we all laughed so much. We were all so thin too; we didn't have very much money, although what we had we all shared. Often we just forgot to eat completely.'

Ibex continued to work hard in rehearsal, playing a selection of cover versions of songs by The Beatles, Rod Stewart and Yes. They opened all their live gigs with their own rendition of 'Jailhouse Rock'. Freddie's stage act had vastly improved, although the other members of Ibex were a little embarrassed by his lively, camp movements and gestures. 'We just used to yell at him, "For goodness' sake, Freddie, just stand still!" He was all over the place, such energy, but it wasn't done then!' says Mike Bersin.

In late 1969, Roger, Brian, Freddie, Pat and Helen were all sharing a flat in Ferry Road, Barnes, along with most of Ibex, Tim from Smile and various others. It was supposed to be home to three people at the most, so when the landlady came to collect the rent they would all hide in the bedroom. Freddie had an early-morning routine, remembers Mick Smith: 'Most mornings Freddie would be up first. He had a white Fender Telecaster and he would walk around the flat, stepping over the various bodies still trying to get some sleep, strumming and singing the Who's "Tommy". He knew every chord and all the words. It was quite a ritual.'

The flat also boasted a beaten-up old acoustic guitar among its clutter, so bad no one could play it. On one occasion, says Geoff Higgins, 'Brian picked up this battered old guitar, and strummed it a bit. He then proceeded to play, perfectly, the Beatles song "Martha My Dear". He played the bass line and the piano harmonies, all on this one instrument. I'm a great Beatles fan, and I just stood there with my mouth open. I was amazed, he was brilliant.'

Many of the earliest Ibex songs were written in that flat, Mick recalls: 'I've never seen anyone write songs quite like Freddie. He would start singing and strumming the guitar, and then someone would have to sit by him and write down what he sang. I never once saw him write anything down, someone else always did. It was spontaneous, but it made sense.'

Most of the flat's residents liked to smoke marijuana, which Tupp used to buy from Kensington Market mixed with jasmine tea – apparently, the smell of the tea disguised the smell of the dope. When he got it home someone would sit and separate the dope from the tea. Once Tupp was in a hurry and when he returned from his shopping spree he simply dumped the bag of 'tea' into the caddy and dashed out again. Freddie hated smoking, particularly marijuana. That day he was alone in the flat and fancied a cuppa; he considered it disgusting hippie tea, but there was no alternative. He made a pot, poured a cup and sat down. His friends came home an hour later to find him smiling, feeling wonderful and saying how great the tea was, completely out of his head. He wasn't so happy when the effects had finally worn off . . .

'We had a party one night,' Freddie recalled. 'Tupp made these cakes, with dope in them. I refused to touch them, but everyone else had some. Then at about midnight the police came, some killjoy neighbour had called them. We invited them in and gave them a drink and a couple of these cakes. We all fell about, but they left, not knowing a thing. I would love to have been a fly on the windscreen of their police car after about half an hour, when the effects of the dope had hit them.'

Ibex were still travelling up and down Britain's motorways in an assortment of borrowed and begged vans, and earning little for their efforts. Ken Testi was acting as their booking agent and managed to get them various pub and club dates, mostly 'up north'. On one notable occasion when the band had a booking in Bolton, Richard Thompson borrowed a transit van from Heathrow Airport, where he worked, and lent it to Ken to drive Ibex and Roger, who was tagging along that day, up the motorway to the gig. They had arranged to pick up Tupp Taylor at Piccadilly Circus. The front of the van was full, and in the back were the rest of the band and various friends. As they drove they played acoustic guitars and sang loudly, and often tunelessly! They arrived at Piccadilly and stopped the van in the middle of the road for Tupp to jump aboard. As they rolled up the clattering shutter at the back the deafening noise of guitars and singing brought Piccadilly to a halt and everyone just stared at this van full of 'hippies'.

On arrival in the quiet northern town it was going-home time for the local miners, many of whom were walking up the main street. The van pulled up, the shutter was raised and out leaped a satin-and-fur-clad Freddie, right into their midst. It was hard to tell who was the most shocked, Freddie on seeing the black-faced, dour-looking miners or the miners on seeing the dashing Freddie. Both just stood and stared at each other for a moment, until Freddie jumped back into the van, yelling, and yanked the shutter down in fright.

The gig that night, 23 August 1969, was at the Bolton Octagon Theatre, and the band also played an open-air festival the next day in Bolton's Queens Park. It was quite a shock for unsuspecting northern audiences to be faced with someone as different in style and looks as Freddie; even Mike stood out during those two gigs, as his mother had made him a gold lamé cloak, which he felt obliged to wear. Unsurprisingly, Ibex received a mixed reception.

Just after that they were booked to play at St Helens Technical College. Freddie's stage wear that night was a pair of skin-tight black velvet trousers, which he'd had made specially with no side seams: instead, they had a seam up the back of each leg. He loudly requested that someone get him a full-length mirror for the dressing room (actually the kitchen). The mirror arrived and he spent half an hour before the show straightening the back seams of his trousers.

Even though the venues Ibex played were small, and the audiences smaller still, Freddie's appeal to the ladies in the audience was legendary. They would flock around him to chat or just to be seen with him. He had an air of mystery: his mode of dress singled him out, but his shyness stopped him being talkative on stage (Tupp did all that) and he came across as aloof and moody because of it.

As nothing was happening for Ibex in London, and they were tired of the endless travelling back and forth to gigs up north, they decided to move back to Liverpool. Freddie didn't like the idea but he thought he'd give it a try. He spent most of his time in Liverpool sleeping on Geoff's bedroom floor in a huge pub called the Dovedale Towers in Penny Lane, renowned for Mrs Higgins' bacon-and-egg breakfasts.

The band had a gig lined up at basement club The Sink in Hardman Street, below the Rumbling Tum club, on 24 September 1969. Richard Thompson drove them all up to Liverpool in his van – so quite a few went along to support Freddie. Brian wasn't free to travel with them, and so decided to take the train up to Liverpool the following day – the day of the gig.

The Sink wasn't licensed to sell alcohol so punters had to swap money for bottle tops in the upstairs club, then use those as 'currency' downstairs. Before the show the band had all gone for a drink in a nearby pub. Roger and Tim were up from London and were wary of walking the streets of Liverpool at night; as they left the pub, a gang of skinheads came around the corner. Members of the newly formed skinhead movement were then threatening anyone who didn't look like them, especially 'hippies' as they called them. Violence was their calling card, and street fights and brawls in pubs and clubs were becoming commonplace up and down England. On this night, when the skinheads came face to face with a bunch of men wearing an assorted array of fur, leather, velvet and jewellery, they must have thought they had hit the jackpot. The skinheads blocked the street and refused to let Ibex pass. Roger, having plenty of Dutch courage, flashed a card at them, stating that it was an ID card to prove he was a judo black belt and that by law he was required to inform them three times of his judo status before he could legally hit them. He gave the three warnings, and the skinheads scarpered. The card he had shown was nothing more than his old student card, and he had never had a judo lesson in his life!

Ken Testi and Richard drove the van to Lime Street station to meet Brian off the train. As they arrived to park up, a policeman asked if they were waiting for the London train. Ken said they were, and the policeman told them to drive straight onto the platform and wait for it there. When the train pulled in, Brian jumped off, saw the van and casually climbed in, as though he was used to getting this kind of treatment all the time!

Ibex were booked to play a gig for the Liverpool University new term intake party – or Freshers Week. During the gig, Tim jumped on stage to help with the vocals. Freddie invited Brian and Roger on stage, too – marking the first time that Freddie, Brian and Roger had played together at a live show.

Life in Liverpool wasn't much better for the band than it had been in London. They were hungry and broke, and the money they made from gigs was being stretched by having to pay two guys to set up and operate a fairly elaborate light show. They began to wonder why, when they needed the money and were only getting £25, £15 of it was going on lights – but Freddie couldn't contemplate performing without lights.

Ibex played their final gig – which included magnesium flares and a light show – at St Helens College of Technology on 26 September 1969. Mike had decided to stay on in Liverpool to attend art college, and Freddie eventually moved back to London.

But Freddie was so determined to make something of himself as a performer, that he couldn't be without a band for too long. So he decided to call all the Ibex members and ask them if they were prepared to change the band name to Wreckage – in fact he had already decided that this *was* to be their new name, so he told each of them that the others had already agreed to it! Mike Bersin and Tupp Taylor were happy with it. Freddie finally had his own band.

Wreckage played their first gig on 31 October 1969 at Ealing College. They had a number of gigs booked over the following weeks, including one at Richmond Rugby Club, where Brian went along to show his support. Wreckage also played at Imperial College supporting one of the first heavy metal bands – Iron Butterfly.

Mick 'Miffer' Smith's family were going through a rough patch at this time, and his recently divorced mother needed financial help. He felt the time had come to leave Ibex and got a job as a construction worker on the new M56 motorway before going back to being a milkman. Some years later he met and fell in love with an American girl called Debbie and went to live permanently in the USA. Ibex replaced him with Richard Thompson, whom they had known for a number of years.

Richard played a couple of gigs with Wreckage, driving the band and their followers to Widnes in Cheshire, for a show at the Wade Deacon Grammar school on 21 November 1969. The gig was actually booked for Ibex, and arranged by John Taylor's sister, so Miffer also went along to catch up with his friends. However, the gig was

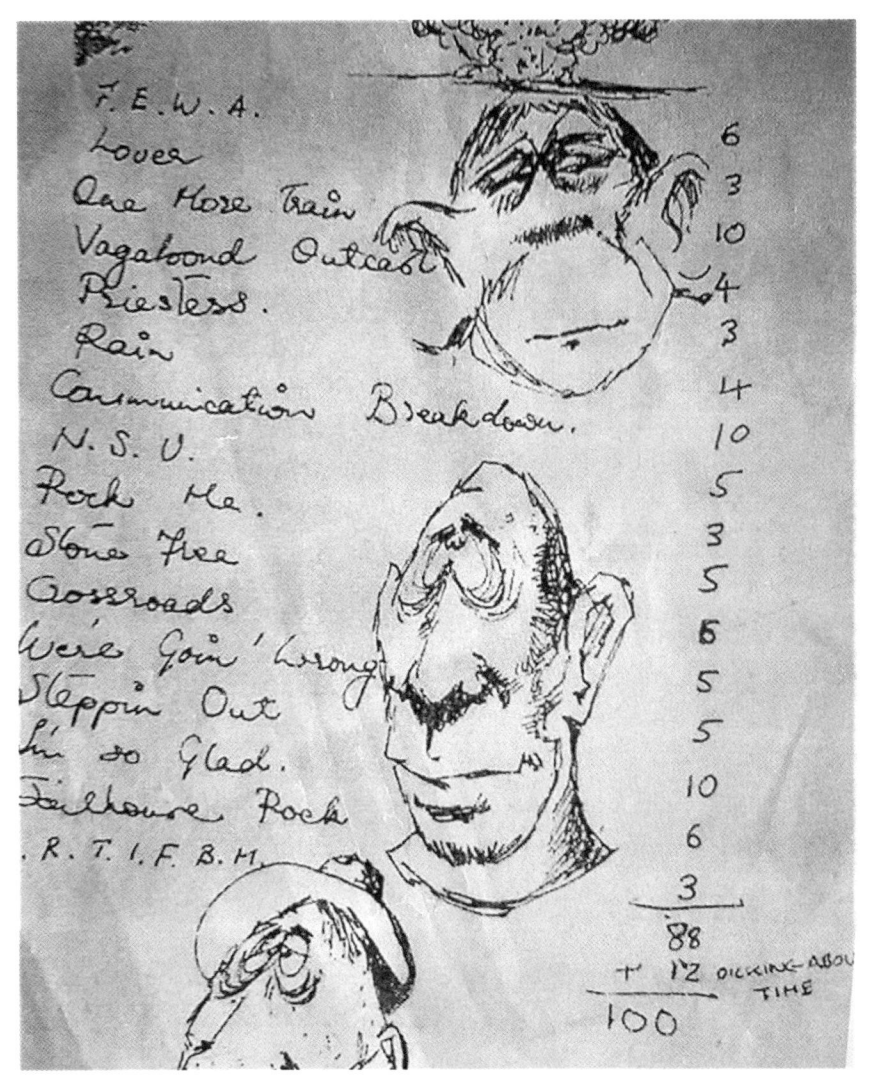

A Wreckage set list, written by Freddie, along with sketches. Note the track timings – and twelve minutes spare for 'dicking about'!

an unmitigated disaster. The sound was awful, the equipment didn't work properly and the audience hadn't a clue who the band were or what the music was. To top it all, Freddie was using a battered old microphone stand with a solid, heavy bottom, which he struggled to manoeuvre as deftly as he would have liked. During one song he grabbed it to try to swing it around, and the bottom fell off. He carried on with the top pole section only, and did so forever afterwards – it became his trademark.

Soon after the fiasco at the grammar school, Freddie was feeling disillusioned, he felt that Wreckage should, by now, have made a name for themselves – but they hadn't. So in December 1969, Freddie left the band.

Richard Thompson stayed on the local music scene, playing with a variety of amateur bands. But Freddie was at a loose end, and he missed performing. He applied for a number of auditions advertised in the music press, one of which was in *Melody Maker*, saying 'vocalist wanted'. Not wanting to go alone, Freddie 'borrowed' Smile's roadie, John Harris, and his van. He also recruited Roger as moral support. The audition was to be held in a youth club in the crypt of a church in Dorking, Surrey, and, equipped with fur coat, best boots and designer trousers (the tightest ones he could get) Freddie set off, with John and Roger in tow. When they arrived, Roger got out first and held open the door. Freddie, resplendent in fur coat, swept into the room, closely followed by John, reverently carrying a small wooden box, which he made a great show of opening. Inside was Freddie's personal Shure microphone. The pomp and ceremony were impressive, and the band he was auditioning for decided that he was the right man, especially when he got around to singing. They offered him the job, and in February 1970 Freddie became lead singer of Sour Milk Sea, alongside Chris Chesney (then known as Chris Dummet) on vocals and guitar, Paul Milne on bass, Jeremy Gallop on rhythm guitar and Boris Williams on drums, although shortly after Freddie joined the band, Boris left (later in his career he was the drummer for The Cure). He was replaced by Rob Tyrell on drums.

After a few rehearsals, the band played a few gigs in Oxford (Chris's hometown), notably one at the Highfield Parish Hall in Headington on 20 March 1970 in aid of the homeless charity Shelter. It came to the attention of local paper *The Oxford Mail*, who printed possibly the only photo taken of Freddie with the band. They also did gigs in London, including one at the Pink Flamingo in Wardour Street. The band's set list included three of Freddie's own songs, written for Ibex, which were 'Lover', 'Blag' and 'FEWA' (which stood for Feelings Ended Worn Away). Freddie also persuaded them to include Elvis Presley's 'Jailhouse Rock' and Little Richard's 'Lucille'.

Freddie and Chris Chesney, who was about seventeen at the time, became close friends and Chris moved into the house that Freddie shared with Smile in Ferry Road, Barnes. The pair started songwriting together. The other members of Sour Milk Sea were more than a little peeved that Chris and Freddie spent so much time together, and felt rather insecure about the future of the band. After just two months, Jeremy, who owned nearly all the equipment, decided to take it back and break up the band. By the middle of April 1970, Sour Milk Sea were no more.

Not long after the band's demise, Freddie's and Chris's friendship began to fade. Chris finally decided to go back to Oxford University to continue the studies he had neglected for a stab at musical stardom.

Up to now Freddie hadn't had an opportunity to exercise his artistic skill commercially; any drawings he produced were usually for his own personal enjoyment or for friends. In early 1970 he visited several agencies who he hoped would find a use for his talents and was taken on by the Austin Knights Agency in Chancery Lane, designing or drawing for magazines, newspapers and books. Little came of it, although he was asked to illustrate a children's futuristic space story. Unfortunately, although Freddie started the work, the book never made it into print. He soon got tired of sitting around waiting for the agency to ring and decided he would be better off as a freelance designer and artist. He advertised locally and in magazines although by now he was convinced that he should be channeling his energies into his music. He remained friendly with the three guys in Smile, who were still doing the very thing he knew in his heart he wanted to pursue.

CHAPTER 5

AS IT BEGAN

IT WAS OBVIOUS TO EVERYONE THAT FREDDIE, BRIAN AND ROGER should combine their talents and work together. Between them, they had enough expertise and ability to cope with the vagaries of the music business. Freddie had some extraordinary and far-sighted ideas for this new venture, but first they had to decide what to call themselves. Brian and Roger had both read the same trilogy of books by C. S. Lewis during their childhood – *Out of the Silent Planet* – from which the phrase 'the Grand Dance' had come, and that was a popular contender for the name. Roger also liked the sound of The Rich Kids and Build Your Own Boat, but Freddie remained unconvinced, and persuaded them at least to consider one of his ideas – Queen.

At first Brian and Roger were unsure about it, perhaps due to its camp overtones, but both could also see its potential. It was short, memorable and had the connotations of royalty, drama and dynamism that they all agreed would be their trademarks for the future. Freddie, on this occasion, got his own way, and in May 1970 the three began life as Queen.

The first task was to find a bass player. Roger called Mike Grose from Cornwall, remembering him from Reaction and PJ's club in Truro. Mike was not only a good bass player, but he also owned a

Roger's band name idea doodles...

huge Marshall amplifier stack and a Volkswagen van, both valuable pieces of equipment for a struggling new band. He agreed to come up to London and play with them, although it meant leaving his current local band, Bent Cement. As an inauspicious start to his career with Queen, the windscreen in Mike's van shattered on his journey up from St Austell, and he drove nearly all the way praying it wouldn't rain.

At that stage, Queen didn't own much equipment, and what they had was a mismatched mixture of old amps and homemade gear, but it was enough to see them through those early days of constant rehearsals. They were lucky in that Brian, who was highly thought of at Imperial College, was given free use of unoccupied lecture theatres and storage space in empty rooms.

Both Brian and Freddie had some experience of songwriting, and through salvaging the songs from Ibex, Smile and Wreckage days, and adapting them to suit their new image, they rehearsed a fair amount of original material. They all felt that this new band should combine the intensity of theatre with strong, powerful rock music. It was important, they agreed, that an audience had something good to watch as well as hear – according to Brian, this was far from fashionable at the time. Freddie's own performance was a practised blend of the strength and grace of ballet – an art for which he had great admiration – and drama.

From past experience the band felt they could handle most of what the music business could throw at them, and they were determined to keep tight control of their career in every aspect. Freddie and Roger were convinced that this was going to be *the* band. Brian was equally as excited and certain of the band's future, although he continued with his thesis, intending to complete it.

Roger and Freddie had become inseparable, and were regularly seen parading along Kensington High Street decked out in the latest fashions. The stall in the market meant they were able to acquire the necessary items and they were not afraid to flaunt them. The two of them spent a lot of time with friends in the Kensington pub in Earls Court and the Greyhound, down a side street next to the market – everyone lived reasonably close to both establishments so they became gathering points. Freddie's promenades along the High Street had another purpose, though, apart from pure exhibitionism. At that time Kensington High Street was a mecca for important music industry people and musicians, and the atmosphere was often likened to New York's Greenwich Village. In his most immaculate apparel, Freddie often bumped into record company VIPs or fellow musicians and always acknowledged them, even if they didn't have a clue who he was, which would give him enough reason to approach them again at parties or gatherings, with the possibility of something worthwhile for Queen coming out of it.

Some months previously, Roger's mother had begun to arrange a Red Cross charity event in the City Hall in Truro, and Roger had agreed that Smile would play. Even though Smile was defunct he

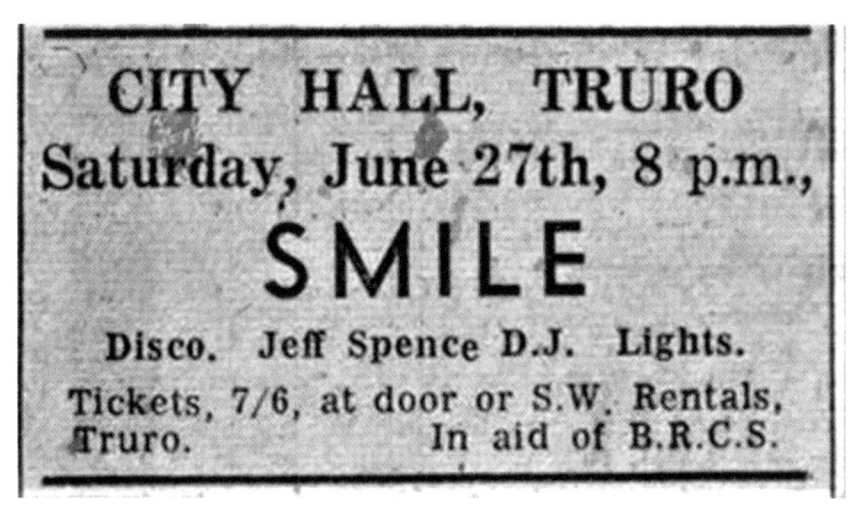

> **CITY HALL, TRURO**
> Saturday, June 27th, 8 p.m.,
> **SMILE**
> Disco. Jeff Spence D.J. Lights.
> Tickets, 7/6, at door or S.W. Rentals, Truro.   In aid of B.R.C.S.

The advert for Smile in Truro, which in fact turned out to be Queen's first public performance.

didn't want to let her or the charity down, and so he took the embryonic Queen to Truro to play the gig. They were accompanied by John Harris. Pete Edmunds and John had ceased to see eye to eye by this time, as, in Pete's opinion, John had got so close to Queen that he almost considered himself the fifth member. Pete had decided his services were obviously no longer required and left just before the first Queen gigs.

It was 27 June 1970 and although in the advertisements they were still billed as Smile, it was their first public performance as Queen. They opened the set with a revamped Wreckage song, 'Stone Cold Crazy'. Freddie was nervous; although well-rehearsed, he hadn't played in front of a proper audience before with this band and his stage performance wasn't as professional as he would have liked. But all in all the band played well and were appreciated – and were even paid £50 for expenses. Queen's insistence that they have a distinct visual style meant they played that first gig wearing striking silk stage costumes, predominantly black and white – certainly a far cry from most other bands then, who wore plain blue jeans and T-shirts. They all wore silver rings, bangles and neck chains, at a time when men didn't go in for much jewellery.

Around this time, Freddie decided to change his name. Bulsara wasn't really the kind of name for someone who was going to be hugely famous – his faith in himself was so strong. He chose Mercury, the mythical messenger of the gods. He thought it was rather apt.

• • •

The band arranged a gig in a lecture theatre at Imperial College for an invited audience of record company VIPs and close friends, to prove how far they had progressed. Shortly after that, on 25 July 1970, they were booked to play at PJ's in Truro. Although by now they had played two concerts as Queen, this was the first time they were billed under that name. That gig, however, was the last for Mike Grose, who had been playing bass for over seven years. He says, 'I was getting tired of playing. I wanted to try other things, get what everyone called a "proper job", and I missed Cornwall. I thought, even then, that this band might one day make it big. But that didn't stop me wanting to get out.' Freddie, Brian and Roger also felt that, for musical reasons, the situation wasn't working. So they amicably parted company with Mike in August 1970. The other three immediately began their search for a replacement – they had a gig booked at Imperial College for late August so time was of the essence. A friend of Roger's knew a bass player called Barry Mitchell and phoned to tell him of the vacancy in Queen. Barry contacted Roger and an audition was arranged at Imperial. They all seemed to get on well, Barry looked the part – blond and handsome – and time was short, so Barry was asked to join, starting then and there.

'I felt like such an outsider when I first joined the band,' says Barry. 'They had everything worked out. Just before my first gig, Freddie suggested we all camp it up and wear women's clothes. He really wanted to play on it, but it just didn't happen, thank God!'

The new line-up rehearsed zealously – still at Imperial – and even played a couple of impromptu gigs for friends to gauge the reaction. All they needed now were some small gigs to get themselves up and running again, starting with the Imperial gig on 23 August. They used simple lighting but all wore fancy stage costumes. Freddie even went so far as to procure the talents of Wendy de Smet, the dressmaker who had provided some of the clothes for the market stall, to design their outfits. Wendy would also later create his 'Mercury suit': a black one-piece outfit with a deep slashed front and 'wings' on the cuffs and ankles, and a white version of it. During the Imperial show the audience were treated to free apple juice and buckets of popcorn, which had been carried from Freddie's flat earlier in the day. The band set out to prove that they were different in all aspects, and that night they went down well – but as the audience were

AS IT BEGAN

friends of the band, they may have been somewhat biased! One friend in the audience that night was producer John Anthony, who was very impressed. A few days later, on 29 August, he turned up at Roger and Freddie's Kensington Market stall and said he wanted to record the band.

They went on to play in Swiss Cottage, London, in September, at a private school for American children whose parents worked at the American Embassy. The audience was young, didn't really like the music and the band didn't do too well – but they were paid, so put it down to experience.

On 18 September 1970, Freddie and Roger closed their Kensington Market stall for the day in mourning for Jimi Hendrix, who died that day. He had been a huge influence on all the members of Queen, and his death was a tragic end to a brilliant, if volatile career. As a mark of respect they played 'Voodoo Chile' during that night's rehearsal.

Freddie and Roger came to a joint conclusion that they'd had enough of sharing flats with the world and his wife and anyone else who needed a bed, and so were on the look-out for a flat they could share. Freddie found the perfect place to rent in Shepherd's Bush, a spacious apartment complete with a grand piano, belonging to the elderly owner.

Queen were keen to do as many gigs as possible, and they booked one at the College of Estate Management in Kensington on 16 October 1970. They invited the 120 people they considered their closest friends, of whom eighty turned up, and most of the Kensington pub crowd. 'That night we saw such an improvement,' says Wendy, Freddie's dressmaker, and who, some years later, married Smile's first roadie, Pete Edmonds. 'They were brilliant; they were happier with each other, they were well rehearsed. It just came across to us, and we felt that we were witnessing the emergence of a band of star status. It was such a good experience.'

Other gigs were provided by ex-Ibex roadie and manager Ken Testi. Ken was studying at St Helens College of Technology on Merseyside and was the college's social secretary. As such, he was in charge of booking bands to play at college balls and dances, and his first task was to ensure that Queen, with whom he was still friendly, were given a few engagements. 'I was in a position to give them work. I knew talent when I saw it, and they had it in abundance, all they needed was a break.'

Soon after gigs began to come thick and fast, in and around London, and on Merseyside in St Helens and Liverpool, including dates at the famous Cavern Club – where The Beatles had first played – on 27 and 28 November 1970. Roger comments in his diary at the time: *'Good gigs, esp. Sat night. Asked back.'* Sadly, they never had the opportunity to return.

An excerpt from Roger's diary.

The day after a gig in St Helens, the band had some time to kill before the drive back to London and decided to visit a local cinema, which specialised in pornographic films. They paid and went in, and the film started. 'We all sat there, and then this huge pair of tits came on screen. That was it, we were in fits, crying with laughter,' said Barry. 'We couldn't stop. Eventually, the manager came up and threw us out. That made us giggle all the more as we staggered up the aisle to the exit!'

During their trips to the north-west the band were forced to rely on the hospitality of friends with spare beds, or floors, as they couldn't afford hotels. On one particularly cold day, Brian was staying with Pat and Helen McConnell's family in St Helen's. He sat down in the living room in front of the fire and stretched out his legs over the grate, feet on the mantelpiece. Says Helen, 'Suddenly we could all smell burning. It was dreadful, an awful smell. My dad was the first to realise that it was Brian's boots – they were melting!'

By January 1971, Barry had decided he no longer fit in. There was tension within the band and things weren't moving fast enough. He was impatient to start earning much-needed money, whereas the other three were prepared to bide their time and work on their material and presentation, knowing it would pay better dividends in the long run. Barry played two more gigs with Queen, 8 January 1971 at the Marquee in Wardour Street and 9 January at the Ewell Technical College in Surrey, where both Queen and Genesis supported Kevin Ayres and the Whole World Band, after which Barry and the band parted company and the search was on for yet another bass player. They auditioned several people, and finally settled on Doug Bogie, mainly because he came equipped with a substantial array of gear. Rehearsals began to initiate Doug into the band, and all seemed well.

In February, Queen played two shows, one at the Hornsey Town Hall, and the other at Kingston Polytechnic – a gig near Doug's home territory – supporting Yes. After cajoling friends into being impromptu spotlight operators at that gig, Queen took to the stage. But Doug had invited all his friends to the show and, not far into the set, he completely took over. He did his own outrageous stage act – 'He jumped up and down in a manner most incongruous,' says Brian – stealing the limelight from the rest of the band. The next day Doug was fired.

It was becoming increasingly disheartening for the other band members as they parted company with their third bass player, and Roger and Brian cheered themselves up by accompanying John Harris, who was still working with them as a roadie, to a disco at the Maria Assumpta Teacher Training College. During the evening they were introduced to a friend of a friend, John Deacon. Talk turned to music, and they soon discovered that John was a bass player. John, who wasn't in a band at the time, was invited to audition. He accepted the offer, and they all agreed to meet a few days later.

CHAPTER 6

JOHN RICHARD DEACON

BSC (HONS)(1ST CLASS)

JOHN RICHARD DEACON WAS BORN ON SUNDAY 19 AUGUST 1951 AT the St Francis Private Hospital, London Road, Leicester, to Lillian Molly and Arthur Henry Deacon. Arthur Deacon worked in insurance for the Norwich Union in Leicester. Quiet, shy John started at his first school – the Linden Junior School in Evington – in 1956, the year his sister, Julie, was born. When John was just seven, his parents bought him his first guitar, a red plastic 'Tommy Steele' special. In 1960 the family moved to Oadby, still on the outskirts of Leicester, and John transferred to Langmoor Junior School.

John's father encouraged his son to get involved in his own hobby, of tinkering with electronics, and the young boy soon became engrossed. He adapted an old reel-to-reel tape recorder and used it to record music from the radio – usually The Beatles and Alan Freeman's hit parade show, *Pick Of The Pops*. In the early sixties, as his interest in music grew, he bought the first two Beatles albums on reel-to-reel tape. Even though he loved music, electronics became his main hobby and he aspired to expanding that hobby into a career.

His father gave him a ham radio receiver when he was ten, and he spent hours with it in the garden shed, picking up different stations and news items. He and his father also spent time together trainspotting, and fishing in the local river and canal.

In 1962, aged eleven, John moved to Gartree High School in Leicester, where he was an average student, working as hard as was necessary. A huge Beatles fan, he had decided that he wanted to learn to play guitar and saved the money from his early-morning paper round and other odd jobs to buy one. He had soon accumulated enough for a basic acoustic guitar, and then had to learn to play it. He applied himself with his accustomed diligence and it wasn't long before he and his school friends were rehearsing together in a friend's garage. It was during these early rehearsals that John began to realise he enjoyed being in a group; it became something for him to look forward to at weekends and after school. He and pal Roger 'Splodge' Ogden would play along to records or listen to tapes to master songs by other bands. They also bought sheet music to learn the chords for popular songs.

Sadly, that year John's father died. They were very close and it affected John deeply. He consoled himself with his music.

John was fourteen when he formed his first band, The Opposition. Lead singer was Richard Young, who was older than the other boys and worked for his father's company. He had a bit more money than the rest of them and owned a Hammond organ and could afford to buy equipment such as microphones and amplifiers. He also helped the others to acquire their own gear. The bass player was Clive Castledine, the drummer Nigel Bullen, with whom John had rehearsed before, and John himself played rhythm guitar. He used a Hofner, borrowed from Richard, with only one working pickup – it originally had three, but Richard claimed two of them to improve his own instrument! John had realised quite early on that his own acoustic wasn't suitable, so had bought a second-hand Broadway Solid in the

JOHN RICHARD DEACON

local music shop sale for £5, which proved unplayable – hence the borrowed guitar.

The band's first full practice as The Opposition was in Nigel Bullen's garage in early 1965. The band played a mixture of pop, soul and Tamla Motown songs, all cover versions of music popular at the time. They wrote one tune themselves, though, called 'Heart Full Of Soul'.

On 25 September 1965, The Opposition played their first public gig at a party at Clive Castledine's house. Just a month later they made their proper debut in the hall at Gartree School, where they went down exceptionally well. So keen were these young musicians to get to work that they advertised in the local *Oadby and Wigston Advertiser* as available for 'engagements, parties, dances etc.', which cost them the princely sum of thirty-two shillings for two weeks.

By November 1965, when The Opposition had done a few gigs, they decided to try out a new singer to add harmonies. Richard Frew became a member, which meant that a new microphone had to be added to the growing list of equipment. However, a December rehearsal was the scene of the first of many line-up changes within the band, and Richard's musical career ended abruptly when they dropped him.

On 4 December 1965 they played their first major gig, as a support to local band the Rapids Rave at the Co-operative Hall in Enderby, and were paid £2. They played many gigs in and around Leicester at Enderby, Wigston, Evington and Countesthorpe. By now they were amassing quite a following, when in April 1966 they acquired a new member, Pete 'Pedro' Bart, owner of a Reslo microphone.

In April, bass player Clive Castledine left the band, leaving the vacancy that John Deacon decided to fill: he bought his first bass, an EKO, in a music-shop sale for £22, leaving Pedro to take over as rhythm guitarist.

Because of the change in line-up, the band changed their name in May 1966 – a daring move – to The New Opposition. The band played every weekend and some weekday nights at clubs, pubs, halls, fetes and weddings, supporting other local bands or as headliners. A notable gig came in August 1966, when they were again supporting the Rapids Rave and many in the audience commented that the New Opposition had outplayed the headliners!

September saw the start of John's first term at Beauchamp Grammar School in Leicester. He was still interested in electronics, and he started the new term full of enthusiasm and great ideas for the future.

In October 1966 the band played at the Leicester Casino in the Midland Beat Championships. The other band booked to play, The Stray, didn't turn up, so The New Opposition won through to the semi-finals – and were paid £5. New Year's Eve 1966 found John and the band seeing in the year at the same place they had seen in the previous year – the Market Harborough Youth Club.

By January 1967, The New Opposition decided they needed another change of name. Several were suggested, including The New Hood and Feelin'. Neither was quite right, and they reverted to their original name. In February that year a photograph of them appeared in the *Oadby and Wigston Advertiser*, to congratulate the 'Oadby Beat Group' on reaching the finals of the Midland Beat Championships, to be held at the De Montfort Hall, Leicester – which never took place as someone forgot to hire the hall. The line-up now consisted of Nigel Bullen, Richard Young, Ronald Chester, David Williams and John Deacon.

Throughout 1967, the refreshed Opposition played gigs at clubs and private parties, RAF bases and the USAF base at Molesworth. Their stage show now included two go-go dancers, Jenny and Charmaine, and the band were concentrating more on their image – they all sported silk shirts in different colours. For such a young band they were earning good wages on the circuit, £10 to £15 per night or more.

In early 1968, The Opposition had bookings every weekend and had earned enough to consider buying their own van – they had had to rely on friends and relatives to transport them to and from gigs up till now. During the break in a gig at the Roundhills Youth Centre they went out and bought a second-hand blue Morris J2 1961 van.

March saw another name change, the band agreeing unanimously on Art, suggested by David Williams. They must have been one of the first local bands to use their own lightshow at gigs that were big enough to accommodate it. Bookings were coming from further afield now – St Neots, Kettering, Melton Mowbray – but things were going too well. In September 1968 one of the longest-serving members, Richard Young, left. He said he had found himself another group.

John was now seventeen, studying for his A-levels and fitting schoolwork in around his playing. He had always thought he would end up in London and had studied hard between gigs. His goal was still to make electronics his full-time career and he left Beauchamp Grammar School in June 1969 with eight O-levels – in English Language, English Literature, Maths, Physics, Chemistry, Biology, French and Special Maths – and three A-levels in Maths, Further Maths and Physics, all at grade A. His results were more than adequate to land him a place at Chelsea College, part of the University Of London, to study electronics. He was due to start his course in October 1969, and in August he played his final gig with Art, at the Great Glen Youth Club. He hated the idea of anyone replacing him in the band, but the move to London was more important, and he left hoping that something great would happen in the Big City. Art replaced him quite quickly, with bass player John Savage.

During his first year at college John wasn't involved with the music scene, although he had brought his old acoustic guitar with him, just in case. The time passed uneventfully and he settled into college life, devoting all his time to his studies.

He did, however, regularly go to gigs at his and other colleges, and saw many local and up-and-coming bands. He was at one in the College of Estate Management in Kensington, in October 1970, to see a band called Queen. He recalls, 'They were all dressed in black, and the lights were very dim too, so all I could really see were four shadowy figures. They didn't make a lasting impression on me at the time.'

As he began his second year at Chelsea College, John realised he missed music and being involved in a band: he had been part of one for so long that he found it hard to give it up completely. He persuaded his mother to drive all his equipment to London even though he had no idea what he was going to do with it. He was sharing a flat in Queensgate with Peter Stoddart, a guitarist and fellow student, and they sometimes played guitar together, to improvise and practise.

They joined forces with a couple of fellow students, Don Cater on drums and Albert, another guitarist, and jammed together, playing covers of popular songs, none of them as yet having ventured into songwriting. They didn't have a name – they'd never done any gigs and hadn't thought they'd need one – but they were approached to play at a concert in the college with a couple of other bands on 21 November 1970. As it was to be advertised, they needed a name and decided on Deacon just for that gig. The band played blues and R&B-type tunes, but although John was playing again, he wasn't happy. The band weren't quite right. He regularly looked through the music papers at the 'Musicians Wanted' advertisements but only went for one proper audition. He wasn't offered the job, so spent his summer vacation working as a tea boy for the British Tourist Authority in London to earn some extra money.

In late February 1971 John attended a disco with Peter Stoddart and a friend of his, Christine Farnell, at Maria Assumpta Teacher Training College. Christine introduced John to three friends of hers, Roger Taylor, Brian May and John Harris. Roger and Brian were both members of Queen, the band John had seen previously – and

JOHN RICHARD DEACON

they were looking for a bass player. They asked John if he was interested in auditioning. On Sunday 28 February 1971, he turned up at a lecture theatre in Imperial College, where Queen had made arrangements to rehearse. The equipment was all set up on the floor – they had AC30 amps, a drum kit and the lead singer, Freddie, had a microphone and a small amplifier. John arrived with his bass guitar and a tiny amplifier (it became known as the 'Deacy Amp') and proceeded to learn 'Son And Daughter' and a couple of other songs that Queen were performing at the time. The audition ended with them playing the blues in a lengthy jam session. John left that evening with the promise that he would be contacted soon, and the rest of the band proceeded to discuss him in depth. Says Roger, 'We thought he was great. We were all so used to each other, and were so over the top, we thought that because he was quiet he would fit in with us without too much upheaval. He was a great bass player too – and the fact that he was a wizard with electronics was definitely a deciding factor!'

The following day, on 1 March, they asked him to join the band – and John Richard Deacon became the fourth and final member of Kensington-based band Queen.

CHAPTER 7

THE TRIDENT YEARS

BRIAN, FREDDIE AND ROGER KNEW THAT THEY HAD FINALLY FOUND the permanent fourth member of Queen, and threw themselves into intensive rehearsals to familiarise John with their repertoire – rehearsals that continued for five months. Although John was busy with Queen and his electronics studies, he still found time to attend discos and dances at other colleges, and it was at one such disco at the Maria Assumpta College in March that he met student Veronica Tetzlaff, after which they began to see each other regularly.

He continued to study, as even though he considered Queen to be his passport to a full-time musical career, he also saw the sense in obtaining the degree he had worked so hard towards. Brian was still working on his thesis, too. They all knew how fickle the entertainment business could be and wanted to ensure they had something to fall back on lest it all come to nothing.

John's first gig with Queen was at Ewell Technical College in Surrey on 2 July 1971. He was quite happy to wear one of his favourite shirts, but Freddie, who didn't like it, insisted on lending him a T-shirt. Not a great start, but it didn't deter them, and the gig, although small, was a reasonable success. Not long after that, on 11 July, Queen played at Imperial College. It was rather a nervous time for John, as most people at Imperial had seen Queen many times with their other bass players – but he proved himself a worthy addition. This was the gig at which the audience were treated yet again to homemade popcorn. The band had spent the morning in Brian's tiny kitchen (a converted corridor), at his flat in Queensgate Terrace, making it. In the audience that night was producer John Anthony, who said to the band as he was leaving, 'I'll call you soon . . .'

At this point Roger decided he needed extra income and registered on a college course for a biology degree – which made him eligible for a grant. He enrolled at the North London Polytechnic in early July 1971. The course he was following involved plant and animal biology, and his first task was to study the exotic plant life at London's Kew Gardens.

Queen wanted to perform as much as possible. Rehearsing was all well and good but the fun lay in playing to live audiences. Roger arranged a short tour of his home turf in Cornwall. His mother wasn't too keen to have the whole band and their convoy sleeping on her front-room floor this time – it was getting overcrowded, with roadies, girlfriends, friends and hangers on – so they rented a small three-bedroomed cottage on the outskirts of Truro.

The tour included such high spots as the Wadebridge Town Hall, RNAS Culdrose and a pub in St Agnes called the Driftwood Spars. The landlord protested that they were far too loud and asked them to turn down the volume, but Queen were resolute – the volume was right and wasn't being touched. After the gig, when the equipment had been taken down and packed away, a lengthy, heated argument ensued. No one knows quite what was said or implied, but finally everything was resolved and the band were paid for the gig – although, as they fled the pub in the van, a posse of local lads in a battered old car gave chase. The band outran them around the quiet, narrow lanes, managing to escape.

Throughout the tour, the posters relentlessly advertised 'Roger

Taylor and Queen' – and on one occasion in Truro, which the others have never let him forget, 'Legendary Cornish drummer Roger Taylor' printed in large capitals 'and his band Queen' printed in lower case.

Their final booking on the 'Cornish Tour' was their first outdoor gig, a festival at the Tregye Country Club, on Carnon Downs outside Truro, on 21 August 1971. Queen were second from last on a bill headed by Arthur Brown's Kingdom Come and Hawkwind. Tickets were £1.25 for nine bands, and the posters advertised 'Food, freaks, licensed bar and lovely things . . .'

When they got back to London in September, Brian decided to arrange a gig at Imperial College as a private showcase for some of the agencies responsible for arranging bookings for bands in the capital. Queen had a number of gigs booked, but at what they considered small, unimportant venues. They felt they should be doing bigger and better concerts. Brian persuaded several agency people to attend the gig in one of the lecture theatres but none of the VIPs were impressed. They didn't get one booking out of it, and began to feel despondent. Fame was an elusive creature.

Around September 1971, Brian called an old friend, Terry Yeadon. He asked him if he knew of anywhere the new band could do some recording, cheaply. Terry told Brian he was now working for De Lane Lea, who had moved their studio complex to Wembley from central London – and that the studio were looking for musicians to test the new equipment they had installed. The criteria was simple: the band had to be LOUD!

Terry asked De Lane Lea studio director Dave Siddell if Queen could be the band to test the gear; he said yes. The deal was that the musicians would record using the equipment, and potential studio users would be on hand to hear and watch them. In return for their services the band could record their demos for free. It was an opportunity not to be missed and, of course, Queen jumped at it. Not only

Driftwood Spars

BARS
ST. AGNES

Special this Monday—FREE DANCING

The Legendary Drummer of Cornwall

ROGER TAYLOR

and

QUEEN

.... FREE ENTERTAINMENT EVERY NIGHT ....

TO-NIGHT	SUNDAY
Dancing to	JACKIE (BABY)
HAIRY MAGPIE	**ARMSTRONG**
	Disco for the over-18's.
FRIDAY	
Sing-along with the	TUESDAY
FERRYBOATERS	It's Folk with
Cornwall's top pub songsters	**IAN**
SATURDAY	WEDNESDAY
MONTY	**SWEET ESSENCE**
on the Wurlitzer.	The Gruesome Twosome.

would they be able to make the all-important demo tapes, but they would have ample occasion to meet producers and engineers, people who could be vital to their future. They went into the studios on 18 September to start their work.

The producer/engineer with whom they were testing the equipment was Louie Austin and, as Roger and Brian already had studio experience, they were able to work together quite closely. They were all concerned that the tapes should be as good and as professional as it was possible to make them and had definite ideas about the way they were recorded and mixed. 'They were very fussy,' Louie recalls. 'The songs were done one by one. They would carry on until they thought it was right. It sometimes took a very long time. But they put up with so much shit too, during that time.'

The sessions in De Lane Lea were arduous. The band had to move constantly from studio to studio, taking down their own gear, moving it themselves and then setting it all up again next door, but the time they had in each of those studios, especially the biggest one, wasn't wasted. They did their demo tapes free – and rehearsed their stage show without disturbance.

However, the problems in the new studios were endless. During one session they kept hearing clicks during the recording and couldn't work out what they were until they realised the clicking happened whenever they touched metal and that the studio floor contained metal ducts to carry cables. When it was time for a 'take' and the tapes were going, everyone had to stand stock-still until it was finished.

Still, they recorded five of their own compositions, 'Liar', 'Keep Yourself Alive', 'The Night Comes Down', 'Great King Rat' and 'Jesus'. Part of 'Liar' had started life as the Ibex track 'Lover', co-written with Mike Bersin. Says Brian: 'I had heard Wreckage play this track in a rehearsal, and particularly liked one riff, but the rest of the song was changed drastically by the four of us, using some of my own riffs and Freddie's words. There is actually an interesting aside to this. "Liar" was one of the first songs that we worked on together, and there was a moment when we discussed if we should all be credited in such cases. Freddie said, "As far as I'm concerned the person who wrote the words has effectively written the song." It may not have been the most logical solution, but it was a workable rule which we used virtually unchanged right up to the last two albums, when we decided to share everything regardless of origin. The rule almost certainly discouraged us from co-operating on lyrics for a long time and started a trend towards separateness in song-producing in general.'

They were all pleased with the final product: their professional attitude had made it easier for producer Louie to work with them. They always knew exactly what they wanted and he had only to guide them in achieving it. Even with the technical problems they faced they had come through it intact and enthusiastic.

By this time Roger had become bored with the Kensington Market scene and the stall – he thought of himself as a musician, not a market trader. So he left the stall in the capable and still willing hands of Freddie. He joined forces with fellow stall owner Alan Mair to make the most of their clothes, jewellery and fashionable boots. Alan's stall was directly opposite a ladies' clothes stall, and it didn't take long for Freddie to realise that with some minor adjustments to the ladies' changing-room mirrors, and by fractionally moving the cash desk on his and Alan's stall, he could get a great view of all the women changing!

Freddie still had many friends on the Kensington scene, and had grown close to one in particular, whom he had met back in 1970 while she'd been on a date with Brian May – the manageress of the Kensington High Street Biba boutique, Mary Austin. 'It took Freddie nearly six months to finally ask me out!' she said, a procrastination that caused confusion. 'I thought he fancied my best friend, so I used to avoid him. One night we were at one of his gigs, and after it had finished he came looking for me. I left him at the bar with my friend to go to the loo, but I actually sneaked out. He was furious!' But finally he had the courage to ask Mary out, and she became an almost constant companion.

On 9 December, Queen played a gig at the swimming baths in Epsom, Surrey. They were supporting Arthur Brown's Kingdom Come again. It was an awful gig: the acoustics were poor and, as always at swimming pools, it echoed even though the pool was covered with boards.

By the end of 1971 Queen were still relatively unknown, except to students at Imperial College and a few fans in Cornwall and Merseyside, but the band were still determined to make it. Said Freddie: 'There was never a doubt, darling, never. I just knew we would make it, and I told everyone who asked just that.'

Queen were still using De Lane Lea, demonstrating the new equipment for possible customers, and recording their own material, when John Anthony visited. He was accompanied by Roy Thomas Baker, who was involved with management company Trident. They were at the studios with the intention of using it for future projects, but when they saw Queen, they stayed for a while and watched and listened with interest. John had of course seen the embryonic Queen at Imperial, and then again at John Deacon's first outing with the band. He realised just how massively Roger and Brian had improved since Smile's first studio sessions. He had a chat with the band and they offered him a demo tape to take away with him.

Roy and John were enthusiastic about the new band they had seen and they listened to the tape to convince themselves that what they heard was as impressive as they thought. They played the demo to Trident boss Norman Sheffield: 'I found that first tape interesting,' he says. 'You could tell there was talent individually, and they could play, they were good musicians. But I was wary of making a full commitment at such an early stage.'

With demo tape in hand Brian, Roger and Ken Testi, who was once again living in London, began to do the rounds of record companies. It was a thankless task, arriving at reception desks and being greeted by uninterested receptionists who wouldn't let them near the man in charge of the Artists and Repertoire section. 'Sorry, the A&R man is at lunch', 'Sorry, you can't see Mr So-and-So as he's got someone with him', and on and on.

THE TRIDENT YEARS

In January 1972, John organised a gig at Bedford College – he had friends there who said it would be good. However, the audience that night consisted of just six people, and John considers it to forever be one of the most embarrassing moments in his life!

Finally, Tony Sheraton-Smith, the head of Chrysalis Records, showed an interest in Queen, and even went so far as to offer them a deal. It was, at least, a break – but after much discussion the band turned him down. Chrysalis had made an offer but the money was not good enough for four broke young men in need of equipment.

Trident were still contemplating getting involved with the band but wanted to see them live before they made any decision. They also wanted to see if any of the major record companies would be interested in signing them. They were booked to play at a hospital dance in Forest Hill, London, on 24 March 1972 and Barry Sheffield, Norman's brother and co-owner of Trident, decided, on Roy Baker's recommendation, to go and see them.

It was a good night. Queen were relaxed and happy, and the audience liked them. Barry was suitably impressed, and there and then offered Queen a contract with Trident Audio Productions.

In May 1972 they were on the verge of signing the deal with Trident but insisted on there being three separate agreements: the publishing rights, recording deal and management contract had to be negotiated separately, or the band were not interested. They were pushing their luck, but Trident were convinced that the band were worth sticking with, and three agreements were drawn up, though not yet signed. Still, Trident bought Queen a brand new PA system and new instruments for all except Brian, who was more than happy with his homemade Red Special guitar.

Barry and Norman Sheffield had long conversations about the prospects of their protégés, both certain they could do something with the band, even though some of their music business colleagues thought they were mad to consider taking on a group with a name like Queen! But they were determined and, although Norman had sworn to Queen that he would personally take care of them and their future, he knew he would need to employ a full-time manager to deal with the day-to-day affairs of the band.

Trident Audio Productions had been set up by Norman and Barry Sheffield with the advice and assistance of an American, Jack Nelson. In the States, Jack had been involved with a small, progressive record company called Blue Thumb. He had been introduced to Norman Sheffield by a mutual acquaintance and was fascinated by the music coming out of Trident Studios, which was considered one of the hottest studios in London, and the work of engineers such as Robin Cable, Ken Scott and Roy Baker, which was highly acclaimed.

Jack had given Norman the idea of setting up a production company, with a view to turning it eventually into a record company. His involvement, however, was in a purely advisory capacity, so Norman's first thought was of Jack Nelson when he found himself in need of managerial advice.

Norman flew to the USA for talks with Jack, taking with him tapes from the three bands he was (unknown to Queen) touting as a package: Queen, Eugene Wallace, and Mark Ashton and Headstone. Jack listened to the tapes and was immediately interested, but particularly in Queen. He said, 'I heard that Queen sound, and I just knew it had promise, how could I not? I knew that John Anthony had a good ear for talent, and this was yet more proof of that.'

Jack agreed to become involved with Trident, and part of the deal he struck with Norman Sheffield was Queen. He took the Queen tape to everyone he could think of, but none of them wanted to know. 'They all told me that Queen just weren't going to happen. They were crazy. But I had to find someone who was qualified – we had an investment in Queen, and their careers.' Jack approached all the best managers he could think of but all of them passed. 'They just didn't have the vision.'

THE TRIDENT YEARS

Soon after, Jack ran into a friend in London, who was working for American manager Dee Anthony. Jack told him about Queen, and the friend offered to set up a meeting with Dee. At midnight that night at his home in Hampstead, Jack was telephoned and told that Dee would see him – right then. He got up and drove down to Park Lane, arriving well after 1 a.m. He played the tape, and Dee's comment was, 'No, no, no. I've got a group called Humble Pie who are going to be MUCH bigger than this group will ever be.' He told Jack he should manage the band himself, reminding him that if he was prepared to have a meeting at that time in the morning for them, he had already begun that management. Driving back home afterwards, Jack decided to follow Dee's advice. He knew the music business as well as anyone, so why not?

'During the summer of 1972 I took the demo tape to EMI to see if I could interest them in giving Queen a recording deal,' said Jack. 'They had already been turned down by Decca but EMI were at the time in the throes of setting up a rock label. Previous artists had been released on the His Master's Voice label, and EMI wanted to distinguish between their more mature ballad-type acts and the new young talent they were aiming for. I offered them the package of three acts that I myself had been offered, but EMI said they only wanted Queen. Trident would not compromise – it was all or nothing – and EMI turned them all down.'

Undaunted, Trident sent Queen into their own 24-track recording studios to start work on an album. Although Trident had high hopes for the band, the studios were very busy and Queen were only given 'down time' to record: they could work only when the studio was not being used by other acts, which meant either late nights or weekends. The artists using the main studio time were the likes of David Bowie, The Beach Boys, The Rolling Stones and Elton John but even so, Queen were more than a little aggrieved at being asked to use spare time. It meant a lot of hanging around at the studios, waiting for other bands to finish, as it was often at short notice that the studio came free, and the band didn't want to miss a minute of precious session time. But they weren't idle, and while they sat and waited they wrote songs and worked together on new ideas.

In another studio in the Trident complex, producer Robin Cable was experimenting with an old Beach Boys song, 'I Can Hear Music'. Phil Spector had been in the studios previously, recording with Ronnie Spector, and Robin was trying to achieve a Phil Spector-type sound as a tribute to the man himself. Robin had heard Freddie singing in the other studio, and as he seemed to have time on his hands now and again, asked him if he would sing that song for him. Freddie didn't mind – why not do something constructive while waiting around at Trident? After the initial recording session he told Robin he thought the track needed something more – and Roger was drafted in to add percussion overdubs, castanets, tambourines and maracas. The original solo break had been played on a Moog synthesizer, which didn't seem to work, so Freddie persuaded Robin that Brian could do the job better on guitar. Brian played a two-part harmony passage, the first example of this kind of work to be released to the public, and a solo on the fade-out. Freddie also recorded a version of the Dusty Springfield classic 'Goin' Back' for Robin,

When it was finished Robin loved 'I Can Hear Music'; it sounded very 'Spectoresque', but he still wasn't sure of what to do with it. The recording, however, had at least given Freddie, Roger and Brian (John had been elsewhere and wasn't involved) the opportunity to garner more studio experience, which was no bad thing. Robin assured them that whatever he did with the tracks, he would be sure to let them know. They went back to working on Queen songs and thought nothing more of it.

The summer of 1972 was a quiet one for Queen. They were still using as much studio time as Trident could provide to work on their album. Freddie was still working with Alan Mair in Kensington Market,

THE TRIDENT YEARS

which was bringing in some money. John graduated from college in June 1972 with a first-class honours degree in electronics. Although he felt happy with Queen and loved the music, things were moving slowly and he was pragmatic enough to think further ahead, to a time when it might all grind to a halt completely. He continued to study and was working towards a Masters degree in Science. Roger left the North London Polytechnic during the autumn of 1972, with his degree in biology.

Freddie decided that Queen needed an emblem, something that people could associate with them, so he began to design one. He had various ideas, all based around the band's birth signs – Brian was a Cancerian, Roger and John both Leos and Freddie a Virgo. He designed a crest featuring two lions holding a Q (complete with crown), a crab and two fairies (for the Virgo, of course). The whole thing was dominated by a huge Phoenix, a symbol of hope which seemed, to Freddie, representative of the dreams and ideals he harboured for Queen.

In September 1972, Trident came to an agreement with Queen that they should be paying them something, even though no deals had yet been signed and no product was available. Much discussion ensued and various amounts of money were offered until, finally, Trident agreed to pay them £20 per week each. It wasn't a vast amount by any standard, and as they all lived in rented accommodation – never cheap in London – it just about covered expenses and day-to-day living.

On 1 November 1972, Queen agreed to sign a legal contract with Trident Audio Productions Ltd. The deal was that Queen would record for Trident, and Trident would get the best recording and distribution deal they could with a major record label. It was the first time an independent record production company had taken on full responsibility for a rock band, but Trident were confident of their reward.

Jack Nelson was still busy trying to get the band a lucrative deal with one of the big record companies and employed Dave Thomas as a co-manager to oversee the everyday requirements of the band – which were considerable. Now they had signed the contract, Queen were determined to make the most of it, and insisted that Barry and Norman Sheffield gave them their maximum backing and commitment.

Trident had booked Queen a gig on 6 November 1972 at the Pheasantry, a huge pub on the King's Road, Chelsea, inviting everyone and anyone from as many record companies as they knew. On the night of the gig the PA didn't turn up until about an hour before the show was due to start: John Deacon and John Harris spent the time frantically trying to set it up, wiring up amps and the mixing desk and getting the monitors to work so that at least the band could hear themselves even if the audience couldn't hear the band. But the PA episode had upset the band and they didn't play their best.

The money that Queen were now earning enabled Roger to find his own flat. He and Freddie were still close friends, but Freddie and Mary wanted to live together, and Roger felt the need for his independence. He found himself a small flat in Richmond, a beautiful suburb of London, and moved in in late November.

By the end of November 1972 Queen at last completed their first album. Trident were very pleased with the results. Although it had been recorded in bits and pieces, mixed whenever there was free time and engineered by such a selection of different people it was surprising each one was able to follow on from the previous one, it sounded professional. But the band felt that the mixes had been rushed, and it was discovered that 'Liar' had been overdubbed onto the wrong backing tape, due to a tape operator's error. Roy and Brian insisted that more studio time be given to bring the album up to scratch. Even a young Mike Stone, studio tea boy at the time, was used by the band to help with some of the final touches. Finally, and having been produced by Roy Thomas Baker, John Anthony and Queen

THE TRIDENT YEARS

themselves to their own, even then, high standards, they all felt that the album represented the music Queen had been playing live in their three years together.

Brian was still working on his thesis, his free time usually taken up with study, but he found time to offer private tutorials in the evenings at Imperial College. He was keen to help students who found the coursework difficult – and, of course, he needed the money.

By January 1973 the album was finished, but as yet, no record company had agreed to press and distribute it, despite Trident's efforts to place it. Jack said, 'It took me over a year to get Queen a deal, and *everyone* turned them down, I mean everyone. I won't name names as some of those people turned out to be my best friends and I don't want to tarnish their reputations! But they know who they are, every one of them.'

It was the time of the annual MIDEM Festival, the trade fair held in Cannes in the South of France, *the* big event in the music industry calendar. A representative of Trident, publisher Ronnie Beck, took along a tape of the new Queen album, with the idea of plugging it to all the record company executives in attendance. Eventually it reached the ears of Roy Featherstone, a top executive for the soon-to-be launched EMI label, and present at the festival to promote it. 'I had been played hundreds of tapes that week, from people's mothers to their howling dogs and by bands and artists interested in the new label,' said Roy. 'None of them grabbed me, I was bored! Then Ronnie Beck handed me this Queen tape, and I listened and was knocked out. What stood out for me was the combination of Freddie's voice and Brian's guitar on a track called "Liar". I have wondered since if that tape would have been so much like a breath of fresh air had the whole atmosphere at MIDEM not been so awful.' Roy was given the biography Trident had prepared and liked what he read. When he was told that 'one or two other record companies' were also interested in this new band (blatantly untrue, but he didn't know that and it certainly grabbed his attention), Roy sent an urgent telegram to Queen via Trident in London, telling them to hold off signing any deals with anyone else until he got back. Jack had been involved in major negotiations with CBS and had had three revisions made on that company's contract. But he finally declined their offer.

In February, Trident arranged for Queen to do a special session for BBC Radio One, to be broadcast on *Sounds Of The Seventies*. It was a great chance for Queen to get some free, and extensive, publicity. The BBC wanted them to record four tracks, and they were given free rein to choose which they would feature. In the end, after a lot of deliberation, they went into the BBC studios in Maida Vale with producer Bernie Andrews and recorded 'Keep Yourself Alive', 'My Fairy King', 'Doin' Alright' and 'Liar'.

The session was first heard on the radio on 15 February 1973, and the response from the listening public prompted EMI to put the wheels in motion to sign Queen. They were still adamant that they would sign only Queen, and not the other two bands in the package, but Trident were equally determined not to let Queen go without selling the other two acts.

Roy Featherstone and his EMI colleague David Croker approached Trident; neither was prepared to let Trident know just how much they wanted Queen at this stage. They offered a contract, which Trident refused, asking for more money. EMI turned them down and offered another, and so on and so on, until they had negotiated the best possible deal for Queen – and EMI had also to accept the other two Trident artists, or deal was off.

It was March 1973 before Queen were ushered into the new offices of EMI Records Ltd to sign their first record contract. It was all over quickly and without much fanfare, but suddenly the band found themselves with a record deal covering the UK and Europe. They were excited; it seemed that at last they were getting somewhere and all that hard work was about to pay off. Brian and Roger were probably a little more apprehensive – they had seen it all go so badly wrong with Smile after it had got this far.

EMI wanted to release the Queen album quickly but, due to problems within the company on the finalisation of the plans for the new label, the release was held up.

On 9 April 1973, Jack Nelson booked the Marquee to hold a 'showcase' gig for the benefit of Elektra managing director Jack Holsten. Mr Holsten was flying back from Tokyo and had agreed to stop off in London en route to New York to see the band. He was interested in signing them, and Jack had told him he had to see the band live before he made a final decision, and that only then could they sit down and talk.

Although only half the invited audience had bothered to turn up and Queen were still finding their feet in their live performance, Holsten was knocked out. Jack Nelson says: 'Jack was a visionary – he could see the real talent. All the trappings are add-ons, and Jack saw through them.'

Queen were booked to play several small gigs over the next few months at various colleges and clubs, including Queen Mary's College in Basingstoke. Freddie was determined that his performance would have a unique style, and he wanted to incorporate drama and dance into the stage show. Those small venues gave him ample opportunity to develop his personal style; after the Basingstoke gig, he almost lost his voice and had bruised his leg badly from hitting it so hard with the tambourine. The band all experimented with stage clothes and make-up, with tight satin trousers, loose, flowing blouses and black and white gear. Freddie also began to paint the nails on his left hand black, as Brian remembers: 'Queen had by now played Liverpool so many times that we had a following there. Among them were some fans who had taken up our black and white theme, and gone so far as to paint their fingernails alternately black and white. One night after a show they produced their nail varnish bottle, and amidst much drinking, painted Freddie's nails black and mine white. It added to the general effect, so we decided to keep it up. I could only keep white varnish on the left hand, though, because playing scratched it all off the right hand. But in the white and violet lights that we used as footlights they glowed strangely. The nails survived the first couple of tours, as did the eye make-up!'

Freddie was sometimes instrumental in choosing the outfits for the rest of the band, often resulting in arguments and cries of, 'I'm not wearing *that!*'

The close friends they had all made in the early days were still very much in evidence and the band still frequented their old haunt, the Kensington, on free nights. Freddie's attention to detail and style were sometimes exasperating – especially one night, when everyone had gathered at his and Mary's flat, ready for a night out. 'Freddie spent a whole hour in front of the mirror in the bedroom, just choosing which belt to wear! He would come out in each one and ask our opinion. We just wanted to go out! He was so vain, but we tolerated it, everyone did. It was part of him, part of his character. He just wouldn't have been Freddie without that vanity,' says close friend Helen McConnell.

The songs that Freddie, Brian and Roger had worked on in 1972 with Robin Cable now reappeared, released as a single by EMI under the name of Larry Lurex. Robin Cable had decided that 'I Can Hear Music' and 'Goin' Back' were too good to sit on a shelf and had convinced EMI to release them. But he couldn't use Queen's name due to the imminent release of their own album so decided to spoof Gary Glitter, immensely popular then, and release it as Larry Lurex. Unfortunately, Gary's popularity went against them: many people were upset by the satire and refused to buy or play the song. The whole thing backfired, and the single was a total failure in the UK. It was, however, the first appearance on record of Queen – or three of them, anyway – and later became a much sought-after collector's

THE TRIDENT YEARS

item. Much later, it was bootlegged and 'released' on the Anthem Records label in the USA, ensuring that the collector's value of the EMI release soared.

EMI were almost ready to release the first Queen album and the band were immersed in the details of the process. They were determined to be involved in every aspect of their first album, from the pressing of the actual vinyl right through to the cover. They all visited the EMI offices regularly to keep abreast of any developments and to maintain a close contact with the company, which, they felt, was important.

The band pulled in a friend, Doug Puddifoot, who Roger had known from Truro and who had photographed Smile and Queen at gigs, to take pictures of them posing in Freddie's flat. They also took snaps of each other and pulled out oldies from previous years. They invited some friends round to Freddie's flat to sift through the mountain of photographs they had accumulated, to find the best ones for the album's back cover. They all chose their own personal favourites (Freddie's queries of 'Do I look gorgeous enough?' fell mainly on deaf ears that night) and Brian and Freddie spent weeks cutting them all out and pasting them into a collage.

They also got Doug to help with the design for the album cover, using one of the group photos he had taken. The idea was to make it look like an old Victorian photograph by tinting it sepia and enclosing it within a deep maroon oval background. Doug was happy to oblige and presented the band with the artwork he had come up with – but Brian had other ideas. He had discovered that if coloured plastic was stretched over a camera lens and the photo taken through it, the result was distorted but strangely effective. Doug spent days and nights in his darkroom experimenting with different coloured plastics and different ways of stretching it but eventually, exhausted, gave up. Then Brian suggested using a photograph of Freddie on stage backed by two powerful spotlights. With a little darkroom wizardry and the coloured plastic, the effect Doug achieved was reasonably close to Brian's idea – and was accepted.

They handed over all the photos and artwork for the cover to EMI.

Freddie and Roger had recently come to the conclusion that John's name would sound much more interesting if it was reversed, and John, still feeling a little like the 'new boy', concurred – even though he disliked the idea – and he was credited as Deacon John on the cover.

Queen were asked to select a track to become their first single – a rare opportunity as the record company usually makes the choice – and decided to release 'Keep Yourself Alive', written by Brian. He was also lucky enough to claim the B-side with his track 'Son And Daughter'. The single was released on 6 July 1973 in Britain, and Trident assured Queen it would appear in Europe shortly after. It was reviewed extensively and mostly, but not exclusively, favourably in the music press. 'A raucous, well built single', said *Record Mirror*. *NME* thought the band held huge promise: 'If these guys look half as good as they sound they could be huge', while the *Daily Mirror* were already excited: 'New male rock band called Queen will blow your head off with a diabolical, high-energy nerve tingler'. However, *Melody Maker* thought the band 'Lacks originality', while *Sounds* commented 'It never really gets going', although in his column in the latter, DJ John Peel added, 'Some pleasing guitar and synthesizer work . . .' Not bad for a debut single.

EMI's promotions manager, Eric Hall, approached Trident to make a promotional film, to send out to agents and publicists in the USA and Europe. It was a new idea, but as Trident had just acquired their own video company, Trillion, it was a chance to test the new camera equipment. So, on 16 July, Queen turned up at London's St John's Wood film studios to make their first ever promotional films, directed by Mike Mansfield.

THE TRIDENT YEARS

They filmed two clips: one for 'Keep Yourself Alive' and another for 'Liar'. The band weren't happy with the filming process though. The lights were hot and the cameras got in the way as they tried to shoot from strange angles. The director had decided to paint the stage a bright and 'poppy' white, despite the band's leanings towards 'mysterious' black. The band were all uncomfortable and it took several takes before Mike was happy with it.

The following day, Norman Sheffield viewed the footage and wasn't pleased with the result, so another session was arranged for the following month.

The single was sent out to all local and regional radio stations for inclusion on their playlists but, with the exception of Radio Luxembourg, it didn't get any airplay at all. BBC Radio One rejected it no less than five times. EMI sent a 'white label'★ copy of the Queen album to BBC Television, in the hope that someone might like it enough to plug it – although they forgot to include the publicity material about the band. There it landed on the desk of Mike Appleton, producer of the BBC's rock programme *The Old Grey Whistle Test*. Mike played the anonymous album out of curiosity and loved it, especially the first track. He didn't have a clue who the band were or whom he should contact about the track but took it upon himself to include the song on the programme. Having no film to accompany the song, he sent it to a friend in the animation department and asked him to cut something to go with it.

On 24 July 1973, *The Old Grey Whistle Test* featured the song 'Keep Yourself Alive', played over a piece of animation once used by US President Franklin D. Roosevelt as part of his election campaign. The BBC received numerous calls about the song, including one from Trident informing them of the identity of the band.

★ A white label copy is an early pressing of a record, used for promotion while the labels and covers for the album are being printed.

EMI released the band's eponymous* debut album on 13 July 1973. The label advertised it extensively in the music press, teenage magazines, billboard posters and record-shop window displays.

The album was a 'thrusting, dynamic, forceful, not to mention heavy' debut, according to *Time Out* magazine. It effectively showcased the songs that Queen had been playing live around the country.† The music was raw, loud and heavy for its time. But the album started slowly and initial sales were low.

By now BBC Radio One had heard the album, and although they were still not giving the single any airplay, Queen were approached by John Peel, who was notorious for picking up on new bands he thought worth recommending to his listening public. His radio show regularly featured 'sessions' by people he considered up-and-coming artists – and he asked Queen to do one.

Having already had experience of recording for the BBC and knowing that such publicity could only be good for them, the band agreed. Again they were given the choice of tracks for the recording, which took place on 25 July 1973, and selected 'Keep Yourself Alive', 'Son And Daughter' and 'Liar' from the debut album, and another track called 'See What A Fool I've Been', on which they had been working.

In August 1973, Trident cloistered Queen in one of the vast sound stages of Shepperton Studios to rehearse and work on new material, and it was while they were there that Trident decided to make a new promotional film.

---

* Roger had wanted to call the album 'Top Fax, Pix and Info' but had been outvoted, and another title they had discussed was 'Deary Me', a favourite phrase of Roy Thomas Baker.

† Whether Queen had anticipated the reaction to their music, or whether it was to let listeners know that the music they played was realised purely through skill, they added the comment 'and nobody played synthesizer' to the album sleeve.

THE TRIDENT YEARS

The camera crews arrived at Shepperton early on the morning of 9 August, with director Bruce Gowers – to find that an over-eager Freddie Mercury had shaved his chest for the occasion. They filmed the band performing to playback tapes of 'Liar' and 'Keep Yourself Alive'.

Good publicity must be properly manufactured and put out to the right places for maximum effect, so Trident employed Tony Brainsby as the band's publicist. Tony hadn't seen or heard Queen before he took them under his wing, but he felt that if they were good enough to warrant Trident spending so much money on them, they must be worth working for. Tony was well known in the music business as his other clients included big names such as Paul McCartney and Wings, The Strawbs, Mott The Hoople, Steeleye Span and Wizzard. 'Oh, they were full of ideas,' Tony says of Queen. 'They knew how they wanted to look, how they wanted to be represented, how they wanted to be packaged. They just came in to see me, plonked a stack of photos on the desk and said, "These are what you can use, and this is our logo." My job from then on wasn't too difficult.' His first task was to arrange for Brian to do an interview with *Guitar* magazine about his Red Special. Brian provided them with his own photographs of each stage of the making of the instrument, and happily divulged all the facts about what went into its construction.

During August 1973 the band went back into Trident Studios to start work on their second album. This time they were booked in as a main act, and could, at last, have all the time they wanted. Given such parameters, they were keen to experiment. They had come up with loads of ideas for new techniques and sounds and had ample opportunity to put them into practice. Recording continued until the second week of December.

Brian decided to take a part-time job in September teaching English at Stockwell Manor Comprehensive School in south-east London. He was entertaining thoughts of a permanent teaching job if Queen didn't work out, so this one was good practice. He was still working on his thesis, too; it was a project close to his heart and he wanted to finish it. During days off from Stockwell, he worked with EMI Electronics, assessing the destructive effects of fragmentation bombs. In odd moments he also found the time to write and run a computer program to calculate the positions of frets on a guitar to twenty decimal places. He says: 'It went somewhat against the grain, and perhaps triggered a growing sense of where my life *ought* to be going.'

Around that time, Roger was introduced to British folk singer Al Stewart, who was recording at Trident's studios. He asked Roger if he would care to add some percussion to the album *Past, Present And Future*, which he was currently working on, an offer Roger quickly accepted. It was the first time a member of Queen had worked professionally with another artist.

The BBC wanted to record a live session with Queen for future broadcast on their *In Concert* series and arranged a gig for them at the Golders Green Hippodrome on 13 September. It was in front of a live audience, as were all the sessions for the *In Concert* series, and Queen opened with a taped introduction, the song 'Procession', which they had just recorded for their second album. It was an innovative idea and impressed the audience, whetting their appetites for the rest of the show, which was received exceptionally well.

In September 1973, Elektra Records in the USA released the first Queen album. It wasn't expected to go far, but its appearance in the chart in those early days was a big thrill. Quite quickly, the radio stations picked up on it and began spinning tracks. They were also getting requests from listeners – this unknown British band were making a name for themselves. The album seemed to gather momentum more quickly in the USA than it had in Europe, entering the *Billboard* chart and climbing to an impressive number eighty-three – a rare achievement for a new British band.

In October 1973, Mott The Hoople were planning a big British

THE TRIDENT YEARS

tour. Jack Nelson knew Bob Hirschmann, Mott's manager and a fellow American, and set about persuading Bob to take on Queen as the support act. It was no easy feat, as Queen were unknowns and Bob was sceptical that they could handle the tour. But Jack's powers of persuasion, coupled with an advance payment of £3,000, convinced him to accept the band as the opening act. The tour was due to start on 12 November.

On 9 October, Elektra Records released the first Queen single in America. They chose 'Keep Yourself Alive' as it had failed to chart in the UK and they had hopes that it might fare better in the States. It didn't.

Before the tour with Mott The Hoople began, Queen had a lot of publicity planned for Europe and, along with Eric Hall, flew out to make TV and radio appearances in Belgium, France and the Netherlands. They also had a couple of gigs set up, again for publicity purposes, and played their first live gig outside of the UK on 13 October 1973, at the Underground Club at Bonn Bad Godesburg, in Germany. This concert was followed the next day by an appearance in Luxembourg at a venue called Le Blow Up. It was supposed to be recorded for a Radio Luxembourg *In Concert* special, but on the night, all the equipment went wrong and they didn't get anything on tape.

The previously recorded UK *In Concert* show was broadcast on Radio One in late October, and the band also played a gig at Imperial College and another at the Paris Theatre in London. The crowds at their concerts were slowly but surely growing in number. Says Norman Sheffield: 'Their following was really strong, even then. We'd have grandparents turning up with their children and their grandchildren, it was amazing!'

In November the band organised another gig at Imperial as the final warm-up show before their first major tour with Mott. It was sold out in advance, and the packed audience was ecstatic. Afterwards the show received rave reviews in the music press, including a review the band continue to cherish, by writer Rosemary Horide.

November 12 saw Queen embarking on their first UK support tour at the Leeds Town Hall. They were nervous, and took the stage as the strains of 'Procession' played through the PA. They played songs from their debut album, from their forthcoming album and one or two covers of other artist's songs. Freddie spoke quietly between numbers, introducing each one with very little chat or banter. Brian baffled the crowd with his guitar solo, as by using echo he created guitar harmonies, making it sound as if there were two guitarists – and many of those present were trying to see the phantom guitarist on stage.

The dates were numerous and took them all over the UK and, as a support act, they were getting a much better reaction than most as their confidence grew. The band had gathered a large following from their first album, and the audience was peopled as much by fans wanting to see Queen as Mott. During the gig at the Southend Kursaal, Freddie, Brian and Roger joined Mott on stage to give them a hand with the backing vocals for 'All The Young Dudes', the band's big hit.

During a few days off in December, Queen popped into the BBC studios again to record four more tracks with Bernie Andrews, for future radio use. This time they chose 'Ogre Battle', 'Great King Rat', 'Modern Times Rock And Roll' and 'Son And Daughter'.

On 14 December, Queen and Mott were booked to play two shows at the Hammersmith Odeon in London, a matinee and an evening performance. It was the first time that Brian's parents had seen him play live with Queen. 'It was all so exciting,' said Ruth May. 'It was such a big place, and we had only ever seen him play at little halls before. We were probably the oldest ones there, and as we were taking our seats a young fan came over and asked us who's mum and dad we were. When we told him, he asked us for our autographs. It

Queen's loyal subjects

"SOLD OUT" said the sign on the door. Amazing, that an unknown (or almost) group like Queen should sell out a gig at Imperial College. But having seen them now, I understand why.

Six months ago, when I last saw the band, they showed promise but weren't very together. This time they were very good. Their leader Freddie Mercury pranced about the small stage, waving his mike both violently and sensually as they performed numbers from their first album; most notable of which were their single Keep Yourself Alive and Son And Daughter.

The atmosphere in the hall was electric. The kids were with Queen all the way, showing a remarkable knowledge of the band's repertoire and greeting each number uproariously.

The group were musically very good, their stage presence was excellent and when you consider that the material was all their own, it was a remarkable performance for a new group. The material was far above average, and it was obvious how hard the band worked at entertaining by the tremendous rapport that was established.

At the end if the set, after a couple of standard rock 'n' rollers to provide a fitting climax, the audience wouldn't let Queen go. They were forced on stage to do three encores, until they finally had to stop—not from lack of demand, but sheer exhaustion. The funniest moment was undoubtedly the first encore—Freddie's Big Spender was done a la Shirley Bassey, and thus was outrageously camp.

On the whole it was a very good night, and a highly creditable performance. If Queen are this good on the tour with Mott the Hoople (which they start next week) Mott had better watch out. Queen could turn out to be a bit more than just a support band.—ROSEMARY HORIDE

Queen
EMC 3006
on tour with
MOTT THE HOOPLE

NOVEMBER
12 Leeds Town Hall
13 Blackburn, St. Georges
15 Worcester Gaumont
16 Lancaster University
17 Liverpool Stadium
18 Stoke on Trent, Trentham Gardens
19 Wolverhampton, Civic
20 Oxford, New Theatre
21 Preston, Guildhall
22 Newcastle, City Hall
23 Glasgow, Apollo Centre
25 Edinburgh, Caley Cinema
26 Manchester, Opera House
27 Birmingham Town Hall
28 Swansea, Brangwyn Hall
29 Bristol, Colston Hall
30 Bournemouth Winter Gardens
DECEMBER
1 Southend, Kursaal
2 Chatham Central
14 LONDON, Hammersmith Odeon

was a wonderful show.' Unfortunately, Mott's afternoon show had run way over time, and Queen's early evening show had to be cut short. Nevertheless they played to over 7,000 people that day, their largest crowd to date. This was the final date on the tour; by the end of it Queen had lived up to all the expectations Trident had for them, and sales of the first album were increasing. They received huge public acclaim, but were either ignored or panned by the press, referred to as 'supermarket rock' among other descriptive phrases. Mott themselves were more than happy with Queen and the way they had supported them, and, as Brian says, 'a great relationship had already grown between the bands off stage. We learned a lot about stagecraft and backstage organisation from Mott and their entourage – as well as having enormous – and outrageous – fun!' Bob Hirschmann asked Queen if they would support them on the forthcoming US tour – and Queen graciously agreed.

EMI were overwhelmed with requests for information about Queen and asked Trident if they could handle the band's mail. Trident asked Queen if they knew of anyone who would like to take on the task. They did. Pat and Sue Johnstone, friends of Roger's from Cornwall, who had known the rest of the band for some time and had worked at Kensington Market, were assigned the task of responding to all the mail that came in. It soon became obvious that the fans wanted to know more than just tour dates and album releases, so Trident paid to set up an official fan club. Queen loved the idea and got closely involved in its inception and promotion.

By the end of 1973 the sales of their first album had established Queen as one of the most exciting new bands to appear in a long time – but the band had also established an often blatantly hostile relationship with the press. Queen were convinced of their future and worked hard towards it, but the press seemed only interested in the band's personal lives and antics, particularly those of the 'camp lead singer' (their description). Their comments and innuendos upset

THE TRIDENT YEARS

everyone, but Freddie wasn't going to let them see he was troubled by their tirades, and indulged them by behaving exactly as they expected, which often antagonised them. Even at this early stage it had become popular for journalists to ridicule the band, to the fury of Queen and their growing army of fans.

The final gig of 1973 was in Liverpool, at the Top Rank club. It was a special Christmas show headlined by 10cc, with Queen supporting and local band Great Day opening the show. It was almost like a homecoming for Freddie after his stint in Liverpool with Ibex, even more so as two members of Great Day had previously played with him in that band: Mike Berin and Queen's friend and early 'manager' Ken Testi.

The headline in *Sounds* in January 1974 read 'Britain's Biggest Unknowns'. Queen were voted as third best new British band, and the top slots were snatched from them by Nazareth at number one and Blue (who?) at number two. Many other British music papers were featuring their 'best of' polls of the previous year; and Queen appeared in more than a few. It was a great start to the new year.

The band had two concerts planned, in Australia in late January, and, as part of the preparations for that trip, they and their crew had the usual series of injections. As a result, Brian suffered from a high fever and his arm ballooned. He was diagnosed as having developed gangrene at the injection site, caused by a dirty needle, and it was touch and go for some time as to whether he would lose his arm.

Their trip started on 28 January. Queen were booked to headline two shows at a big open-air festival in Sunbury – their first taste of trouble. The local bands and promoters couldn't understand how a totally unknown English band could take precedence over established Australian bands.

Queen took their own lighting rig with them – they were proud of it and wanted to impress the audience – but as it was so complex, they also took with them their own crew to operate it. That was

GREAT XMAS SHOW
STARRING
10 C.C.
Queen
Great Day
FRIDAY 28TH. DEC. 8PM.-1AM BAR TO 12.45
TOP RANK SUITE L'POOL
TICKETS 100P FROM RUSHWORTHS COSMOPOLITAN VIRGIN PROBE

their second mistake: the local crews were angry they were losing work, and therefore money, and refused to co-operate with the English crew, going out of their way to be unpleasant and disruptive.

Their third mistake was to do things in style. They hired white limousines to take them from their hotel to the concert venue, and when they arrived made a big entrance, which the Australians hated, dismissing these 'Pommies' as just too clever.

To cap it all, the band were not feeling their best. Brian was still in a lot of pain with his arm and Freddie had an ear infection, for which he was taking antibiotics that made him feel drowsy and out of sorts, and he couldn't hear properly.

Queen wanted to make full use of their lights and waited until it was getting dark before they went on stage, by which time the audience were stamping and slow-clapping them. Finally the Australian DJ who was acting as compere walked on to introduce them, and announced them as 'stuck-up Pommies', turned his back to the audience and dropped his trousers in a 'moon' to demonstrate his contempt of the band.

Freddie couldn't hear himself singing at all, Brian's arm was making it difficult for him to play and the lighting rig gave up the ghost as the equipment had been sabotaged, but despite everything, fans reported that it was, in all, a great show. From a grudging start, the audience warmed to the band and were wildly enthusiastic by the time they had finished, demanding the obligatory encore. The DJ, however, had other ideas. He came back on stage and said, 'Hold it! Do you want more Queen?' There were uproarious cries of, 'Yeah!' from the crowd. Mr DJ continued, 'Do you want more of those Pommy bastards?' There was some confusion in the ranks. 'Or do you want a good old Aussie band?' More confusion and cries of 'Yeah!' 'How about Madden Lake?' and the audience were with him and yelling wildly. He manipulated Queen effectively out of their encore.

The next day the press slated the band and printed 'comments' from them that they hadn't made. There was a strong anti-British and anti-Queen feeling, not just in the papers but in the reactions of people they met. They were due to play another show that night but, as Freddie was in severe pain and running a high temperature, it was called off, much to the anger of the promoters. As far as they were concerned, it was just another black mark against the band.

Queen were only too relieved to get out of Australia and flew back to the UK with the minimum of delay. It had been an experience they were not likely to forget, and one that cost them dearly, not only in financial terms – they had paid their own return airfares – but in peace of mind and bad publicity. As a finale, when the plane landed at Heathrow Airport the band were faced with a barrage of photographers – all waiting for Her Majesty The Queen, whom they had thought was arriving, and none too happy when four exhausted musicians appeared.

Despite all the aggravation, though, something positive and optimistic occurred in a Melbourne hotel room. The band were awaiting the arrival of the first test pressings of their second album, which were being flown out from the UK for their approval. When they appeared, the band and Jack sat round a portable record player to listen. After the first play-through, they all felt that, at last, they had come very close to realising their full studio potential (the complex and multi-layered voices and guitars were close antecedents of 'Bohemian Rhapsody' and the *Night At The Opera* album, which would later take the world by storm.) For the time being, the band felt that they had taken recording to a new level. It was a high they needed given the dire circumstances of the 'Down Under' trip.

In mid-February the *New Musical Express* readers' poll showed Queen as the second Most Promising New Name – at the time they hadn't even had a hit single. In the USA, Elektra Records decided to release another single from the Queen album, an edited version

THE TRIDENT YEARS

of 'Liar', which was released on 14 February, again with little chart success.

The next single was scheduled for late February. Prior to its release, a white label copy was handed to Ronnie Fowler, head of the promotional department at EMI. Ronnie was charged with promoting both Queen and another new band, Cockney Rebel. He played the single to death, loved it and, not being aware at the time of the 'third party' involvement with Trident, took it upon himself to 'break' Queen, launching himself into it twenty-four hours a day.

Ronnie spent over £20,000 in expenses on the band, taking key people from radio and TV out to lunch and dinner, usually ensuring that one of the band made an appearance at the meetings. He became close to Queen over the time he worked on their behalf – and a pain to the media. He pestered and cajoled them into playing Queen, promoting Queen, anything – as long as it was Queen.

Ronnie recalls: 'One Tuesday evening I was working late in my Manchester Square office – which was infamous for having the biggest free cocktail bar in the business; I'd get everyone there, producers, DJs, artists, everyone. The windows were wide open and I had the Queen white label on, again! A security guard had just been in to tell me that it was 7.30, and didn't I think it was time to go home, people were complaining all over the Square about the music. As I was about to leave, the phone rang. It was Robin Nash, the producer of BBC's *Top Of The Pops*. They had a last-minute space in that Thursday's show, and did I know anyone? I said yes. His comment was "Give me two guesses who the band is?" He knew I meant Queen!'

Ronnie rushed the demo disc round to them, they listened to the track and liked it. He then had to check with Queen that they could appear at such short notice, which, of course, they could. The only problem was that *Top Of The Pops* would not use the actual single as a backing track (artists rarely sang live on the show, usually miming), which meant that a special backing track had to be recorded. Ronnie had to find a studio for them to record the track – that night. He contacted The Who's Pete Townshend, who was recording in London, and he agreed to let Queen use some of his own studio time. The following day, 20 February, completed backing tape in hand, Queen went into the BBC's Rampart Studios to prerecord their appearance on the show.

Queen appeared for the first time on *Top Of The Pops* on 21 February 1974 with a song that hadn't even been released as a single, 'Seven Seas Of Rhye'. They watched the show on a TV in the window of an electrical shop. Ronnie said, 'The day after *Top Of The Pops*, Steve Harley from Cockney Rebel came storming into my office. He was furious, he slammed his fists on the desk and told me all I cared about was Queen, what about *his* band? I just looked him in the eye, and said, "It's your turn on the *Pops* next week." I hadn't a clue! I was just trying to placate the man. But believe it or not, by sheer fluke, Cockney Rebel *were* on the following week. Boy, was I relieved!'

Jack Nelson rushed ten white label copies of 'Seven Seas Of Rhye' round to Ronnie the day after *Top Of The Pops* aired, and Ronnie promised to ensure they got to Radio One. He was as good as his word, and delivered them in person. Clever timing and persuasion of key DJs to play the track at specific times meant that the song was on the air almost all day the next day – and Ronnie had negotiated as many plays in a week as it was possible for one song to have. He went home exhausted but elated. At ten that night the phone rang. Ronnie continues: 'It was Jack. He said he'd had Freddie on the phone, who, after listening to the white label test pressing, said it was the wrong mix and that there was no way that mix could be played on the radio.

'Jack said I had to go back to Radio One the next day, retrieve the ten white labels he'd given me, and replace them with the correct

THE TRIDENT YEARS

ones, which were, as we spoke, being pressed. The next morning, early, the new pressings came and I went down to Radio One. I managed to get back all but two of the wrong mixes. So, somewhere, there are just two different mixes of that single – it seemed like the advent of the remix!'

The single was rush-released by EMI on 23 February. The record company had never worked so fast to get a single into the shops. As the B-side they chose 'See What A Fool I've Been', which never made it onto the album, making the single highly collectable. *NME* said of it: 'This single showcases all their power and drive, their writing talents, and every quality that makes them unique.'

It was just after the single was released that Freddie finally gave up working in Kensington Market. He had held onto the job with Alan Mair until now, although he would often not open the stall until 11 or 12 instead of the more usual 9 a.m. Even then he didn't entirely forsake the market, still visiting both place and people – it was a stimulating, exciting place to be.

The new album, *Queen II*, was ready for release but the band spotted a spelling error on the cover and, although it was a minor one, they insisted it be corrected before the album went on sale; John's name was printed the correct way around – he'd put his foot down, as he didn't like being Deacon John. Finally, *Queen II* was ready – but this was the time of the oil crisis, and most of England was suffering the effects of the three-day week. A government restriction on the use of electricity by major companies held up the album release yet again, with the band's first headlining tour of Britain due to start in a few weeks' time. Stage clothes were still an important part of the Queen 'package' and just before this tour, Freddie and Brian had met with top fashion designer Zandra Rhodes. Working on basic ideas they had given her, Zandra designed and made several stunning outfits, featuring beading and intricate embroidery, velvet, satin and yards of pleated silk.

The band went into Ealing BBC studios to begin rehearsals in earnest for the tour. They had a lot of new material to practise and perfect as they wanted to feature as many of the new songs from the new album as possible – even though it was now obvious that none of the audience would have it at the start of the tour.

On 1 March 1974, they played the first of their headline gigs at the Blackpool Winter Gardens. They had no support band for that or the following night's gig at Aylesbury Friars (which was cut short as Brian's arm was still painful). In Plymouth, however, they were joined by the Liverpool band Nutz, who supported them throughout the rest of the tour.

Freddie's preoccupation with his appearance delayed the start of one of the shows. During the soundcheck, in a particularly energetic piece, Freddie flicked his arm and his silver snake bracelet flew off his wrist and disappeared behind the amps. He stopped rehearsals while he retrieved it. He didn't care about the sound or the show, just if he got his bracelet back (which he did, after some time spent searching).

The band played a much longer set than previously, giving Roger an opportunity to show off his drumming prowess during 'Keep Yourself Alive' with a ten-minute drum solo. The audiences were enthusiastic during those early gigs, and at one point they all began singing 'God Save The Queen' as they were waiting for the band to come on stage. It soon became a regular feature at the start of all Queen gigs.

On 5 March, the single 'Seven Seas Of Rhye' entered the official UK chart at number forty-five. It was their first-ever chart entry, and they were over the moon. It coincided with a change in personnel at EMI: Ronnie Fowler had taken up a post at Elektra Records. He says: 'When I left, I still maintained contact with the band for a long time; we were friends. Roy Featherstone called me into his office when I finally left and threatened to sell my expense account to Steven Spielberg as a science fiction epic!'

THE TRIDENT YEARS

At long last, on 8 March 1974, *Queen II* was released, and again the cover carried the comment 'no synths'. It also broke with tradition by having a white and a black side, instead of the more normal A and B. At the concerts following its release it became increasingly apparent that most of the crowd had gone out and bought it immediately as they all seemed to know the songs. Queen realised that they really were on their way, especially when on 20 March it reached number thirty-five on the album charts. But reviews were mixed. From *Melody Maker*: 'It's reputed Queen have enjoyed some success in the States, it's currently in the balance whether they'll really break through here. If they do, then I'll have to eat my hat or something. Maybe Queen try too hard, there's no depth of sound or feeling.' *Record Mirror* pulled no punches: 'This is it, the dregs of glam rock. Weak and over-produced, if this band are our brightest hope for the future, then we are committing rock and roll suicide.' However, *Sounds* were more positive: 'Simply titled Queen II, this album captures them in their finest hours', and *Disc* appreciated the album's production values: 'The material, performance, recording and even artwork standards are very high.'

At the time, John was still studying; he had begun an MSc course, as he was still in two minds as to Queen's future, even after the success of the second album. It was during that first headlining tour that he finally gave up: he had completed most of the theory for the course and a good proportion of the practical, but the touring was interfering with his work, so he became, at last, a full-time musician.

Suddenly, after the concert at Cheltenham Town Hall on 14 March, the lighting crew quit following more than a few internal problems and arguments. Thankfully, Trident called in lighting director James Dann, who took over at short notice, and the shows went on. The following night's gig was at Glasgow University – where the lighting rig, for the first time on the tour, played up. It was later discovered that it had been plugged into the university's ordinary mains supply, overloading the circuits and causing the fuses to blow – with unavoidable breaks in the show.

Still in Scotland, the band went on the next night to Stirling University. The gig itself went ahead without incident, and the audience were in high spirits by the final song. The band left the stage, the crowd stamped and yelled for more, and were given an encore. The audience continued to shout for more and back came the band for another two songs – but it was after they refused to come back for a fourth that trouble flared. Fights broke out in the crowd; the police were called and for their own safety the band members were locked into a backstage kitchen. Two members of the audience were stabbed and two of the road crew, who tried to intervene to calm the situation, were hurt and taken to hospital. It took the police and security some time to bring a stop to the outbreak, and it was decided that the next night, due to be played in Birmingham, would have to be cancelled and rescheduled for the end of the tour. This brought the band sudden, huge publicity in the music press, with headlines of 'Queen Concert Riot'.

This wasn't the only untoward event in an otherwise triumphant tour. After their gig at Manchester University it was discovered that thieves had broken into the band's vehicle and stolen John's case. It had contained personal items, including some treasured photos he'd taken in Australia. The police were informed but nothing was ever retrieved.

Queen flew out to the Isle of Man on 26 March 1974 for a concert at the Palace Lido in Douglas. They weren't really expecting it to be much of an event – the island is small and not heavily populated – but it turned out to be a memorable gig that they all thoroughly enjoyed. And they were not forgotten by the hoteliers: the aftershow party got totally out of hand and a room was wrecked. The Manx people weren't impressed. However, on leaving the island, the band received the news that *Queen II* had leapt up the UK charts to number seven and, on the strength of that, their first album had, finally, debuted at number forty-seven.

It was around that time that Elektra released the first Queen album in Japan, the start of a long and fruitful relationship with Japanese audiences. They took to Queen with such ardent enthusiasm that it wasn't long before the album was climbing the charts there, too.

On 28 March, Queen were at Aberystwyth University to play at a college ball. Nutz opened to a small, bored audience, most of whom were in the bar, and those who were in the hall showed little or no interest until the last song when the applause was half-hearted. Queen followed them at about 2 a.m. By this time, almost all the people who had been crowding the bar were crammed into the hall. Queen played a blinding set and the audience, with much yelling and stamping, wouldn't let them go, and were treated to three encores. The band were on a real high after that gig, as fans were being turned away from all their shows, tickets were all sold out and they were going down a storm.

What was to have been the final gig on the tour was held at London's Rainbow theatre on 31 March. During the day, the band had a row. Norman Sheffield says: 'Freddie was just being so pedantic, so Brian told him he was an old tart. He got really upset and stormed off. He went out to the van, I think. When it came to the soundcheck we couldn't find him anywhere, so they turned up the volume on the mic and Brian started yelling "Freddiepoos, where are you?" He was livid, but it worked, and he came flouncing back in and the band just got on with it.'

Sound engineer John Harris experimented with the Rainbow's acoustics during the soundcheck. He set up two mixers, one high up in the gods section of the hall, and one at floor level. He equipped the lower one with a graphic equaliser to balance the sound, and the result was much better than the hall's original acoustics. During the set Roger, too, decided he wanted to experiment with sound and poured beer onto his drums. It looked great when he hit them, with all the spray, but the jury is out as to whether it made them sound any better.

Queen played to yet another capacity crowd – of 3,500 – that night and were thrilled that they had filled such a famous venue. Press reaction to that gig was largely incredulous at the way the band were received. But one journalist was not at all surprised. Rosemary Horide was at the gig and, again, her review was one the band took to heart:

> *What a night! It was the culmination of Queen's country-wide tour . . . for their reputation it was a make or break night – their rise has been so meteoric and many doubted Queen's ability to justify playing a such a prestigious venue as the Rainbow so early in their career. Sartorially outrageous in his new white 'eagle suit', Freddie pranced and posed with even more enthusiasm than usual and sang better than I've ever heard him. One would never have believed that this was the first time Queen had headlined at a major venue. After a while they became accustomed to the huge stage and used it to its best advantage. After two encores they finally left the stage to a standing ovation with much cheering and shouting for more.*

On 2 April the postponed gig at Birmingham Barbarellas was slotted in as the final date on the tour. As it was the last night and spirits were high, Roger bet the roadies and the support band a bottle of champagne that they wouldn't 'streak' across the stage during the set. The roadies, of course, weren't daunted by several hundred people staring at them, and nor was Dave, the lead singer with Nutz, who loved champagne. He and one or two of the roadies stripped off and sprinted from one side of the stage to the other during Queen's set. But they apparently never got their promised champagne – and although Freddie and Brian turned up at Nutz's

THE TRIDENT YEARS

first headline gig at the Marquee in London sometime later, Roger stayed away . . .

With such a successful UK tour behind them, Queen were now getting excited about their forthcoming trip to America supporting Mott The Hoople. The reaction they had inspired in British crowds had given them a taste for adulation, and they were looking forward to the bigger gigs in the USA – they couldn't wait to be let loose. Even as the support band they knew they could fire people's imaginations and win them over, such was their faith in themselves.

Freddie said: 'When we had toured with Mott the first time, the audience were really only interested in us as a support band, but this time we all knew they would come especially to see us, and it was a great feeling! In Plymouth, we were late getting on stage, and the whole audience began singing "God Save The Queen"! It was ridiculous, and we loved it!'

On 12 April they left for America with high hopes of success. They had got to know Mott well from their first tour supporting them and were expecting this one to be a lot of fun. 'They were great,' enthused Roger. 'A real "sex, drugs and rock and roll" band. We knew we were going to have a great tour!'

Elektra released *Queen II* in the USA three days before they flew out, and Queen played their first gig in America on 16 April in Denver, at the Regis College. They were received rather quietly at first; the audience had obviously heard of Mott but weren't too sure of the English newcomers wearing satin and nail polish. By the end of the set, however, they'd been won over.

It was a strenuous tour for Queen; the venues were bigger, the audiences harder to woo and impress, and the travelling between gigs was a lot tougher and longer than the relatively short distances between dates in Britain – but they had a ball.

On 1 May, Mott, Queen and the American band Aerosmith were all booked to play the Harrisburg Farm Arena. It hadn't been settled, though, as to who, out of Queen and Aerosmith, would play first, Mott being booked as headliners. When they arrived at the venue – which was nothing more than an enormous cowshed, from which the cows had only been moved the day before, leaving behind the legacy of their scent and other little gifts – the two supporting bands began to argue about who should go on first. Brian quickly got bored with the quarrelling and wandered off backstage, where he came across Joe Perry, the guitarist with Aerosmith, who had also had enough. 'I introduced myself to him,' says Brian, 'and we just sat down together and decided we really didn't give a damn who went on first. Joe brought out a bottle of Jack Daniel's whiskey and we proceeded to get really, really "relaxed". We were so drunk we could hardly walk by the time the argument finished. We've been friends ever since!' Eventually a compromise was reached, with a local band opening the show, then Queen, then Aerosmith. Brian says: 'When we finally went on, I remember, through a haze, whacking the first chord and realising that, among the echo, I couldn't hear a thing. I played the whole show from memory and decided to compensate by giving it lots of action. Everyone thought it was wonderful! So I decided two things for the future: (1) I would always "give it action" and (2) I would never drink more than a pint before a show. I have since stuck by both of those resolutions.'

From 7 to 12 May, Mott and Queen were booked to play in New York, at the Uris Theater on Broadway, which had never held a rock concert. The owners were a little apprehensive but promoter Ron Delsener calmed their fears and all six nights were sold out. Sadly, the theatre suffered quite a bit of damage, as some members of the audience stubbed out their cigarettes on the carpet instead of in the ashtrays. Ron, however, had gone around it before the show and counted all the existing burn holes and checked again afterwards so they wouldn't be charged for them all.

On the final night Brian, who hadn't been feeling too well for a

THE TRIDENT YEARS

few days, collapsed, and was told to get some rest before playing the next gig, which was Boston – the one region, apart from Japan, where Queen were already hot news. The band anxiously awaited confirmation on Brian's health to see if they would have to cancel the shows. But it was even worse than that: they'd not only have to cancel the Boston dates, but all remaining US concerts – as Brian had hepatitis. He recalls: 'The first morning I woke up in the Parker House in Boston, I felt like my whole body was made of lead. I tried to eat a grapefruit, which someone had said would make me feel better, then I dragged myself to the bathroom mirror, and saw that I was a deep shade of yellow. That was the end of our dream of conquering America at one shake. I felt I had let everyone down. They smuggled and carried me on the plane back to England, where I was ordered to bed for six weeks. But that was only the beginning!' Elektra Records had to contact everyone who had been in close contact with Brian to ensure they were all inoculated against the hepatitis virus, which meant the band, all press, Mott, the road crew and many others. The doctors at the hospital received details of Brian's injection prior to travelling to Australia and concluded that he'd been infected by the dirty needle that had caused all the other problems with his arm.

Roger said: 'I don't think any of us ever felt so down in the dumps. The news that Brian would be in isolation for over a month just shattered us. We really felt we were breaking through in the States . . . we just didn't know what was going to happen.'

To add insult to injury, on 20 May, Elektra Records released 'Seven Seas Of Rhye' in the USA. As with the band's previous singles, it didn't hit the chart.

Mott The Hoople had to continue with the tour, and Queen were replaced by Canadian band Kansas. The band flew home, and Brian took to bed as ordered. He was very seriously ill and there was concern over whether he would ever recover completely. In the meantime, the *Daily Telegraph Magazine* ran a photo of him on their front cover for a feature called 'Geared into the teen scene: young fashions that Mother might allow'. They considered Brian a perfect role model for young teenagers, dressed soberly, intelligent and trendy. However, the article also featured two young models, with Freddie standing menacingly over them wearing a white satin winged stage costume designed by Zandra Rhodes and resplendent in black eye liner and nail polish . . .

Brian spent his time in bed working on new songs, as Queen were due to start recording their third album in July. In early June the band worked together on new material for the forthcoming recording sessions. They rehearsed at Rockfield Studios in the heart of Monmouthshire in Wales and began working out the way they wanted the songs to sound. It also gave them a chance to write more new material and lay down the backing tracks. But in between each take Brian disappeared into the bathroom to throw up, still not at all well.

They went into Trident Studios on 15 July 1974, and work was progressing well when, in early August, Brian was suddenly taken ill again. He was rushed into King's College Hospital and had an emergency operation for a duodenal ulcer. Queen had to cancel a planned North American tour in September due to his operation and convalescence. Brian was devastated. He felt responsible for the cancellations and worried that the band might replace him, but they had no such ideas and carried on working on the third album without him, knowing that he could come along when he was better and play his guitar parts to fit. Roy Thomas Baker, who was producing the album, tried hard to keep it all together, which was not an easy task when they had to leave gaps and spaces to be filled later by Brian. He worked so hard that for a time he became known as the Fifth Queenie.

Brian recalls: 'When I finally got out of hospital there was, of course, a mountain of playing to catch up on, plus the vocal harmony parts that needed the depth of the three voices. We did much of the overdubbing in London. We finished off "Killer Queen", "She Makes

THE TRIDENT YEARS

Me" (complete with authentic New York nightmare sounds) and "Brighton Rock". "Now I'm Here" was started and finished in the last couple of weeks, since I'd finally got my ideas straight for the song while in hospital, reflecting on the Mott tour and the future.'

By September 1974 *Queen II* had sold over 100,000 copies, enough for the band to be presented with silver discs. The presentation was made at London's Cafe Royal, arranged by Tony Brainsby, and they were handed the discs by Jeanette Charles, a Queen Elizabeth II 'look-alike' – she even made a Royal-style speech for the occasion. It was Brian's first appearance in public since his illness.

The band were now being noticed and taken seriously, the fan club they had set up was growing daily and the press, although still taking sly digs at them, were beginning to realise this 'flash in the pan' might be around for a bit longer. They were invited for interviews on radio and television as well as for newspapers; but having been chewed up so often, they had become reluctant to have any contact with the press.

On 11 October 1974, EMI released the band's third single, their first double A-side, 'Killer Queen' and 'Flick Of The Wrist', tracks taken from the album they were still working on. 'Killer Queen' was a huge success, reaching number two in the official BBC charts and hitting the number one slot in the music paper charts. The single got rave reviews: from *Sounds*, 'Freddie Mercury comes through as a distinguished rock vocalist, and the backing, although complicated at times, is heard loud and clear'. From *NME*: 'Queen have come up with a sound that'll prove they aren't any one-hit band'.

'Killer Queen' was the band's first big hit and, coming just before a tour, it encouraged them immensely. Their publishing company, Feldman, were so impressed by the band's success in the UK and Europe that, in an unusual gesture, they presented the band with engraved pewter tankards as a mark of their respect.

When they were looking for somewhere to rehearse for their

forthcoming British tour, Roger approached his old friend and roadie from the Smile days, Pete Edmunds. He had gone on to set up his own company, Live Ware, hiring PA systems, and had a warehouse in Ealing, which Roger persuaded him to allow Queen to use for rehearsals.

This tour started on 30 October at the Palace Theatre in Manchester. Queen had splashed out on a new lighting rig and had added new pyrotechnic effects, all very different from what most bands were doing at the time. Their aim had always been to give their fans a spectacle, a real 'show', and they were sure the audience would go for it. They had also prerecorded a special version of the National Anthem to play at the end of the shows – they felt it made a perfect finale, and no insult intended to Her Majesty The Queen. They played six songs from their new album on this tour and included their own 'Queen' medley (in which John Deacon got to hit a triangle) ending with 'Bring Back That Leroy Brown', featuring Brian playing a ukulele solo.

The gigs this time were slightly bigger than previously, and the crowds larger and louder. Brian was now fully recovered and playing well, and with the band flaunting extravagant stage wear, particularly Brian and Freddie, alongside the

THE TRIDENT YEARS

new lights, flash bombs and dry ice, it was an impressive production. The audiences were even more enthusiastic than before – resulting in a few incidents such as the one at the Liverpool Empire on 1 November, when the fans rushed the stage during the introduction tape. The safety curtain was lowered and the manager walked on stage to calm the crowd. The following night, in Leeds, the fans again rushed forward, risking crushing those at the front. Freddie was on stage and with a few words was able to quash the problem swiftly. (Both events made headline news in the music papers the following week.) At Leeds, Roger had somehow damaged his foot before going on stage and played a painful set, afterwards being whisked off to Leeds hospital for an X-ray and treatment. Luckily it was nothing more serious than severe bruising, resulting in a temporary limp.

The tour progressed without further mishap until Glasgow on 8 November, also the day on which EMI released the band's third album, *Sheer Heart Attack*. Freddie was dragged into the audience during the latter part of the show and had to be rescued by security guards. The chaos that night resulted in damage to ten rows of seats, but the manager of the venue, the Apollo Centre, presented the band with silver statuettes for the hall's first complete sell-out.

The press liked *Sheer Heart Attack*, with the *NME*'s reviewer writing: 'A feast. No duffers, and four songs that will just run and run: Killer Queen, Flick Of The Wrist, Now I'm Here and In The Lap Of The Gods . . . revisited. Even the track I don't like, Brighton Rock, includes May's Echoplex solo, still a vibrant, thrilling experience whether you hear it live or on record.' An American music paper said: 'This is a testament not only to Queen's immense talent, but to their versatility as well. Queen will be playing Madison Square Garden as headliners by the time their fourth album comes along.'

Queen's only London date was at the Rainbow Theatre for one night on 19 November, but the tickets completely sold out within two days, so promoter Mel Bush added a second night. Sometime previously, discussions had turned to a potential Queen feature film, which would be excellent publicity. Consequently, it was arranged for both nights at the Rainbow to be filmed in their entirety. Both shows were also recorded with the idea of possibly releasing a 'live' album. But after much discussion, the band themselves voted against the idea; they loved to play live but didn't like the idea of a live album – they didn't think it was good value for money.

An 'end of tour party' was held at the Holiday Inn in London's Swiss Cottage. It was probably the first time Queen had held such a party, but it certainly wasn't the last. Mel Bush presented the band with a brass plaque to commemorate selling out all shows.

Although Queen were now secure in the knowledge they had finally made it, their relationship with the press had deteriorated still further. The band's complete lack of enthusiasm for giving interviews irritated journalists all the more and gave them what they considered valid reasons for the persistent insults they aimed at the band. They even began to invent – largely uncomplimentary – quotes and interviews.

The band were due to start their European tour in late November. They first flew out to the Netherlands, to Hilversum Avro studios, to film an appearance on Dutch pop show *Top Pop*. They then travelled on to Gothenburg, Sweden, in preparation for the tour. They were to be supported by American band Lynyrd Skynyrd, who were, although largely unknown in Europe, huge in their native country, and therefore popular with GIs stationed in Germany. However, Queen only got to play Gothenburg, Helsinki and Lund in Scandinavia, as their equipment truck was involved in an accident and they couldn't get the gear to the other planned gigs. The truck had been loaded up for the drive to Munich. However, the driver misjudged the height of the vehicle when, halfway there, he managed to get it stuck under a low bridge.

Farrokh Bulsara, aged one – the photo that won him first prize in a Zanzibar baby contest.

John Deacon as a toddler.

Roger Taylor and his sister Clare.

Freddie at St Peter's School, Panchgani, India, with his Junior All-rounder trophy, 1958.

Freddie (right) in the boxing ring at St Peter's School.

Freddie (middle) with his first band, The Hectics, at St Peter's School.

Brian, aged fourteen, with his mother, Ruth.

Roger, aged fifteen, with one of his first drum kits.

Roger, Mike Dudley (guitar) and Dave Dowding (bass) in Beat Unlimited, 1964.

1984 in 1964. (L–R) Tim Staffell, Dave Dilloway, Richard Thompson, John Garnham, Brian May.

Brian (far right) as the Lady Mary Lasenby in *The Admirable Crichton*, 1964.

John, aged fourteen, at his parents' home in Oadby, Leicestershire.

John (top right), with The New Opposition: Nigel Bullen, Richard Young, Pete 'Pedro' Bart and David Williams.

'The Wandering Minstrel'. Brian, 1966.

Tim Staffell during the Smile era, 1966.

1984 in 1967.

Freddie with Ibex, Queens Park, Bolton, 1969.

Roger in Smile, 1969. DOUG PUDDIFOOT

THE TRIDENT YEARS

They travelled back to the UK for a few days while the truck was replaced. Luckily, UK-based Edwin Shirley, who was new to the trucking business and had only a few vehicles, turned up with another lorry to take over. Fortunately, it arrived just in time to set up for the 2 December gig, and Edwin' s company continued to supply trucks for the rest of that tour – and every other tour Queen undertook.

The band flew back out to Munich on 1 December to continue the tour – which culminated in Barcelona, where the venue's 6,000 tickets had sold out in one day. In late December, *Music Week* ran a headline declaring 'Queen Conquer Europe!' It was fair comment, as the band's gigs throughout Europe had all been sell-outs, album sales were soaring, local people loved them and it seemed they could do no wrong.

Back in the UK by the end of 1974, Queen finally agreed to do various television and newspaper interviews, and appeared on Granada Television's Christmas Special of the pop show *45*, performing 'Now I'm Here'. They wanted as much exposure as possible as their popularity was on an upward spiral, even though the press were still knocking them. Publicist Tony Brainsby was determined to *try* to change all that, and worked with the band to improve their image within the media. It wasn't an easy task.

Queen's relationship with Trident was souring. The band had had lengthy meetings with Norman Sheffield, concerning their 'wages'. At the start, Trident felt £15 per week appropriate, but the band insisted on £20 a week as more realistic, and just after the release of *Sheer Heart Attack*, this went up to £60. After the success of both 'Killer Queen' and 'Now I'm Here', Queen felt they should be earning far more. Everyone they met assumed that the band were millionaires, which was far from the truth. The friction became unbearable, so Queen approached a young, emerging music-business lawyer, Jim Beach, to see if there was any way they could cut the ties that bound them to Trident. He immediately began negotiations with Trident to sever the three agreements Queen had signed. That was in December 1974. The matter was not to be resolved until August 1975.

By the end of December, success for Queen was assured on both sides of the Atlantic as the single 'Killer Queen' and album *Sheer Heart Attack* both reached the Top 10 in the USA. Any success for English bands in America was hard won indeed, and possibly harder still for Queen, as their image was so out of keeping with US artists at the time, most of whom were wearing nothing more exciting than jeans and T-shirts.

Early January 1975 was a quiet time for Queen, and Brian made the most of it with a short holiday in Tenerife, an island he had loved since his student days.

January 17 saw the release of their fourth single, 'Now I'm Here', from the *Sheer Heart Attack* album, and next day John married his long-time love Veronica Tetzlaff at the Carmelite Church on Kensington Church Street, London.

The problems with Trident and their management of the band's money were now coming to the fore. John wanted to buy a small house for himself and his wife, but Trident refused to advance him the money for the deposit. Freddie wanted a piano and Roger a car but neither request was granted and relationships between the band and Norman Sheffield became even more strained.

On 31 January the band left for the USA and their first headlining tour, amid much excitement. They were looking forward to being top of the bill and finally putting all the new light and sound technology into action. They were all slightly apprehensive, too. 'Killer Queen' had been released a couple of months previously and had sold well, reaching number five in the rock charts, but they still didn't know how they would be received.

They needn't have worried – the tour sold out so quickly that several extra dates had to be added to cope with the demand. They

THE TRIDENT YEARS

often found themselves playing two shows in a day, both to sell-out crowds.

The band's first gig was at the Agora Theater in Columbus, Ohio, supported by Kansas,* whom they had met during the Mott tour, and Mahogany Rush. The American press received the first concert enthusiastically.

However, within the first three weeks of the tour Freddie started to have problems with his voice, and after the second show in Philadelphia, barely able to speak, he had to consult a throat specialist at the University City Hospital. Jack Nelson and Dave Thomas stayed in Philly with Freddie while the rest of the party travelled on to Washington DC, the next stop. The specialist told Freddie he might have two throat nodes, caused by him having strained his voice. He recommended that Freddie didn't sing, and spoke as little as possible, for at least three months. The next night, 24 February 1975, Freddie went on stage at the Kennedy Centre in Washington DC. He and the other band members knew this would be their last show for some time, as Freddie was suffering, but whether it was the thought of not being able to do anything for a while that did it, or whatever, they played one of the best shows they had ever given.

The next day Freddie saw another specialist, in Washington, for a second opinion, and was told that although he didn't have nodes his throat was badly swollen and he should rest his voice as much as he could. Everyone was relieved: nodes might have meant an operation and the swelling, though inconvenient and painful, was easier to cope with. A silent Freddie reluctantly agreed to cancel the next few shows to give his throat time to heal. He flew into New Orleans, where a top show-business throat specialist confirmed the diagnosis and again told Freddie that complete rest was the only cure. He also gave him

---

* American band Styx occasionally stood in for Kansas when they were playing gigs of their own.

a course of antibiotics and painkillers to try to ease the pain and take down the inflammation.

The next six shows were cancelled, but finally the swelling subsided and Freddie was back on stage. He tried to keep quiet between shows, however, as he was worried about it flaring up again. The rest hadn't been sufficient, though, and a few days after resuming the tour Freddie was ill again. It became increasingly obvious that too much strain was being placed on his throat, and several more concerts were cancelled. The band continued with some shows, but with longer rest periods, which seemed to be the only solution.

His throat problems might have rendered Freddie speechless between shows but certainly didn't reduce him to helplessness, as an unlucky lady thief found out in Seattle. Freddie disturbed her in his hotel room pocketing his money and jewellery, and gave chase. She was apprehended and arrested in the lobby.

During the tour Queen had met and talked to show-business manager Don Arden, who offered them a lucrative deal once they were free from Trident. Negotiations with Trident were only in their infancy, however, and the band couldn't accept his offer. Don said he could speed up the Trident business, and contacted Norman Sheffield. Trident agreed, in principle, to his 'suggestions' for releasing Queen, and the band signed a letter authorising him to proceed on their behalf, on the understanding that he would become their manager when it was settled.

One of the bigger venues on the tour was the Santa Monica Civic Auditorium, in California, and during the show, in front of a capacity crowd, John split his trousers. Freddie found this extremely funny and taunted him mercilessly throughout the show until he could sneak off and change.

The final date on the tour, during which they had played thirty-eight gigs in eight weeks, was to have been 7 April in Portland, but again it was cancelled. Back in the UK, the problems with Trident

THE TRIDENT YEARS

were growing. The long negotiations for getting out of the original contracts were still in progress, so the band adjourned to Kawai, in Hawaii, for a short and well-deserved holiday before their first venture to Japan.

CHAPTER 8

CONQUERING JAPAN

QUEEN'S JAPANESE RECORD SALES WERE STILL VERY HIGH, AS WERE expectations for ticket sales. When the band flew into Tokyo Airport on 18 April 1975 they were greeted by over 3,000 screaming Japanese fans, all holding banners and records, and chanting and calling to them as they disembarked.

They were taken by surprise at the strength of their reception, even though they knew *Sheer Heart Attack* and 'Killer Queen' were both riding at number one in the charts there. 'It was amazing,' said Brian. 'All these Japanese people screaming and yelling for *us*. We couldn't take it all in, it was like another world, but we loved it!' The Japanese magazine *Music Life* had arranged a press reception to present them with special awards for their high record sales and popularity, and they were hailed as heroes throughout the country.

The band's first concert was at the Budokan Martial Arts Hall in the capital on 19 April 1975. It was a sold-out show, with 10,000 people packed into the hall, and the sheer weight of numbers was a problem. The organisers had employed Sumo wrestlers to stand behind a barrier in front of the stage to stop people rushing onto it. Within minutes of the show starting, the crowd surged forward, and it became obvious that the wrestlers were unable to hold them back. By the time the band took to the stage, the seats in the arena had begun to collapse, resulting in panic and hysteria. A seething mass, mostly of young girls, was swaying, like a wave. It carried them about ten feet from side to side, and the screaming all but drowned out the music. It was becoming dangerous for the fans and Freddie stopped the show to calm the audience before serious injury befell anyone. The fans listened to him, settled down, and the show – which was being filmed for Japanese television – continued without mishap. When it was over, the band were driven from the hall in an armoured vehicle, to ensure their safety.

Eleven days later, after a concert each day in various parts of Japan, the band were back in Tokyo at the Budokan, having featured on television across the country. As a tribute to the vast crowds who had seen them, they decided to finish the last show in Japanese style, and all took to the stage for the encore dressed in kimonos. The audience was thrilled and went wild.

The tour caused nationwide hysteria: not since The Beatles had Japan seen anything like it. It was the first country to recognise Queen as a major rock band, and treated them accordingly, showering them with expensive and extravagant gifts; and it marked the beginning of the band's deep regard for the country and its people. Freddie was particularly taken with Japan, and bought several silk kimonos and dolls, and started a collection of Japanese art.

The band arrived back in the UK with heavy hearts; they'd had such a good time that it was depressing to be back in the midst of their management traumas. They had some serious decisions to make regarding their future. Their lawyer was still trying to get Trident to relinquish their hold, but as yet nothing had materialised.

In early May, *Disc* magazine readers voted Queen as the top band in no less than four categories of their annual poll: live group, British group, top single for 'Killer Queen' and top international group. They were now featured regularly on radio and television, too, and Freddie was asked to appear on DJ Kenny Everett's radio show, an experience that forged a firm friendship between them.

On 22 May, Freddie was presented with an Ivor Novello award by the Songwriters Guild Of Great Britain for 'Killer Queen'. It was the first time he had received anything so prestigious, and he was immensely proud of it.

During the summer of 1975 the band continued to work hard on new material for their fourth album. They had many new ideas and new songs. Brian was experimenting even more with guitar harmonies and orchestration, as they still resisted using synthesizers. They all considered that the sound of real instruments was far preferable and, besides, Brian could make his guitar do amazing things.

Some months previously Freddie had been introduced to Eddie Howell, a singer-songwriter who was about to start work on recording a single. He asked Freddie if he would consider producing it for him. Freddie had never ventured into producing another artist's music before, but he thought it might be a good experience and accepted. The work was done during the summer, and Freddie, who was also playing keyboards and singing backing vocals, enlisted the help of Brian to add guitar. The finished track, 'The Man From Manhattan', was a minor hit in several countries, although it made little impression in the UK

On 18 July 1975, John and Veronica became the proud parents of their first child, Robert. The band also received a Golden Lion award for 'Killer Queen', which was presented at the Golden Lion festival in Blankenberge, Belgium, Roger and Brian flying out to receive it on everyone's behalf.

The management severance agreements were ready for signature in August, and finally there was light at the end of the tunnel. A major sticking point, however, was that Jack Nelson had already booked venues for a Stateside tour, and tickets had been sold – but the management problems had to be solved. The tour was cancelled, resulting in a substantial loss of revenue for all involved.

CONQUERING JAPAN

Rumours began to circulate that Queen were about to split up due to internal problems – rumours with no truth to them whatsoever. Although the difficulties were real enough, and caused disagreements within the band due to the pressure they were under, the foursome themselves had no intention of letting it destroy their future. Finally, in late August 1975, Queen signed an agreement with Trident that freed them from the three deals. Their publishing company, Feldman, was taken over by EMI, their recording deals were no longer to be channelled through Trident and were signed directly with EMI and Elektra, and they were free to find new management. In return, the band agreed to give Trident a severance payment of £100,000 and the rights to 1 per cent of the royalties on their next six albums. The only remaining problem was that Queen had no money at all.

The band and their lawyer Jim Beach then began the search for new management – the previous written agreement with Don Arden was no longer in effect, by mutual agreement. Together they drew up a shortlist of three people. The first was Peter Grant, then managing Led Zeppelin. Peter was interested but wanted Queen to sign to Swan Song, Led Zeppelin's own production and record company. Queen, understandably, wanted to sign directly with one of the major record companies, and turned down Peter's offer. Peter, however, gave them free and good advice on their future, for which the band were all grateful. Jim then tried to contact Peter Rudge, who managed The Who and The Rolling Stones, but as he was on tour failed to reach him. The third was Elton John's manager, John Reid. At that time Elton John was enormous worldwide, and Reid said, when approached, that he was unsure if he could take on another band. His attitude changed, however, when he found out it was Queen.

CHAPTER 9

THE JOHN REID EPOCH

HAVING ACCEPTED THE MANAGEMENT JOB, JOHN REID'S FIRST TASK was to team up with Jim Beach and negotiate the band's music publishing deal, as they had to find £100,000 by November to pay off Trident. They arranged that EMI Music Publishing would advance them the amount against future royalties.

John threw a huge party at the London Coliseum to celebrate his union with Queen and during the party the band were presented with an array of gold and silver discs for sales of 'Killer Queen', *Sheer Heart Attack*, *Queen* and *Queen II*. They also received a rather different award: a 'Carl Allen Award', which was presented to bands for their outstanding contribution to the ballroom dancing industry . . .

As Trident before him, John realised that he would need a 'day to day' manager for his new signings, and pulled in Pete Brown, who he'd worked with extensively on other projects. Pete was to handle the band's personal lives and business as John wanted them to be properly looked after in every respect.

One of the most popular bands in British music at the time, apart from Queen, was Sparks, which consisted of two brothers, Russ and Ron Mael. During mid-1975 they approached Brian and asked him if he would consider joining them, saying, 'Queen are obviously all washed up, come and conquer the world with us!' Brian was flattered – he liked Sparks immensely – but he turned them down. Queen were well on their way and he was more than happy to stay where he was.

The band had been working hard on their next album in various studios in and around London, and Roger was asked to provide the backing vocals on a song for pop band Fox, who were working in Sarm Studios at the same time as Queen. 'Survival' finally ended up on the album *Tails Of Illusion* (1975). He also agreed to play drums on an album track for singer Eugene Wallace, at Trident Studios, which later appeared on *Dangerous* (also 1975).

In October the band presented John Reid with the track they wanted as their next single, an almost six-minute-long operatic epic entitled 'Bohemian Rhapsody'. John was incredulous. He remonstrated with them, saying they couldn't possibly release something that long, it just wasn't feasible – no one would play it. However, the band were unanimous: it would not be edited. John knew they wouldn't budge, so the single was pressed.

Freddie and Roger, who were still close friends of DJ Kenny Everett, gave him a copy of the single before its release and told him it was for his personal use only, and that he wasn't to play it on the radio. But never one to toe the line, and because he loved the song so much, Kenny couldn't resist giving it a spin on air – fourteen times, in fact, in two days. His listeners' response was incredible: the phone lines were jammed with callers asking where they could buy this great new single.

Finally, 'Bohemian Rhapsody' was released on 31 October. They even gave it a picture cover, the first time they'd done so in Britain. The single was a unique blend of rock and opera; beginning with plaintive ballad, merging into multi-tracked harmonic operatics, then thundering into a heavy rock ending. It was Freddie's magnum opus, and everyone wanted to know what on earth it was all about. He would never say, except that it was a personal song, about relationships. He was never drawn any further. No matter the meaning, the song took the country by storm. Reviewers either loathed it or were euphoric. Some reactions, though, were predictable. Everyone in the media said that no one would play it all the way through on air and that it would never be a hit. They were wrong: the radio stations played it from start to finish every time – it was never cut.

The media previewed the album from which the single was taken at the Roundhouse Studios in London, where those attending were welcomed by a huge sign which simply stated 'Welcome to A Night at the Opera' and where it was announced that this was the most expensive album ever made. When the Queen version of the national anthem, the album's last track, was played, Freddie made everyone stand to attention until it was over.

That preview brought a particular track to the attention of Norman Sheffield, one of the Trident brothers. The track in question was 'Death On Two Legs', the title suffixed by the words 'dedicated to . . .'. Norman saw red and assumed that the song was about him. He could read all the ill-feeling that had arisen between himself and Queen during, and after, their acrimonious parting in lines such as 'You've taken all my money, and you want more' and 'Put your money where your mouth is, Mister Know All.' He threatened to sue both Queen and EMI as he considered the song libellous. Queen refused to do anything: they had never stated anywhere, or to anyone, to whom that song was dedicated. EMI fended off the court action and, in return for an undertaking that Trident would never bring another action in connection with the album, agreed to pay Norman Sheffield a substantial sum, which seemed preferable to ignoring the situation and allowing it to escalate, and certainly better than having the album's release prevented by an injunction.

Queen were due to begin a long UK tour in mid-November, and 'Bohemian Rhapsody' was steadily climbing the charts. The band

THE JOHN REID EPOCH

wanted to be sure the song was played on TV, including on *Top Of The Pops*, if the opportunity arose while they were on the road, so they talked to Bruce Gowers, who had directed *Live At the Rainbow*, about making a short promotional film to accompany the song. It was a new idea, but the band felt sure they could make it work. They were going into Elstree Studios on 10 November to rehearse for the tour and took the opportunity to film the promo video. The band worked out each shot before the cameras started rolling, shots which included bringing the *Queen II* album cover to life. The video for 'Bohemian Rhapsody', now referred to as Bo Rap, took just four hours to film, cost £4,500 to make and a day to edit.

Within two weeks of its release, 'Bohemian Rhapsody' had sold over 150,000 copies – Freddie predicted number three in the charts – and it's possible it ensured that the UK tour Queen were about to embark on was a sell-out. As Kenny had been a great help in the single's success, Freddie asked him to record an introduction they could play at the beginning of the shows. He did so, in his inimitable wacky style.

This tour boasted the most elaborate stage set yet with even more lights and pyrotechnics and dry ice than usual. Roger extended his already extensive drum kit and added an enormous gong (which was suspended behind him and which had to be held from behind by the drum roadie when Roger hit it, for fear of it flying backwards and disappearing into the wings), and there were three new songs in their repertoire.

The tour began at the Liverpool Empire on 14 November 1975, with Mr Big as support. On the third night, in Coventry, Freddie went on stage in his Japanese kimono, much to the audience's delight. Queen crowds were used to Freddie's remarkable costumes; he wore the black nail polish for some time and had sported diamonds and chains, leather and studs and flowing gowns. Brian's stage wear, too, was never dull – he had some amazing winged costumes and tight-bodiced embroidered jackets with flowing sleeves. People expected something different every time and they got it.

On 20 November, *Top Of The Pops* premiered the 'Bohemian Rhapsody' promotional film, to great media and public interest. Using a video instead of appearing in person was such a novel idea and it was a turning point in the history of pop music on television and film, many attributing the launch to the boom in the promo film business. Now bands had to have a good video to accompany their songs – and a couple of years later, along came MTV in the USA . . .

On 21 November, EMI released Queen's fourth album, *A Night At The Opera*. All the band members were great fans of the Marx Brothers and titled their album after what they considered to be one of the brothers' best films. *Melody Maker* wrote: 'The overall impression is of musical range, power and consistently incisive lyrics. My hair is still standing on end – so if you like good music and don't mind looking silly, play this album.'

November 25 saw Queen celebrating their first number one single in Britain with 'Bohemian Rhapsody'. They were ecstatic. 'We were in a hotel in Southampton, we were there for a gig or something, as the band were all staying in the same place, and I had popped out,' recalls Roger's mother. 'When I came back, I bumped into John Deacon in the lobby, and he said they were number one. I was really pleased, and Roger was excited, but it didn't really sink in. Then, on the way home in the car, they played the song on the radio, saying it was Britain's number one. I suddenly realised that my son was a huge success, he really had made it. It was quite emotional.' Brian's and Freddie's parents had never been in doubt, and John's mother, although pleased and excited, said it was nothing more or less than she had expected. But it was an ambition realised.

After five sold-out nights at the London Hammersmith Odeon on 29/30 November and 1–3 December, and dates in Wolverhampton, Preston and Birmingham, Queen were playing in Newcastle at the

THE JOHN REID EPOCH

City Hall. As they were leaving that city en route to Dundee, the band's coach was stopped by a police roadblock and they were escorted to the local constabulary to be searched, ostensibly for drugs. None of the band was particularly interested in drugs: having been students and getting into the music business rather older than some, they'd had ample opportunity to experiment with various substances and found none of them particularly inspiring. The police let them go after their search revealed nothing more than a couple of aspirin, a reality the police found hard to believe.

On 24 December the band played a one-off concert at London's Hammersmith Odeon, which was televised live on *The Old Grey Whistle Test* and broadcast simultaneously on Radio One. It achieved a huge audience, and the bootleg tape of the radio broadcast soon became – and remains – a collector's item among diehard fans.

A Night At The Opera was the band's first album to reach platinum status, for sales exceeding 250,000. The band were pleased but as far as they were concerned it was no more than the album deserved. On 27 December, they celebrated their first UK number one album when it stormed to the top, bringing an added edge to their festive season celebrations. *Opera* was released in the USA on 2 December and marked the beginning of Queen's longest reign to date in the US album charts, at fifty-six weeks.

January 1976 dawned well for Queen as they again cleaned up in the music press's annual polls. In the *NME*, they appeared in eight categories, including best single, for 'Bohemian Rhapsody', and best British stage band. In *Record Mirror* and *Disc* they were in no less than ten categories, among which were best British group, best world group and best single, again for 'Bohemian Rhapsody'. To top all that, Freddie was awarded another Ivor Novello, for, needless to say, 'Bohemian Rhapsody'.

On 19 January 1976, Queen signed the contract for their new management deal with John Reid Enterprises.

By 24 January 'Bohemian Rhapsody' had sat at the number one slot in the UK charts for nine weeks, the first time a single had been at the top for so long since 1957, when Slim Whitman had held it with 'Rosemarie' for the same length of time. John announced that it had sold over a million copies in the UK alone, and that *A Night At The Opera* had then sold over 500,000. He even took an advertisement in *Sounds* to congratulate the band on their achievements.

The band were planning their second headlining tour of North America during January 1976, organised by a new face to the Queen team, Gerry Stickells. 'Promoter Howard Rose put me in touch with Queen when they were looking for a tour manager for the States. I didn't have a clue who they were!' Gerry had previously been roadie, then tour manager for Jimi Hendrix as well as arranging and managing the tours of several other American bands.

On 20 January, Queen flew out of the UK bound for New York and the start of their third US tour, hoping that this time they could get through it without any illness or serious problems. The first gig was in Waterbury, Connecticut, at the Palace Theatre, and the band were received rapturously. One of the songs they performed live was 'Now I'm Here': for the introduction, the band's personal assistant, Pete Brown, would dress in an outfit identical to Freddie's and stand on one side of the pitch-black stage with Freddie on the other. As Freddie sang the opening line to the song, 'Now I'm here . . .' the spotlight would quickly illuminate him and fade. As he sang the next line, 'now I'm there . . .' it would flash on Pete and highlight the echoing, ventriloquist quality of the song. Pete said: 'I had to wear one of Fred's frocks! Apart from having to be a Freddie clone for a while, my other job was to pull all the thorns off the dozens of red roses that Freddie would later throw out into the audience. They wanted to be sure that no one in the audience was hurt, but really it was Freddie who was worried about getting thorns in his fingers.'

It was to be a long, long tour: Queen were set to cover nearly every state in the country. The crowds were huge, and fans were tireless in their efforts to find out which hotels the band were staying at in each town and hovered outside in the hope of seeing and meeting the band. In New York City three young ladies nearly brought the Queen era to a sudden and painful end when they almost succeeded in strangling Freddie while haggling over his scarf.

Queen's after-show parties were becoming notorious: they were long, loud and outrageous and usually attended by local stars and VIPs, and some less desirable types, too. They gave a party after most shows: as Brian once said, after performing the adrenaline was pumping, and they still needed to be surrounded by a mass of people to wind down.

While in New York Freddie, Brian and Roger called into the Electric Ladyland Studios to see Mott singer Ian Hunter, who was working on a solo album, with Roy Thomas Baker producing. Says Roger, 'We spent plenty of time catching up on gossip and tour news, and we all ended up singing backing vocals on one of the tracks, 'You Nearly Did Me In', which also featured the late great bass player Jaco Pastorius.'

In the UK in early February, even though the band were away, Queen were again breaking records – all four of their albums were in the Top 20 at the same time, which was a previously unrivalled feat – and in early March the film *Queen At The Rainbow* was released in the UK and shown at cinemas alongside the movie *The Hustle*, starring Burt Reynolds and Katherine Deneuve. The Rainbow film didn't set the movie world alight, but it caused a stir among some audiences, and a lot of new fans were recruited after seeing it. The power of Queen's live stage act even came across on film.

Back in the USA, record stores were selling out of Queen albums fast, and radio stations were inundated with requests for their tracks. After five sold-out concerts at the Santa Monica Civic Auditorium in LA, the band flew out of the States to Japan, where they were again greeted with riotous adulation by fans at the airport. Tickets had sold out so quickly that Queen again added shows, playing two on the same day in some venues. It was only a fleeting visit this time, though – fourteen days and eleven gigs – but it was enough time to add to their Japanese collections, especially Freddie, who loved shopping at the best of times but particularly in Japan. He bought several more kimonos, including a bright red pure silk one, which he wore on stage on the last night of the tour. He and Brian had also learned a few words of Japanese to say to the audience between songs, which gained them even more kudos.

Next stop was Australia. They all felt a little wary of returning after their initial experience Down Under, but as both the single and album were at the top of the Aussie charts, they returned with more confidence. The trip proved trouble-free: Queen were accepted as the superstar band they had purported to be on their first visit. The locals welcomed them with friendliness and enthusiasm. Eight sold-out concerts later, they flew back to England to start work on their next album. On 29 May 1976, Brian married long-time girlfriend Chrissy Mullen in St Osmund's Roman Catholic church, Castlenau, Barnes.

June 18 saw the release of their sixth single by EMI, 'You're My Best Friend'. It was the first time a John Deacon composition had been released as a single, and it was also the first time they'd considered releasing a ballad – it must have been a popular combination, though, as the single climbed into the UK Top 10 to settle at number seven. *Sounds* wrote: 'It'll be an absolute smash, beautiful harmonies, strident guitar chords and Freddie in superb voice. Instant number one!'

After the success of the 'Bohemian Rhapsody' promotional video, Queen decided to make another video, to accompany the new single, and once again called in Bruce Gowers.

The band's fan club had been running smoothly all this time, coping with the ever-growing demands of Queen fans for in-depth

THE JOHN REID EPOCH

information. They wanted to know everything from the band members' shoe sizes upwards – and some questions were rather personal. The pressures of coping with such demands grew too heavy for Pat and Sue, and they finally quit, none too amicably. They felt they weren't getting the credit they deserved and were being ignored now that Queen had become famous. There was also pressure from fan-club members, some of whom felt that Pat and Sue had perhaps become overprotective of the band, and Therese Pickard took over.

During routine work on their next album in August 1976, the band decided that they would love to repay their English fans for their loyalty and support and came up with the idea of a huge free concert. Venues big enough to hold the vast amount of people they had in mind were few and far between, so, assisted by Virgin Records' Richard Branson, they approached the London Parks Committee for permission to stage the concert in Hyde Park. Permission was granted, but only after the band agreed to certain conditions set out by the Metropolitan Police regarding start and end times, security (which the band would have to provide), facilities for the audience and so on. The date was set for 18 September. Queen decided that they wanted to do more than the Hyde Park gig and planned a mini tour of Britain to precede it, booking the Edinburgh Playhouse and Cardiff Castle. Rehearsal time was also booked at Shepperton Studios for the band to practise the material they had been working on for the new album, and they decided to include some of the new numbers in the set.

The two Edinburgh concerts were played as part of the Scottish Festival of Popular Music, and, as the Playhouse had been closed for some time for refurbishment, Queen were there to relaunch it. They played a set similar to their previous tour, with a couple of additions to the medley section. They also introduced an acoustic set for the first time: all four band members were at the front of the stage for '39'. Freddie played the maracas in this number, and afterwards threw them out into the audience, a practice he continued, getting through rather a lot of maracas. The set also featured the haunting 'You Take My Breath Away' from the forthcoming album, with Freddie alone on the darkened stage, playing the piano. 'Tie Your Mother Down', a new rocker written by Brian, had the audience dancing in the aisles.

The Cardiff concert was an open-air affair, and the weather in the preceding days had been glorious – but the day of the show dawned grey and overcast. The 12,000-strong audience started to arrive as the first drops of rain began to fall. And the rain didn't stop all day. The support bands – Manfred Mann, Andy Fairweather Low and Frankie Miller's Full House – all went on to a wet, dispirited audience. But they had paid to see Queen and, despite the weather, they waited all day, giving damp encouragement to the support bands.

When Queen finally took to the stage, with the rain still falling and the field reduced to a mud bath, the crowd were on their feet cheering, forgetting their discomfort and the appalling conditions.

Everyone was worried that the weather for the Hyde Park show would mirror Cardiff, and the band took out weather insurance to ensure that if the concert had to be cancelled or cut short, they could recoup some of the costs. Before the weather had changed, the concert had been under threat due to drought – so if it hadn't rained, it would have been called off anyway.

Richard Branson had been involved in organising the Hyde Park event and it was during the pre-production discussions that Roger met Branson's personal assistant, Dominique Beyrand, a beautiful young French woman. Roger was smitten and often called and dropped in with a variety of excuses to see her. It wasn't long before they began to see each other regularly.

As it turned out, September 18 was a glorious day. The sun shone as the massive audience, estimated at between 150,000 and 200,000, converged on the park. Traffic was brought to a standstill and public transport was overcrowded as the concertgoers made their way through

THE JOHN REID EPOCH

London. The gig was being recorded for live transmission on London's Capital Radio and the outside broadcast trucks, cables and technicians added to the chaos. The support bands – Kiki Dee, Steve Hillage and Supercharge – were all received loudly and to enthusiastic applause, as the crowd were enjoying the day and were happy enough to show their appreciation. When it was dark, the crowd surged to its feet as the lights came on and the opening chords to 'Bohemian Rhapsody' echoed around the park. Freddie burst onto the stage wearing a specially made white leotard. The band gave an energetic performance, with Freddie exchanging his skin-tight white leotard for an identical black one with a diamante-studded crotch half-way through the set. After the show, the crowds refused to leave and stamped and shouted for an encore. However, Queen were under strict police orders not to return to the stage. Said Gerry Stickells, 'The police threatened to arrest Freddie if he tried to go back out on stage, as he was furious at having no chance for an encore and was going to go back on and give the crowd what they were yelling for. But the thought of being in jail in tights didn't appeal to him at all, so he gave up!' The police switched off the power to make their point. But the same power source had also been used to light the audience and the park exits, and that huge body of people had to find their way out of the park in darkness. The day had been such a success – apart from the lack of an encore – that Queen and John Reid placed a huge 'Thank you' advertisement in the music press for their fans. They also issued 'Thank you' plaques to the entire road crew.

The Hyde Park concert was filmed, as DJ Bob Harris was working on a documentary of the band with their permission and co-operation, and he wanted to include the show in the new film. Some of the footage was also used as promotion for singles and the album.

Over in the USA at the same time, Queen received a Don Kirshner/CBS Rock award for the best-produced album of the year with *A Night At The Opera*.

Work on the new album had been progressing fast and it was wrapped up by mid-October. The band had decided to stay with the Marx Brothers theme and so they christened it *A Day At the Races*. As pre-publicity for the album the band and press attended a race meeting at Kempton Park. A special race, the Day At The Races Hurdle, was run in their honour, sponsored by EMI Records. Two live bands, Marmalade and The Tremeloes, were booked to entertain the crowds between races. It was a beautiful day and attendance was high. The proceeds from the meeting went towards the Sports Aid Foundation Charity, which helped to pay for the training of international athletes for the Olympic and Commonwealth Games. When the Day At The Races Hurdle was being called, all the band members had a bet – and unbeknownst to each other, all backed the same horse, Lanzarote, ridden by champion jockey John Francombe – which won!

The first single chosen from the new album was the ballad 'Somebody To Love', written by Freddie. Roger and Freddie drove to Kenny Everett's country house with a white label copy, as a 'teaser'. Once again, Kenny adored it and played it constantly on his show. The Capital Radio Hitline was a day-to-day chart compiled from calls made by listeners phoning in and voting for their favourite songs, and the first day that Kenny played 'Somebody To Love' on the show, the phone lines went mad. By the time that day's Hitline was broadcast, 'Somebody To Love' had already got to number three. The following day it was played constantly again and made it to number one – all this before being released.

By now the band had all moved out of their rented flats and houses; John had a house in Putney with Veronica, Brian had a modest house in Barnes with Chrissie, Freddie had a flat in Kensington with Mary, and Roger had bought himself and Dominique a house in Fulham, and a beautiful country house in Surrey with acres of garden and woodland, a real 'star's retreat'. As part of the refurbishment of the house, Roger had the basement converted into a recording studio, to work there on his own songs and demo tapes, which he found easier than trying to write in the studio or anywhere else.

'Somebody To Love' was finally released on 12 November 1976, and again the band decided to make a promotional film for it, with Bruce Gowers directing as usual. Within its first week of release the single reached number four in the UK charts, but Radio Luxembourg's individual chart placed it at number one. The first time it was played on *Top Of The Pops*, Pan's People, the resident dance group, gyrated to it. The next few weeks was spent in a whirlwind of interviews and personal appearances on television and radio shows, all pre-publicity for the imminent release of *A Day At The Races*, which finally hit record stores on 10 December. Pending release, EMI had received the highest advance orders ever for an album. But the reviewer in *Sounds* commented: 'It is too formulated, too smartass, too reliant on trickery as a substitute for inspiration. Although I believe that Queen have produced some of the most impressive, majestic, sophisticated music of the decade over the last few years, there must be a substance behind the frills. If I am wrong about this album, then apologies to anyone misled by premature opinion.'

Despite the lacklustre reviews, the album still had its fans in high places. Groucho Marx was kept informed of the release of both *A Night At The Opera* and *A Day At The Races*, due to the connection with his films, and he sent Queen a telegram congratulating them and wishing them as much success with the album as he had enjoyed with the film.

Between the album's release and Christmas the band were again involved with publicity campaigns, appearing on children's television, late-night talk shows, music shows and magazine programmes. Even the reticent Freddie guested on Kenny Everett's *Be Bop Bonanza* radio show. Also, on 28 December, by public demand, the BBC repeated the band's Hammersmith Odeon concert from the previous year. All that publicity must have worked, as *A Day At The Races* became the band's second number one album in the UK.

At the beginning of 1977 Queen were en route to Boston for ten days of rehearsals for an even more extensive tour of North America, covering forty-one concerts. Their first night was at the Milwaukee Auditorium on 13 January, the coldest night in Milwaukee for a hundred years. They were supported on the first few gigs by Cheap Trick and Head East, but after a while British rock band Thin Lizzy took over. The band had added four new songs to the set list for this tour, all taken from *A Day At The Races*, and they included 'Bohemian Rhapsody' in its entirety for the first time. During the multi-tracked operatic section the band left the stage and the light show, dry ice and pyrotechnics took over.

The weather in North America was temperamental, to say the least, and during the drive from a gig in Montreal to another in Chicago one of the equipment trucks was blown off the road by gale-force winds, and another PA had to be flown in.

Queen achieved another ambition on 5 February: they played to a capacity crowd at New York's Madison Square Garden. The band were joining the 'big leagues' now, and with one other major US venue about to be conquered, they were on an all-time high.

'Tie Your Mother Down', written by Brian, was released in the UK on 4 March, and Queen flew Bruce Gowers out to Miami to film a promotional video for it. It was worth the expense, as they knew that the single was being released while they were still in the States and they didn't want to lose television publicity by not being at home. Of the single, the *NME* wrote: 'Back to their roots with some tasty hard rock.'

In early March the tour took the band to Los Angeles, and the home of Groucho Marx. When he found out they were in town, Groucho invited the band to his house for afternoon tea. The band presented him with a tour jacket and a specially engraved gold disc,

THE JOHN REID EPOCH

in recognition of his inspiration and genius. He asked them to sing for him, and they obliged with an *a capella* rendition of Brian's song '39' from *A Night At The Opera*. Groucho repaid the compliment by singing one or two songs of his own . . .

That night the band were at another big US venue they had dreamed of playing, the Los Angeles Forum. Again, it was a capacity crowd, and yet again they performed with their usual *savoir faire* and were received euphorically.

Midway through the US tour, however, Freddie began to have voice problems again, and shows in Sacramento and Fresno had to be cancelled so he could rest his throat. He took advantage of the free time and went sightseeing in Hollywood. Brian went to San Francisco while Roger and John rested and recouped some energy.

The music scene in the UK was changing rapidly. The Sex Pistols had turned 'pop music' on its head. The kids were all emulating the newcomers' image, with chains, ripped denim jackets, spiky hair and Doc Marten boots. And 'punk' was in full swing. A string of punk bands were now releasing their own raucous brand of music to great acclaim and chart success, and the music papers were claiming 'rock is dead' and that the huge rock bands of the last decade – Queen, The Who, Led Zeppelin and Genesis – were has-beens and would fade to oblivion. Strong words, which did nothing to help sales of the Queen single, which only reached number thirty-one in the UK chart.

The band flew back into the UK on 20 March to discussions with Elektra about releasing a different album track for the Japanese market. One track on the album, 'Teo Torriatte', had been written by Brian for the Japanese people, and it therefore featured a chorus in that language. It was decided that it would be a perfect single and was released in Japan on 25 March.

During a quiet period in early April, Roger decided he wanted to record a solo single. He had written several songs that he didn't think were suitable for Queen and wanted to use them. He had the limited facilities of his home recording studio and set to work, fitting in the recording with whatever Queen had planned.

Queen again left the UK on 7 May for the start of their European tour in Stockholm, Sweden. The tour kicked off at the Ice Stadium, and Freddie pranced on stage wearing an exact replica of a costume once worn by the great dancer Nijinsky. As the introduction the band used the album intro for 'Tie Your Mother Down'. Brian explains: 'The intro featured multi-tracked guitars climbing a "never ending staircase" *a la* Mr Escher. "Tie Your Mother Down" became the stage opener at that point. It was actually written with this in mind.' They had also added the scathing 'Death On Two Legs' to the show. For the encore Freddie revealed the latest in outrageous stage wear – a dazzling silver lurex leotard – and the audience went wild as soon as he stepped into the lights.

The Continental leg of the tour was a complete sell-out – tickets for the gig at the Ahoy Hall in Rotterdam had all gone within one hour of going on sale, which had never happened before. At a huge party after the show, held on board a boat, the band were presented with no less than thirty-eight silver, gold and platinum discs for monumental record sales in the Netherlands.

On 20 May, when Queen arrived back in the UK to start the British section of the tour, EMI released the first Queen EP (extended play) single. It wasn't a new idea, many artists in the fifties and sixties had released EPs, although Queen insisted that the four-track single was sold at the same price as the normal two-track. The tracks featured were 'Good Old-Fashioned Lover Boy', 'Death On Two Legs', 'Tenement Funster' and 'White Queen'. Although the fans loved the idea, and the EP climbed to number seventeen in the chart, the music press were less impressed. *NME* had this to say: 'This is called "Queen's First EP", no prizes for an original title for what is probably their first EP. And no stars for releasing four tracks that all their

THE JOHN REID EPOCH

loyal fans will already possess on their long players. A royal shame that', while *Sounds* were even more blunt: 'Enough to make one paint "Art Rock Sucks" on a tee shirt. Destroy!'

The band launched into the UK tour on 23 May, starting at the Bristol Hippodrome. Queen wanted to do something special for their London shows, so they designed and built a 'Crown' lighting rig. The Crown rose from the stage and a sea of dry ice and smoke at the start of the show, ascending to its full height of 40 feet, then descended again at the end. It was 26 feet tall, 54 feet wide, weighed in at 5,000 pounds, cost the band £50,000 to construct and was unveiled at Earls Court in London on 6 June, to an amazed audience. In those days anything that 'moved' in lighting rigs was something new. They did two shows at Earls Court, on 6 and 7 June. On both nights entertainers kept the audience amused in the foyer as they filed in, and pipers played in the auditorium before the show started. Another innovation were the two huge screens flanking the stage, so that those at the back of the hall could still see what was happening on stage. 'Procession' opened the show at the 18,000-capacity auditorium. It was an enormous, lavish production, which included 5,000 red, white and blue balloons being let loose, and the band donated all proceeds from the second night to the Queen Elizabeth II Jubilee Fund. The after-show party on the 7 June was held in a marquee erected in the floodlit Holland Park Gardens.

On 7 June, Elektra Records released 'Long Away' as the band's next US single. It was the first single to feature Brian on lead vocals throughout. Then, on 15 June, Queen went into the BBC television studios to record a special version of 'Good Old-Fashioned Lover Boy', from their EP, for *Top Of The Pops*, broadcast for the first time the following day.

During the next few months the band were ensconced in London's Basing Street Studios working intensively on their next album. While in the States, Roger, a keen science fiction fan, had seen a copy of

QUEEN – AS IT BEGAN

> **A new single from QUEEN on Elektra.**
>
> Due to requests from radio stations across America, we're releasing
>
> # LONG AWAY
> E-45412
>
> Produced by QUEEN
>
> Management: John Reid Enterprises

the magazine *Astounding Science*. On the cover was an illustration of a robot wreaking havoc among the human population, drawn by science fiction artist Frank Kelly Freas. Roger was convinced that the robot, with a little adaptation, would make an excellent cover for the next album. It took some time, but they succeeded in tracking down the elusive Mr Freas. He loved the idea of his robot being used as an album cover, and willingly agreed to alter the picture, so that the people held in the robot's giant hand resembled the members of the band. He also created a new scene for the inside of the album sleeve.

Among all the touring and recording work with Queen, Roger had found time to finish his solo single, which was released on 26 August. 'I Wanna Testify' was an old song, first performed *a capella* by the American band The Parliaments. He had reworked it, made some major changes, and played all the instruments on the song himself. He also paid for everything, from recording costs to getting it released on vinyl – over £5,000, for a single that didn't chart, although he did perform it on Marc Bolan's television show.

The Queen recording sessions jumped from Basing Street to Wessex Sound Studios, where Brian met Lonnie Donegan, whose music had inspired him in his teens. Lonnie was working on a new album, *Putting On The Style*, and invited Brian to work with him on two tracks, 'Diggin' My Potatoes' and 'Rolling Stone', along with Elton John, Ray Cooper and Rory Gallagher.

The release of the band's next single was imminent, and as Bruce Gowers wasn't available to make the promo video for it, they used Derek Burbridge. The single was the anthem 'We Are The Champions', and Queen felt that the song demanded a film that featured a crowd or audience, to give it a 'live' feel. It was far too complicated and expensive to recruit paid 'extras' to play the audience, so the fan club was asked to find a few hundred fans to help out – not a difficult task. The New London Theatre was taken over for the day, and the band were set up to film the video live, although most videos were filmed using taped 'playbacks' – as such, the song was pre-recorded and the band mimed to the track while being filmed. However, the members of Queen felt it would be much more realistic and atmospheric if it was filmed live. So, Bob Harris, who was still working on the documentary he had planned, brought along an extra film crew to record and film it separately, and acted as compere. The shoot was over quite quickly and after they had enough footage, the band decided that they wanted to say thanks to the fan club members for helping, and launched into an impromptu gig, much to everyone's delight.

'We Are The Champions', written by Freddie, was released on 7 October, backed by an equally rousing Brian song called 'We Will Rock You'. The two songs matched each other so well that Elektra in the USA requested permission to release the single in North America as a double-A side; they felt that both tracks would get equal amounts of airplay. A couple of weeks later the single came out in the States, in a picture sleeve for the first time.

In the UK and the USA the single began to climb the charts steadily. Queen hadn't made much impression on the US singles chart thus far, even though their tours were sell-outs and the albums were also selling well. Only 'Bohemian Rhapsody' had breached it at number nine – until this single. However, the British press, as was quite usual, took a profound dislike to 'We Are The Champions' and the reviews were vicious. *Sounds* wrote: 'Too much Queening around seems to have sent these guys permanently soft, they have lost their edge', while *Disc*'s review was to the point: 'Grisly monomania from Mercury's crew.' However, *NME*, with a certain amount of prescience, added: 'Sounds like it's intended to be adopted by football fans all over the country, making it an instant hit on the terraces. Not a bad idea for a load of balls.'

The single finally came to rest at number two in the UK chart, and an impressive number two in the US *Billboard* chart where it was released as a double-A side, but Queen scored their first US number one when it reached the top in the *Record World* chart. *Record World* was, at that time, the most influential trade magazine in the States. Eventually 'Champions'/'Rock You' became Elektra's biggest selling single to date, with sales of over 2 million, and it remained in the US singles' chart for over twenty-seven weeks. The *NME*'s prediction also proved to be spot on, with 'We Will Rock You' being taken up as an American football supporters chant, and 'We Are The Champions' being adopted by the New York Yankees as their anthem and by the Philadelphia 76ers as a warm-up song to raise team spirits before a match.

The Britannia Awards are presented by the British phonographic industry to artists who are voted for by BPI record company members, and on 17 October 1977, Queen received an award for the best British single for the past twenty-five years, for 'Bohemian Rhapsody'. It was a high accolade, and all the band members turned out to the event, where broadcaster Michael Aspel presented them with the award.

Two days later the band played host to the media, to celebrate not only winning the award but also to publicise the release of their forthcoming album *News Of The World*. The album came out on 28 October and the front cover featured the Frank Kelly Freas robot plucking the band from a destroyed auditorium. The album had taken only two and a half months to record; one track, 'Sleeping On The Sidewalk', was recorded in only one 'take' – the band were playing it spontaneously and didn't know the tapes were rolling. Music press reviews were, as ever, mixed. 'This is Queen stripped down to almost basics', said *Record Mirror*. 'The track "Sheer Heart Attack" is a Queen attempt at new wave, a classy version of the Sex Pistols with some very heavy lyrics. It's not a bad album by any means, but it could have been better.' *Sounds*' reviewer was torn: 'Aw, Queen, why did you do this to us? Why doesn't this album say "No Synthesizers"? Side one is foreboding, side two much better after a disillusioning beginning with "Get Down Make Love"... but how nice of Queen to finish so exquisitely with "My Melancholy Blues". Sweet fantasy.' The *Daily Mirror* were generous, but cautious: 'In many ways this is the most intriguing Queen album since their finest, *Sheer Heart Attack*. Whether all the obvious tension within the band will spur them on to greater things, or simply pull them apart, remains to be seen.'

Just before the album's release, the band and their advisers had decided to sever all remaining ties with Trident. Queen had enjoyed so much success that they were able to afford to buy from Trident the ongoing 1 per cent royalty that they had agreed to pay in severance of the original contract.

The BBC approached Queen again and asked them to record another session for radio use. They went into the BBC studios with producer Jeff Griffin. The songs they chose were two versions of 'We Will Rock You' (a slow one and a fast one), 'Spread Your Wings', 'My Melancholy Blues' and 'It's Late'.

However, by now John Reid's management had become a problem for the band. In the beginning Elton John had taken an altruistic view of John's management of another band, but as Queen grew more and more successful, and therefore more demanding of his time, it became evident that it was almost impossible to manage both and give them the kind of attention each deserved. It was this fact which finally united Queen in their decision to break away from John Reid Enterprises. Lawyer Jim Beach was asked to negotiate their release from the contractual agreements.

It didn't take long and wasn't as acrimonious as the split from Trident. The band were in Surrey filming videos for 'Spread Your Wings', the next single, and 'We Will Rock You' in Roger's back garden, working outdoors in the snow. John drove down and he and the band all clambered into the back of Freddie's Rolls-Royce to sign the required severance agreements. Queen had to pay a considerable amount of money to John Reid Enterprises for the privilege of freeing themselves from his management contracts before their expiry date, plus they had to sign over to him 15 per cent of the royalties generated by future sales of those albums already released ad infinitum, all of which contributed to the band's decision to manage themselves. They would be helped by Pete Brown, who decided to remain with them as their personal manager, and Paul Prenter, who had been a close friend of John's and had needed a job, which John had found him with Queen and Jim Beach in the business and contractual areas. Gerry Stickells continued to head the touring organisation.

CHAPTER 10

FINANCIAL INDEPENDENCE

IN NOVEMBER 1977, QUEEN FLEW OFF TO THE USA YET AGAIN FOR another tour – two US tours in one year was unheard of. *News Of The World* had just been released and was well on its way to giving them their first-ever American platinum album.

Rehearsals began at the Metro Coliseum in New Haven (home of Yale University) on 7 November, and the band all flew in separately, as they'd been involved in various personal activities beforehand. This time around the tour budget was extended to include a private plane. Not only did it minimise travelling time, but it also made it possible to 'commute' to the concerts from a few different bases within the USA, where the band felt at home.

The 'Crown' lighting rig that had been debuted at London's Earls Court was far too big to transport to the States, so Gerry Stickells had arranged for a Boston sail-making company to work with the US lighting crew to re-create it in a smaller and more portable form. The band were keen that the American fans should see it in as much of its glory as the British fans had.

The tour started in Portland, Oregon, on 11 November, the show

FINANCIAL INDEPENDENCE

opening with Freddie and Brian on steps at opposite sides of the stage belting out 'We Will Rock You'. At the end of the song the auditorium resounded to deafening thunderclaps, the curtains opened and Roger and John were revealed as the band powered into a heavy, frenetic repeat. The crowds were wild after such an incredible opener – and the band went on to add seven new tracks to their set. Roger took lead vocals on stage for the first time during the self-penned 'I'm In Love With My Car'. That night Freddie, for the first time on tour, sang the beautiful ballad 'Love Of My Life'. The entire audience began to sing it too, and Freddie stopped and let them carry on. They were word perfect. Audience participation on that song became an integral part of the Queen show from then on – and not one crowd let them down by not knowing it, whatever their native language.

As the travelling between cities was so much quicker, the band found they had more time to see the places they were playing in, rather than just the venue and the inside of a hotel room. They took advantage of it as much as possible, including touring the CNE tower in Toronto, Canada, and any other famous and fascinating sights they could find.

In Norfolk, Virginia, Frank Kelly Freas was holding an exhibition of his work at the Chrysler Museum of Art, to which the band were invited. The original robot drawing from which the *News Of The World* cover had been taken was on display, and the artist presented the band with limited editions of his book featuring it.

Next stop was Cleveland, Ohio, where they made a short detour to the control tower at the airport – particularly interesting for John because of his background in electronics.

December in New York was a cold, damp time, but the warmth of the audiences and the band's reception ensured they weren't too uncomfortable. Liza Minnelli was in the Big Apple at the same time as Queen, performing in her own stage show, 'The Act', which Freddie, an extremely keen Liza fan, had to attend.

For the band's first night at the Madison Square Garden, Freddie came on for the encore dressed in a jacket and hat borrowed from the New York Yankees baseball team, who had just won the World Series, and the audience went wild. Brian's and Roger's parents, who had never seen Queen abroad, were invited to the Madison Square Garden concert, as it was so prestigious. Brian's father said, tongue in cheek, that he would only go to the States if he could fly by Concorde. Brian took him at his word, and both his and Roger's parents were booked on the supersonic plane for the trip.

New York's shops held too much temptation for Freddie, but this time he settled for just one item – a 9-foot lacquered Japanese piano. The band couldn't take it with them on the rest of the tour, so arrangements were made to ship it to England.

On 4 December the band were due to play at the University of Dayton arena, in Ohio. The weather was atrocious, and the powers that be at the venue declared that the concert had to be cancelled. The band protested, and despite the weather and the fact that the hall was unheated due to power shortages, decided to go ahead. They chartered a private plane into Ohio, as scheduled services had all been cancelled, then took a minibus to the gig. The promoters did everything they could to show their gratitude, including laying on a huge (cold!) buffet. Queen played to an appreciative crowd of 2,000 people (the audience capacity was 2,800). The better part of them had braved the weather too, and the concert was a great success.

Many other British bands were touring the States at the same time as Queen, and while they were in Houston, Rod Stewart was playing in Los Angeles. Roger hopped on a plane to Rod's gig, flying back next day in time to see the spectacular musical revue 'Hallelujah Hollywood' at the MGM hotel.

After a particularly loud and late party in San Diego and slightly too much alcohol, John put his right hand straight through a plate-glass window. He was rushed to hospital where he had nineteen

FINANCIAL INDEPENDENCE

stitches, causing panic among the tour entourage over whether he would be able to continue playing. They needn't have worried – his arm was sore, but still quite usable.

It was nearly Christmas and the California weather was customarily mild, so mild that a huge party was held in Hollywood, featuring conjurors, belly dancers and other strange entertainments.

The last gig of three at the Los Angeles Forum on 22 December featured an unusual encore. The stage was suddenly invaded by dancing girls complete with scanty costumes and ostrich feathers, a capering elf – brilliantly portrayed by John Reid, who had remained friends with the band and was at the gig as a guest – walking Christmas trees, a gingerbread man played by the director of EMI Records, clowns and reindeer. A huge Father Christmas (a well-disguised 6-foot-plus bodyguard) walked on stage carrying a bulging sack, out of which leapt Freddie. All incredibly camp and very Queen. During that encore 5,000 balloons were released along with mock snow and glitter all over the audience and Brian and Freddie performed a special version of 'White Christmas'. A Christmas treat for the fans and obviously, after a show like that, the band had a party planned – a glittering festive special.

Queen flew back into Britain on Christmas Eve to spend the holiday with family and friends and wind down after the successful but exhausting tour. 'We Are The Champions'/'We Will Rock You' had made the number one slot in many countries worldwide but scored a breakthrough for Queen in France. The country had previously been a weak territory for the band, up to *News Of The World*, but 'We Will Rock You' picked up extensive radio play and was used as the A-side there. It stayed at number one for twelve weeks, after which, because no record was allowed to be number one for any longer, the French media published their chart with 'We Are The Champions' as number one instead! After this, Queen were huge in France for a couple of years, a dramatic change which was borne out by concert attendances.

FINANCIAL INDEPENDENCE

Two one-hour radio specials were broadcast on Christmas Eve and Boxing Day on BBC Radio One, hosted by Tom Browne. They featured interviews with all of Queen, giving an insight into the band and their music. It was a splendid end to a successful year – Queen were now so established they knew they could put bums on seats worldwide, sell singles prolifically and be received as heroes everywhere they went. They had all worked hard for this, and now they had made it they were prepared to work even harder to hang on to it.

January 1978 began quietly. Roger flew to France for a short break and to look at venues for possible concerts there. It was also an opportunity to visit Dominique's parents, who lived just outside Paris. The annual music business festival, MIDEM, was also taking place in the South of France, and Radio Europe One, the second largest European radio station, presented Queen with an award for the rock band with the most potential, collected on their behalf by Pete Brown.

Since the split with John Reid the band had discussed the pros and cons of managing themselves, which they all thought preferable to signing another managerial contract. They had been represented for accounting and tax purposes by Keith Moore, from Moore Sloane and Company, but felt that they weren't getting the advice they needed from that quarter, so John Deacon brought in Thornton Baker, a firm of accountants who specialised in tax advice, represented by Peter Chant.

With the advice and help of Peter and Jim Beach the band proceeded to set up their own management structure. Peter came in as business, tax and accounts adviser and Jim left Harbottle and Lewis, where he was a partner, to take over the business management of Queen Productions Ltd. They also set up Queen Music Ltd and Queen Films Ltd. The idea behind Queen Films was that the band would finance their own videos and any movies, and then license them to EMI for promotional use only, in return for a contribution towards the costs of making them. It was an unusual set-up, as most record companies owned the audio and visual rights to their artists, but by doing it this way Queen were free to do whatever they wished with their own videos. It was on Peter's advice that the band planned to take their first 'year out'. The reasons for this were entirely tax related, as UK tax regulations state that tax is not payable if a person spends at least 300 in any 365 days out of the UK.

John and Veronica became the proud parents of their second son, Michael, on 3 February 1978, and on the 10th, before the band could leave the UK for that 'year out', Queen released their tenth UK single, a track by John called 'Spread Your Wings'. *Record Mirror* were predictably caustic: 'As both sides of this single have been available for some time on album, I can only assume that this is primarily aimed at new Queen fans. But I didn't think there were any.'

The band also went into Shepperton Studios for intensive rehearsals to ensure that they were keeping the show up to date and playing material from the new album as well as the others.

On 9 April 1978 they flew out of the UK to Stockholm to begin another European tour, opening at the ice stadium on 12 April. To advertise Queen's imminent arrival, EMI in Brussels hired a public-relations company, Lion Promotions, to drive trucks around the city, on the backs of which they had stuck giant robots. They played tracks from the album through loudspeakers as they went, which was hard to ignore. Unfortunately, they had to fly out and begin the tour minus John Harris, who had gone everywhere with them since Smile days. Sadly, John had developed an illness and was unable to accompany them: it was the first time they had been anywhere without him and he was much missed.

This time round, the band had managed to take with them a special 60-foot version of the 'Crown' lighting rig to impress the crowds, although at some venues the ceilings weren't high enough to use it, and they had to make do with the base.

FINANCIAL INDEPENDENCE

The venue in Brussels was the Forest Nationale, a huge hall used by most bands who played Belgium. Queen were the first band ever to play three consecutive sold-out nights there, such an achievement that the promoters took space in the local music press for a congratulatory advertisement.

Their first gig in Paris was at the Pavilion de Paris on 23 April and, as there had been trouble there in the past with other bands, the police had put a limit on the number of people allowed in, resulting in a lot of disappointed fans stamping and shouting outside. Fortunately the first night was trouble-free, and the police relaxed their limitations for the next concert.

West Berlin was the home of a famous, or infamous, drag club and after their gig at the Deutschlandhalle, the band were treated to a night out. Advance notice of their visit had reached the club, and the resident drag artists featured a rather rude parody of 'Bohemian Rhapsody' in their act, which was greeted with a raucous ovation. While in West Berlin, Roger and Brian crossed Checkpoint Charlie in the Berlin Wall into East Berlin, an experience that moved them deeply.

On 25 April, Elektra Records released an edited form of the track 'It's Late' as a single in the USA. Not very successful, its highest *Billboard* chart position was just seventy-four.

On 4 May it was back to England for a run of five gigs, starting at the Bingley Hall in Stafford for two shows on 6 and 7 May. For the first time anywhere, Freddie came on stage not wearing the accustomed leotard, but instead a shiny black PVC jacket and matching trousers, while for the encore he flounced on, clad in a bright red sequin-encrusted hot-pant jumpsuit, with a low plunge neckline, which left little to the imagination.

Daily Mail readers had voted Queen as the best group in a reader's poll, and the band were invited to a ceremony on 10 May to collect the award at a plush Knightsbridge restaurant — but it got out of hand and by the end of the evening every glass in the place had been smashed.

On the final night of the tour, 13 May, at the Empire Pool, Queen played a breathtaking version of 'White Queen', which delighted the audience. It was a perfect song to showcase the band's individual talents and went a long way towards proving to everyone that those talents, however good they had been originally, had been honed to perfection after so many arduous and demanding tours. That night, the *Daily Mirror* presented Queen with an award for the best British rock group at a party after the show, at which the glasses, or most of them, remained intact.

Roger and John both flew out of the UK shortly after the end of the tour to start work on the next album at Mountain Studios in Montreux while Freddie stayed on in the UK to co-produce with Roy Thomas Baker an album for a close friend, actor Peter Straker. Peter had proved he had a fine voice when he'd appeared in the stage musical *Hair*, but this was his first venture into vinyl in his own right. Freddie had such faith in his ability that he invested £20,000 of his own money in the album, *This One's On Me*, which was released later in the year. Brian also stayed in the UK for the birth of his first child; on 15 June 1978, Chrissie gave birth to James, known as Jimmy. Within days of the baby's birth Brian flew to Canada to visit friends and continue his 'year out'. He celebrated his own birthday on 19 July in Toronto. Eventually Brian and Freddie both joined John and Roger in Switzerland to work intensively on the new album.

Roger held a birthday party in Montreux, an extravagant affair in the local hotel, to which all the 'beautiful people' were invited. Freddie was in high spirits and at one point was found by some bemused guests swinging from a huge chandelier. 'I have *always* wanted to swing from a chandelier,' he said. 'And when I saw this exquisite cut-crystal thing dangling there I just could not resist it!'

At one point during the recording in Montreux a violent

FINANCIAL INDEPENDENCE

thunderstorm cut all power in the town; Brian dashed outside at the height of the storm with his portable tape recorder and taped the thunderclaps, using them on the album at the end of 'Dead On Time'.

The album recording switched from Mountain Studios to SuperBear in Nice, in the South of France. The band had been advised by their accountant not to record the entire album in one country, as that country might have reason to assess them for tax. While in Nice, they celebrated Freddie's birthday party, in St Paul de Vence and, as usual, it was outrageous. Everyone stripped naked and cavorted in the swimming pool, much to Freddie's amusement, as he was the only one who stayed dry. He had invited over a lot of close friends from England for the party, including Peter Straker, and during the evening the pair treated the guests to their own renditions of Gilbert and Sullivan arias.

While the band were working at SuperBear, a bicycle tournament passed through the city, and all those hunky chaps on bikes inspired Freddie to write a new song, 'Bicycle Race'. It was decided that the track would be the next single release, a double-A side with Brian's 'Fat Bottomed Girls'. The band's publicity company hit on the idea of hiring Wimbledon Stadium in London and getting sixty-five naked girls to hold their own bicycle race, and using the photos and film footage as promotion for the song. The band jumped at the suggestion and it was put into practice. On 17 September the sixty-five naked girls, all recruited through various model agencies, had assembled at Wimbledon Stadium and were lined up for their race – luckily it was a warm and sunny day. The film crew and photographers were ready (there were more than a few unpaid camera assistants that day) and the race was on. Unfortunately for Queen there was one unforeseen expense: Halfords Cycles, who had provided all the bicycles, refused to take back the used saddles and had to be paid for replacements.

October 13 saw the release of the single 'Fat Bottomed Girls'/'Bicycle

Race'. Its cover featured the rear view of the winning naked cyclist and caused such outrage that later copies had to have black panties drawn onto them. The band couldn't understand the outcry; it was, after all, simply a naked bottom and much worse than that could be freely seen on the top shelf of any newsagents. Some of the single reviews were kinder than in the past, but most were just as condemning. From *NME*: 'Queen loathe the music press. They deserve all the vitriol that may be further hurled at them if this is an accurate preview of the new album.' *Sounds*, however, was more generous: 'FBG opens up like something out of a Harlem Episcopal church meeting and breezes into the heavy, honey dripping hard rock at which the band are so surprisingly successful.'

Quite unsurprisingly, to their fans, the single came to rest at a solid number eleven in the UK charts.

In mid-October the band flew directly from France to the States to start another US tour. They were all shocked when John turned up with an almost shaven head. He had never been one to care much about his appearance – he dressed comfortably rather than fashionably – so such a drastic step as this, as though to conform to current punk trends, amazed everyone. To him, of course, the haircut was practical and he denied accusations that he was 'going punk'. The haircut did earn him a new nickname among the band and roadies, though: 'Birdman' – as applied to the one who'd been incarcerated in Alcatraz.

Before kicking off in Dallas they filmed promo videos with American director Dennis De Vallance for both 'Fat Bottomed Girls' and 'Bicycle Race', which was to be a double A-side single in the States. The tour opened on 28 October at the Dallas Convention Centre, with another impressive new lighting rig and, as the band had got into the habit of naming them, this one became 'The Pizza Oven'. Why? 'If you'd stood under it, you'd know why,' said Brian. It was bigger than anything Queen had previously used, and it took the crew eight hours to set up, and another eight to take down. It used 600 individual lights in seven separate banks and was operated by hydraulics. At the start of the show the 5-ton rig was held at a 45° angle over the stage and as the opening music was played the rig was slowly lifted. During the show it moved constantly, all seven banks of lights shifting position separately. At the end the whole lot were facing the audience, and the colours were changed to bright white spotlights which shone directly at them. Another innovation introduced was a small platform on which was a scaled-down drum kit. It was lowered from the roof (where the size of the hall permitted it) and the band stood on it to perform their acoustic medley. Roger had extended his drum kit again, with a pair of enormous timpani, on which he delivered an energetic solo each night.

For the encore of the Memphis gig, as a tribute to Elvis Presley, they played 'Jailhouse Rock', a song they had often featured live in the past.

After the New Orleans show on 31 October, and as a pre-launch party for the new album, *Jazz*, the band had planned a huge, expensive and outrageous party at the New Dreams Fairmount Hotel, organised and paid for by them rather than the label, as they wanted to invite both of their record companies, EMI from the UK and Elektra from the USA. It was the first time the companies had ever met in relation to their joint interest in Queen – and each one ensured the maximum turnout of its executives so as not to be outdone by the other. The band invited over 400 guests, including press from England, South America and Japan, not to mention local and national US press. The party was to start at midnight, and on the stroke of the witching hour the Olympia brass band marched into the hall at the head of a procession containing Queen and other bizarre revellers. Guests were entertained by naked female mud wrestlers, dwarfs, fire-eaters, jazz bands, steel bands, Zulu dancers, voodoo dancers, strippers, drag artists and unicyclists to name but a few. Members of the British press, accompanied by Tony Brainsby, had flown into New Orleans in time to see the show, then went on to the party, stayed up all night and got a mid-morning plane back to the UK.

The party ended up going down in rock history as the most over-the-top one the band had ever hosted. It made headlines from coast to coast and across the world. The next day the band held a more sedate press conference, at the elegant Brennan's restaurant in the French quarter of the city.

Again, this US tour was undertaken in the most relaxed and time-efficient manner, by private jet. The band were even able to stop off at Disney World, Florida, for a whole day of childish fun.

Back in the UK on 10 November, EMI released *Jazz*, Queen's seventh album. Roger had seen both the title and the cover design, a whirl of concentric circles, painted on the Berlin Wall. As soon as he saw it, he knew it was right for the album, and none of the others disagreed. A free poster featuring a bevy of beauties from that famous nude bicycle race was included with every copy. In the States the poster caused a public outcry: it was seen as pornography and banned. Instead they replaced it with an application form so that anyone wanting the poster could send away for it. Again the band were nonplussed at this cry of immorality: as far as they and their record company were concerned, the race, the photos and film clips were all in the best of taste and merely harmless fun; the girls had taken part voluntarily and enjoyed themselves. No harm had been done, and the majority of those who bought the album weren't in the least offended.

One of the credits on the album read 'Thunderbolt courtesy of God', which related to the clap of thunder that Brian had recorded during the violent storm in Montreux and used at the end of 'Dead On Time' – it sounded remarkably impressive. But the critics were, again, blunt. From *NME*: 'Cue the third rate Gilbert and Sullivan, if you have a deaf relative buy them this for Christmas.' Even *Sounds*

FINANCIAL INDEPENDENCE

couldn't bring themselves to be positive this time: 'I would dearly love to like Queen as much as I did in the early seventies, but the task is becoming increasingly impossible.'

But, as always, the album was well received by the public, selling in high enough quantities to hit number two and remaining in the chart for twenty-seven weeks.

The fan club, now run by Amanda Bloom, was keen to keep the band in the forefront of fans' minds while they spent so much time abroad and hit on the idea of an entire day dedicated to Queen. They acquired the services of DJ Alan Freeman, a fan himself, and took over the Empire Ballroom in Leicester Square. The band sent a telegram wishing everyone well, and provided promotional videos. It was a great day and one that the fan club vowed to repeat.

Meanwhile, back in New York, the stage of Madison Square Garden was taken over during 'Bicycle Race' by naked young ladies riding around on bikes ringing their bells. Backstage after the show the band were presented with 'golden tickets' by the management of the Garden to commemorate ticket sales more than 100,000 at the venue – a rare achievement.

The tour drew to a close with a final night in Los Angeles at the Inglewood Forum, and the band flew back to England in time to celebrate Christmas.

Never content to rest for long, 12 January 1979 found Queen bound for Hamburg and the start of another European tour, their biggest yet with twenty-eight gigs, beginning on 17 January at the Ernst-Merck-Halle. This tour included two concerts in Yugoslavia for the first time, in Zagreb and Ljubljana, both sold out in advance. The Yugoslavs weren't used to big rock bands appearing in their country and were astonished by it all.

On 26 January 1979, EMI released the band's twelfth single in the UK, a track from *Jazz* called 'Don't Stop Me Now'. They recorded a video with Jogen Kliebenst while they were in Brussels. And – shock horror! – the music press liked it. 'Despite everything, Freddie has one of the best voices in rock, and Queen know how to change chords intelligently. Do they own EMI yet?', said *Record Mirror*. The *Daily Mirror* were even more effusive: 'Queen let rip with an exciting song which will surely be a cracking hit.'

It was a hit, breaching the British Top 10 and settling at number nine.

During the three concerts at the Pavilion de Paris Freddie noticed that every night the front row of seats contained the same group of English fans, all carrying bicycle bells to ring at the appropriate time. He got so used to them being there that he even gave them a name – the Royal Family (co-founded by co-author of this book, Jim Jenkins) – and greeted them every night, usually with jocular remarks like, 'Oh, fucking hell, are you lot here again?'

The final night was out of control and the local *gendarmes* were called in to restore order, but not before an unfortunate incident led to members of the road crew being sprayed with tear gas – no serious injuries though, and they were all fit enough to attend the end of tour party that night. At the party the band were presented with silver statuettes of naked girls on bicycles to commemorate such a successful tour. Each show had been professionally recorded as Queen had been asked by their record company to release a live album. Public demand had been huge so although the band still weren't keen, if it was what the fans wanted and if it would stem the illegal trade in bootlegged tapes, they would do it.

They flew from Paris to Montreux with the tour tapes to begin work on editing them for the album. They wanted to achieve something as close as possible to a live show but with the music 'touched up' a little to improve sound quality. Working with producer John Etchells, it took them a long time to choose which tracks to use from which shows, but after that it was reasonably simple to put it all together.

FINANCIAL INDEPENDENCE

The band loved working at Mountain Studios, on the shores of Lake Geneva, and Montreux itself was a small, peaceful town. They liked being there so much, that they decided they should buy the studios, and their tax advisers agreed with them.

The studios were owned by a group of Dutch shareholders, who were not in the music business and who weren't very happy about the way the studio had been run. Alex Grob, who had built the studios with Dutch backing, spent more of his time in Los Angeles with his American wife than he did running Mountain, so when Jim Beach approached him about selling, he was happy to negotiate – as were the shareholders. The deal eventually went through in 1979 and when Queen were asked by resident engineer David Richards what they intended to do with Mountain, Freddie answered, 'Throw it in the lake, dear, what do you think?'

Just before they were due to leave Switzerland for a tour in Japan, the group were asked to consider writing the theme music for a futuristic feature film, produced by Dino De Laurentiis and based on the classic comic book hero Flash Gordon. They had all been keen to write a film score, so Jim arranged a meeting with the producer. When he mentioned Queen and their interest, De Laurentiis' first reaction was simply, 'Who are the Queens?' They were, in fact, the first rock band he had ever listened to. The outcome was that Queen were commissioned to write the *Flash Gordon* soundtrack.

Flying into Tokyo was like a homecoming for Queen, and they were greeted again by fans at the airport with banners and photos. The gigs all sold out well in advance, and people were still queuing outside each night in hopes of getting in. Major Japanese music magazine, *Music Life*, held a ceremony for the band during their trip, and presented them with awards for top group, top single, top album and each member topped their own musical category – other bands and musicians hardly got a look-in. The tour opened on 13 April at the Budokan in Tokyo, and the show was filmed, to be broadcast across Japan at a later date. An addition to the usual set was 'Teo Torriate' from A Day At The Races, which had Japanese lyrics – and another first was Brian taking over on piano for that song.

On 27 April, Elektra Records released another single, 'Jealousy', from *Jazz*, which failed to chart. Meanwhile, EMI's territories in Germany, Yugoslavia and Spain were under public pressure to release 'Mustapha' as a single, which they did.

CHAPTER 11

CRAZY IDEAS

IT WAS WHILE THEY WERE WATCHING THE MEN'S SINGLES FINALS AT Wimbledon, that Freddie and Roger came up with an idea. In June 1979, Queen approached the All England Lawn Tennis Club for permission to use Centre Court, which is only ever in use during a few weeks of every year during the Wimbledon Championships, for a concert. The Club gave the matter 'serious consideration', but they turned it down saying they didn't think a rock concert was a fitting event for the hallowed turf of Centre Court.

Live Killers, the band's first live and first double album (to date), was released on 22 June 1979. It featured songs from sixteen European concerts and sold swiftly; Queen's live shows were by now legendary and millions of fans wanted to re-create that sound in their own homes. *Live Killers* filled the gap, although there was still a market for the bootleggers, who could command huge sums for badly recorded tapes of Queen shows. The band hoped to lessen demand with this album but couldn't stop it completely.

The album gained some critical acclaim. 'I don't find the obligatory post-77 groan rising to my lips at the mention of their name, and this package is a perfectly adequate retrospective on most of their best songs', said *Sounds*, while *Record Mirror*'s review was positively glowing: 'Bring out the champagne and roses, this is a triumph. This album enhances Queen's songs and isn't a mere fill in until the next studio project. Listen and you'll not be disappointed.' Fans agreed, and *Live Killers* reached number three in the UK chart.

Veronica gave birth to the Deacons' third baby on 25 June, a girl, Laura. John and she were overjoyed; after two boys a girl was most welcome. Quite appropriately, Queen's thirteenth single, the live version of 'Love Of My Life', taken from *Live Killers*, was released just four days later. *Melody Maker* was disparaging though: 'Once upon a time "Love Of My Life" was a gorgeous ballad on the *Night At The Opera* album. Now it sounds like an upmarket football chant.'

It wasn't a commercial success either, only reaching number sixty-three in the UK chart.

In 1979, EMI Records were one of the biggest major record companies, and in June that year their achievements were recognised when they received the Queen's Award to Industry. To celebrate the fact, they decided to re-press just 200 copies of their top-selling single, 'Bohemian Rhapsody', on blue vinyl and release it as a numbered limited edition. They presented the members of the band with the first four copies, framed, and then ensured that the staff, management and key members of EMI all got copies too, leaving few of those 200 to make it to the shops and guaranteeing that it would become a rare collector's item virtually immediately.

Queen spent the summer of 1979 working on their new album, mostly at Musicland studios in Munich. The band's usual way of working was to go into the studios with set ideas and almost finished tracks to perfect and complete, but this time they had very little: no set songs, no half-finished tracks, just some vague ideas. It meant starting from scratch with each song. They were also working with a new producer, Rheinhardt Mack (known as Mack). In addition, they slotted in work on the score of the *Flash Gordon* movie – and producing two albums simultaneously didn't prove easy.

CRAZY IDEAS

In mid-August they were headlining a huge open-air festival in Germany, for which rehearsals began in early August at Shepperton Studios, just outside London; its size and acoustics made it the band's preferred place to practise, as they could erect a stage of the size they would be working on for the show, and the crew could set up and test the lighting rig and stage equipment. They flew out to Saarbrücken on 17 August for the gig the next day at the Ludwigsparkstadion, in front of 30,000 people, a record crowd for a German festival. The other bands on the bill were Red Baron, Voyager, Molly Hatchet, Lake, Alvin Lee and Ten Years After, The Commodores and Rory Gallagher.

Earlier that day, Roger had attempted to bleach his hair; he'd been doing this for some years, since his naturally blond locks had begun to darken. This time he had drastically overdone it: 'It was just dreadful,' Roger recalls. 'It was bright, nauseating green. But it was too late to do anything about it, I just had to go on stage with it like that. It was so embarrassing and Freddie took the piss all night.'

Their set went down a storm, and when the band left the stage during the operatic section of 'Bohemian Rhapsody', which had proved impossible to re-create live and was done with backing tapes, they let off hundreds of fireworks, creating a real party atmosphere in the crowd. At the end of the show, during 'We Are The Champions', they let fly with high-powered water jets, which, as it was a hot night, was welcome relief for the packed audience.

On 24 August, Elektra in the USA released the fast version of 'We Will Rock You', taken from *Live Killers*, as a single in North America. As with the previous singles, it failed to chart.

Roger decided to take a holiday in early September, during a break from recording the new album. He had recently indulged in one of the recognised trappings of success, a new Ferrari, and decided to drive himself and Dominique down to the rich man's playground of St Tropez. Roger loved fast cars, but as they drove flat out down the autoroute through France, the engine caught fire. Luckily both he and Dominique escaped unhurt, but the car was a write-off. That wasn't the end of the bad luck, though: Roger hired a speedboat to take some friends out for a day to a nearby island. They got to within sight of their destination when the engine gave out. They radioed ashore and, after drifting for three hours off the coast, were finally rescued by the coastguard and towed back to the mainland.

Freddie had always been a fan of ballet and opera – in particular the Royal Ballet. He frequently attended performances and knew several of the dancers, and had become firm friends with Wayne Eagling, one of the principals. When the Royal Ballet organised a special performance to raise money for the City of Westminster Society for Mentally Handicapped Children, Freddie was asked if he would consider dancing a special piece, choreographed by Wayne. He had never done any ballet, although he had used some of the exercises practised by dancers to keep fit for his energetic stage performance. But as it was something he had always wanted to try he agreed to take part.

Freddie began practising a few weeks before the performance, to tone up and get more supple, and then a few days before the performance he rehearsed with Wayne, another principal dancer, Derek Dane, and the *corps de ballet*. The two songs he had chosen to dance to were 'Bohemian Rhapsody' and a new song, 'Crazy Little Thing Called Love', both to be played by the orchestra with Freddie doing live vocals as he danced.

The performance took place on 7 October at the London Coliseum, with Roger in the audience for moral support. Freddie's first dance was 'Bohemian Rhapsody', and he performed with skill in front of a packed house of enthusiastic balletomanes. They loved him, and he received a standing ovation for both his cameos.

Freddie not only stole the audience's affections that night, but he also stole the Royal Ballet's best wardrobe man and dresser, Peter

CRAZY IDEAS

Freestone. When Freddie asked 'Phoebe', as he was known to his friends, to leave the ballet and work for him, he jumped at the chance. Needless to say, the Royal Ballet loved Freddie's performance on stage, but were none too pleased with his backstage deals.

On 5 October, EMI released the band's fourteenth single, 'Crazy Little Thing Called Love', with 'We Will Rock You' on the B-side, again taken from *Live Killers*. It was released in Europe as a twelve-inch single too, the first time Queen had used such a format on the Continent. *Record Mirror*, surprisingly, liked it: 'Well done, Queen. This is totally unlike any other singles you've released. It's slick, smooth, finger snapping and Freddie's voice suits it down to the ground.'

Queen joined forces with director Dennis De Vallance for the promo video, featuring black leather, dark glasses and scantily clad male and female dancers – plus several pairs of clapping hands sticking up through holes in the floor of the catwalk on which Freddie strutted. As the hands were a last-minute addition, they hadn't arranged for any extras to be available, so members of Queen's personal staff were recruited to lie flat on their backs under the stage. To make the situation more bearable, they took with them a bottle of Jack Daniel's whiskey, which was passed around under the boards. Much giggling ensued, and it was by sheer luck that they managed to get those handclaps in the right places. The single was a big hit, reaching the number two slot in the UK charts.

The band decided that as they had been playing bigger and bigger venues, they wanted to go back to something smaller. Brian says, 'We had played the big places, and although we loved them, and felt it was good that more and more people could come and see us, we also felt we were losing touch with the audience. Our whole show was about audience contact – we felt close to them, they felt close to us. But with those big places they were so far away, so distant. So we got Gerry Stickells to find some small, silly venues for us. We didn't want just ordinary little theatres, we wanted places that were different. We played the medium-sized places first, then the daft ones, we called it the "Crazy Tour" and thoroughly enjoyed it!'

First, Queen played at the RDS Simmons Hall in Dublin. It was the first gig of their career in Ireland and they treated the audience to their own version of that old Irish classic 'Danny Boy'. They also played their next single live for the first time, a haunting, angst-filled song by Brian called 'Save Me'. Freddie also took up a guitar on stage for the first time, for 'Crazy Little Thing Called Love'. Although Freddie was a great pianist, he wasn't so good with six strings and a plectrum, but they felt that 'Crazy' just needed something a little different. For the encore, 'We Will Rock You', Freddie came back on stage on the shoulders of a huge 'Superman', alias the on-tour bodyguard Alan Robertson.

The British tour started at the biggest of the planned venues, the Birmingham National Exhibition Centre, on 24 November; Queen were able to claim the highest attendance record for an indoor concert with 14,000 people. They had taken with them on this tour a scaled-down, but still impressive, version of the 'Pizza Oven' lights.

Their stage outfits had changed over the years, not too dramatically in the cases of Roger, Freddie and Brian, but John was now often seen in a most un-rock-like collar and tie. Freddie was well into his 'leather' period, with red or black leather trousers, caps and blue or red knee-pads. That well-known exponent of black leather and chains, Judas Priest lead singer Rob Halford, said in an interview that if Freddie wanted to wear the leather gear, he would challenge him to prove his machismo by competing in a spin around the Brands Hatch racing circuit on a powerful motorbike. Freddie was perturbed, though he accepted Rob's challenge – but only if Mr Halford would take a turn with the Royal Ballet first. Strangely enough, Rob declined and no more was said about Brands Hatch.

Queen went on to play two nights at the Manchester Apollo, and two nights at the Glasgow Apollo, on the second of which Roger forgot the words to 'In Love With My Car', compelling Freddie to take over. Two nights at the Liverpool Empire followed (on the second Freddie wore one red and one blue knee-pad, to keep the Everton and Liverpool football supporters happy), then one in Bristol and two at the Brighton Centre. After that, they were due to appear at the HMV record store on London's busy Oxford Street but the Metropolitan police were so concerned about the disruption to traffic, and the chaos that huge amounts of fans might cause, that they banned the appearance, much to everyone's disappointment.

The Crazy Tour of London began on 13 December at London's Lyceum Ballroom, a venue more used to dances and discos than big rock bands. The crew had to cut two holes in the roof of the hall to 'fly' (or hang) the lights and the PA – holes which had to be paid for, but as Paul McCartney was due to play the venue some days later Queen got him to foot half the bill.

After that show the band hosted a 'silly hats' party, special guest at which was Mrs Gertrude Shilling, herself famous for wearing fabulous hats, designed by her son. Mrs Shilling presented the members of the band with gold discs celebrating sales of 'Crazy Little Thing Called Love'.

The next gig was at the Rainbow Theatre in north London, then on to Tiffany's in Purley, a nightclub and another strange place for a big rock band. On 19 December they played the Mayfair in Tottenham, which was so small they couldn't use a lighting rig and had to make do with the minimal stage lights provided by the venue.

The Lewisham Odeon followed and then they moved into Alexandra Palace, along with a film crew, as they intended to make the video for their next single, 'Save Me', there. At that concert Freddie threw bananas to the audience during 'We Will Rock You', for reasons only known to himself.

Gerry Stickells, Queen's tour manager since 1976, collapsed backstage during the Crazy Tour and was rushed into hospital, suffering from total exhaustion brought on by the endless touring he'd undertaken, with Queen and various other bands in between; he hadn't taken a proper break in years. After a few days in a hospital bed, on hospital food, he was up and about pretty swiftly and back on the road, although under doctor's orders to take things easy – advice he, of course, ignored. 'The doctors told me to take it easy for a while,' Gerry said, 'but none of them have ever been on the road with Queen. That advice is almost impossible to take. The tour might have been small in venue size, but it was a hassle. Some of the places were just so tiny that trying to cram in a band the size of Queen was nigh on impossible. But that's what they pay me for, working miracles. So we did it.'

In July, Paul McCartney had approached Queen and asked if they would be interested in playing a charity concert; all the proceeds would go towards helping the people of Kampuchea, who were still trying to recover from the horrors of a bloody war and mass genocide at the hands of the Khmer Rouge. A series of gigs was to be staged, starting on Boxing Day at the Hammersmith Odeon. The band readily agreed to be a part of it.

Queen were the only band to play on the night of the 26th, treating the audience to a full set. In the following days a variety of bands, including Wings, The Who, The Clash, Ian Dury and The Blockheads, The Specials, Rockpile, Elvis Costello, and The Pretenders played, performing for about forty minutes each. The high point of the last night was a 'supergroup' featuring an impressive line-up of famous faces. The event was filmed for later broadcast on television, and an album was released featuring songs from each of the bands who had given their time. Queen's contribution was the track 'Now I'm Here'. A considerable amount of money was raised to help the starving people of war-torn Kampuchea.

'Save Me' was released as Queen's fifteenth single on 25 January 1980 ('Tat music from a tat band' was *NME*'s eloquent comment) and

CRAZY IDEAS

climbed to number eleven in the charts, while 'Crazy Little Thing Called Love' was setting the charts alight worldwide. In the USA it gave them their first number one; it was number one in Australia for seven weeks and reached the top spot in New Zealand, Canada, Mexico and the Netherlands, an amazingly high-selling single everywhere.

The early part of 1980 was spent on the new album and the *Flash Gordon* soundtrack. The band went back to Munich to work, as musically they found it a stimulating and inspiring place, and obviously the nightlife helped.

Freddie nipped back over to the UK in February to appear on Kenny Everett's television show. He usually avoided television appearances – he loathed them – but as Kenny was a friend, he agreed, and appeared in his leather stage outfit, proceeding to leap on an unsuspecting Kenny and knock him to the floor, where the two of them rolled around in an unrehearsed mock fight.

While in England Freddie saw a beautiful house for sale. It was a stunning, eight-bedroomed Victorian mansion, set in the middle of a quarter of an acre of landscaped garden in the heart of Kensington. He fell in love with it immediately, and paid cash for it – over half a million pounds. He had always promised himself that one day he would own a mansion, but just owning it was enough. He had no inclination to live in it, as the flat just off Kensington High Street was more than comfortable. So the house remained empty.

During a break in work on the album Roger flew up to Montreux and Mountain Studios to produce two songs for singer Hilary Vance, known as Hilary Hilary; he co-wrote 'How Come You're So Dumb' while 'Rich Kid Blues' was written by Terry Reid. Roger also played on the track, arranged them and provided backing vocals. Back in the UK his girlfriend Dominique gave birth to their son, Felix Luther, on 22 May 1980. He arrived ten weeks prematurely, weighing in at only two pounds. He was kept in an incubator for some time, until he was finally declared fit enough to leave hospital.

It was around that time that Freddie decided on an image change: he cut his long, thick, black hair, much to the grief of many of his female fans. In 1980, for the making of the video for 'Play The Game', their forthcoming single, he upset them even more by growing a moustache, and gave up painting his nails. The result was that gifts of razors and bottles of black nail polish flooded the band's offices.

'Play The Game', the band's sixteenth single, was released on 30 May. Press reviews constituted the usual odious drivel, but as they'd given up believing them sometime previously, they weren't too bothered. *NME* wrote: 'Another three minutes of indulgent, over-produced trivia just like I expected.' It was their first single to feature a synthesizer, while the cover included a photo of the band with Freddie sporting the offending moustache – and it still got to number fourteen in the UK chart. Roger sang lead vocals on the B-side, 'A Human Body', although that track was not included on the forthcoming album.

CHAPTER 12

TRIUMPH OVER AMERICA

ANOTHER TOUR OF NORTH AMERICA HAD BEEN PLANNED FOR THE summer of 1980, and on 19 June the band flew to Los Angeles to begin rehearsals. The lighting company again came up with something different and, after months of planning, unveiled the new rig – the 'Fly Swatter'. It had a number of separate sections that were all independently mobile – and known to the crew as the 'G2 Razors' – another innovative move towards 'interactive' lighting rigs, which seemed almost alive. Some described them as 'like praying mantises' and they provided not only washes of bright light but spotlighting too – all very mean and moody.

Just as they began the tour, the band's ninth album, *The Game*, was released in the UK on 30 June. It went straight into the UK charts at number one, but that didn't stop *NME* slating it: 'Old and tired and bland and blinkered. It purrs with self satisfaction.' But *Sounds* loved it, beginning the column in capital letters: 'I LIKE QUEEN, I LIKE QUEEN . . . This album is a straight kick into the goal, it's like winning the men's singles at Wimbledon.'

This album also made use of synthesizers. John says, 'We wanted to experiment with all that new studio equipment. We had always been keen to try out anything new or different while recording. The synthesizers then were so good, they were very advanced compared to the early Moogs, which did little more than make a series of weird noises. The ones we were using could duplicate all sorts of sounds and instruments – you could get a whole orchestra out of them at the touch of a button. Amazing.'

The 'new' sound they had achieved upset some of the older Queen fans, who just didn't expect them ever to dabble in synthesized music, but Freddie said that Queen didn't want to get into a rut and wanted to move with the times. It drew a lot of new fans into the Queen circle, too, giving them their third UK number one album.

Queen's first gig on that tour was at the PNE Coliseum in Vancouver at which the audience bombarded Freddie with disposable razors and razor blades – an unheeded hint that he might remove the offending moustache.

During a tour break the band flew back to the UK to spend time with their families, and Roger decided to start work on a solo album. 'I'd had these ideas for years, and I just thought the time was right to start putting them into some sort of order. I'd had a go with the single, but I had an album full of songs that I knew couldn't be done by Queen. I don't really know why they were not suitable for us as a band, they just weren't.' But after fifteen days at home, they had to fly back to the USA to recommence in Memphis.

August 12 1980 was the release date of the single 'Another One Bites The Dust' on Elektra in North America. Says Brian: '"Another One Bites The Dust" was never an easy song to pull off on stage – the drums didn't have the "snap" of the record, and some audiences evidently found it "not very rock and roll". But we persevered, feeling it was an important song – Freddie especially felt this. What happened independently was that the song was picked up by a major black radio station in New York City – apparently, they thought we were a black act. The response they got was so enormous that other stations followed suit, and Elektra were forced into releasing it. It was a giant

TRIUMPH OVER AMERICA

"cross-over", our only one really, and more than doubled our album sales in only a few weeks.'

The tour continued across the USA and Canada, during which 'Another One Bites The Dust' became a colossal hit in America, hitting the number one spot and staying there for five weeks. It was one of only three Queen singles to go platinum in the USA and it topped the charts right across the board: in rock, soul and disco. Queen were given a *Billboard* award for top Crossover single and were nominated for Grammys and Canadian Juno awards. It became the band's biggest selling single to date, staying in the US charts for 31 weeks, and gave Elektra their first ever 3-million-selling single – while *The Game* became Queen's first number one album in North America. 'Another One Bites The Dust' was also a huge number one hit in Guatemala, Argentina, Mexico and Spain – and at home in the UK, where it was released on 22 August, it got to a credible number seven.

After a six-day break back in England, the tour rumbled on, culminating in a whopping four sold-out nights at Madison Square Garden, at a venue they had once only dreamed of headlining. Those concerts signalled the end of the longest tour the band had yet undertaken, a staggering forty-six gigs in all – every one of which was sold out.

They all took a well-deserved holiday for most of October, then set to work on completing the *Flash Gordon* soundtrack at Anvil Studios in London. They decided the first and only single from the soundtrack album would be 'Flash' and began work on the promo video with director Mike Hodges. They were given permission to use clips and dialogue from the actual film in the video, as the film itself was virtually ready for release.

They were off to Europe again on 20 November, to rehearse in Zurich, Switzerland, for the tour, where the first gig was scheduled, in the Hallenstadion, supported by British band Straight Eight. For the encore this time around, Freddie came on stage on the shoulders of 'Darth Vader', again played by a bodyguard, this time 'Big' Wally Verson – which led to trouble.

George Lucas's company heard about the Darth Vader sequence and, as they owned the copyright to the character, decided to press charges as Queen had not paid the appropriate fee for its use. Queen's lawyers stepped in, however, and were able to settle amicably out of court. That was all well and good, except that that quarter's fan club magazine had already been printed, featuring a short introduction to some of the Queen road crew, including Mr Verson. He had listed one of his jobs with Queen as 'part-time Darth Vader' and every copy of that issue (some 10,000) had to have that line blacked out.

'Flash', the band's eighteenth single, was released on 24 November while they were still touring in Europe, so *Top Of The Pops* had to make do with a promotional video of the new song, which reached number ten in the UK chart. In the USA, Elektra chose a different single, 'Need Your Loving Tonight', which peaked at forty-four.

On 5 December, Queen were the first band to play at the new all-seated Exhibition Centre in Birmingham. It had been purpose-built for bands and exhibitions and, so that audiences could see from wherever they sat, a revolutionary new design was used: the roof was suspended from huge supports outside the building, instead of pillars inside the structure. Queen made the opening night at that venue a fitting one and sold every seat in the house. They sold out the following night, too. An addition to the usual Queen stage set on this tour was . . . a synthesizer, essential for the band to play tracks from the *Flash Gordon* soundtrack. Freddie decided to try to shock the audience with his stage outfit for the encore: by donning the shortest, tightest pair of black leather shorts he could find – they didn't leave much to the imagination, but no one complained . . .

The band's tenth album, the soundtrack to *Flash Gordon*, was released on 8 December. It was a new concept in soundtrack albums, as they had incorporated in the music snatches of dialogue from the film, to add authenticity. It reached number ten in the UK chart. The review in *Record Mirror* was excellent. After raving about the whole album, it finished: 'This is the sort of stuff I haven't heard since Charlton Heston won the chariot race in Ben Hur. An album of truly epic proportions that warrants an equally epic five out of five.' *Sounds* wrote glowingly too, concluding: 'As a film soundtrack, Flash Gordon is something extraordinary.'

On 9 December, the second night of their three-night stint at the Wembley Arena, it was announced that John Lennon had been shot dead by a fan outside his apartment in New York. The band were devastated – Lennon had been a hero to all of them, and to be gunned down by someone purporting to be a fan brought home their own vulnerability. They played a moving version of 'Imagine' that night as a special tribute to John, reducing the audience to tears. Freddie seemed to forget the words of the song, but Brian says: 'It was my fault. I forgot the chords and got to the chorus too soon.'

On 11 December the band were back in Brussels for the last few dates of the tour, during which *Flash Gordon* premiered in London. The movie was well received by the press, and each review made special reference to the soundtrack music, commenting on its atmospheric qualities and its ability to reflect and enhance so perfectly the film's action and dialogue.

The tour finished on 19 December 1980 and Queen flew back into the UK for a quiet Christmas at home. They had been discussing with EMI the possibility of releasing a *Greatest Hits* album in time for Christmas, but as *Flash Gordon* was still new they decided it was the wrong time to do so, and the idea was temporarily shelved.

It was the time of year once more for awards and polls, and Queen were nominated for three Canadian Juno awards, for best single, 'Another One Bites The Dust', best album with *The Game* and best band. In the American *Record World* poll they won top male group, top producer, top disco crossover, top crossover single and a special achievement award. They received the best band honour in the Dick Clarke awards and were up for two Grammys for best-produced album with *The Game* and best performance by a group with 'Another One Bites The Dust'. The accolades continued in the American *Circus* magazine where they picked up top votes for best band, and best live show, best album for *The Game*, best single with 'Another One Bites The Dust' and they each came third in their own musical category. 'Another One Bites The Dust' and 'Crazy Little thing Called Love' were two of the five top-selling singles in the States during 1980. 'Dust' alone sold over three and a half million copies in the USA and received a 'NARM' award.

By the end of 1980 Queen entered *The Guinness Book of Records* as the highest-paid directors of a company. But those earnings weren't director's fees: they were tax-free royalties still coming in from the two albums *Jazz* and *Live Killers*, which had been recorded outside the UK. Also by the end of 1980, Queen had sold over 45 million albums and 25 million singles worldwide, and *The Game* had gone platinum no less than *five* times in Canada alone. Amazing.

CHAPTER 13

SOUTH AMERICA BITES THE DUST

FOR SOME TIME QUEEN HAD BEEN DISCUSSING NEW PLACES TO PLAY. Almost as a joke, someone suggested they try South America. Bands had played there before, but in a low-budget way with minimal equipment. They decided that if they could do it with their usual full complement of equipment, and perform at the major outdoor stadiums in Argentina and Brazil, then they should go ahead. Gerry Stickells and Jim Beach were on the case: 'There was no one at all in South America who had the experience to promote anything as huge as a Queen tour,' said Jim, 'so I personally flew down to Rio, and set up a temporary production office at the Rio Sheraton Hotel for three months. From there I could easily commute to Buenos Aires to keep an eye on the proceedings.'

Jose Rota, now based in Buenos Aires, had been a leading record company executive in Los Angeles and was recommended as the right man to become the overall promoter and Queen's liaison with local promoters: Alfredo Capalbo, inexperienced, although he had put on concerts before with Julio Iglesias of a much less technically demanding nature, took on the job in Argentina. In Rio de Janeiro the local promoter was Marcus Lazero, who was well known there and, compared to the other two, was a hardened professional.

It wasn't until all negotiations were well underway and the concerts had been advertised and tickets gone on sale, that Queen discovered Alfredo didn't have the money to pay their guaranteed fee and was skimming the profits off ticket sales to pay it. Concerned, they asked Jose how he was paying for the tour, and he said he was crediting it all to his American Express card. Marcus intended to cope with the guarantee payments by paying nothing up front at all, but would make the venues available to the band, with which they couldn't argue.

Before all that, the band had concerts planned for Japan. The Nottingham Forest football team were on the same plane as Queen on the flight over and invited them to watch the match they were playing in Japan against a team from Uruguay. The band had a few free days before the gigs began, so John and Roger went along – sadly, Nottingham lost 1 – 0.

Flash Gordon had its Japanese premiere on 10 February, which Queen attended as guests of honour. After the film they were called up onto the stage, an event they weren't expecting, and interviewed. It is never easy to be interviewed in a foreign country as the interpreters can be off-putting. None of the band spoke a foreign language fluently – and this time, as this was, of course, Japan, there was also much screaming, which didn't help.

On 12 February, Queen played the first of five sold-out concerts at the Budokan Hall, to an audience of 60,000 people over the run. They again received the best band award from *Music Life*; John and Freddie were voted top of their respective categories and Brian and Roger second in theirs. They were also awarded gold discs for sales of *The Game*.

Freddie had a little time left before leaving for the States to prepare for the South America tour, and he spent it indulging his passion for shopping. One of the biggest stores in Tokyo, the Shibuya Seibu, closed entire floors so Freddie could receive a bespoke personal service, without being bothered by other shoppers.

The problems with South America began before the crew and the equipment had even loaded up for the long flight from Japan, when production manager, Chris Lamb, flew into Argentina as the advance party. He was stopped at customs, his cases searched, and the tour passes discovered. Queen were renowned for the 'aesthetic charm' of their tour passes, and this one was no exception: it featured two beautiful ladies, one Japanese and one South American, sharing a banana. Nothing wrong with that, except they were both naked from the waist up. In South America the pornography laws are strict, and the passes were classed as pornographic pictures. Chris spent the next few hours with a black marker pen, drawing a line across the ladies' chests.

With that problem solved, the crew and over twenty tons of equipment flew out of Tokyo airport in giant Flying Tiger planes destined for Buenos Aires, taking the longest city-to-city air route in the world. Another forty tons of gear was flown into Rio from North America.

The band took a short holiday while all this was going on: Brian went off to Disney World in Florida, Roger to Los Angeles, Freddie to New York, where he was negotiating to buy an apartment, and John flew home to England.

The venues in Argentina were the gigantic Vélez Sarsfield football stadium, the Municipal Stadium in Mar del Plata and the Athletic Stadium in Rosario, which were all sold out in advance. As football is almost a sacred game to the South Americans, they also had to take three tons of artificial grass to cover and protect the real turf in the stadiums they were booked to play. Jose Rota had already had his own nightmares when he was approached by the Argentinian intelligence service, who were worried that terrorists could easily mix with the band's road crew and pass undetected. They asked him what he would do if someone put a gun to Freddie's head in the middle of a show and ordered him to say *Viva Perón*. Jose couldn't give exact answers; nothing on the scale of this tour had ever taken place before, but his response was, more or less, that if 60,000 young people couldn't gather for a concert, then it was a very sad day. His own diplomacy and enthusiasm, however, convinced the authorities that everything would go according to plan, and he even secured the necessary airspace to enable the Flying Tigers to transport the gear unhindered.

When the band arrived on 24 February, Buenos Aires airport was filled with fans, the realisation of a dream. Queen were the most popular rock band in South America, and rumours about their concerts had been circulating on and off for years – advertisements for tickets had even appeared in local newspapers. But each time the rumours had proved false. Even for those standing at the airport and in possession of a ticket, the thought that it might be more hearsay was at the forefront of their minds. When the plane landed and the mass of security guards drove up to it, there was an air of tense expectancy. The steps were wheeled up as the aircraft door swung back. The airport sound system began to broadcast Queen music, and then the fans knew that the foursome had finally arrived. The whole place erupted. At the request of the Argentinian president, a government official met the band and sped them through the arrival formalities. Bandairantes Television, the main Argentinian station, transmitted their arrival on live television, and showed regular bulletins of Queen news. From that day forward, the tour was known as the 'Tour Of A Million No Problems'. Once the equipment arrived it had to be road-hauled to the first venue; the trucks duly arrived and were loaded with the containers. No problem – except that once the trucks were out of sight of the airport the haulage company transferred the containers to smaller, inadequate ones to save money. All went well until the last bend before the stadium, when one of the trucks tipped over, spilling the container and its contents into the road. It was two days before a crane large enough to lift it upright arrived. From then on, all road trips were closely supervised.

As the temperature in Buenos Aires was touching 100 degrees Fahrenheit, the crew wore their usual hot-weather attire of tiny shorts, no shirts and knotted handkerchiefs on their heads. The local people who had been drafted in to help also adopted the same outfit. But a local who was sent 'downtown' on an errand was arrested and promptly thrown into jail, as Argentina has a strict dress code with laws forbidding men to wear shorts in public. The man was held for a couple of days before being released.

On 28 February 1981, it seemed all the problems had been ironed out: everything had gone to plan as Queen took to the stage in front of 54,000 fans at Vélez Sarsfield for their first concert in South America, and although bands had played indoor venues on the continent, none had aspired to the huge stadiums that Queen were filling. The band were nervous and apprehensive. They were under the spotlight from all quarters, as the entire music industry waited to see if their ambitious plans would bear fruit or if they would fall flat on their faces.

Queen needn't have worried, the fans went crazy, every song they played was recognised and ecstatically received, and the crowd even sang along in English, though few spoke the language. When it came to 'Love Of My Life' Freddie stopped singing and the audience took over, word perfect all the way through. It was, for Queen, a very moving experience, and Freddie wasn't the only one to wipe a damp eye.

The following night the show was broadcast live on television to over 35 million people in Argentina and Brazil. After each show, the band were escorted out of the stadium by military police, in some thrilling manoeuvres that would have put movie car-chases to shame. The only reason for such measures was that the local people were concerned for the band's safety among such joyously riotous crowds – but the band never felt in any danger. The vibes were all good.

The president of the Vélez Sarsfield stadium threw a party for Queen at his home where they were introduced to the footballer – and almost demigod to the Argentinians – Diego Maradona; Brian swapped his Union Jack T-shirt for Maradona's football-team shirt. They were also invited to meet General Viola, the president of Argentina, at his house. He had specifically requested a meeting with them as the shows they had given were thought of as a major cultural event in his country. Brian, Freddie and John accepted, but Roger did not agree with the president's political views, and so declined the invitation on principle.

There was a short break between the concerts in Argentina and those set for Brazil, which was fortunate for two reasons. The band had wanted to play at the biggest stadium in the world, the famous Maracanã Stadium in Rio, but the promoter had been unable to book it; the governor of Rio had changed the law to specify that the stadium could only be used for football matches and cultural or religious events, and Queen didn't qualify. The band offered to donate a substantial sum of money to the special charity run by the governor's wife, but that offer fell on deaf ears, so they finally had to admit defeat.

Negotiations took place to play instead at the second biggest stadium in the world, Morumbi in São Paulo. Eventually, just ten days before the show was advertised to take place, the promoter managed to secure permission for them to perform there. The tickets went on sale immediately and sold out so quickly that a second night was organised, for which tickets sold out in the thirty-six hours prior to the show.

The band's equipment, all 110 tons of it, had to be road-hauled through the jungle from Argentina to Brazil. When it got to the Brazilian border, customs wanted to examine every single piece on every truck, which would have taken three months, when they had only three days. On being informed of this one of the customs officials, quite literally, had a heart attack, although thankfully not fatal.

Luckily Jose knew several customs agents in Rio. The agents sent a representative to the border to explain that the inspection simply could not be done, and the trucks were allowed through, with just thirty-six hours to go before the show.

While all this frantic negotiation was taking place, the band and their crew were taking a rest – and Rio couldn't have been a better place to relax, with two of the world's most beautiful beaches, Copacabana and Ipanema, and some of the best and most exotic nightlife. When it was discovered that the Rio date could not take place, everyone began preparations for Morumbi, somewhat reluctantly, as life in Rio was sublime and none of them wanted to move on.

Local security was hired for the band members during their stay in São Paulo, and John's 'guard' introduced himself by saying he had killed 212 people so therefore must be good at his job.

Plans were going well, apart from a small matter that registered with Gerry and Jim. The concert organisers couldn't have been more helpful – everything the band required they were provided with. However, Gerry spotted something odd: 'I noticed the equipment they were providing us with had, in every case, always belonged to someone else,' he observed. 'We were using huge, Super Trouper spotlights, and they all had Earth, Wind and Fire stencilled on the side. Some other piece of equipment had another band's name on too. It just dawned on me that they had obviously "confiscated" this gear during previous tours.'

This caused serious worries about whether Queen's equipment would be seized at the end of their tour – and the band had with them virtually every piece of equipment they owned. They couldn't take any chances and after the second Morumbi concert, they decided the gear would be removed with great speed. They chartered a Flying Tiger 747 cargo plane and arranged for it to be on the runway at São Paulo after the show.

Meanwhile, the concerts at Morumbi went ahead. The band walked out on stage on 20 March 1981 to deafening cheers and thunderous applause from 131,000 people, the largest paying audience for one band anywhere in the world to date. Before the show the following evening, while the band were in the dressing room, Gerry was trying to make a phone call. After the seventh telephone he tried failed to work, he grew angry, an unusual occurrence, ripped the telephone from the wall and threw it out of the window. The police were called and the band locked into the dressing room until the incident had been resolved – but the promoter had failed to realise that they were due onstage at any moment. The band were eventually released to take the stage in front of another 120,000 people. In total, Queen had played to a staggering 479,000 fans on the tour and had grossed over three and a half million dollars. Immediately afterwards the crew stripped down the stage, loaded the gear and took it to the waiting plane, which left at 6 a.m., before anyone knew what had happened – the security and stadium staff were too busy stealing the artificial turf Queen had left behind to notice.

The first section of that inaugural tour of South America was over and the gear made it to the USA, to be held in storage at the airport ready for the band later in the year. During that tour every one of the band's albums were in the Argentinian Top 10 and the single 'Love Of My Life' spent a year in the singles charts – a feat never before accomplished by any band, British or otherwise. Gerry Stickells was the head of what was, perhaps, the best touring organisation ever seen on the road: it comprised a hand-picked team, including Trip Khalaf and the Clair Brothers Audio team, TFA lighting with Jimmy Barnett in charge, and Queen's own personal and permanent crew of Jobby, Ratty, Mr Modem and Crystal, all experienced technicians.

SOUTH AMERICA BITES THE DUST

South America had been a triumph for the band and the crew. It had been evident right from that first gig in Buenos Aires, when the band had astounded the Argentinian organisers with not only their stage performance and the response of the audience, but with their organisation from beginning to end. Band and crew flew back to the UK, tired and elated, and knowing that, in a few short months, they would be doing it all again in Venezuela.

CHAPTER 14

A CHANGE OF DIRECTION

ROGER RELEASED HIS SECOND SOLO SINGLE ON 30 MARCH 1981, A track called 'Future Management' with a B-side of 'Laugh Or Cry'. Both were taken from his solo album, which was released a week later. The single charted, although only at forty-nine. The music press reaction to Roger's solo single was, in some cases, predictable, although, oddly enough, one or two of the papers that had generally disliked Queen were uncharacteristically kind. *Sounds* said: 'It's a reggaeish song which is bearable enough. A laudable attempt to step out of the shadow of the toothy one.' But *NME* remained true to their colours, saying: 'Roger does a Rundgren and plays everything apart from Scrabble. A plodding regatta de blanc that drags rather than just lays back.'

On the album, *Fun In Space*, Roger showed his musical versatility by playing all the instruments, with a little help from a friend on some of the keyboards. He recorded it mostly at Mountain Studios in Montreux, slotting it in between Queen work and touring, and, as he had a few spare weeks, he fitted in as much publicity as possible. The album fared little better than the single in the press. 'This is Son of Flash Gordon; it has similar comic book style characteristics.

A CHANGE OF DIRECTION

Listening to this is the most fun you'll have apart from playing Space Invaders', said *Record Mirror*. *Melody Maker* was rather more cutting: 'Revelling in bombastic arrogance, so redolent of Queen. A rich man's self-indulgence run riot over two sides of an album.'

But the press didn't count on Roger's avid Queen following, and his debut album climbed the UK charts to rest at a praiseworthy number sixteen.

The following month EMI Records took out a double-page spread in the April edition of *Music Week*, congratulating Queen on their achievements in South America – the headline ran 'South America Bites The Dust'. The music industry and many other bands had all been watching the tour's progress with bated breath, as they all knew that if Queen succeeded, it would open the way for others to follow. And when Queen got back in one piece, with a full complement of equipment and their crew intact, other top bands began planning.

Brian's wife Chrissy gave birth to their first daughter, Louisa, on 22 May 1981. He was in the UK for the birth, but shortly afterwards had to fly out to Montreux as work had begun on the next Queen album. During early May, Elektra Records released 'Let's Get Crazy', from *Fun In Space*. It was Roger's solo debut in the USA – but, sadly, a commercial failure. Roger released another single from the album in the UK on 29 June, a track called 'My Country', his third solo single, which went the same way as the others – into obscurity, as far as the majority of the record-buying public was concerned. It did, however, attract one decent review from *Melody Maker*: 'Queen aren't my favourite band, but there is no doubting their drummer's multi-instrumental and vocal prowess. A worthy bit of barrier breaking, but hardly top 40 material.'

Roger also found time to produce two songs for comedian Mel Smith, who had become a good friend. They were titled 'Richard And Joey' and, rather oddly, 'Julie Andrews' Greatest Hits', on which Roger also provided backing vocals and all the instrumentation.

While Queen were working on the new album in Switzerland, Roger and Freddie socialised frequently with Montreux resident David Bowie. He visited the studios several times, and on one occasion his visit developed into an impromptu jam session. No one had any intention of making anything out of it but as the day wore on a song emerged, later to become 'Under Pressure'. The trio finished it off in New York sometime later and Bowie also provided backing vocals for another track, 'Cool Cat', but that version wasn't used on the final album.

Freddie's birthday on 5 September was celebrated in his usual inimitable style: he bought Concorde tickets for all his closest friends and flew them to New York. He was living in a huge suite in the city's Berkshire Hotel at the time, and that was where the party was held. It eventually ground to a halt *five days* later. Freddie flew back to the UK for a few days' rest and recuperation, before flying back to the USA with the rest of Queen on 15 September, bound for New Orleans and rehearsals for their second tour of South America.

The crew and equipment were already well on their way to Caracas in Venezuela, for what had already been dubbed the 'Gluttons for Punishment' tour. In Venezuela they had secured the services of a very good local promoter, Enzo Morera. The only problem was that while they were there the country's President, Rómulo Betancourt, referred to as 'the Father of Democracy', was dying. Enzo had explained to the band that if he did die then the whole country would go into mourning and the five planned concerts would have to be cancelled. The band played their first night on 25 September at the Poliedro de Caracas, where everything went well and Betancourt was still alive. They played their second and third nights, and the ex-president held on.

September 28 was a day off, and Jim Beach persuaded John, Brian and Roger to go down to the Venezuelan equivalent of *Top Of The Pops*, a television show filmed live. Freddie wanted nothing to do

A CHANGE OF DIRECTION

with the venture and remained behind at the hotel. The band walked on stage and were introduced as Queen – but the audience couldn't tell whether they were the real thing as all the other guests were lookalikes shipped in from a Californian company who specialised in celebrity doubles ('Yul Brynner' had just been introduced before Queen). The three of them stood there on live television, feeling a little embarrassed, when suddenly a man rushed onto the stage, pushing past Jim who was in the wings, and started yelling in Spanish into the microphone. 'I was standing with an interpreter, and managed to discover that the chap had, in fact, announced that Betancourt had died,' said Jim. 'He said there would be a two-minute silence. But none of the band could understand any of this, and I couldn't go and explain as the TV cameras were still filming. They just stood there, looking nonplussed. After a couple of minutes, another chap ran on stage, and the audience began to cheer. My interpreter said that *this* chap was telling everyone that Beancourt wasn't dead. And still the band all stood there, looking nervously around, and at each other, not knowing what on earth was going on around them.'

Later that night Rómulo Betancourt died, and the next two shows were cancelled. The country shut down for a period of mourning, including the airport. The band felt like prisoners, knowing they were trapped in Venezuela until the people decided to reopen for business. It was a frightening time, as none of them understood the political situation – whether a revolution was about to take place or what would happen next.

The cancellations resulted in a battle with Enzo Morera, who didn't want to pay them for the two shows. He eventually paid up, much to everyone's relief, as the political situation was so unstable and stories about strange 'disappearances' and people being pushed down lift shafts had reached them from various sources, stories that were quite easy to believe in the atmosphere of unrest surrounding the country at that time.

When the airport reopened the band and crew all flew to the USA, from whence the trip to Mexico would take place. The band took a few days' break; the crew and Gerry Stickells headed for the border.

Once there, the problems continued. The eighteen-strong advance party arrived at the border at 3 p.m., complete with passports and work permits, only to be told that the border was open between midday and 2 p.m. and that even if it had been open, they could only issue six visas a day and the most they could allot to one party was three. The crew booked into a local hotel, to try again the next day. They were met with the news that they would have to have their fingerprints taken before the visas could be issued. Frustration was at an all-time high, as schedules had to be kept and time was running out. After another night in the hotel, someone suggested that monetary inducement to the border guards might speed matters up. Next day they trooped back to the border, a short conversation took place, eighteen visas were exchanged and the crew crossed into Mexico without further hindrance – albeit £500 poorer.

October 9 was the band's first gig in Mexico, at the University Stadium in Monterrey. All went well, and the Mexicans gave Queen an enthusiastic welcome – they had never seen anything quite like it before, as major rock bands just didn't play Mexico.

However, promoter Jose Rota was arrested while the band were in Mexico and thrown into jail the day before the Pueblo gig. They had to bail him out to the tune of $25,000 so the tour could continue.

On 16 October, Queen played their first night at the huge Estadio Cuauhtémoc in Pueblo, just outside Mexico City. The stadium had been in a terrible state when the crew had arrived, and they'd had to repaint signs and clear rubbish from the pitch. As the fans began to pour in, they were searched and checked for radios and tape recorders; if they had either, the batteries were removed – ensuring that bootleggers couldn't make tapes, or so everyone thought. Inside the stadium,

Smile outside the Royal Albert Hall, London, 1969. (L–R) Brian May, Roger Taylor, Tim Staffell. DOUG PUDDIFOOT

Freddie, Roger and Roger's girlfriend, Jo Morris, in Roger and Freddie's Kensington Market stall, December 1969.

Freddie with Sour Milk Sea, 1970. (L–R) Freddie Bulsara (vocals), Chris Chesney (bass and backing vocals), Paul Milne (bass), Rob Tyrell (drums) and (sat) Jeremy Gallop (guitar).

The earliest photos of Queen playing live, St Helens, Merseyside, 30 October 1970.

The earliest photo ever taken of Queen, 1970. Original bass player Mike Grose is first from left. DOUG PUDDIFOOT

Third bass player, Doug Bogie, 1971.

Freddie at the Marquee, 1972. DOUG PUDDIFOOT

Experimental photo session by Doug Puddifoot, in Freddie's flat, 1972. DOUG PUDDIFOOT

Freddie's flat, Holland Road, 17 March 1973. DOUG PUDDIFOOT

Queen's first promotional photo, taken in Freddie's flat, 1973. DOUG PUDDIFOOT

The proposed cover of the first Queen album, which never made it to the finished product. DOUG PUDDIFOOT

The band on their American tour, Chicago, March 1975. MICHAEL MARKS

Queen signing their music publishing deal with EMI, November 1975. New manager John Reid is on the far right.

Queen at Hyde Park, 18 September 1976. The free concert drew a crowd of 150,000.
GODDARD ARCHIVE/ALAMY STOCK PHOTO

Roger and Freddie, Hyde Park, 1976. KEYSTONE FEATURES/GETTY IMAGES

Queen with Groucho Marx, 3 March 1977.

Freddie with his parents, Bomi and Jer, 1977.

Roger with his mother, Winifred, when he flew her out to the USA for some of the shows.

A CHANGE OF DIRECTION

fans were greeted by a stall selling batteries at astronomical prices – the same batteries that had been so recently confiscated . . .

Apart from that, everything seemed to be going well until the band walked out. The massive crowd began to throw all sorts of rubbish onto the stage, not, as was at first thought, out of contempt because they didn't like the show, but out of appreciation because they loved it. They launched everything from shoes to bottles – and batteries. It was hazardous for the band, who were in danger of being seriously hurt but luckily, with a bit of ducking and diving, they survived the set – all except personal manager Paul Prenter, who was hit by a battery. He was often pompous and dismissive of the road crew, looking on them as mere underlings, so the direct hit raised a loud cheer. Thankfully it did him no serious or lasting damage.

After the gig, at a hastily convened production meeting in the early hours of the morning, it was decided to ban all alcohol from the stadium, assuming that this would stop the rowdiness and rubbish-throwing. Long meetings with the police ensued to ensure that the audience the next day was searched as they arrived, and all bottles and cans of drink were confiscated. The theory was that if the fans were relieved of such items, it would minimise the danger of missiles being aimed at the stage. Gerry and Jim supervised the operation, standing by while fans were deprived of their drinks. It all seemed to be going well, until the band's sound engineer, Trip, dashed up and asked why everyone inside the stadium was getting drunk on tequila. They all went back inside and discovered that a stall had been set up on the other side of the gates, which was selling back, at high prices, the booze that had been taken away outside.

The concert went ahead as planned, and the audience showed their appreciation as before, and again the band miraculously escaped unhurt. But after that show which, due to tax and currency problems, the band weren't being paid for, they decided they'd had enough and cancelled the remaining shows. It was all too much. The truck drivers were given triple pay to pack up and drive non-stop to the border – and the band told the promoter that they were flying on to another gig in Guadalajara. Instead they were smuggled aboard a flight bound for New York and left, vowing never to set foot in Mexico again. The promoter was furious, but he'd made enough money out of the two shows they had played to cover his own expenses. After it was all over and everyone had had a chance to reflect on it, they agreed it was an incredible experience but one that might not bear repetition too soon.

CHAPTER 15

A CLASSIC COLLECTION

WITH THE IMMINENT RELEASE OF A *GREATEST HITS* ALBUM, THE BAND decided to go one further. Because Queen had been far-sighted enough to make videos for all single releases after 'Bohemian Rhapsody', and because Jim Beach had been prescient enough to make sure the band maintained ownership of them rather than turn them over to the record company, they were able to release the whole lot on a compilation video: it was the first time such a comprehensive collection of promotional videos had been made by any band, and on 19 October 1981 *Greatest Flix* was released in the UK.

Several books had been written about the band and their musical careers, all unofficial as the band wouldn't give permission to publishers. As the band had had no dealings with the authors, they were concerned that the contents might not be accurate. One in particular, *The First Ten Years*, came to their attention because it was credited on the cover as 'official'. The band were concerned not solely about its content, but that it was purporting to be something it was not, so took the publishers to court. Unfortunately they lost the action and the book was published: it set a precedent for Queen in that they never again tried to sue an unofficial publication – it was obvious to them that it was a useless and time-wasting exercise.

The song that Queen and Bowie had worked on together in Switzerland was so good that the band decided to release it as a single. The original working title, 'People On Streets', was replaced with 'Under Pressure' and it was released on 26 October 1981, with 'Soul Brother' on the B-side. It was an immediate bestseller – Queen fans and Bowie's own army of followers rushed to record stores, ensuring the single made it to number one, Queen's second sojourn at the top. The press reaction? 'Queen's performance is surprisingly good, it's Bowie and Mercury's vocals and words that let the whole thing down,' said *Sounds*. 'Something deep and significant going on here. Rage and pathos bubbling in Bowie's performance, not to mention the squeaking of Mr Mercury's accompaniment,' added *Melody Maker*.

As Bowie was unavailable to make the music video, Queen asked director David Mallett to compile something to accompany the track on television. He cut together footage of rushing commuters, buildings being demolished, explosions, all along the themes of stress and pressure.

Queen had commissioned Antony Armstrong-Jones, First Earl of Snowdon, to take special portrait photos of them for the front cover of the *Greatest Hits* album and, to maintain continuity, the photo was used on the *Greatest Flix* cover, too, and on the cover of the accompanying book, *Greatest Pix*. The latter was a pictorial history of Queen's ten years together, compiled by Jacques Lowe, who was, at one time, personal photographer to President John F. Kennedy during his term of office. Jacques had been given hundreds and hundreds of slides, photographs and transparencies taken of Queen over the ten-year period, and personally spent hours going through them to select what he considered the best ones, and those that represented what Queen had achieved over the decade.

The album, released on 2 November, was a collection of seventeen hits, but because different tracks had been hits in different countries,

A CLASSIC COLLECTION

various versions were released simultaneously. Some included the latest hit 'Under Pressure', although the UK version did not.

On 7 November 1981, *Greatest Hits* ('an album with class all the way through', said *Record Mirror*) entered the UK chart at number two; sales had reached platinum status, as it had already sold over 300,000. The following week, Queen were still number one in the singles chart, occupied the top slot in the video chart and the album had climbed to number one as well. It was an amazing achievement, echoed around Europe as the single and three compilation releases took the charts there by storm.

The band had decided sometime previously that they would like to make a feature film of a live concert, and talks were instigated with various directors and production companies. After much discussion a company in Canada, MobileVision fronted by director and documentary filmmaker Saul Swimmer, offered the best deal. Saul had previously co-produced, among others, The Beatles' film *Let It Be*. MobileVision's innovative concept was to show films at gigs on a massive outdoor screen which could be transported from venue to venue – theoretically a great idea.

It was agreed that the band would perform two special concerts in MobileVision's home city of Montreal, which would both be filmed, so on 24 and 25 November they played to 18,000-capacity packed houses. Queen were hot then in Canada, and tickets for the special shows sold at an incredible speed. It was the band's first rendition of 'Under Pressure' without David Bowie, and was well received.

The concerts were shot using 70mm film, unusual in that most films are shot using 35mm, but because it was to be shown eventually on a screen measuring 90 by 120 feet, this meant the film had to be larger to maintain quality. The two concerts were then edited and the best bits from both were used to make the film (unfortunately, in one or two places the synchronisation leaves a lot to be desired). It was originally planned for release during the summer of 1982 in the USA and Canada, and would head to cinemas in the UK and Europe later that year, but early problems with finances and arguments as to who would pay caused delays right from the start.

In early December the band flew out to Munich to start work on their next album. Although all of them were resident in London, Munich had become a firm favourite. Freddie in particular spent much of his time there – he was almost a resident at the Arabella Haus Hotel where he rented the entire top floor for himself and his entourage, and he had made a lot of close friends in the city. Brian says:

> *Munich had a huge effect on all our lives. Because we spent so much time there, it became almost another home, and a place in which we lived different lives. It was different from being on tour, where there would be an intense contact with a city for a couple of days, and then we would move on. In Munich we all became embroiled in the lives of the local people. We found ourselves inhabiting the same clubs for most of the night, most nights! The Sugar Shack in particular held a fascination for us. It was a rock disco with an amazing sound system, and the fact that some of our records didn't sound very good in there made us change our whole perspective on our mixes and our music. 'Another One Bites The Dust' and 'Dragon Attack', on* The Game *album, both showed a trend towards more 'rhythmic' rock. And* Hot Space *[the band's tenth album] became almost totally oriented that way. Freddie in particular was keen to explore that avenue to the extreme! ('Body Language', 'Staying Power' etc.) The multitrack of 'Staying Power' was sent to Arif Mardin in the USA (famous for Aretha Franklin, Chaka Khan productions, etc.) and he put a live horn section on using his own arrangement. This was a very different approach for us.*
>
> *In retrospect it's probably true to say that our efficiency in Munich was not very good. Our social habits made us generally start work late in the day, feeling tired, and (for me especially, and perhaps for Freddie) the emotional distractions became destructive.*

A CLASSIC COLLECTION

Many times it had been mentioned that Queen's music was somewhat orchestral and talks had been undertaken with the Royal Philharmonic Orchestra, with a view to them performing a selection of Queen tracks at the Royal Albert Hall in aid of a charity for people with leukaemia. Queen were enthusiastic about the idea, and on 8 December a Royal Promenade Concert was held at the Royal Albert Hall with the RPO and the Royal Choral Society. The event was a sell-out, at a minimum of £50 per ticket, and the audience was made up largely of diamond and fur-clad ladies, and gents in formal dinner suits. To augment the charity's fund the event was filmed and recorded, with the hope of releasing an album and video, with profits from both being donated to the charity.

The band all flew home for Christmas – and to reflect on a tenth anniversary year that was one of their most successful to date.

In January 1982, the band returned to Munich to concentrate on their new album. Also working there was American artist and good friend Billy Squier; Roger and Freddie found time to give him some 'emotional support' and sing backing vocals on the track 'Emotions In Motion', from the album of the same name that Billy was working on.

Time off was spent in Los Angeles, where Roger, Brian and John had all bought houses – a combination of the love of sunshine and good living, and the chance to write off some money against UK tax bills. They spent their time discussing the forthcoming European tour, and the video they would make for their next single, 'Body Language'. They were in Los Angeles only for a few days, then jetted into the UK for a brief stay – during which Roger found time to work with Gary Numan on his forthcoming album *Dance*. He popped into Rock City studios in London and played drums on three tracks, 'Crash', 'Morals' and 'You Are You Are'. Gary had been a Queen fan since he was a boy and had met Roger during recording sessions, when he and Queen had been in adjacent studios – they shared an interest in fast cars and boats.

The new Queen single was due for release on 19 April, and the band, with director Mike Hodges, decided to fly to the Magdar Studios in Toronto, Canada, to make the video. 'Body Language' had given them several ideas and they finally settled on featuring naked bodies, painted with arrows and liberally covered in baby oil, in a variety of provocative poses. The band themselves remained fully clothed.

Just before the single was released, their contract with EMI for the UK and Europe had to be renewed. They signed on 1 April 1982 for a further six albums, beginning with the one they were working on at that time. 'Body Language' came out on 19 April in a sleeve featuring two people from the video, a man and a woman, their glistening bodies painted head to toe, with the mysterious arrows. Unfortunately, in the USA the cover was considered too risqué, and after many complaints, Elektra withdrew it and put it out in a plain blue cover. The British press quite liked 'Body Language'. 'Good, electronically pulsed cooled-out slick 133 bpm 7in white disco smash', said *Sounds*. 'Not since they had all those ladies riding bicycles have Queen been so outrageous. The picture sleeve apart, this is an excellent single. Don't think Mary Whitehouse will like it though!' said another.

However, the band's fans didn't take to it, and it went no higher than number twenty-five in the UK chart. The video for 'Body Language' was, like the cover, similarly censored – MTV refused to show it as it was thought too explicit for family viewing.

The band flew to Gothenburg on 8 April to begin their tour the following night at the Scandinavium. They again had a completely new lighting rig, which, although large, was not quite as over the top as it had been previously. The music itself had a 'funky' feel to it this time around, displeasing those fans who'd bought tickets to see the hard rock band they had grown up with. Their support act for the tour was British band Bow Wow Wow, whose music could be described

A CLASSIC COLLECTION

as 'lightweight pop' and whose stage dress leaned towards punk. Unfortunately, that band weren't well received by European audiences, and after several shows of booing and bottle-throwing, Bow Wow Wow were forced to withdraw from the other shows. Queen liked the band and thought the audiences were being narrow-minded in not giving them a chance, but they were replaced by another British band, Airrace, featuring, on drums, Jason Bonham, son of the late great Led Zeppelin drummer John. That gig was also the first to feature a 'fifth member' on stage. Queen decided that as they were using synths in their music now, they needed to introduce keyboards to their live work. As neither Brian nor Freddie could devote full stage time to playing them, they drafted in the talented Morgan Fisher, who for many years had been with Mott The Hoople, which is where Queen met and got to know him. He was, by all accounts, a strange character, always dressed in weird and wonderful 'hippie' fashions and bright colours – he loved orange.

During early 1982, England and Argentina were engaged in conflict over the sovereignty of the Falkland Islands, off the Argentinian coast. In late April, Queen were in the number one slot in Argentina with, appropriately for the time, 'Under Pressure'. The Argentinian government weren't amused and subsequently banned Queen from ever again appearing in Argentina and their records from being played on the radio for the duration of the conflict.

The European tour was still underway when the band's twelfth album was released on 21 May. They had called it *Hot Space*, a title drawn from an inebriated late-night conversation about the many musical open spaces this album contained, which were definitely hot.

Hot Space was a distinct turn away from the hard rock image with which Queen had, up to then, been associated – and for many fans it was too much of a turn. It seemed as though Brian's guitar work had been sacrificed to some extent in favour of the ever-present synthesizer, and to a large majority of fans his guitar was an integral part of Queen's music. Brian himself admitted publicly that he wasn't keen on the album, but in its defence, he said that Queen had to try new avenues and new techniques, that there was truth in the old cliché about not being stuck in a rut.

The album was reasonably successful, reaching number four in the UK chart – but lost those Queen fans who thought the band should stick to rock and steer clear of what they called 'disco'. On the other hand, it gained them a degree of respect within the music press. 'New styles, and a whole new sense of values. You'll love *Hot Space*, eventually,' said *Record Mirror*. 'Queen have never made particularly blinding albums, but you'll have to agree that *Hot Space* shows more restraint and imagination than tripe like *Jazz*,' said *Sounds*. *NME* loved it, adding 'The production of the whole album is really a peach.'

The album was released at about the same time in the USA and proved a turning point in the band's popularity there, too. It reached number twenty-two in the chart, but the reaction of the rock radio stations and their listeners – always important to album sales – was, some said, predictable. The DJs loathed it, and their listeners wouldn't request tracks from it; the album nose-dived and the band's reputation as a solid hard rock band bombed too. Queen had a tour planned for later in the year and hoped the gigs would help to reassure their fans that, live, they were still hard and heavy.

The band flew back into Britain on 23 May for a few days' break before setting off on the UK leg of the tour. The first show, on 29 May 1982, was held at Leeds United's football ground Elland, in front of a capacity crowd of 38,000 people. ('One of our best gigs ever,' said Brian.) Three days later their twenty-first single was released in the UK, a poignant track written by Brian called 'Las Palabras de Amor (The Words Of Love)' ('A down tempo moody with Freddie playing the part of a Spanish choir boy', said *Sounds*), which climbed to number seventeen in the UK chart.

June 1 and 2 were spent in Edinburgh, playing two concerts at the

A CLASSIC COLLECTION

Ingliston Agricultural Hall. Then it was back down south to the huge Milton Keynes Bowl, a relatively new outdoor arena set on the outskirts of the town. The venue was not much more than a huge hole in the ground, although it was being called a 'natural amphitheatre'. The show wasn't completely sold out, but Tyne Tees Television were on hand to film the event for a future broadcast. 'None of us thought it was a very good gig at the time, we were wishing they had filmed Leeds,' said Brian. 'I particularly found it hard to get the sound right and couldn't hear the monitors very well. But Tyne Tees filmed it, and mixed it themselves, with no help from us; and we now think it's one of the better videos of our live shows. "Staying Power", especially, sounds even tighter than the record (and heavier).'

The band flew into Milton Keynes by helicopter from Battersea in London. It was Freddie's first experience of a helicopter. 'I was terrified,' he said. 'I don't like flying in anything smaller than a jumbo jet, darling, and this thing was so small! But I was told we had photographers and the like at the other end waiting for us to arrive, so I couldn't possibly let them see how shaken I was! My knuckles were white from gripping the arm rests. But when we arrived, I stepped out of that machine with a smile on my face looking like I did it every day, no one was any the wiser.'

The support for Milton Keynes were American bands Heart, and Joan Jett and The Blackhearts, and British band the Teardrop Explodes. Heart were reasonably well received, Joan Jett slightly less so, and by the time the Teardrop Explodes took to the stage the audience just wanted Queen. They thought they'd waited long enough and showed their annoyance by pelting Teardrop with bottles and cans – abysmally poor behaviour from usually well-behaved fans, and the band left the stage early to shouts of abuse and a further hail of bottles.

The original plan for this tour had been to play Old Trafford in Manchester and Arsenal football team's home stadium in Highbury, north London, as well as Leeds and Milton Keynes. Unfortunately both shows had to be cancelled, Manchester through lack of portable toilet facilities (the Pope was touring the UK at the time and his 'venues' had snapped them all up), and Highbury because the residents complained it would be far too noisy and the venue had not been granted a licence.

Milton Keynes was the last night of the tour, then, and of course they had a party. The Embassy Club in London was booked for an exclusive 'Shorts and Suspenders' celebration. As the name suggests, everyone was to attend suitably attired in one or the other or both, depending on individual taste. It was a wild night and carried on well into the early hours of the morning. That evening, support band Heart were playing at London's Dominion Theatre in their own right, and Brian showed his support for them by going to the gig and getting on stage with them for their encore.

For the first time in five years Queen decided to appear on *Top Of The Pops* with 'Las Palabras de Amor'. They had avoided it for the last few singles, due to touring or recording commitments, but they were free to record the show in person this time. They appeared on 10 June, and the same footage was shown again two weeks later.

A tour of North America was scheduled to start in mid-July, and just before they left for Montreal to prepare for it, the band went into film studios with director Brian Grant to make two promotional videos, for 'Back Chat' and 'Calling All Girls'.

They arrived in Canada on 18 July and the first gig was at the Forum in Montreal on the 21st, supported by their good friend Billy Squier. They had again employed an 'extra member' on keyboards. This time they took on Fred Mandell, usually part of Elton John's touring band, as the band had decided that Morgan Fisher didn't quite 'fit', and seemed to not be enjoying the tour . . . in an interview he gave many, many years later for the fan club magazine, Morgan said:

A CLASSIC COLLECTION

Although they were perhaps too embarrassed to speak frankly to me at the end of the European leg, I think they realised I wasn't enjoying it so much and that I didn't feel very comfortable. It made sense to part company and they almost did it to be kind to me. But rather than try and explain it all, they sent me a telegram saying they'd decided they didn't need a keyboard player for the next tour – I didn't know until later that they got someone else in. I wasn't heartbroken because of the way things had transpired and I don't feel any grudge whatsoever . . . it was almost a relief.

From Montreal they went on to Boston, where the city declared 23 July an official 'Queen Day' and the band were handed the keys to the city by the Lord Mayor of Boston, and an official declaration was signed, stamped and presented to them. The enthusiasm carried on throughout the day and on to the gig that night; the atmosphere was electric, quelling the band's apprehensions that the US public's adverse reaction to *Hot Space* would influence ticket sales and the eagerness of the audiences. 'Boston had been one of the first American cities to really break for us,' said Brian. 'They were all so enthusiastic, they had parades and Queen events, it was just great, they loved us.'

On the 27th they made a rare 'in store' appearance at Crazy Eddie's record store in New York, which was inundated with fans all clamouring for their copies of Queen albums to be signed. The concerts in New York were again at the Madison Square Garden, and after both shows, on 27 and 28 July, backstage parties were held, featuring such delights as naked female mud wrestlers and endless supplies of champagne.

Back in the UK, EMI released Queen's twenty-second single on 9 August, a track from *Hot Space* called 'Back Chat', which only got to number forty before quickly disappearing without trace. Said the *NME*: 'This is possibly a parody of the disco format, and one wonders if Freddie Mercury had got his tongue firmly in his cheek.'

Elektra Records chose a different single from the album as their release – 'Calling All Girls', a track written by Roger and the first of his songs to be released as an A-side. But although the band were on tour at the time, the single fared worse than the one in the UK, struggling to number sixty for a very brief stay of just five weeks. The band did make a futuristic video for the single, directed by Brian Grant and based on *THX 1138*, George Lucas's feature film directorial debut from 1971.

After the first few gigs in North America, Queen's private plane was blown off its chocks outside its hangar, rendering it useless, so the band hired another. But this new one was no ordinary plane. It was Elvis Presley's last private jet, a snazzy little thing called the *Lisa Marie*, after his daughter. It was fantastic apart from one thing: Elvis had apparently had a strong aversion to bright light, including ordinary daylight, and he'd had all the windows blacked out. It was like flying in constant darkness, so they decided to change it for a decent, ordinary little jet in which to continue the tour.

During a short break before the shows in LA, Roger found time to slip into a recording studio and provide backing vocals for old friends Kansas. He sang on three tracks for their *Vinyl Confessions* album, 'Play The Game Tonight', 'Right Away' and 'Diamonds And Pearls'.

The tour finished on 15 September at the Inglewood Forum and Queen flew back to the UK the next day for a brief five-day stay. They had agreed to appear on the US television chat show *Saturday Night Live*, so flew back to New York, where they performed 'Crazy Little Thing Called Love' and 'Under Pressure' live on television. They also made a fleeting appearance on another chat show, *Entertainment Tonight*, before flying back home.

It was the shortest of rests, as they were due to return to Japan on 15 October for yet another tour. Just before their arrival the album *Gettin Smile* was released by Mercury Records in Japan. It featured six

A CLASSIC COLLECTION

tracks recorded by Smile from way back in the sixties, four of them previously unreleased. Roger and Brian were concerned that it might not be the real Smile, as neither of them recalled ever having recorded that much material, but on hearing a copy they had to admit that it was genuine. The album had been released without permission, but after they listened to it, and having had the cover notes translated into English, they agreed not to act, allowing the album to remain on sale. It wasn't easy to get hold of, anyway, as it was only available on import, meaning it quickly became a collector's item.

The first concert of the Japanese tour was held at the Kyuden Auditorium in Fukuoka. As had become customary on Queen's arrival in Japan, fans were at the airport and Queenmania surrounded them wherever they went. A few nights later the band were playing in Sapporo where, after the show, everyone – band, crew and management – were involved in a beer-drinking contest. The heats were hard fought between crew, band members and the local 'experts', and after the consumption of vast amounts of Japanese beer the finals took place. The outright winner was personal manager Paul Prenter. He stayed standing just long enough to down the last pint before he ended up under the nearest table!

The final night of the Japanese tour was at the Seibu Lions stadium in Tokyo. The gig was filmed by a Japanese film company, to be released on video in Japan at a future date.

After it was all over Brian and John flew back to the UK, but Roger stayed on in the East and became a tourist for a few days. He visited Hong Kong, Bangkok and Thailand, taking in the temples, gardens and palaces. He also sampled the exotic food – and the nightlife. Freddie flew to New York directly from Japan, although he had stayed on an extra day to fit in the obligatory shopping. By now he had acquired his New York apartment, which was on the forty-third floor and commanded stunning views of the river and Central Park.

In November, the finished print of the Montreal film finally arrived in England – almost a year after it had been filmed. It was to have been released in British cinemas before Christmas 1982, but problems were discovered with the sound.

On 13 November, Roger held a late fireworks party in the garden of his Surrey house. He used the occasion to premiere the *Live In Milton Keynes* film to his guests, including Brian and John.

In the USA, on 23 November, Elektra Records released what was to be their final Queen single, the track 'Staying Power', which failed to chart. Queen's contract with Elektra, covering Australia and New Zealand, expired in December 1982, and after lengthy and involved talks and negotiations, the two parties agreed to separate. Queen were no longer happy with the way that Elektra were representing and promoting them in those territories and decided to sign with EMI for future albums.

CHAPTER 16

GOING SOLO

AT THE END OF 1982 ALL FOUR MEMBERS OF QUEEN AGREED THEY wanted to take a break: they were beginning to get on each other's nerves and arguments were becoming more and more frequent. They had been recording and touring together for twelve years without a break, and they all felt it was time for a rest. It was a unanimous decision, and they announced they wouldn't be touring throughout 1983. They agreed to go their separate ways that year and see what happened. They didn't look on it as a 'split', although that's the way it was reported by the press, and none of them wanted to call it a day completely – to end it finally would, they felt, be madness. It was merely a pause for reflection.

Freddie had been thinking of making a solo album for some time, and at last he had time to do something about it. He booked studio time at Musicland in Munich and got to work in early 1983. During that time in the studio he was introduced to Giorgio Moroder, who was working on a re-release of the 1926 Fritz Lang silent science fiction film *Metropolis*. He wanted to put a contemporary musical score to the film, which was, at the time of its release, intensely futuristic showing an uncanny prescience for later inventions and events. He asked Freddie to consider collaborating on a track for the film, to which Freddie agreed. He had never co-written with anyone outside Queen, and had not recorded anyone else's compositions, apart from Larry Lurex. This was a great opportunity for him to be involved with the film, which fascinated him, and was a new avenue to explore.

John spent the first part of 1983 at home with his wife and family. He was quite content to do very little: he couldn't make a solo album without a singer as he, by his own admission, couldn't sing a note. But it wasn't all homely events for him: he met up with friends, tennis players Vitas Gerulaitis and John McEnroe, and fellow musicians Scott Gorham, Simon Kirke, Martin Chambers and Mick Ralphs. They all gathered in a rehearsal studio for a day-long marathon jam session. Some of the songs they played were recorded for posterity, but none saw the light of day. John also played bass on the song 'Picking Up Sounds', by a group who called themselves Man Friday & Jive Junior.

Roger decided to spend his time skiing but thought he should get in some practice first and flew up to Aviemore in Scotland accompanied by his personal assistant, Chris Taylor (always known as Crystal). On their first night in the quiet Scottish town they decided to have a bit of fun and posed as vacuum cleaner salesmen. After a few days finding his feet on the nursery slopes and then on to the more difficult *piste*, Roger flew to Switzerland to put his new-found skills to the test. While he was there, he took a detour into Mountain Studios, where he wanted to try out several solo ideas. Rick Parfitt of Status Quo was also in Switzerland at the time, and as he happened to have a day or so free, he called in to Mountain to help Roger.

Roger had stacks of ideas for a second solo album in the back of his mind, but yet wasn't too sure that they would all work. He knew he would forget them if he didn't commit them to tape soon, though, and he wanted to have something to work on at a later date. John flew out to Switzerland during those few days to join him and Dominique, and apart from them all becoming competent skiers, John worked with Roger on his recording.

The weak winter sun was then replaced by the heat of Los Angeles for both Roger and John and their families, and in March the band's Montreal film *We Will Rock You* premiered in the States at Daytona Beach, Florida.

The problems with that film rumbled on: the huge screen on which they wanted to show the film – now reduced slightly to 60 by 80 feet – was, because of its size, susceptible even to the slightest gust of wind and kept blowing over. The Daytona premiere was cancelled at the last moment while experts tried to work out how to keep a screen of that size upright.

After a brief stay in Paris, Brian and his wife also flew out to California. Brian wanted to take his Red Special to the States with him, as he was planning to go into a studio and work on a solo project he had in mind. The guitar was far too precious to him to have it thrown into the aircraft hold, so he asked if it might be taken on board as hand luggage. However, the airline refused, saying it was far too big to be stowed either under the seat or in the overhead locker as hand luggage. The only alternative was to give it a seat, and if he wanted to do that, he would have to *pay* for it. It seemed that this was the only way, so Brian agreed and paid a child's fare for his precious guitar. Once in Los Angeles he wasted no time in getting to work – but not yet on his own project. He met up with friend Jeffrey Osborne in the Mad Hatter Studios in LA and played on two tracks for Jeffrey's forthcoming solo album, the title track 'Stay With Me Tonight' and another called 'Two Wrongs Don't Make A Right'.

Then he contacted several friends who all lived in LA and asked them if they fancied getting together for some musical fun: Eddie Van Halen, a guitarist who Brian respected and admired greatly; Fred

Mandell, keyboard player of repute who had played with Queen on stage and was a regular with Elton John; Philip Chen, bass player with Rod Stewart; and Alan Gratzer, the drummer from REO Speedwagon, came together at the Record Plant studios in late April.

At first the intention was to do nothing more than jam and have fun, and Brian had in the back of his mind the theme tune to the children's television series *Star Fleet*, which his son Jimmy watched. The sessions went on all day, they played everything from rock'n'roll to blues to jazz. Brian kept the tapes rolling the entire time. He had begun the session with definite ideas as to the direction the 'jam' would take and had no intention of allowing musicians of that calibre merely to hang around and play twelve bars. They played his own arrangement of the *Star Fleet* theme song, plus 'Let Me Out', a track he had written sometime previously but had never had a chance to use, and finally a lengthy blues jam. When it was all over, they still weren't intending to release it, but Brian gained the permission of all the others to mix the tracks and do further work – just in case . . .

Queen's recording contract with Elektra covering Japan expired at this time, and, for the same reasons they had not renegotiated with Elektra for the Antipodes, they decided to sign a new deal with EMI Toshiba.

Freddie, meanwhile, spent time in New York relaxing, of which his idea was to visit loud, late-night clubs until the early hours of the morning and spend the rest of the day in bed. He then flew to Los Angeles to see close friend Michael Jackson, who was recording a new album. They worked together on two songs, with a view to both being included either on Michael's new album, or if that failed, on the album Freddie had been working on. After the recording sessions and subsequent discussions, however, it was finally decided that neither track would see the light of day.

After their rest, relaxation and individual projects, the band members flew back to the UK separately. Brian had been approached by Polydor Records about the possibility of producing one of their newly signed bands, a group of young Scottish lads called Heavy Pettin'. It was a new step for him as, although he had co-produced Queen albums alongside the other band members, he had never produced anyone else, so he readily agreed to give it a try. The work began at London's Townhouse Studios in May 1983, and he was aided by Rheinhardt Mack, usually resident at Munich's Musicland Studios.

Roger, an avid fan of fast cars and motor racing, was invited to be a guest at the Monaco Grand Prix, an offer he *had* to accept. He went to Monaco with Crystal and Rick Parfitt, who was also a racing fan. Putting those three together was probably a mistake, as the sunshine, racing cars and a little too much wine resulted in Roger being arrested. It was nothing more serious than inebriated high jinks, but Jim Beach had to be summoned from holiday in Montreux to pay the quite substantial fine to release him from jail. Then Roger had to get out of Monaco within a matter of hours, a condition of his release, and as there were no immediate flights out, Jim had to arrange for a chartered helicopter to collect them all.

On 5 May, the film *We Will Rock You* received its European premiere at the prestigious Cannes Film Festival in the South of France, and on the 6 May it was shown for the first time in San Diego, California, but on an indoor screen. The problems with the vast outdoor MobileVision screen were insurmountable and that idea was scrapped. From San Diego the film toured America, mostly at colleges and universities, using a new sophisticated mobile film unit.

The film had a mixed reception: many applauded it for what it was – a real-life portrayal of Queen on stage. But others criticised it for lack of quality in film technique and even more for failing to capture the excitement and audience atmosphere of the shows.

Freddie's love of opera was well known, he particularly liked male voices, never having been a great lover of the female operatic voice. Pavarotti was a firm favourite. Around this time, he and Feebie attended a performance of Verdi's *Un Ba/lo In Maschera* given by Pavarotti at the Royal Opera House sometime in May. In act two, the female soloist was Montserrat Caballé, and Freddie was awestruck. It was the first time he had ever seen her, and the sheer power and beauty of her voice mesmerised him.

In the UK, the television show *Pop Quiz* had become popular. Hosted by DJ Mike Reid, it featured pop and rock stars in two teams of three, answering questions on music. Both Roger and John, on different occasions through May, were in teams on the show, and Roger was twice team captain. It was during one show that Roger met Robert Plant, former vocalist of Led Zeppelin, who had released a solo album and been asked to perform a couple of tracks from it on the Tyne Tees television show *The Tube*. He asked Roger if he would accompany him up to Newcastle as guest drummer for the session. As Roger had a free day, he made the trip. The programme was prerecorded for broadcast the following night, but due to another section of the show overrunning, Robert's session was never shown.

Roger was also approached to take part in a charity power boat race in Poole, Dorset. Never one to ignore a challenge and being a lover of fast boats, he readily agreed, and along with friend and fellow musician Gary Numan trekked down to Dorset in July. The boat they were to crew was the *Air Canada Cargo*, and was driven by a friend, Tony Fletcher, with Roger navigating. They came a close second and all received medals and a trophy.

Meanwhile, Jim Beach, who had business interests in the film world as well as with Queen, had been in discussions about producing a movie, *The Hotel New Hampshire*, based on the novel of the same name by John Irving. He asked Queen if they would be interested in recording the music for the film and in mid-July, John and Freddie flew out to Montreal for a meeting with the director, Tony Richardson.

GOING SOLO

The band agreed to work on some of the music for the film and left the meeting with several ideas and copies of the novel. By this time they had all realised they missed recording together and arranged to meet in Los Angeles to discuss their future.

CHAPTER 17

BACK INTO ACTION

THAT MEETING TOOK PLACE IN MID-AUGUST AND IT WENT WELL — THEY booked recording time immediately in the Record Plant in Los Angeles. It was the first time they had ever recorded as a band in America but they all felt that LA's atmosphere might bring a fresh approach, and perhaps even redirect them musically towards the US market.

Says Brian: 'We went into the studios for this album with the definite agreement among ourselves that it would not be delivered to Elektra Records. Freddie, in particular, was adamant that to do so would be throwing it away, since he felt the company no longer seemed capable of doing their job. However, we also realised that to buy our way out of the existing deal was going to be expensive, and John, particularly, felt that it may be a huge waste of money. While we recorded, Jim was delegated to sort it out. In the event, we paid $1 million to get out.'

The band signed a new deal with Capitol Records on 26 October, with the album in production, *The Works*, to be that label's first release. Brian also signed a solo deal with them for the promotion and distribution of Star Fleet Project and any future solo plans.

Some of the original ideas for the new album were based on the book *The Hotel New Hampshire*, which they had all read, but as work progressed the band realised the music wasn't right for a film, and thought they might record two albums, a Queen album and the film soundtrack.

But it wasn't to be; finally, and regretfully, they pulled out of the film project to concentrate on finishing their own album. They were all so enthusiastic and excited about it that they put everything into it, inspiring its title, *The Works*. One track that had been written for the New Hampshire film remained, 'Keep Passing The Open Windows', a phrase used throughout the book as words of encouragement in bad times.

Back in the spring of that year Jim Beach and Gerry Stickells had flown to Brazil to negotiate another Queen tour in South America, fuelling rumours that the band were all mad. They even booked six gigs at five venues – all stadiums – with an estimated audience of 700,000 people. One of those venues was Maracana, the largest stadium in the world, holding 206,000 people, which had been the one place they couldn't use on their first time round in South America. But the venture was beset with problems revolving around promoters, money and equipment right from the start – problems that even the well-oiled and efficient Queen machine couldn't cope with. In the autumn, the entire tour was cancelled.

Meanwhile, in North America, *The Game* was the first Queen album to be released on the new compact disc format in mid-September.

On 24 October 1983, Brian's first solo single was released in the UK. The track was 'Star Fleet', from the jam session with his friends in Los Angeles, and as such it was released under the name Brian May and Friends. It wasn't very successful, entering the UK charts at number sixty-five. October 31 saw the UK release of the rest of the tracks recorded by Brian May and Friends, which was the Star Fleet Project, a mini-album of three tracks – the title track, Brian's track 'Let Me Out' and the jam session they had recorded, now titled 'BluesBreaker', and dedicated to Brian's hero, EC, Eric Clapton. Most members of the British press either ignored it, or criticised it, but the reviewer in heavy metal magazine *Kerrang!* probably spoke for many fans when he wrote: 'BluesBreaker' is on side two, and here we find the real jam. This is something of an epic, with each of the participants digging deep down into their collective musical vocabularies to produce an extended repartee that is a must for all fans of the blues. This could have been awful, but instead it's an extremely enjoyable interlude for Brian May, and anyone who cares to join in. I just hope that Queen let him back in now.'

The mini-album reached number one in the British Heavy Metal chart, and later became a collector's item for guitarists worldwide. It was released by Capitol Records in the USA the following day, their first Queen-related release.

Work on the new album was progressing so well that they all decided to take a short break back in the UK, to spend time with their families. John took the opportunity to spend another day jamming with John McEnroe and Vitas Gerulaitis, as both tennis players were in London for a tournament. It was obvious that McEnroe was really a frustrated guitarist – maybe his first swipes with a tennis racket had been when he was using it as a makeshift guitar . . . But everyone involved enjoyed the session, although this time none of it was committed to tape.

On 20 November Brian was involved with London's Capital Radio in something called the Rock School. The idea was that top musicians demonstrated before an audience how they played their instrument and the techniques and equipment they used. Brian took the stage at the Duke of York theatre with two guitarists chosen by Capital from the many who had applied to be a part of the class. He showed the audience and those on stage with him the tricky technique of playing with a sixpence, and he explained how and why he used the

BACK INTO ACTION

AC30 amplifiers, which few people still used, and how he achieved the strange and wonderful noises from his instrument. He also gave a rendition of 'Love Of My Life'. It went out live on Capital and made an informative and interesting class.

Queen had decided that the first single release from the new album was to be a track called 'Radio Ga Ga'. Written by Roger, the song was inspired by his young son Felix, who had one day commented, on hearing something he didn't like on the radio, that it was all 'radio ka ka' – 'ka ka' being a term he usually used to describe something he might find in a toilet bowl. But Roger amended it slightly, thinking that it was quite possible the radio stations wouldn't be able to play 'Radio Ka-Ka'. They all wanted an epic video to accompany the new track and were keen to work with director David Mallett. They had discussed using some of the footage from the film *Metropolis*, for which Freddie had been writing a song, and they bought the rights to certain scenes of that film directly from the German government. Another idea was more ambitious, needing about 500 people to make it work. The director approached the Queen fan club and asked them to provide the extras – it was easier and cheaper to use fans, and the fans loved it. There were, however, only four days in which to recruit them.

Queen fans were known to be loyal, though, and at 10.30 a.m. on 23 November 500 of them arrived at Shepperton Studios. They all put on white boiler suits, which were then sprayed with silver paint. Then they assembled in regimental rows to await instructions and the arrival of the band. They had to stand in line, heads bowed, for a whole day, under hot lights, with just a short break for lunch. During the chorus of the track they had to clap their hands in time with the band members, who were on a raised stage in front of them. The crowd were great and picked up the idea quickly – it was the band who kept getting it wrong. The filming finished at about midnight. When it was finally completed and edited it was one of the most ambitious and expensive videos Queen had ever made – it even featured clips from a few of the band's previous videos in a 'picture book' sequence – and cost more than £110,000.

John and Veronica Deacon's fourth child was born on 13 December – a boy they called Joshua. And it was the last event in what had been a very quiet Queen year.

In January 1984, Freddie flew out to Munich to do some more work on his solo project. He settled himself into his accustomed rooms at the Arabella Haus and began work with Mack at the Musicland studio. His own ideas had been demanding expression for some time, but they were ideas he knew he couldn't have used within Queen. He had confessed to being an incurable romantic, and the songs he was working on for the solo album were mainly love songs and ballads.

'Radio Ga Ga' was released on 23 January 1984 by EMI with a non-album track, 'I Go Crazy', as the B-side. It was the first Queen single to carry a personal catalogue number – Queen 1 – and was also the first Queen product to be released in the relatively new 'cassette single' format. It went straight into the UK chart at number four. Publicity for the single included a phone-in where fans dialled to hear a song, and the record company also took advertising space on the sides of London buses.

The press reaction was indifferent. NME were predictably sniffy: 'Displays a lack of substance, intention, cohesion or spirit. Arrogant nonsense, it quite upset my afternoon', while *Record Mirror* were not much more complimentary: 'After a long absence Queen come bouncing back. All we're going to hear from our radios for the next few weeks is 'Radio Ga Ga, Radio Goo Goo'.

On 3 February the band flew out to Italy to perform at the annual song festival in San Remo. Queen had never played in Italy in all their years of touring, and the excitement of the locals was running high on their arrival. The festival was like a huge version of *Top Of*

BACK INTO ACTION

The Pops, with many bands performing one song each. Queen were the main band of the evening and played 'Radio Ga Ga' for 2,000 screaming Italians.

Four days later, Capitol Records released 'Radio Ga Ga' as their first Queen single. Compared to the last few releases from the band, it was reasonably successful, clocking up thirteen weeks in the chart and climbing to number sixteen.

As plans were being discussed for a 1984 tour to promote the forthcoming album, ideas were tossed around about new places to perform. The band wanted to play a gig in the Vatican in Rome. Permission was sought and, at first, not refused outright, but physical problems manifested themselves. No motor vehicles were allowed inside the city, which would mean the crew driving the trucks up to the wall and then humping in the gear manually, and the provision of power was anything but straightforward. It was soon felt that maybe it wasn't such a great idea after all – so everyone breathed a sigh of relief when the Pope refused permission.

The Works was released in the States by Capitol Records on 24 February. Brian says: 'In spite of an enthusiastic start with the new company, *The Works* did, if anything, worse than *Hot Space* overall in the USA. But this must be balanced against the fact that Freddie was so depressed about the Elektra situation, it was doubtful if he ever would have agreed to make the album at all.'

The UK release followed on EMI on 27 February. It was Queen's thirteenth album, but unlucky it certainly wasn't: *The Works* entered the UK album chart at an impressive number two. Its cover was by legendary Hollywood photographer George Hurrell, who, in his time, had taken pictures of all the Hollywood greats, including Marilyn Monroe, and whose art lay in retouching them to perfection by hand.

The music press reaction was a surprise to everyone especially the band. 'The comfortable yet demanding 'Radio Ga Ga' is brought down to earth by the hot and oily 'Tear It Up', with its catscratch fever guitar. Another jewel in the crown,' *Record Mirror* said. 'It's all there I can assure you: spurious social comment in 'Machines', slight Fred ballad via 'Is This The World We Created', and even a nip of the old Brian May metal with the excellent 'Hammer To Fall',' *Sounds* gushed.

'Radio Ga Ga' stayed at number two in the singles charts in the UK but reached number one in nineteen other countries.

Brian had a little spare time on his hands at this point, and so agreed to help his good friend, Manfred Mann vocalist Chris Thompson, on his new album. Brian played on a beautiful track called 'Shift In The Wind', which was released as a single, all proceeds of which were donated to the Save The Children Fund.

The follow-up single to 'Ga Ga' was to be 'I Want To Break Free' and the band again recruited director David Mallett to make the video. The first day of filming took place at a new studio called Limehouse in London's newly refurbished Docklands on 22 March. At short notice again, the fan club provided 400 extras, who this time wore black boiler suits and miners' helmets. The shoot took place in a massive warehouse next to the main studios, which was freezing, but the extras played their parts well, surrounding the band and moving down steps en masse on cue. The next day the band went into a smaller studio in Battersea to film the main part of the video, which involved them all dressing as women. The idea came from Roger's girlfriend Dominique: she had suggested they do a spoof of the long-running British soap opera *Coronation Street*, and each member of the band was to portray a character. When Freddie appeared, everyone cracked up. He was wearing black fishnet stockings, a pink skin-tight 'skinny rib' jumper and the shortest of leather miniskirts, plus black wig and make-up. But he still kept his moustache! He came out of the dressing room in six-inch heels too but found he couldn't walk down the stairs in them so swapped them for two-inch ones. Roger was beautifully made up as a teenage schoolgirl – he even shaved his legs, as the cuts testified. John was the grandma, make-up ageing him to somewhere around eighty. Then Brian appeared – in nightgown, face cream, hair rollers and fluffy rabbit slippers.

There was more filming to be done to complete the video, but it didn't involve Roger or John, so on 24 March the two of them embarked on a short but strenuous promotional tour of the Far East and Australia to plug the new album. They started off in Japan on 25 March with the first of six interviews a day, remaining in Tokyo until 30 March, when they flew to Seoul, in Korea. None of Queen had visited South Korea, and their welcome was warm and enthusiastic. They appeared on television live – a disconcerting experience as they were surrounded by a crowd of interviewers, only one of whom spoke any English, and that haltingly. Questions were fired at them and they were handed the microphone to reply. Their every word was met with sounds that they found uncannily like sheep bleating, which they discovered afterwards was the Korean word for yes.

They arrived in Sydney, Australia, on 2 April for more press and TV interviews, then on to Melbourne on the 5th. They had one free day in Australia, and while John slept or did nothing, Roger and Crystal, his personal assistant, hired a seaplane to visit a small, exclusive restaurant that could only be reached by that mode of transport.

All in all, John and Roger covered 112 interviews in just sixteen days and were exhausted after they had finished, so much so that they both flew to Spain for a holiday.

On 5 April, while Roger and John were still away, Freddie went into the film studios to finish the video for 'Break Free'. He wanted to re-create Debussy's *L'Après-midi d'unfaune*, the ballet made famous by Nijinsky and rehearsed for some time with the Royal Ballet *corps de ballet*, before going back to film at Limehouse. But firstly, he shaved off his moustache, much to the delight of most of his fans.

The section with the ballet took a full day to film, and yet only occupied a forty-five-second slot in the finished video.

When completed, 'Break Free' was the most outrageous video they had ever made, and the most expensive, even topping the cost of 'Ga Ga'. But the band's critics were quick to find supposed fault: the video was meant to be funny but the press called them 'transvestites', 'blatant homosexuals' and even accused them of corrupting their young fans.

The band and their fans, however, loved it. Roger says: 'We had done some really serious, epic videos in the past, and we just thought it was time we had some fun. We wanted people to know that we didn't take ourselves too seriously, that we could still laugh at ourselves. I think we proved that.'

'I Want To Break Free', the band's twenty-fourth single, was released on 2 April with 'Machines – Back To Humans' on the B-side. EMI's marketing ploy was to release the single in no less than six different covers, the four seven-inch singles featuring individual photos of the band, and two twelve-inch singles with the entire band on the cover: true fans bought all six. *Record Mirror* described the single as 'A big, fat dud', but the fans loved it, and it reached number three in the UK charts and was a huge success in every European country, making it to number one in some – as well as being a smash in the relatively new South American market, where it became an anthem for freedom. In the USA the B-side was an instrumental version of 'Machines', which has since become a collector's item.

In late April 1984, Freddie was approached by *Vogue* magazine to appear in an issue with various other famous faces, in an article they were doing featuring diamonds. They wanted him to pose wearing a diamond stud. He agreed to the photo session, as it was something

BACK INTO ACTION

new for him, and of course he loved diamonds. The photos were taken in Munich and appeared in the June 1984 issue. The diamond stud he was wearing was valued at several thousand pounds, but as it was so small it wasn't easy to see what he was supposed to be modelling.

After *Vogue*, Freddie stayed in Munich to continue work on his solo project, which was taking him much longer than he had first anticipated. Being a perfectionist didn't help: he was determined that it was going to be faultless.

Meanwhile, since Billy Squier was in London working on his new album, Brian popped into Battery Studios in late April to play guitar on the track '(Another) 1984', for the forthcoming *Signs Of Life*, and Roger flew out to Montreux to finish work on his second solo album. He had already scrapped a lot of the original material and rewritten several other songs for it, but it was finally getting close to completion.

Switzerland was also the setting for the Golden Rose pop festival, at which Queen were asked to perform. It was an event in which many top bands were invited to participate, although none of them ever played live. They were asked to mime to backing tracks to make things easier for 'everyone concerned': meaning no equipment, apart from drum kits and backline amps, would need to be moved between bands. The festival took place on 12 May and was filmed and recorded, to be televised throughout Europe at a later date. Queen did four numbers – 'Radio Ga Ga', 'Tear It Up', 'It's A Hard Life' and 'I Want To Break Free'. None of the band had ever liked miming to playbacks but realised this time that it would make their life easier.

After the festival, Freddie flew back to Munich to get on with his album. He made close friends in the city and spent many nights at the Henderson's club: a favourite haunt of the rich and famous. On one night in late May, he got involved in late-night drunken revelry with a few friends, which resulted in him taking a bad fall and tearing the ligaments in his leg. He ended up in a plaster cast from toe to hip for three weeks, able to do very little for himself.

On 14 May, EMI chose to release *The Works* as the first of the Queen back catalogue on compact disc, while 4 June saw the release of Roger's fourth solo single in Britain, a track called 'Man On Fire' taken from his forthcoming album. He decided, with the help of director Tim Pope, to make his first promo video as a solo artist. Unfortunately, they included in it some footage of a burning building, which, earlier in the video, had been occupied by a little girl. As the film didn't show her getting out of the building before it burst into flames, the video was banned by MTV.

Moreover, the single, which reached no higher than sixty-six in the UK chart, was reviewed by few of the music papers, most of them choosing to ignore its existence. Even those who did acknowledge it were not flattering. *No. 1* said: 'This ghastly song chucks Meatloaf and Springsteen into the blender and emerges with a messy spread. Nasty.' *Sounds* were equally caustic: 'He can write the songs, but he can't sing them like Freddie does. Which is why Queen get the hits.'

On 25 June Roger's solo album, *Strange Frontier*, was finally released in the UK. It featured a couple of tracks written by other artists, namely 'Racing In The Streets', a Springsteen song, and Bob Dylan's 'Masters Of War'. In content the album was very 'anti-nuclear' and Roger's lyrics reflected his strong views. But the album failed to climb higher than number thirty in the charts. Sounds described it as 'The product of a talented guy with no reason to do anything ever again. Empty.' The album was released later in the USA and Japan.

Queen had often been nominated for many of the music awards that abounded, but hadn't received any for some time, until 28 June.

BACK INTO ACTION

At a celebrity dinner they were awarded a Silver Clef by the Nordoff Robbins Music Therapy charity. The charity used music to help children and adults living with disabilities or life-limiting illness and gave Queen the award for their 'Outstanding Contribution to British Music'.

Roger released another single from *Strange Frontier* on 30 July – the title track. ('Explodes into life and gives Roger the chance to show off a big rock voice', said *Sounds*.) He again decided he wanted to make a video and flew to Los Angeles to work with director George Bloom. The idea was to base it on the cult James Dean film *Rebel Without A Cause* (1955), and they took a full crew down to the cliffs of Malibu, the location of the Dean film. Roger was filmed in a race like that seen in *Rebel*, speeding towards the cliff top and certain disaster for one of the two rivals.

Over the previous few months Guild Guitars in New York had been working on a replica of Brian's Red Special, for sale commercially, and Brian had been closely involved in all aspects of the work. He regularly visited the factory to check on progress and make sure they were getting it right – he was adamant that he wouldn't give his name to a product that was in any way inferior. The pickups for the new model were specially produced by DiMarzio and named after Brian. They were to be made available separately from the Guild model, to enable guitarists to convert or adapt their own instruments. The Guild copy was launched in Chicago in late June 1984, as the BHMl. Brian was really pleased with the finished instrument and attended the launch party, at which Guild gave him one of the very first copies. Brian regularly used the guitar on stage and in the studios. But the relationship with Guild was short-lived. The company sold few of the instruments, as it was on sale at £1,200 – an exceptional amount for an electric guitar of any calibre. They decided to make several alterations to it, ostensibly to improve it, but mainly to try to lower the price to one at which they could feasibly sell it. Brian was told of the changes, with which he strongly disagreed. However, Guild insisted, and Brian withdrew his support of the instrument, terminating the agreement, and halting the production of the BHMl.

CHAPTER 18

CONTROVERSY REIGNS

IN MAY 1984 QUEEN ANNOUNCED THE DATES FOR THEIR FORTHCOMING European tour, beginning in August and taking them through to the end of September. For many years Hazel Feldman, the head of business entertainment at the Sun City Superbowl, a multiracial venue in South Africa, had been trying to persuade Queen to play there. In July 1984 the band announced that at last they felt the time was right and accepted the offer. They would be going to South Africa after the European tour had finished. The announcement alone caused a stir among the press and the Musicians Union, and several anti-apartheid groups throughout the UK and Europe. Brian says: 'We had heard so much about South Africa, about the troubles there, but we had also heard a lot about Sun City, and we wanted to go and see it all for ourselves.'

Their twenty-fifth single, 'It's A Hard Life', was released on 16 July. The video was made by Tim Pope in Munich and featured the band at a masquerade ball. Freddie wore a weird red off-the-shoulder outfit with a line of huge eyes snaking down the front, and Brian used a guitar, specially made for the video, with a skull-shaped body and a long, bone-shaped neck. It was a small instrument, and impossible to play, but Brian paid over £1,000 for it to be made. But, when the video was finished, it was far from being one of the band's favourites. It had taken ages to film, and Roger, John and Brian were all dressed in tight, heavy costumes with ruffles and brocade and wearing thick make-up. It appeared to them to be a Freddie-showcase with them as extras. But after some lightweight leg-pulling about Freddie dressing up as a giant prawn, they let it pass and looked ahead to the forthcoming tour.

The band flew out to Brussels on 23 August, as the European tour was due to start the following day at the Forest Nationale. For this tour they had procured the talents of keyboard player Spike Edney, who had in the past played extensively with The Boomtown Rats and various other top bands. The band were all pleasantly surprised when during 'Radio Ga Ga' the entire audience raised their hands and emulated the handclaps that had featured in the video.

The gig that night was filmed as they wanted to use parts of it in the video for their next single, hard rocker 'Hammer To Fall'. They invited members of the audience back the following day to complete the video shoot, with David Mallett directing.

Brussels was used almost as a warm-up gig for the rest of the tour, as Queen knew they would always get a great reception at that venue. The stage backdrop was based on Fritz Lang's film *Metropolis*. It had steps either side of the drum riser linking a catwalk behind Roger. Two enormous cogwheels were hung at the back, both of which turned towards the end of the show (these were worked by hand from behind the backdrop, as it was felt that mechanical wheels might prove less reliable). The lighting rig covered the entire stage, top and sides, and each bank of lights was worked by computer to turn, tip and swivel during the set, while a massive column of lights flashed at the back between the cogs.

After Brussels they flew back to the UK on the 26th in preparation for the short hop over to Dublin, their first visit to Eire since 1979. The tickets for the shows in Britain had gone on sale and sold

CONTROVERSY REIGNS

out in record time; box offices and ticket agents countrywide were declaring phenomenal sales just hours after opening.

At the same time as the band were breaking box office records, the BBC held a twenty-four-hour rock marathon, which opened with the video for 'Bohemian Rhapsody'. One of the 'events' was a phone-in for viewers to vote for their all-time favourite live shows: the winner by a substantial margin was Queen live at the Hammersmith Odeon, Christmas 1975. But the BBC showed only twenty minutes of the gig, much to the viewers' disappointment.

After three days at the Birmingham National Exhibition Centre, Queen played their first night in London at the Wembley Arena on 4 September. During the first encore Freddie walked on stage dressed in his 'Break Free' outfit, complete with false breasts, which caused good-natured uproar.

After the gig at Wembley on 5 September, Freddie hosted a late-night birthday party at Xenon nightclub in London. As usual, it was well attended by the show-business fraternity, many of whom had been at the gig earlier in the evening. Most of them didn't arrive until after midnight, and many didn't leave until dawn. But the band had planned things well and took the next day off, so had plenty of time to recover.

On 10 September, EMI released the twenty-sixth Queen single, 'Hammer To Fall'. The papers, for once, were impressed. 'Brian May has plunged Queen's fingers back into the rock and roll mains socket and charged up glorious memories of the band pre-76', said *Kerrang!*, while *Melody Maker* called it 'A very good pop rock song'.

Also released that day was Freddie's first solo single, the track he had co-written with Georgio Moroder for *Metropolis*, 'Love Kills'. It was released in the USA the following day.

September 10 also saw the release of Queen's first full-length concert video, the Montreal film *We Will Rock You*. The public loved it – at last, Queen live in your living room! It sold so well that it entered the UK video chart at number one.

The tour continued in Dortmund on 12 September, and during that tour Queen had no fewer than nine albums in the UK Top 200, something which few other bands could emulate. September 21 was the day that the *We Will Rock You* film, and *The Works EP*, began a six-month, late-night cinema tour in the UK, opening at the ABC Cinema in London's Edgware Road.

The tour went well until Hannover, on 22 September, when Freddie slipped on the steps on stage during 'Hammer To Fall', landing awkwardly and again damaging the ligaments in his knee. He couldn't get up, and one of the road crew had to run on and help him to the piano stool, where he remained to perform three more songs, before the pain forced him to stop. He was taken to hospital immediately after the show and the leg was X-rayed, strapped up and he was told to rest it completely. Not being one to heed doctors' advice, he was back on stage in Berlin on the 24th, albeit moving a little more slowly and cautiously than usual.

The European section of that tour finished at the Vienna Stadhalle on 30 September, and Queen flew back to the UK for a couple of days, then off to Bophuthatswana in South Africa for their historic string of shows there. The band had agreed to play twelve dates at the Sun City Superbowl, for which tickets had sold out in one day – the fastest ever for that venue. Fifteen minutes into the gig on the third night, disaster struck when Freddie's voice gave out. They managed to finish, but it was hard on Freddie, who was in great pain. He'd been having trouble with his throat before the show, but thought it was just a mild strain and ignored it. Because Sun City's own medical staff were unqualified to treat throat problems, a specialist had to be flown in to examine Freddie and once again he was told that absolute rest was the only answer. It was a recurrence of the same problem that had dogged him in the USA some years before, aggravated by the dry air of Bophuthatswana. Queen had to cancel the next two nights, which cost them and the Superbowl dearly. Brian was upset at having to cancel and during the enforced break he decided to get outside the insular Sun City complex to see more of South African life.

In Soweto, just outside Johannesburg, an annual Black African Awards Show was held in October, specifically to honour black musicians. The organisers approached Brian and asked if he would like to attend and present several of the awards. He was more than happy to accept, but the authorities at Sun City were nervous about the idea: there was a safety risk involved in Brian travelling anywhere outside the complex, and they also felt it might jeopardise the subsequent dates, which still stood. But Brian had made up his mind and travelled to Soweto, accompanied by Jim Beach.

It was a warm night but pouring with rain. The stage was set up in an open field, with thousands of spectators sitting or standing, watching the proceedings. The atmosphere was moving, deeply felt by Brian as he presented the awards. The winner was Margaret Singamo, who was confined to a wheelchair, the original lead in the hit musical *Ipi Tombi*. 'It was quite amazing,' said Brian. 'The whole atmosphere, the warmth, the great friendliness of the people. You could feel it, it was almost a tangible thing. It was a night I will never forget. I promised those people that one day, Queen would go back to Soweto and play the stadium for them.'

Freddie eventually recovered enough to continue, and the final six dates at Sun City went ahead as planned. While they were there, they decided they wanted to do something to help underprivileged children and were told about the Kutlawamong School for deaf and blind children in Bophuthatswana. It had been founded several years earlier but struggled on a shoestring to help and educate children with disabilities. After discussions with EMI South Africa and the school patrons, Queen decided to release a special live album in South Africa, all royalties from which would go directly to the school. EMI agreed to donate their own cut from the album, too. The money that was raised enabled them to build a new wing on the school, which was badly needed because of overcrowding since the school never turned anyone away. Money continues to be donated each time a copy of the album is sold.

When Queen got back to England, they were in serious trouble with the Musicians' Union. South Africa was the one place in the world that they banned their members from playing and Queen had contravened all the Union's guidelines and edicts. Brian attended a meeting of the MU General Committee where he gave a lengthy speech about the band's reasons for the trip and what they felt they achieved there. 'I told them we believed that we achieved more in the fight against apartheid by going, and insisting on mixed audiences, than by staying away; that we had been able and willing to have our anti-apartheid views printed in the South African press [unusual at that time], that we had been able to give moral support to many minority groups by being there, and had been praised for our courage in going there by all who were trying to break down the barriers, and that if we were to refuse to play to people suffering under a government we didn't approve of, there would be very few places we could go (maybe not even Britain). Finally, I upheld our belief that music should transcend all barriers, unfettered by race or politics.

'This was a view which ran against much of the popular opinion whipped up by the press at that time, but many artists and musicians have since expressed similar ideas (including Cliff Richard and Paul Simon). Thankfully the world is, overall, taking a more considered view.'

Brian received a standing ovation from the members present for his speech, but the Committee were unmoved and Queen were heavily fined. The band agreed to pay only on the condition that the money would be donated to a worthy charity and didn't find its way into the coffers of the Union. The problems didn't end there. The trip also resulted in the band's being included on the United Nations blacklist of organisations and musicians who had visited South Africa. Some people complained about the band's visit after the event, but many more stood by them and even supported them. Queen didn't regret going – it had been a great experience – but they were saddened to be banned from visiting South Africa again unless the situation there changed dramatically. The promise to play in Soweto could not be fulfilled.

After South Africa, Freddie flew back to Munich, which had become a second home to him, to continue work on his solo album.

Meanwhile, Henry Crallan, who for some time had been the keyboard player for the Kevin Ayers band, offered John a partnership in a commercial twenty-four-track recording studio in London's East End. It was a type of project John had not previously considered, but, as ever financially astute, he realised it could be a good investment. The studio opened for business the following spring.

On 19 November, Queen released their first video EP. *The Works Video EP* featured the four videos they'd made for the singles released from the album of the same name. The video had previously only been shown at cinemas, supporting *We Will Rock You*.

Queen had never released a single specifically for Christmas, as many other bands had, but in 1984 they decided, rather tongue-in-cheek, to do so. Brian, John and Roger all went into Sarm Studios in London in early November to start work on it, then Roger and Brian flew out with the tapes to join Freddie in Munich to complete it. The single, the band's twenty-seventh, was released on 26 November, entitled 'Thank God It's Christmas'. It wasn't a resounding success, only getting to number twenty-one in the charts, but it became something of a collector's item, for the simple reason it never appeared on any Queen album, only on a compilation Christmas album.

By December 1984 Queen had done something they had never done before and released every track off an album as single A- and B-sides. It didn't go down well with their critics, who accused them of cashing in on fans' loyalty by expecting them to buy all the singles as well as the album.

CHAPTER 19

FROM RIO TO HISTORY

GERRY STICKELLS, QUEEN'S LONG-TIME TOUR MANAGER, NOT ONLY coped with Queen but other huge events and bands as well. One of them was an enormous festival planned to take place in January 1985 in Rio de Janeiro. It was billed as 'Rock In Rio' and many of the world's top bands were taking part over an eight-day period including ACDC, Def Leppard, Iron Maiden, Yes, James Taylor, George Benson and Ozzy Osbourne – and Queen, due to their previous successful tours of South America, were asked to headline the event, which was to be the biggest rock festival ever held in the world. The band, of course, agreed as, even though they'd had some traumatic experiences during their own tours there, they considered this festival just too good, and too big, to miss. They left for Rio on 6 January 1985, Freddie having to travel via Paris from Munich due to bad weather. The festival site, the Barra da Tijuca, in Rio, was specially built and could hold an incredible, record-breaking 250,000 people. The Brazilian television station, Globo, had set up cameras to televise the festival across South America.

It was a colossal event, with local bands appearing alongside the top names. Queen closed the show on the first night, walking on stage at 2 a.m. on 12 January. They couldn't believe the sight that greeted them – they had played to huge audiences before, but never this big. The crowd stretched from the front of the stage way back as far as the eye could see. Their reception was deafening, and the audience was with them all the way, singing along and clapping – until the encore. Freddie came back on stage in the top half of his 'Break Free' outfit; tight jumper, false boobs and wig, and the audience started to throw rubbish – bottles, cans and stones – at the stage. Freddie whipped off the offending items, laughed uproariously, and thought no more of it for the rest of the encore, which was free of incident. The band left the stage in triumph. After the show the local people explained to the band that 'Break Free' had become a liberation anthem for them, a message against dictatorship. They couldn't bear to see it mocked in that way.

It also didn't help when one of the security guards at the front of the stage had been rather heavy-handed with one or two of the excited revellers during Queen's set. The crowds at the front had witnessed the violence and began to throw missiles at the guards, which was when people further back had hurled things at the stage. Luckily no one was hurt but a distorted version of the incident appeared in the British press.

On the night of the 12th, EMI Records held a huge party for the Rio artists at the Copacabana Beach Hotel. Most of the famous faces who were part of the festival attended, and the party was shown on live television all over South America. Many guests ended up jumping into the large hotel pool fully clothed, including Brian (who had been the first in). A minor altercation took place between Freddie and Rod Stewart – both volatile characters and sitting at opposite ends of the party area, when they found out that the other was there. Neither would walk over to say hello to the other, and a few bad-tempered comments were passed, but nothing serious, and they laughed about it afterwards.

On the beautiful sandy beach directly outside the Copacabana, hundreds of Queen fans had gathered to hold their own celebration party. They spelt out 'Queen' in the sand using 1,500 candles. When Brian was told, he left the glittering celebrity affair to join the fans on the beach for a while and have some fun with them. Meanwhile, back in the UK, the press focused on the 'near riot' that had supposedly been caused by Freddie's 'boobs', and not the fact that Queen had just headlined the world's biggest ever rock festival.

On 19 January, again at two in the morning, Queen took the stage as the closing act for the festival. The only thing that had marred it was the weather: it had rained almost constantly for eight days, after which the festival site looked more like a muddy swamp than a field. Oh, and the smell. According to those who were there, it was an all-pervading stench: the toilet facilities for 250,000 people left a lot to be desired.

Negotiations started directly after the festival for Queen to purchase from Globo Television the rights to their section of the show, with the possibility of releasing it on video at a later date. Queen could do no wrong in South America, and the rights were quickly granted – many other bands at the festival had made similar requests but were refused.

John had always been quite careful with his choice of cars, mostly settling for Volvos, but after Rio he decided to treat himself to a Porsche. Shortly after buying it he went to see Phil Collins at the Albert Hall and joined him for a few drinks after the show. He was stopped for speeding later that night in The Mall, notorious for police vigilance and justifiably so as it is the 'front drive' for Buckingham Palace. He was breathalysed, failed, fined £150 and banned from driving for twelve months. Needless to say, he sold the Porsche.

Brian was approached in mid-February and asked to contribute a chapter to an Oxford University Press publication called *The Guitar Teacher's Handbook*. The book featured chapters dedicated to different guitar skills – classical, folk, flamenco, jazz and rock. Brian was asked to write a piece concerned with the teaching of electric guitar in schools and colleges, a relatively new phenomenon, as many of the 'old school' guitar teachers had never considered the electric instrument worthy of serious study.

On 25 February, Brian helmed a two-hour special show at London's Capital Radio. The original idea was that he would sit in as guest DJ but that someone else would cue up the records and push the right buttons. He insisted on being let loose on the controls. The result was a creditable radio show. His mistakes seemed to add to his enjoyment and it came across as fun. He played a selection of his own favourite songs and received a good review from veteran DJ Alan Freeman.

In early 1985 the UK Music Video Awards were held for videos released during the past year. Queen were honoured in two categories: *The Works Video EP* won a highly commended prize for best compilation and 'Radio Ga Ga' was voted best promotional video.

On his travels, Roger had met Jimmy Nail, a Geordie actor playing Oz in the very popular British TV series *Auf Wiedersehen, Pet*. Jimmy wanted to make a single and asked Roger if he would produce it for him, which he agreed to do, along with David Richards. The song was the oldie 'Love Don't Live Here Anymore', which Jimmy sang well, surprising many people with his heretofore unrecognised talent. Roger arranged it and played drums, so when Jimmy wanted to make a video, he agreed to appear in that as the drummer too. Roger was trying to build up the production side of his career, in partnership with David Richards, so when he was asked by Virgin if he and David would produce one of their new signings, Scottish band Sideway Look, he agreed and started work with them in March 1985. But they hadn't got very far when Virgin dropped the project. Roger was rightly peeved, as he thought the work they had done was good and worthy of release, but the record company held the purse strings and the recording was cancelled. Roger went on to produce 'Loving You', by ex-Undertones singer Feargal Sharkey, and played drums on the

Roger Daltrey track 'Under A Raging Moon', featuring Roger and seven other drummers, and dedicated to the late Keith Moon.

Although Freddie spent a lot of time in Munich, he flew to London frequently, and was a regular on the London club scene, at the Embassy Club, Xenon and Heaven. He had a large circle of friends and it wasn't unusual for them still to be drinking and dancing into the early morning. It was during one such night at Heaven in March that Freddie met Jim Hutton, an Irish men's hairdresser working at London's Savoy Hotel. They had briefly met some years before, but Jim had told Freddie, quite bluntly, to 'fuck off'. This time, however, they hit it off and became friends.

From 2 to 4 April, Freddie took over London's Limehouse Studios to make a video for his forthcoming single 'I Was Born To Love You' with director David Mallett. One of its strangest scenes was hundreds of women 'goose-stepping' towards and around the camera, all wearing red plastic shaped breastplates, black tights and high heels.

The band flew into Auckland on 5 April. They had never played in New Zealand and were excited by the prospect. They were met by a small crowd of anti-apartheid demonstrators when they arrived and found more outside their hotel.

During the few free days they had in New Zealand, Spike Edney received a phone call from Boomtown Rats vocalist Bob Geldof. Bob asked Spike if he would sound out Queen to see if they would be interested in an event he was trying to put together at London's Wembley Stadium, with all proceeds going to famine relief in Ethiopia. He didn't want to call the band direct if they weren't going to be interested. Spike asked Queen, and at first, they refused – it sounded to them like a pie in the sky idea that probably wouldn't get off the ground. But Spike told Geldof to call them direct and try his powers of persuasion. Bob phoned back and nagged them into saying that they might appear if the event materialised.

Back in the UK, Freddie's second solo single was released on 8

April, a track called 'I Was Born To Love You' taken from his long-awaited solo album, which, at last, was nearly ready for release. The B-side was non-album track 'Stop All The Fighting'. The single reached number eleven in the UK and was released in the USA later that month, but without chart success.

Queen's first concert in New Zealand was on 13 April at the Mount Smart Stadium in Auckland. The crowds were ecstatic, aside from another small group of anti-apartheid demonstrators outside the venue. The show was televised all over the country, and they were joined on stage for the encore of 'Jailhouse Rock' by Spandau Ballet's singer Tony Hadley, a keen Queen fan, who had flown over from Australia to see them.

They went on to Melbourne, Australia, on 16 April for the first of four nights at the Sports and Entertainments Centre. After two shows the band had a day off and, as Phil Collins was also in town and playing that night, they went to watch his show. Two nights later he repaid the compliment. But from the day they set foot in Australia, things started to go wrong. Within minutes of the band walking onto the stage the lights began to misbehave, before packing up halfway through the set. The sound wasn't too good either and, all in all, it was a dreadful night. Phil enjoyed the gig, though, and said afterwards in the dressing rooms that they'd played well despite the problems.

Next day they flew to Sydney for a short break before the beginning of a four-night stint at the Entertainments Centre there. Brian's wife Chrissie joined him, and the two of them flew up to the idyllic Heron Island, on the Great Barrier Reef. They spent their free days learning to scuba dive, which was by far the best way of seeing the amazing reef life. Brian got quite good at it, and by the end of that short holiday had qualified as a 'padi diver' by diving to 60 feet and passing the written exams.

The rest of the band spent their free time in Sydney, a city lively enough to keep them and their crew occupied. They decided one day to hire a pleasure cruiser, the *Matilda*, and take a trip round Sydney harbour. Of course, the boat had a well-stocked bar – this *was* Australia – which, during the course of the day, became seriously depleted. At one point, the band's sound engineer, Tony, was offered $100 if he would jump into the harbour from the boat. Sydney harbour has, as most people know, its quota of sharks but Tony wasn't going to let that bother him and, without a backward glance, he leapt overboard. He wasn't in any fit state to swim anywhere, and couldn't get back to the boat, so an SOS was sent out to the harbour police who were quickly on the scene to rescue him. But it proved an expensive jape. The rescue had held up a Russian trawler and the hydrofoil and hovercraft services; the statutory fine for delaying shipping in the harbour was then $5,000. No amount of pleading helped and Tony paid up – but was only $4,900 out of pocket, considering his $100 winnings.

The band played the first night of four at the Sydney Entertainments Centre on 25 April. Elton John was also in Australia, and his manager, John Reid, took Brian and John for an evening at the Sydney Opera House on the 27th while Roger, Freddie and Elton, who were good friends, enjoyed the Sydney nightlife.

Back in England on 29 April, Freddie's debut solo album was finally released on CBS Records. He called it *Mr Bad Guy*, the title of a track from the album which referred in its lyrics to himself. It was dubiously received by the press, many of whom were surprised at its content – a mixture of love songs and ballads with a touch of funk. It certainly wasn't what anyone had expected from the lead singer of a rock band, but, as Freddie said at the time, it was very 'him'.

Sounds were thoroughly unpleasant about it: 'This album is nothing more than a wimpy work-out of soft rock and dated disco.' But *Record Mirror* were more positive: 'Freddie has produced a diverse album filled with dextrous tunes that are infinitely more pleasurable than the last 17 Queen albums.'

Directly after Australia, where they had endured the highest rainfall in the country for 150 years, Queen flew into Japan for six shows and Brian spent time visiting the Aoyama Recording School to talk to pupils about the techniques and skills of guitar playing.

While they were in Japan, on 13 May, Picture Music in the UK released *Live In Rio*, the edited footage of the band's celebrated performance at the Rock In Rio Festival. It was an immediate success and went straight into the video chart at number one.

CHAPTER 20

LIVE AID

THE BAND ALL RETURNED TO THE UK ON 17 MAY – BUT NOT FOR LONG. Roger and John immediately took off for the Balearic island of Ibiza for some rest, while Freddie went back to Munich. He still spent a lot of his time there – he felt relaxed and happy in a city that had excellent nightlife and some of the closest friends he'd ever known, and it didn't do his tax situation any harm. But he loved London too, and was a regular 'commuter' between the two cities. He had also developed a close friendship with Jim Hutton and they were almost constant companions.

Freddie and Mary Austin were still great friends, but no longer shared a physical relationship; he had bought a flat for Mary near his own house, and she continued to be very much a part of his life, dealing with his day-to-day business affairs and the running of the house and its staff.

Meanwhile, lawyer Jim Beach held a meeting with Harvey Goldsmith, who was to promote Bob Geldof's proposed Wembley Stadium charity gig in aid of Ethiopia. Queen had now decided that they would like to appear; over the weeks they had been away, news had filtered through to them that the gig, now being billed as 'Live Aid, The Global Juke Box', was going ahead and a parallel gig was to be held simultaneously in Philadelphia.

At the start of the meeting Jim told Harvey that he wanted to discuss Queen's time-slot for the concert. Harvey hung his head and said, 'Not another band who wants to close the show.' All the bands approached to play had said yes, but they had all wanted to close the event – in other words, be what they considered the headliners. Queen had other ideas: they asked to go on at 6 p.m. Harvey agreed immediately.

Freddie had never been one to do interviews at any stage in the band's career; he was frequently quoted as saying he hated them. As he had a solo album out, however, he allowed himself to be persuaded into doing just one, an interview with DJ Simon Bates, to be broadcast in three parts on Radio One. His only proviso was that it be recorded at the band's offices in Notting Hill Gate.

Simon duly turned up on 22 June and was shown into a top-floor office, where he was joined a short time later by Freddie. The interview began promptly, after Simon had been supplied with a coffee, and Freddie a vodka and tonic. By the end – and nearly a bottle of Stolichnaya vodka later – Freddie was answering more questions and chatting more freely than he had in years, and the interview gave a wonderful insight into the man and his album – much to Simon's relief.

'Made In Heaven' was Freddie's third solo single in the UK and came out on 1 July with a non-album B-side, 'She Blows Hot And Cold'. He decided to make a completely outrageous video and, once again with the help of director David Mallett, his ideas slowly became reality. The film company built a replica of the Royal Opera House in a warehouse in north London (none of the film studios had high enough ceilings), and Freddie re-created excerpts from both *The Rite Of Spring*, the ballet by Stravinsky, and Dante's *Inferno*, using a troupe of barely clothed dancers and props including a 60-foot high rotating globe and tons of dried leaves. Unfortunately the excesses of the video didn't help to sell the single, and it only charted at fifty-seven. Meanwhile, in the USA, Columbia Records released Freddie's 'Living On My Own' single on 2 July. It peaked at eighty-five in the chart.

LIVE AID

On 10 July, Queen disappeared into the Shaw Theatre in King's Cross, London, for three days of intensive rehearsals for Live Aid. The event was going ahead as a 'Global Jukebox', and each band had been allotted twenty minutes. Queen spent hours arguing over which of their many hits to play. Finally, they decided on their set list: 'Bohemian Rhapsody', 'Radio Ga Ga', 'Hammer To Fall', 'Crazy Little Thing Called Love', 'We Will Rock You' and 'We Are The Champions'. To ensure they could fit them all in, they rehearsed them in shortened form. During rehearsals they had clocks set around the stage to hone their set down to the second. With just forty minutes to set up their entire show, they used several of their own crew, secure in the knowledge that their equipment would be working properly when they took to the stage – important, as they would get no soundcheck and no second chance. All the crews involved were working for free and helping out across all the bands, so as little time as possible was wasted changing equipment between acts.

Finally, the day of the show arrived: 13 July 1985. Wembley Stadium was packed and the weather, which had been dull and chilly for days, brightened into glorious sunshine. The event started at midday, with Status Quo appropriately belting out 'Rocking All Over The World', and flowed along beautifully without mishap or incident. The crowds received all the acts enthusiastically and the atmosphere was electric.

At 6.41 p.m., Queen took to the stage, one minute late... Not only was it prime time in the UK, but it was also when the show went live around the world, meaning they were one of the first bands seen by the audience watching the Philadelphia broadcast.

After Elton John's set, and just before the finale, Brian and Freddie took to the stage with their acoustic rendition of 'Is This The World We Created'. Freddie later remarked, 'It looks as if we wrote the song for this event – but we didn't, even though it seems to fit the bill.'

After the show Elton John rushed into the band's dressing room with the words 'You bastards . . . you stole the show!'

Live Aid was broadcast to over one billion people worldwide and made history that day. Queen secured their own place in history, as every media person, journalist, fan and critic unanimously agreed with Elton that they had stolen the show. Even Bob Geldof gave them that distinction in a later interview: 'Queen were absolutely the best band of the day. They played the best, had the best sound, used their time to the full. They understood the idea exactly, that it was a global jukebox. They just went and smashed one hit after another. It was the perfect stage for Freddie: the whole world. And he could ponce about on stage doing "We Are The Champions". How perfect could it get?' He went on record as saying Queen were 'the biggest band on the planet'.

Classic Rock magazine later said, 'The performance helped transform them into a wonderfully camp, sleek and ubiquitous rock band, and the biggest British live act of the 80s.'

Prior to Live Aid, the band had found themselves feeling slightly disillusioned with the way their lives and careers were going. In an interview with *Classic Rock*, Freddie explained, 'We were all forming a sort of rut. I wanted to get out of this last 10 years of what we were doing. It was so routine. It was like, go to the studio, do an album, go out on the road, go round the world and flog it to death, and by the time you came back it was time to do another album.'

But after Live Aid, they had a massive resurgence and were introduced to a new generation of fans, cementing their 'legendary' status and giving them renewed faith in their music and their relationship as a band. And almost before the dust of Live Aid had settled, the band were starting to think about new music and touring.

But normality soon resumed. Freddie flew back to Munich, and Brian started work on a proposed solo album. Roger was approached by Jason Bonham – son of Led Zeppelin drummer John Bonham – to produce an album for Virginia Wolf, his new band. Roger agreed and work began in Eel Pie Studios in London, moved on to Munich

LIVE AID

— and then the sunshine of Ibiza. Roger also found time to fly out to Mountain Studios to co-produce with David Richards a record by Camy Todorow. Camy was from East Berlin and had defected from East Germany to become a singer. Roger played the drums on the song too, a track called 'Bursting At The Seams'.

Elton John was recording at Sol Studios in London in early September, and John and Roger popped in to visit him during the sessions. They were asked to play on the album, and both contributed by playing on 'Too Young', which eventually appeared on Elton's album *Ice On Fire*, and another track, 'Angeline', which featured on his next album *Leather Jackets*.

Freddie's fourth solo single, 'Living On My Own', was released in the UK on 2 September — and three days later he held another of his infamous birthday parties. As he was still in Munich, he hired Henderson's, his favourite night club. The theme was to be a black and white drag ball and he paid several thousand pounds to have the club completely redecorated in black and white. He invited all his friends from Germany and England, paying for them to fly over just for the night and to be put up at the Munich Hilton Hotel. Everyone had to dress in drag so it was hard to tell, as people began arriving, who were men and who were women. The only male not dressed as a woman was Freddie himself. The small club was full to bursting with guests in all manner of outrageous outfits, and the whole thing was captured on film, as Freddie wanted to use some of it in a video for his latest solo single. He went back to the club the following day to shoot several sexy scenes, and the video was cut and edited. But his record company, CBS, banned it. They said it was too lewd and suggestive ever to be shown in Britain, as it featured men dressed rather convincingly as women — and Freddie diving through the fishnet-stocking-clad legs of a dancer, also a man!

Their appearance at Live Aid had given Queen the urge to perform live and record again, and plans were afoot for a 1986 European tour. It was to be an immense affair, and in late 1985, Gerry Stickells set the wheels in motion.

In September the band were approached by director Russell Mulcahy, a well-known promotional video director, who was making his first major feature film, and he wanted Queen to write and record some of the music. They initially agreed to provide at least two tracks, as long as one was used as the title track.

Filming had already begun and Russell gave them definite ideas about the type of music needed. *Highlander* was a strange story about an immortal man, his life over the 2,000 years he had so far lived and his subsequent meetings with other immortals to gain mastery and win 'the prize'. Queen went into the studios in September to begin work and quickly completed a track that they felt just had to be released as a single – and that had no bearing whatsoever on *Highlander*. The idea for 'One Vision' had come from Roger and was based on Martin Luther King, Jr. and his 'I have a dream' speech.

When it was released on 4 November, the band were slated, as the media immediately associated 'One Vision' with Live Aid. The aim of everybody who took part that day had been to raise as much money as possible in a common goal, to help the starving people of Ethiopia. The lyrics to 'One Vision' – 'One heart, one soul, just one solution' – were similar sentiments indeed, but those of a man whose own dreams had been voiced many years before. The media decided that Queen should have donated all the royalties of the song to Live Aid as, they said, it had been directly inspired by the event – and especially as the song had climbed to number seven in the UK chart. They completely ignored the fact that the Queen song 'Is This The World We Created', which featured at Live Aid, was earning money for the Save the Children Fund every day – and still is.

After deciding to release 'One Vision', Queen invited Rudi Dolezal and Hannes Rossacher, a director and producer team better known as the 'Torpedo Twins', into the Munich studios to film them at work and play, for a video to accompany the song. During editing, Rudi and Hannes cut two different versions, one for the seven-inch single, and another to go with the twelve-inch, which they called 'Extended Vision'. It was a light-hearted look at the band 'behind the scenes'.

Freddie was disinclined to get involved with very much outside Queen, and certainly not if the media were involved, but he agreed to attend 'Fashion Aid', a charity event on 5 November held at the Royal Albert Hall, with proceeds going to the Ethiopian Famine Appeal. He wore a suit made by David and Elizabeth Emmanuel – the designers responsible for the exquisite dress worn by Lady Diana Spencer for her wedding to the Prince of Wales. He was accompanied by stunning actress Jane Seymour who wore a wedding dress also designed by the Emmanuels, and they walked the catwalk as though it were a wedding aisle.

Dave Clarke was another of Freddie's close friends. He had been famous in the sixties as the singing drummer of his own band, The Dave Clark Five, and was now working on the stage musical *Time*, which was to star Cliff Richard, a mutual friend of his and Freddie's. Dave was responsible for writing all the music, and the songs that Cliff sang on stage were to be recorded by various other artists, to be released on an album. Dave asked Freddie to sing 'In My Defence'.

CBS records released Freddie's fifth solo single on 18 November, another track from *Mr Bad Guy* called 'Love Me Like There's No Tomorrow'. In an attempt to increase sales, the record company decided to offer the twelve-inch version of the previous single, 'Living On My Own', free with this single. Unfortunately, the ploy didn't work and the single failed to chart.

EMI, always with an eye for new marketing and packaging ideas and a nose for making money, decided to release a boxed set of all of Queen's albums. The box contained thirteen albums, including *The*

Works, but it did not include *Greatest Hits*. They also included a world map to show Queen's domination, which John hated – he thought it made them look like they were taking over. There was a discography, complete with glaring errors and a 'tour date' itinerary. The albums were re-sleeved in white with gold roman numerals, embossed with the famous Queen crest, packaged in a classy black box with gold lettering, and released on 2 December at the phenomenal price of £70.

But the fans bought it. EMI had included an album in that set which couldn't be bought anywhere else: *Complete Vision* featured B-sides to singles that had never appeared on albums, plus that dear old chestnut 'Thank God It's Christmas'.

One of the strangest things to happen in December 1985 was the inclusion of Queen's name on an obelisk erected in Antarctica by Greenpeace. Queen, along with many other bands, had donated a track, 'Is This The World We Created', to *Greenpeace – The Album*, to raise funds for Greenpeace's conservation work. All those involved in the album project were commemorated on the obelisk. Why, no one was quite sure – grateful though they were. After all, who on earth was going to *see* it?

All the controversy over Sun City was still having far-reaching effects, and in December, Queen were forced to make a full press statement to the effect that they had no intention of visiting South Africa again, were completely against apartheid and were not in any way a political band. Even though they had said all this once, it had apparently fallen on deaf ears. They were upset by having to state so categorically that they would never go back there, but it seemed the only way to silence the critics.

CHAPTER 21

A MAGIC YEAR

IN JANUARY 1986 THE BAND WERE INVOLVED IN INTENSIVE WORK ON the songs for *Highlander*. They had now agreed to provide the entire soundtrack to the film and release the songs as an album. Russell made available rough edits of the film and Queen set to work, inspired by the on-screen action. Driving home after seeing one particular episode, Brian wrote a song he called 'Who Wants To Live Forever?' He sang and hummed the idea into a small portable tape recorder, arriving home with an almost complete song.

Even though the work on the soundtrack album was time-consuming, the band members felt they needed to take an occasional break. Freddie sloped off to work on a song for a German movie, *Zabou*. 'Hold On' was co-written and sung as a duet with a friend of his, Jo Dare. He also squeezed in work with Billy Squier on his forthcoming album *Enough is Enough*, singing on 'Love Is The Hero' and co-writing another, 'Lady With The Tenor Sax'.

Roger wasn't idle either. He was approached by Birmingham-based rock band Magnum and asked to produce their new album. He and producer David Richards together produced the excellent *Vigilante*, with Roger also providing backing vocals on two tracks, 'Sometime Love' and 'When The Night Comes Down'.

Elsewhere, John had been friendly for some time with Errol Brown, lead singer with seventies chart-topping band Hot Chocolate, and when Errol began work on a solo album, he asked John to co-write a track with him, which became 'This Is Your Time'.

EMI and Capitol Records had both heard rough edits of the new Queen album, and both wanted different singles. They had supposedly done in-depth market research and knew just what the current sales on various singles were like and could usually judge what type of song would sell best – not that they had always got it right in the past. Capitol wanted the powerful, rather heavy track 'Princes Of The Universe', and EMI wanted the more pop-oriented 'A Kind Of Magic', which was also going to be the album's title track.

The band agreed to let both companies have their choice of song, and proceeded to make a video for 'Princes', directed by Russell Mulcahy. The star of the *Highlander* film was a French actor called Christophe Lambert (he'd previously played Tarzan in 1984's *Greystoke*), and Queen asked whether he would appear in the video, portraying the character he had played in the film, the Highlander McCleod. He loved the idea and flew in from his home in Paris for the shoot. The single was released by Capitol in North America on 7 April, where it failed to chart.

Two weeks later Queen were back with Russell in a disused theatre in north London, filming the video for the British single 'A Kind Of Magic'. In the video Freddie portrayed a magician while the others were vagrants whom he transformed into musicians. During editing special effects and computer animation graphics were added, making it the first 'animated' Queen video since 'Save Me' many years previously. The single was released on 17 March, to some acclaim, and featured an instrumental B-side, 'A Dozen Red Roses For My Darling'. *Sounds* wrote: 'The enduring Queen produce another slick piece of cabaret and vaudeville'. The single reached number three in the UK chart, but number one in a staggering thirty-five countries around the world.

Another film, *Biggles*, based on the classic children's books by W. E. Johns, was in the making in April 1986. John was asked to work on the music and decided to form a new band for the project. He called them The Immortals; other musicians were good friends Robert Ahwai and Lenny Zakatek. They worked on several songs, but only one, 'No Turning Back', was used on the film, as the theme song. It was released as a single on 19 May and the video depicted them all wearing the famous Biggles flying helmets and goggles and featured a guest appearance by Peter Cushing – a video John prefers to forget.

Roger took some time off from recording to participate in the Trustee Savings Bank sponsored Rock School competition as a judge. The event was the culmination of many months' work by regional judges, choosing, from hundreds of entries, the best area winners in a competition open to all amateur bands, the finals being held at the Camden Palace in north London. Roger was astounded at the high level of musicianship he witnessed and commented, 'All the bands involved have paid a lot of attention to their stagecraft and the delivery to the audience. They were all really good.'

Highlander had already been premiered in the USA and Paris but not in the UK. The Queen fan club, now run by Jacky Gunn, requested permission to show the film at a small cinema in Great Yarmouth, Suffolk, as part of a weekend Queen convetion being held in a holiday camp there in April. The idea was discussed with the film's distributors, who at first weren't keen as a premiere had been arranged in London. They were finally persuaded that no harm would come to the print and that it was excellent publicity, so *Highlander* got its first British showing in sunny Great Yarmouth.

'Time', the track that Freddie had recorded for the soundtrack album of the stage show, was released as a single on 6 May. Freddie wanted to make a video for it and gained permission to use the stage set of the musical, which had opened at the Dominion Theatre on Tottenham Court Road. As there was a matinee each day as well as the evening show, the only time that the set was free was very early in the morning so Freddie, Austrian director Rudi Dolezal and a film crew were assembled at 6 a.m. for filming.

Freddie and his personal assistant, Joe Fanelli, went back to the Dominion that evening to watch a performance of the show, arriving backstage early to have a chat with Cliff Richard. They watched the first half from the wings. As it was coming to an end, Freddie decided he wanted to sell ice creams during the interval. 'I did try and point out it wasn't one of his better ideas,' says Joe. 'Especially as he wouldn't have a clue what a pound coin looked like, so how on earth was he going to make sure the people paid the right price and were given the correct change?' Freddie's solution was simple: 'I bought the whole lot, so I wouldn't have to charge anyone anything,' he said. He donned a white coat, took his tray of ice creams and walked out into the audience. At first, no one had a clue who he was and he happily wandered around, handing out the treats. Then he got bored and began to throw them: 'He was hurling ice lollies and tubs and Cornettos all over the place,' continues Joe. 'They were landing in people's laps, on their heads, it was chaos. Some people even threw them back!' Eventually, supplies exhausted, Freddie retired backstage, to thunderous applause, as by now almost everyone in the theatre had realised who he was.

Every year Montreux was taken over by the Golden Rose rock festival (as well as the annual jazz festival) and in 1986 Queen were asked to perform. The festival featured a lot of top bands, all miming to backing tracks, and was filmed for a later broadcast throughout Europe. Queen 'played' four songs in all: 'One Vision', 'Friends Will Be Friends', 'A Kind Of Magic' and 'Hammer To Fall'.

The band went into rehearsals in May for their next European tour. The dates they had arranged were huge and included two nights at Wembley Stadium in London, although they had provisionally booked dates in both Manchester and Newcastle upon Tyne in the event of a complete sell-out of both those nights. Tickets sold out at Wembley in a matter of hours.

The dates at the Maine Road stadium in Manchester and St James's Park football ground in Newcastle upon Tyne were confirmed, and tickets for both of those also sold in record time – at Manchester the tickets were the fastest-selling ever for that venue, 40,000 in twenty-four hours. Promoter Harvey Goldsmith had also 'pencilled in' a further date in England at the enormous open-air site at Knebworth Park in Hertfordshire, 'just in case' the entire tour sold out. The dates in Europe were some of the biggest venues the band could get, including a French racetrack and plenty of football stadiums. Nearly all the venues were outdoors, so everyone was praying for a great summer weatherwise.

Meanwhile, at the London film premiere of *Down And Out In Beverly Hills*, Brian bumped into vivacious actress Anita Dobson, who was starring as Queen Vic landlady Angie Watts in one of television's most popular soap operas, *EastEnders*. He invited her to watch Queen play at Wembley Stadium in July, an offer she accepted.

The forthcoming single release in the UK was to be 'Friends Will Be Friends', and for the video the band again got fans to stand in as extras. This time, though, they decided they needed a small thank you for being there and printed several hundred T-shirts which announced, 'I am a Queen Friend'.

On 29 May, Roger's girlfriend Dominique gave birth to their second child, a girl they called Rory. Just four days later EMI released the band's fourteenth album, *A Kind Of Magic*, the soundtrack album for *Highlander*. But this 'soundtrack' album was different from most: rather than release an album of 'incidental' music that sounded remote when removed from its original context within the film, they re-edited a lot of the music and released it in the form of proper 'songs'.

The album entered the UK charts at number one – as usual, to mixed reviews. 'A pot pourri of musical styles. And it's quite probably only a band of Queen's stature and breadth of appeal who could put out an album of such diverse songs without disappointing a sizeable portion of their fans', *Kerrang!* said. *Record Mirror* were more snide: 'Queen have been plying their trade profitably for so long that there's really no point in becoming incensed at their one (lack of) vision. The only strong emotion Queen now evoke in me is a fervent wish that Brian May would cut his hair.'

Queen flew to Stockholm on 6 June in preparation for the start of the 1986 'Magic Tour' in that city the next day. The stage they were carting around Europe was the biggest they had ever used. It was 64 feet long, with 40-foot wings on either side, and from ground level to the top of the lights it was just over 52 feet high. The lighting rig used six computerised control desks and weighed over 9 and a half tons when hoisted.

The start of the tour was marred by a group of anti-apartheid demonstrators outside the venue chanting anti-Queen slogans but the Rasunda football stadium was packed to capacity, and the crowds were in fine voice. The band had combined older Queen classics with new material, in a set designed to appeal to 'newcomers' to Queen music and those who had been around much longer. They added a rock'n'roll medley to the set, which brought the entire band down to the front of the stage for the first time in years. Freddie ran to the back of the stage at the end of show as the others took their bows, to reappear swathed in a deep red velvet cloak with ermine trim and bejewelled gold crown, doffing said headgear at the audience as though he were the King of England. As many of the newspapers commented, only Freddie could have got away with that.

On a rare few days off in the Netherlands, Brian nipped into a recording studio and did a demo tape of two songs, one for Japanese singing star Minako Honda, by request, and one for Anita Dobson, who had decided to take the step into recording music, after having been part of many musical theatre productions.

In England, Queen's thirtieth single, 'Friends Will Be Friends', was released on 9 June. For the B-side EMI had used an old track, 'Seven Seas Of Rhye', as they thought that after so many years the band would have new and younger fans who might like to own a copy of it on a single. *Kerrang!* said of it: 'The same as usual and not as good as "Night At The Opera". And oh, look, "Seven Seas Of Rhye" providing a bit of B-side justification!'

By 21 June the band had reached Mannheim, and the huge open-air venue Maimarktgelände. Before the show Freddie had asked if it could be arranged for him to come on stage in the bucket of a huge crane. If that was what Freddie wanted, then all attempts would be made to accommodate him: the necessary equipment was hired locally and set up near the stage. During the soundcheck Freddie climbed into the crane bucket, which was then winched up some distance above the stage. He was terrified: the crane driver lowered the bucket and a trembling Freddie climbed out and refused to have anything more to do with the 'stupid idea'. The show took place that night with no crane in evidence.

One of the other bands on the bill was Marillion, and then lead singer Fish joined Queen on stage during their rendition of 'Tutti Frutti'. The show was broadcast live on German radio.

After two nights in Zurich the band flew back to the UK, and on to Dublin, where they were playing an open-air gig at Slane Castle, just outside the city, on 5 July. The weather on the morning of the show was appalling – wet, windy and decidedly chilly – but the crowds started arriving by the bus, coach and carload early in the day. There were three support bands, Irish band Fountainhead, all-girl band The Bangles and the gravelly voiced Chris Rea, who was immensely popular in Ireland. When Queen came on the audience were drenched and cold – from the stage the field looked amazing due to the rainbow crowd of umbrellas. Midway through the gig, though, trouble flared in the audience, and Freddie had to stop the show to calm things down.

Queen's first British concert on the Magic Tour was 9 July at the St James's Park stadium in Newcastle. Negotiations had taken place previously with the Save The Children Fund, as Queen wanted to donate money to the fund, and it was decided that all proceeds from the Newcastle show would be given over to them. Promoter Harvey Goldsmith agreed to waive his considerable cut and hand that to charity, too.

A MAGIC YEAR

Brian had flown up to Newcastle the previous day to appear on a local television show to be interviewed about the concert and Queen's involvement with the charity, while the rest of the band flew up by private plane on the day of the show. During the flight Freddie asked the size of the venue for that day's gig. On being told 38,000, he joked it was one of their 'smaller venues'.

Then it was back to London. On 11 and 12 July Queen played Wembley Stadium to a capacity crowd of 72,000 per night. The band were all excited: they were used to playing the biggest venues, but this, for them, was different – this was their hometown in front of a home crowd. Despite the rain the crowds went wild, especially when, halfway through the gig, four enormous, helium-inflated caricatures of the band members were let loose into the night sky. Only one of them – Freddie – escaped the stadium, coming to rest in someone's garden some miles away in Chelmsford, Essex, where it was held to ransom by the householder the next day. The other three were pulled into the crowd and disappeared without trace.

After the Friday show a backstage party was held for the road crew, as a thank you and for the band and crew to unwind. Roadcrew parties are usually rather sordid, and this one was no exception: it featured sleazy strippers recruited for the occasion, who 'performed' a variety of weird acts for the people attending – nearly all of whom were, of course, male.

The Saturday night concert was filmed in its entirety by Gavin Taylor and his Tyne Tees Television crew for transmission at a future date. At the start of the show there was a tremendous cloudburst, drenching crowds and band alike, but halfway through the sky cleared. Afterwards the band held their own party, a slightly more restrained affair than the crew's. They invited 500 people to the beautiful Roof Gardens restaurant and club in west London. The restaurant was situated on the roof of Marks and Spencer in Kensington High Street, and once up there, it was almost impossible to tell that you weren't in a mature, landscaped garden somewhere in the middle of the British countryside.

The party started at about midnight and arriving guests were greeted in the lifts to the gardens by girls wearing skin-tight uniforms – or what seemed to be uniforms until the guests took a closer look, and discovered it was nothing more than body paint and that the girls were stark naked. The party also featured dwarfs, drag artists, topless girls in the gents lavatory and a man in a G-string in the ladies. During the evening, Queen got up and played a short session as Dicky Heart and The Pacemakers, joined by scantily clad Page Three model Samantha Fox, Marillion singer Fish, Gary Glitter and many more of the celebrity guests. A good night was had by all – and a good morning, too, as most of the revellers didn't leave until 6 a.m.

Queen played one more date in England, at Maine Road in Manchester – where it didn't rain. They then flew out to Germany for a concert in Cologne on 19 July, a gig at which Brian repaid the Marillion compliment and joined them on stage for their own 'Market Square Heroes'. Then it was on to Vienna for two more shows there. From Vienna they had to get to Budapest and, as the Danube flows through both cities, they decided to take a river cruise. The vessel they hired was none other than President Gorbachev's personal hydrofoil. Their arrival inspired the British Embassy in Budapest to hold a special party in their honour.

Because no other major rock band had played a stadium date in the Eastern bloc, Queen had decided to film the gig. They contacted the Hungarian government to request permission and to enlist their help with the project – the only major film company in Hungary, Mafilm, was government owned. Mafilm were asked to provide cameras, lights and other equipment, which they willingly did, commandeering virtually every film camera in Hungary. The band's arrival on the Danube and their soundcheck was filmed, and a lot of

A MAGIC YEAR

backstage and more personal footage was taken too, much of which was used by television news around the world. Tickets sold out incredibly fast, people travelled from all over the Eastern Bloc to attend, including some from Russia, and several hundred fans turned up on the day of the concert hoping to get in, or at least to be able to hear the show from outside.

The support bands for that concert were Dutch band Craaft, who had been with Queen for many of the gigs on the tour, and local band Z'zi Labor, consisting of about thirty matronly ladies in beautiful national costume, a full band of musicians similarly attired, and a lead singer. They sang Hungarian folk songs and waved handkerchiefs and went down a storm. Freddie and Brian had been learning a verse or two from a local folk song, which Freddie sang, reading the words off the palms of his hands as he couldn't remember them.

It was an incredible concert; most of the crowd had probably never seen a rock band before in their lives, but they still sang along with songs such as 'Love Of My Life', and they all went wild when Freddie and Brian dedicated the folk song to them. They raised their hands and clapped in all the right places for 'Radio Ga Ga', although most of them had probably not seen the video.

Back in the UK on 21 July, EMI released Freddie's first video EP, featuring three tracks from his own *Mr Bad Guy* album and the video he had made for the 'Time' single. A week after its release it entered the video charts at number one.

The next port of call was France for one concert, then on to Spain; there were a few days' rest in the sunshine at the exclusive Marbella Club, followed by what was to have been the final concert, in Marbella. Due to the phenomenal success of the tour, the decision was made to confirm the date Harvey Goldsmith had been holding at Knebworth Park. The concert was announced immediately, and even at such short notice the official limit of 120,000 tickets went in a matter of days, although in reality well above that number were sold.

The final gig of what Freddie christened the 'Queen Tornado' at Knebworth Park in Hertfordshire on 9 August was officially billed as 'A Night of Summer Magic'. Knebworth is a beautiful old mansion house set in acres of grounds, where the stage was erected in the middle of a field. The site was gigantic; several sets of delay towers ensured the crowds at the back didn't get the sound a long time after those at the front, and an enormous screen, first used at Wembley, was hoisted over the stage.

Backstage a funfair, including dodgems, kept everyone happy all day, and several beer tents were set up in the overcrowded 'special enclosure' area, for friends, colleagues, hangers-on and record company executives. It was a gloriously sunny day and people began arriving at the crack of dawn. They were the lucky ones: as the morning wore on, traffic jams into the site grew longer and slower, until the police were claiming they were witnessing the worst in British history. The band had been forewarned of traffic problems and had arranged for a helicopter to fly them in from Battersea Heliport. Not wishing to arrive completely unannounced, however, they paid £3,000 to respray the helicopter with the easily recognisable 'Kind Of Magic' cartoons and logo. When they flew overhead during the set of support band Big Country, the entire 120,000-strong crowd all looked up and cheered.

This was the biggest paying audience Queen had ever played to in the UK – figures quoted afterwards by the police suggested 200,000 was probably nearer the mark. Queen gave what was later classed as one of their finest performances. Another four inflatables had been secreted in the audience and were launched halfway through

A MAGIC YEAR

– all four made it above the crowds this time, to land who knows where.

Sadly, a young Status Quo fan was stabbed during the concert, and as the crowds were so tightly packed he bled to death before he reached an ambulance and hospital. On a more optimistic note, though, a baby was born in the crowd.

The band were completely unaware of the death of a member of their audience at this point, and so after the concert everyone packed into the backstage area for the second 'end of the tour' party. Mud wrestlers and strippers added Queen's usual 'high-class' touch to the proceedings, as did trucking company boss Edwin Shirley as he frolicked in the mud pool with the naked girls – fully clothed. Everyone drank and danced until the early hours – several people for the single reason that they couldn't get out.

The traffic jams at the end of the concert were as bad, if not worse, than those beforehand and as the car park areas (more fields) were without any lighting, some were still trying to find their cars in the acres of vehicles the next morning. Others gave up trying to leave and slept in their cars.

During this tour Queen broke the all-time attendance record in the UK by playing to over 400,000 people and that tour grossed more than £11 million for twenty-six concerts. The band were now able to take a breather to reflect and look ahead to their future. They had enjoyed the touring, as they always did: although it was tough on them physically, in some ways it made life easy. It meant that everything was planned for them, their day-to-day lives were timed and scheduled. Real life was much harder. However, they all felt that the time was right for them to take another break from each other. They needed a rest and some time alone. The pressures of touring weren't easily surmounted by even the best of friends, and they all felt at snapping point. John, particularly, had been going through a rough time, feeling as though he was verging on a nervous breakdown;

his personal life had been suffering to the degree that he and Veronica were considering separation and he needed to get away from it all for as long as it took to sort himself out. The band agreed to take a break for most of 1987, to 'play it by ear' and see how things worked out.

Freddie's mansion in Kensington, Garden Lodge, had stood empty since he had bought it back in early 1980. He had been offered over a million pounds for it, unseen, by an Arab buyer, but he had refused to sell. He had hired top interior designer Robin Moore-Eade to demolish and rebuild the interior, and an army of gardeners to landscape the gardens and construct a huge fishpond. He had been closely involved in all the work, his taste was impeccable and he knew exactly how he wanted the house to look. He even went along with Robin to the stonemason's yard to choose the particular black marble, shot through with gold, that he wanted for his en-suite bathroom.

He was still living in the same flat in Kensington, also bought in 1980, and was more than happy there, but once the work was finished on the house, he decided to move in for a weekend to see if he would be comfortable there – so successfully that he never moved out. He negotiated to buy the two small mews houses next door so that he could have guest rooms, and had a large conservatory built behind them and linked to the main garden. It was a stunning house, and he and his two assistants, Feebie and Joe, had more than enough room to spare. His love of cats was well known: Oscar and Tiffany had been with him for many years and now that he had the space, he acquired several more. Some months later, Jim Hutton also moved in.

In the States, Capitol released the band's thirty-third US single, 'Pain Is So Close To Pleasure', which failed to make any impression on the *Billboard* chart. Meanwhile, in the UK, Queen's thirty-first single was released on 15 September 1986, a beautiful ballad, written by Brian, titled 'Who Wants To Live Forever'. The video for the song, shot with director David Mallett, was filmed using the National Philharmonic Orchestra, forty choirboys and 10,000 candles. The song eventually reached number twenty-four in the UK charts.

On 16 October Queen received an award for the best live performance video, for *Live In Rio*, at the British Video Awards ceremony. Roger and Brian collected it on behalf of the band, from presenter Mike Smith.

Due to a decided lack of television programmes showing videos in the UK 'A Kind Of Magic' and 'Who Wants To Live Forever' were destined to be hidden away in the recesses of the band's offices indefinitely, so the band released them as a video single. It was a brand new concept: no other band had yet done such a thing. That, however, had never stopped Queen before, so on 20 October the first Queen video single was released, and entered the video chart, previously filled with live concerts and compilations, at number one. It didn't take long for other bands to follow suit.

Gavin Taylor's film of the Wembley Stadium show had been bought by Channel 4, and talks had taken place about how and when it should be shown on television. The band wanted it to be played on radio simultaneously with any television broadcast, but as Channel 4 is an independent television station, it couldn't involve the BBC, who had the experience and technical facilities for simulcasts. They approached the forty-eight independent radio stations and negotiated with them to broadcast the show. They all agreed, but to enable it to work efficiently the sound had to be transmitted via satellite to each of the stations, no landlines being available to link all of them, with a built-in quarter-of-a-second delay, so that the sound people heard on their radio matched exactly the pictures they were watching on television. On top of that, special permission had to be obtained from the ACIT, the television crew union, as the independents had never done a simulcast before. On 25 October 1986 the Real Magic show from Wembley was shown on Channel 4 and simultaneously broadcast on all the independent radio network stations. It clocked up 3.5 million viewers, a figure only marginally topped on the channel by soap opera *Brookside*.

On 8 November, Queen had no less than five videos in the Top 10 of the UK video chart, something no other band had been able to achieve at that time – no other band had released so many.

In November, Brian was asked if he would consider being a guest guitarist on stage with 'spoof' heavy metal band Bad News. They were, in fact, four talented comedy actors more usually known as the Young Ones, and whose television series became compulsive viewing. Brian loved playing live, with anyone, and readily agreed. He would be guesting along with Led Zeppelin guitarist Jimmy Page. The concert was at the Hammersmith Odeon on 9 November, and Bad News were on the bill with Sampson and headline band Iron Maiden in a special matinee performance in aid of the NSPCC. The idea was that the Bad News guitarists would begin a guitar duel – Jimmy Page and Brian would stand behind the speakers on stage and actually play the solos, and then walk on, still playing, much to the consternation of the Bad News boys. The band got on so well with Brian that they asked him if he would produce their album, if they ever made one. He said, of course, not thinking for a moment it would ever happen – but it did eventually, in May 1987.

He had never wanted to produce other people as he preferred playing, but when he was asked to write and produce some songs for beautiful Japanese singer Minako Honda, he said yes. Minako was a huge star in Japan, although she had never been heard of in the UK. She flew to England to work with Brian at Sarm Studios in London, on the two tracks: 'Golden Days', a song he had written on tour, and 'Crazy Nights'. He produced the two songs, and played guitar and sang backing vocals, which were released as a 12" single in 1987. Minako's album *Cancel* also featured a track called 'Roulette', which had started life as an Immortals song, co-written by John

A MAGIC YEAR

Deacon and Robert Ahwai, called 'No Turning Back', on which John had played bass.

Brian's personal life was far from quiet at the time. He and his wife were not getting on particularly well, which was throwing him into deep depressions. His work with Anita Dobson brought the two of them together, and that friendship inevitably grew into a closer affection. The newspapers and media were quick to latch on to them and they were photographed together at various events. They managed to keep a low profile on the whole affair and denied the rumours emphatically. Brian was concerned that it would affect his children, for whom he cared deeply, and went to any lengths to protect them, so they managed to keep up the pretence that Brian was happily married and he and Anita were just good friends.

During the quiet stretch, Freddie went to Japan. He became a tourist, albeit a pampered one, and shopped to his heart's content. He bought more porcelain and antiques for his collection and tried in vain to purchase some of a priceless collection of Japanese Imari plates – which the owner refused to sell. He was also a special guest at the Japanese opening of the musical *Cats* but wasn't actually told he was guest of honour. He turned up late to discover the entire performance had been held up for him. When asked, on his return, how the trip had been, Joe Fanelli said, 'Shopping with Freddie is like hitting yourself on the head repeatedly with an ice pick. It feels so good when you stop.'

By late November EMI had released every one of Queen's albums on compact disc: they were the first band to have their entire back catalogue available on CD. But EMI's remastering of the original tapes using the latest digital technology left a lot to be desired. The collection was released with flagrant errors, mistakes easily noticed by fans and anyone else with the newer 'programmable' CD players: many tracks started and finished in the wrong places.

Several shows on the Magic Tour had been recorded and edited to form a single live album, which was released on 1 December as *Live Magic*. The idea of editing the songs was to try to create the impression of the live show on just one album. (The band didn't want to have to release another double live set – they still loathed live albums.) Unfortunately, their fans weren't impressed. Their idea of a live album was the double set, full-show version they had been given with *Live Killers*, not a one-album edited version. Queen had committed the ultimate sin, as far as the fans were concerned, by cutting 'Bohemian Rhapsody'. But, despite the objections and its critics, the album entered the UK chart at number three, with sales of over 400,000 and no single to promote it.

The band's popularity in America at the time was low. They hadn't toured there since 1982 and the last two album releases had failed to make much of an impression on either the fans or the charts. As Brian put it, 'Queen couldn't even get arrested in the States right now.'

Capitol Records in the USA were reluctant to release the live album since, they said, there was little demand for it. The band felt there was little point in trying to force the record company to release something against their will as Capitol would, of course, put little effort into promoting it. The live album never appeared in the USA, a decision that was not well received by the many American fans still loyal to Queen, which was, perhaps, the fatal blow to Queen's relationship with Capitol.

The film that Queen had made during their visit to Budapest was finally finished and Brian flew out to the country's National Convention Centre for its premiere on 12 December. The first showing was private, but it opened to the public at 9 a.m. the next morning. In one day a total of *nine* sold-out screenings took place, followed by seven screenings a day for the next week, all of which were sold out.

CHAPTER 22

BARCELONA OR BUST

THE EARLY PART OF 1987 WAS VERY QUIET FOR QUEEN, SO FREDDIE took the opportunity to go into the Townhouse Studios to do some solo work. He hadn't really considered a second solo album at this stage but had several ideas he wanted to commit to tape. Roger and John had both decided to take a winter break in Los Angeles, where both owned houses, and flew out in late January. Brian remained in England, still trying to sort out his personal life: Chrissy was heavily pregnant with their third child, but life at home was still up and down. His relationship with Anita was developing, if a little explosively, and he was in turmoil. A ray of sunshine in his otherwise troubled life appeared when his second daughter, Emily Ruth, was born on 17 February.

The Budapest concert film was released on video in the UK on 16 February. Queen had been involved in extensive negotiations with the Hungarian government about releasing the film, due to Mafilm's involvement, but were eventually granted permission to release it throughout Europe.

Freddie's work in the studio resulted in a remake of a great old Platters song, 'The Great Pretender' – and he decided to make a video for it. His ideas were outrageously extravagant and production costs began to mount even before filming began. He wanted 400 identical cardboard cut-outs of himself, and another six or so made in the outfits he had worn in previous Queen videos. He wanted to recreate several past Queen videos and one or two of his solo ones, so new sets had to be built. *And* he wanted his friends Peter Straker and Roger Taylor to dress up in women's clothes and appear in it with him. Originally he had wanted to fly over the white cliffs of Dover too, but that idea was scrapped. Director David Mallett didn't bat an eyelid – accustomed as he was to the excessive demands of Queen videos – so everything was prepared. On the day of the shoot Roger, who had just flown back from LA, Peter and Freddie all dressed in several different women's outfits – and stunning they all looked, too. The single was released on 23 February, and provided Freddie with his best solo chart position to date when it climbed to number four in the UK chart.

In late February changes within Hungary and its government meant that the band's *Greatest Hits* album, and their *Greatest Flix* video, could finally be released there. It was their first official release in Hungary and sales were phenomenal.

Elsewhere, when the announcements were made of the nominees for the annual British Phonographic Industry Awards, Queen were nowhere in sight. So to compensate, the band's record company EMI compiled an advertisement featuring Queen's achievements during 1986, which they placed strategically in the award ceremony's programme and in the major British music magazines. That advertisement read:

1. Queen sold 1,774,991 albums in the UK alone.
2. 'A Kind Of Magic' entered the UK album chart at number one and remained in the top five for thirteen consecutive weeks.

3. The 1,828,375th fan in the UK bought a copy of Queen's *Greatest Hits*, and the album continued in the UK Top 100 charts throughout the year, where it has been for 268 weeks.

4. Queen sold out two nights at Wembley Stadium, one at Newcastle St James's Park, one at Manchester Maine Road and one at Knebworth – total in excess of 400,000 people – an all-time UK attendance record.

5. Queen's *Real Magic*, directed by Gavin Taylor, became the first ever stereo simulcast on independent television and the independent radio network when a satellite link-up took place on 25 October.

6. Queen's 657th performance became the first ever major stadium concert in the Eastern bloc on 27 July at the Nep-stadium in Budapest, filmed with 17 35-mm movie cameras by the Hungarian State Film Agency, Mafilm.

7. Queen's *Magic In Budapest*, directed by Janos Zsombolyai, became the first full-length feature concert film to be premiered in the Eastern bloc in Budapest's National Congress Hall on 12 December.

8. Queen released their first ever video single in the UK, entering the video charts at number one on 27 October.

9. Queen's Magic Tour of Europe played to over a million people in June, July and August in twenty-six dates, grossing in excess of £11 million.

10. *Daily Mirror* readers voted Queen the best band of 1986 by 50 per cent more votes than any other band.

11. *Daily Mirror* readers voted Freddie Mercury best male vocalist for 1986 'by miles'.

12. Freddie Mercury's video EP entered the UK video chart at number one on 21 July.

13. Queen held their first ever three-day fan club convention at Great Yarmouth on 25 April.

14. Russell Mulcahy's second feature film, *Highlander*, with a music score by Queen and Michael Kamen, went on general release in the UK on 29 August.

15. Queen threw 28 parties.

16. Queen gave the proceeds of their Newcastle football ground concert to the Save The Children Fund.

17. Richard Gray spent 918 hours working on Queen artwork and received the best album cover award from the *Daily Express*.

18. Queen released *Live Magic* on 1 December and sold over 400,000 before Christmas without a single.

19. Queen hits were released on no fewer than fifty-three compilation albums in twenty-three countries throughout the world.

20. Freddie Mercury was forty.

21. Queen refused to ban their videos from appearing on British television.

22. Queen Films had five videos in the UK top twenty-five on 8 November.

23. Freddie Mercury was voted best male vocalist of the year by the readers of *The Sun*.

24. Queen were voted best group of the year by Capital Radio listeners.

25. Mary Turner described Queen as a national institution.

26. Queen's 'We Will Rock You' re-entered the *Music Week* top ten video charts in July, where it remained for the rest of the year.

27. Queen's *Greatest Flix* remained in the *Music Week* top thirty video charts all year, totalling 115 consecutive weeks since being the first ever number one video in the UK.

28. Queen's *Live In Rio* remained in the *Music Week* top thirty video charts all year, totalling eighty consecutive weeks since its debut at number one on 20 May 1985.

29. Queen were awarded top music video for *Live In Rio* at the British Video Awards on 16 October.

30. Shell adopted 'I Want To Break Free' as their theme song for a nationwide television and radio campaign.

31. Hannes Rossacher and Rudi Dolezal nearly finished post-production on their mammoth video cassette – *Queen – Magic Years (A Visual Anthology)* – due for release early 1987.

32. Yet again Queen fail to win a BPI Award.

Thank you Brian, John, Freddie and Roger – we at EMI appreciate you.

In the early part of the year Brian flew to Los Angeles to work with oversized rock singer Meatloaf. The pair collaborated on the track 'A Time For Heroes', which became the theme song for the Paralympic Games being held in the city later in the year.

In March 1987, Picture Music International released two videos. The first was Freddie's outrageous 'The Great Pretender', featuring an extended version showing clips from the making of the film, including Roger, Freddie and Peter getting dressed in their outfits, and the second was a 'blast from the past' on EMI's Gold Rush video label, featuring the videos for both 'Bohemian Rhapsody' and 'Crazy Little Thing Called Love'.

Back in July 1986, during a television interview in Barcelona, Freddie had said that the only reason he was in Spain was to meet Spanish opera diva Montserrat Caballé. He had fallen in love with her voice a few years earlier, after seeing her at the Royal Opera House in London's Covent Garden, with Luciano Pavarotti. His comment in the interview was perhaps not strictly true, but it came to the notice of influential people. Carlos Caballé, Montserrat's brother and manager, approached Jim Beach and suggested that perhaps Freddie might write a song for Montserrat to sing, entitled 'Barcelona', which could be an anthem for the Barcelona Olympic Games, due to take place in 1992. Freddie, after much persuasion, agreed.

The first person Freddie turned to with his task was Mike Moran, as they had a good working relationship and were good friends. The initial collaboration produced three rough tracks, 'Exercises In Free Love', 'The Fallen Priest' and 'Guide Me Home', on which Freddie had sung in a falsetto voice, as an approximation of Montserrat's part.

In March 1987, Freddie flew out to Barcelona to meet Montserrat, accompanied by Jim Beach, Peter 'Phoebe' Freestone and Mike Moran.

Lunch was arranged for 2 p.m. at the Ritz Hotel, where the management had arranged the Garden Room, equipped with a very basic speaker system and a grand piano.

Freddie was incredibly nervous. Phoebe said, 'Freddie paced the

BARCELONA OR BUST

room like a caged tiger. He was chain smoking, and, unusually, he was early. Montserrat was late, and at ten minutes after one, when he was convinced she wasn't going to come, she walked into the room. She and Freddie stood and stared at each other – two musical giants meeting for the first time. But once the introductions were over, neither of them could stop talking!'

Lunch over, Freddie leapt up and said, 'I've got a couple of things here dear, would you like to hear them or not?' She said she would love to, and the tape of the three rough songs were played, the idea being that she would choose one as the B-side to 'Barcelona' (which didn't actually exist yet). Freddie had only planned on working on one single with her, but she was very excited by what she heard, and asked if there was any more. Freddie said there wasn't as to do any more would have meant an album. She then asked how many tracks an album would require, and why didn't they record one together? Freddie, according to Phoebe, almost fell off his chair at her suggestion. Regaining his composure, he said with a nonchalant wave of his hand, 'Oh, why not dear?'

Montserrat was due in England a few days later to perform at London's Covent Garden, and invited Freddie and his entourage to see the show. Without Freddie's knowledge she contacted his co-writer on 'Exercises In Free Love', Mike Moran, and asked him to help her learn it for performing that night. Mike obliged and even agreed to accompany her – and Freddie was completely taken by surprise when Montserrat performed his song.

In the past Queen had often been asked to visit sick fans or record messages for them. None of them ever particularly liked doing this: it is not easy to sit with a tape recorder and talk as if everything is all right with the world when the person you are talking to might be in a coma. On one occasion Freddie heard that a young fan from Plymouth was in a coma following a road accident. Colin was only twenty-five and considered himself a Freddie 'lookalike'. Freddie had booked studio time to work on songs for Montserrat and took advantage of that to write a song for Colin called 'Keep On Smiling', which he recorded on tape and sent to Plymouth. Colin recovered a little, but sadly not enough, and died shortly afterwards. His family, however, said the tape had made a difference, and that it would be buried with him so that no one could copy it.

On 15 April 1987, Queen received an Ivor Novello award for their outstanding contribution to British music, after fifteen years and thirty hit records.

In early April, Freddie began work on the album he had agreed to record with Montserrat Caballé. After their initial meeting in March, Montserrat had bought Queen's entire back catalogue – albums and videos – so that she would be fully aware of the person she was to work so closely with. She had, over the course of listening and watching, become a great fan of Freddie's and could not believe that he would want to write songs for her.

The way they worked on the album was completely different from what Freddie was used to. Montserrat had little time to devote to actually being in the studio and wasn't prepared to just go in and sing until she had it right. She preferred to know exactly what was required of her beforehand. So Freddie and Mike Moran would complete a track at a time, including a 'guide vocal' for Montserrat's part. Freddie would then send her the tape, wherever she happened to be, she would learn her vocal, go into the studio at the next opportunity and record it in virtually one take. This was to be the format for the entire album, which proved at times to be incredibly frustrating. But it was hugely rewarding nonetheless; when the first track was finished, Freddie sat back and said, 'I've done it. I have captured *her* voice, on my tape.'

The album was finally finished over nine months later, and both Freddie and Montserrat were both more than happy with the result. What they'd captured was exactly, to the note, what Freddie had envisaged when he began the project, and he commented on this achievement, 'What else is there left for me to do?'

During the penultimate weekend in April 1987 the fan club held its second weekend-long convention. Among other delights planned for the weekend was the British premiere of the band's *Live In Budapest* film, at a small cinema in Southport, Merseyside, an incongruous start for a film that had taken a government to help make it.

On 30 May the island of Ibiza staged Ibiza 92, a huge festival at the outrageous Ku Club, to celebrate Spain staging the Olympics and Paralympics in 1992. Freddie had agreed to be guest of honour and close the event with Montserrat Caballé singing the song he had written for her and her home city, 'Barcelona'. It was a magnificent setting, and Freddie and Montserrat performed flanked by glittering fountains and backed by the magnificent night sky. As they finished to tumultuous applause, the sky exploded with one of the biggest fireworks displays ever to have been staged in Europe to date.

Back in England, Brian was tracked down by 'spoof' heavy metal band Bad News, with whom he had played live in 1986. They were making their debut album and were badgering Brian to produce it. After all, he had said he would . . . way back then, when he thought it would never happen. But it was a project he couldn't refuse; he had the greatest respect and admiration for the guys in the band – Adrian Edmondson, Nigel Planer and Rik Mayall, who had collectively appeared as 'The Young Ones' in the incredibly popular television series of the same name. The lads were also joined by Peter Richardson, who had been director and producer of *The Comic Strip Presents* . . . which was responsible for making household names of not only the three 'Young Ones' but French & Saunders too. Brian knew that the project would prove to be an 'interesting' experience.

They began work at Sarm Studios in London in May 1987. Once in the studios, the band lived and breathed the heavy metal rock star image, although none were all that proficient at playing their instruments. But the idea was that the album should sound amateur – it was meant to be a joke. Brian remembers, though, that by the end of the hilariously funny recording sessions they had all improved so much that they had to force themselves to play badly.

CHAPTER 23

A DIFFERENT PERSPECTIVE

ANITA DOBSON'S SINGLE, 'TALKING OF LOVE', WAS RELEASED ON 6 JULY and she and Brian flew to Vienna to film a video to accompany it, still denying emphatically the rumours of a romantic link – even during an interview on the BBC's *Wogan* chat show.

Back in May, Roger had begun work on a third solo album, with David Richards. His previous two had been reasonably successful, although none of the songs had ever been played live. This was another of Queen's 'quiet' periods. Brian was producing, Freddie was working with Montserrat and John was somewhere in the world on holiday, which was increasingly becoming one of his favourite pastimes. Roger decided to form a band so that he could play live the songs on his first two albums and the tracks he was currently working on. He discussed it, of course, with the other members of Queen, and they all gave him their blessing and wished him luck, as long as Queen came first and his solo project second if the two ever clashed.

First, advertisements were placed in all the major British music papers, stating 'Drummer of a top rock band looking for musicians'. (He wanted to keep his name out of it at this stage, as he thought it might attract the wrong sort of people.) The replies were thin at first, so it was printed again a week later in a bold boxed setting, with a catchy 'If you think you're good enough and you want to be a star call this number' type text. It worked, and letters and calls flooded in. Some of the demo tapes sent were brilliant, and were kept aside; others were mediocre, and more were dreadful. After weeks of listening Roger shortlisted twenty bass players, twenty guitarists and twenty drummers. He hired Paramount City, a theatre turned nightclub in Soho, for three days, and each musician was given a set time at which to appear. It wasn't easy for them: they were played, just once, a backing track to one of the songs Roger was working on, and then had to play along with it. It was particularly difficult for the guitarists as, unknown to them, they were trying to outplay Brian May. Roger kept out of sight for most of the auditions, so the musicians were also playing to a faceless critic. Finally, after three days, Roger had made his choice. It hadn't been easy, and he favoured two from each instrument right up until the last minute. He finally picked Clayton Moss, one of the best guitarists he saw over those three days, drummer Josh Macrae, blond, sporting sunglasses, almost a clone of Roger himself, and finally Peter Noone on bass. Peter had auditioned with his brother, a guitarist, and they were almost identical, which Roger thought would look great on stage, but unfortunately Roger didn't think Peter's brother quite as good as Clayton, and didn't select him. The final member of the band was keyboard player Spike Edney, a friend of Roger's who had played keyboards with Queen on their 1984 and 1986 tours.

They began rehearsals almost immediately, during which they argued about their name. Finally they decided to call themselves The Cross. It was short and memorable, and despite comments to the contrary, had no religious connotations. Roger took the band out to Ibiza, where he had purchased a holiday villa, to rehearse and record. The album he had begun earlier in the year was complete, and he

A DIFFERENT PERSPECTIVE

had secured himself a record deal with Virgin Records on the strength of it. But he wanted the new musicians to change one or two of the mixes and play on some of the tracks, which also meant they were entitled to 'points' on the album and would be paid royalties against sales. While they were in Ibiza, ostensibly working, Roger bought a new toy – a speedboat which he named 'Ga Ga'.

Brian's work with Bad News was almost finished. Contrary to newspaper reports that he felt 'drained and exhausted' by the sessions and had to leave the country to recuperate, he had thoroughly enjoyed working with the band. On 29 August, at the annual Reading Rock and Jazz Festival, Brian joined them on stage, and learned rather quickly how to dodge the hail of bottles and cans hurled by heavy metal fans who didn't find the spoof funny. To upset music fans even more – and horrify Queen fans in particular – Bad News decided to release their own version of 'Bohemian Rhapsody', which even featured, among others, John Deacon on backing vocals. It was appalling – tongue in cheek, perhaps, and very funny, although many fans didn't think so. It was nothing less than sacrilege as far as they were concerned and they made their views known vociferously. Most of them were calmed somewhat when told that Freddie, who had written the song, thought it amusing and wasn't upset in the slightest.

Freddie's birthday parties were legendary by this time, and as if to outdo all his previous efforts he held his forty-first birthday party in the exclusive hotel Pikes, Ibiza, where he was spending a couple of weeks in the sun with friends. Most of his other friends, however, were still in London. Not a problem really – or, at least, not when you're as wealthy as Freddie – you simply charter a private plane. It was left up to his secretary Julie to contact the airlines, as the plane needed to be a big one, about DC9-sized. Negotiations were opened and closed quickly, and a plane was made available to fly from London's Heathrow airport early on the morning of 5 September, and to leave Ibiza at midday the following day. It was champagne all the way on the flight, with snacks and canapés to accompany the drinks. The flight was uneventful, as far as the guests were concerned, apart from Anita Dobson trying to ply the pilot with champagne in order to steal his cap. It wasn't until the pilot was seen at the party later on that the drama was uncovered: the plane had landed with only one engine when the other had developed a fault.

As soon as they arrived the guests were shown to their rooms – Freddie had booked the entire hotel for those two days. The party began later that evening, and among the posh party frocks was a contingent from the nearby Ku Club, dressed outrageously in very little, but all wearing the most amazing hats, including one complete with a live songbird. For a lot of the guests the party didn't have a definite ending: many of them climbed back aboard the plane next day without having slept at all.

The Cross flew from Ibiza straight to Montreux to continue work on album tracks, and then into the UK and a succession of London studios, starting at Maison Rouge. Freddie and Brian both called in to listen to the new material and make contributions. Freddie sang lead vocal on one track, 'Heaven For Everyone', and Brian played guitar on 'Love Lies Bleeding'. The first single, 'Cowboys And Indians', was released on 21 September on Virgin. They had made a video for the song just before its release, featuring three tall, long-legged blonde models miming to the backing vocals to add glamour. Glamour wasn't all they added: Roger and one of the models, Debbie, struck up an immediate friendship, followed not long afterwards by romance.

Also on 21 September, Freddie's duet with Montserrat, the single 'Barcelona', was released in Spain. Unprecedentedly, it sold over 10,000 copies within just three hours. Lots of Spanish record shops couldn't get extra stock as not many more than that had been pressed: the Spanish public were not notorious for buying singles. The Official Olympic Committee, having heard the song, declared that they had chosen it as the official anthem for the 1992 Olympics to be held in Barcelona.

A DIFFERENT PERSPECTIVE

Freddie and Montserrat wanted to make a video to accompany the single's release in the rest of Europe and approached David Mallett. The idea was to re-create the backdrop that Freddie and Montserrat had used during the Ibiza 92 festival, and David drafted in 300 Queen fan club members to wave disposable cigarette lighters around at appropriate moments to add 'atmosphere'. It resulted in a great video – and a lot of burned fingers . . .

The single was eventually released in the UK on 26 October and everyone was rather shocked by it. It was the first time that anyone who sang with a rock band had ever diverted into the world of opera, and Freddie was in turn hailed as a genius, dismissed as an eccentric or slammed as a disgrace to the world of rock music. *Kerrang!* were in awe: 'This is sensational. Quite extraordinary and the ultimate in high camp'. *Sounds* were also fans: 'This will appeal to real music lovers'. Surprisingly, the *NME* were very complimentary: 'The A-side remains breast-beatingly impotent, but the B-side is dead refreshing, interesting at the very least.' *Record Mirror*, however, were less so: 'In the most curious matching of talents known to man, Freddie settles back in the armchair and whinges a bit while the weighty Montserrat woman leaps around the room, yodelling and warbling wildly. He's never been the same since "Bohemian Rhapsody".'

During November, Richard Branson's airline, Virgin Atlantic, opened a new route to Florida; the inaugural flight was a private one for a planeload of celebrities, including John Deacon. During that flight John met the band Morris Minor and The Majors, who were just about to release a rap single in the UK, 'Stutter Rap (No Sleep Til Bedtime)', a parody of the 1987 Beastie Boys track 'No Sleep Til Brooklyn'. Jokingly they asked John if he would like to appear in the video – just for fun. He agreed, and they decided that from then on, they would try to find him a cameo role in all their videos.

Meanwhile, Roger and the other members of The Cross were busy getting their faces known on as many television programmes as they could find, including children's pop shows, and they made their live TV debut on 6 October on the Roxy music show.

On 6 October, for the second successive year, Queen picked up an award at the British Video Awards, this time for Best Video (Music) for their *Live In Budapest* film. Exactly a month later, The Cross performed their first ever live gig, filmed live for *Meltdown*, at Teddington Lock Studios in front of an invited audience, mostly consisting of Queen fan club members, who'd had advance notice and a few hundred free tickets to distribute. Needless to say, it was a well-received inauguration.

Over the last year or two, Rudi Dolezal and Hannes Rossacher, a film director and a producer, had been trailing Queen all over the world, from gigs to hotels to parties, walking, shopping, talking and drinking. They had filmed interviews with the band and with hordes of other celebrities to put together the definitive documentary about the life and times of Queen. But this was no ordinary 'rockumentary': they had scoured the archive film vaults, rummaged through the boxes and boxes and reels and reels of film and video stored at the band's office, and even asked for fans' help in obtaining rare footage. Then they had edited the whole lot, plus the new film they had shot, into an enjoyable, watchable film. The finished product was unveiled to the public on 30 November 1987. *Queen – The Magic Years, a Visual Anthology* was a mammoth epic of three hours' duration, divided into three hour-long 'episodes' and sold either as a boxed set, or individually.

At the end of 1987, the band members were still involved in their separate projects, Brian still working with Anita Dobson (and still denying those rumours . . .), Freddie was with Montserrat, Roger was with The Cross, and John was writing new material for the next Queen album.

CHAPTER 24

PERSONAL TURMOIL

THE YEAR APART HAD PAID OFF. ALL MEMBERS OF THE BAND HAD flexed their individual creative muscles enough to think more coherently about Queen and its future, and they decided it was time to work together again. They went into Townhouse Studios in early January to begin recording.

On 4 January, The Cross decided to release a second single, the title track of their forthcoming album, *Shove It*. They had filmed a video for the track back in November in the Chelsea club Crazy Larrys, inviting around a hundred friends to take part, the invitation suggesting to 'dress wild'. The Cross supplied the wine and the friends supplied the lively, dancing audience.

Roger's relationship with model Debbie Leng had developed to the stage where they wanted to move in together – and his relationship with his girlfriend of many years, Dominique, broke apart. But the couple had two children to consider, whose future was of paramount importance. To ensure their safety and security, at least financially, Roger and Dominique were married on 25 January at the Kensington and Chelsea Register Office. Freddie and Mary Austin, his companion of many years, were witnesses. Twenty-three days later Roger moved out of the home he shared with his wife and children and into a house he had bought for himself and Debbie, only minutes away.

The UK press were quick to catch on to the story, and it made headlines in most major newspapers. Twenty-five-year-old Debbie had been appearing in an advertisement for Cadbury's Flake and the press harassed her and Roger relentlessly for the story of the 'Flake Girl' and the 'older' rock star – proof, if nothing else, of the small-mindedness of some tabloid journalists.

During the furore, The Cross released their debut album on Virgin Records on 25 January. Its title, *Shove It*, was a phrase often employed by Roger's personal assistant, Chris 'Crystal' Taylor, but one that increasingly applied to the drummer's reaction to the press when asked to comment on his personal life.

The music press were, in the main, keen on The Cross's debut album. *Kerrang!* commented: 'Judged objectively and on its own terms, this debut is a beautifully produced slab of super sophisticated pop rock. *NME* was particularly complimentary: 'All in all (with the exception of a horribly gloomy sleeve – shoot that artist!), *Shove It* is a nifty little debut and, I'm sure, the start of a fruitful new era in Roger Taylor's career.

The following day, the debut single in North America – the album's title track – was released. It featured a B-side that was left off the European album release, a track called 'Feel The Force'.

The Cross were now ready for their first tour, which began in the early hours of the morning of 20 February at a Leeds University student ball. There were several other acts on the bill, and The Cross featured quite low down, but it didn't worry them: they used the gig as a warm-up for the first real show that evening, held at the Queen Margaret Union in Glasgow. The majority of the audience were Queen fans wanting to see Roger – which was, of course, inevitable

PERSONAL TURMOIL

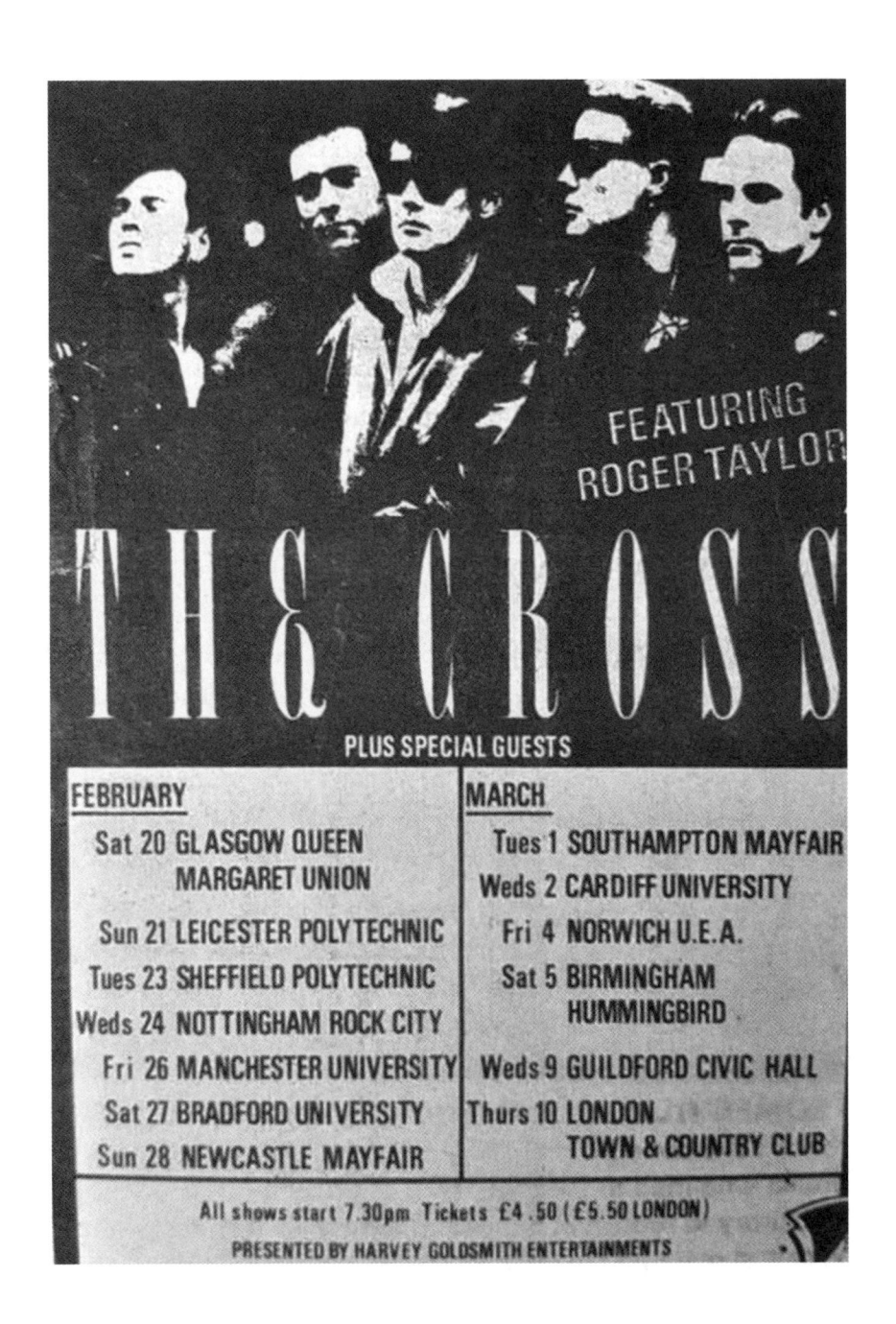

FEATURING ROGER TAYLOR

THE CROSS

PLUS SPECIAL GUESTS

FEBRUARY
- Sat 20 GLASGOW QUEEN MARGARET UNION
- Sun 21 LEICESTER POLYTECHNIC
- Tues 23 SHEFFIELD POLYTECHNIC
- Weds 24 NOTTINGHAM ROCK CITY
- Fri 26 MANCHESTER UNIVERSITY
- Sat 27 BRADFORD UNIVERSITY
- Sun 28 NEWCASTLE MAYFAIR

MARCH
- Tues 1 SOUTHAMPTON MAYFAIR
- Weds 2 CARDIFF UNIVERSITY
- Fri 4 NORWICH U.E.A.
- Sat 5 BIRMINGHAM HUMMINGBIRD
- Weds 9 GUILDFORD CIVIC HALL
- Thurs 10 LONDON TOWN & COUNTRY CLUB

All shows start 7.30pm Tickets £4.50 (£5.50 LONDON)
PRESENTED BY HARVEY GOLDSMITH ENTERTAINMENTS

– but he insisted they be billed as 'The Cross' – with 'featuring Roger Taylor' in small print below – and not, as the promoters wanted, 'Roger Taylor and the Cross'.

There was one strange phenomenon that occurred at many of the Cross dates on this tour . . . the band were showered with Cadbury's Flake bars!

The UK tour concluded on 10 March at the Town and Country Club in north London, an important gig for the band, as all their friends and family were in attendance, including Brian May and ex-Led Zeppelin lead singer Robert Plant. The band were nervous about the concert, but they played well and went down a storm.

Just before they were due to fly to Germany for a short tour, beginning on 8 April, they released a third single from *Shove It*, the ballad 'Heaven For Everyone', which they had re-recorded with Roger on lead vocals instead of Freddie, as in the original album version. Reluctantly, Roger had to succumb to a change in the billing: the German promoters knew they wouldn't attract the audiences without Roger's name. So, after much discussion with the rest of the band, he reluctantly agreed to 'Roger Taylor and the Cross'. It worked to a certain extent, as although the venues weren't filled to capacity, the crowds were bigger and more enthusiastic than expected.

Around this time, *Record Collector* announced that Queen had become the third most collectable band, following The Beatles in first place and U2 in second. Elvis Presley came a close fourth.

On 14 April, Freddie did something he had always said he would never do: appear in a stage musical. *Time* starred Cliff Richard, and Freddie joined the crooner on stage for a special charity performance. The proceeds from that show were donated to the Terrence Higgins Trust for research into AIDS.

A few days later, Freddie flew to Madrid to attend a gala performance at Teatro Real, staged in honour of the 25th anniversary of Montserrat Caballé's operatic career. There she performed several

PERSONAL TURMOIL

of the songs that she and Freddie had worked on together before a capacity audience, including the King and Queen of Spain – and, without her knowledge, Freddie himself. After the show, to her complete surprise, Freddie walked on stage to congratulate her in person and present her with a bouquet.

On 2 May, Jim Beach flew out to Marbella with some of the Freddie–Montserrat songs and previewed them to the international conference of Polygram Records, who were planning on signing Freddie as a solo artist for this album. They were all astonished by the material, and keen to release the album as soon as possible.

During the weeks preceding the annual Montreux Rock Festival, The Cross were approached and asked to appear. They agreed in principle, but only with the proviso that they could play live; it was more usual for acts taking part to mime to backing tracks, which meant they didn't have to ship equipment (it made the lives of the crews and engineers easier, too – it's far simpler to tweak a few knobs to make a tape sound good than to make an entire live band sound great). The controversial request was not looked upon favourably, but as they were co-managed by Queen's manager, Jim Beach, and Jim was closely involved with the rock festival and its organisation, they were granted their request. On 12 May they played just two songs, 'Manipulator' and 'Heaven For Everyone'. Roger mentioned in his fan club letter, 'We were one of only two acts, out of 54, to appear completely live.'

• • •

OVER THE YEARS, QUEEN HAD DONATED A LOT OF TIME AND MONEY to charitable causes without fuss or fanfare, from gifting signed photos and albums for auction, to their profits from the Newcastle concert. When they were asked to participate in the Prince's Trust Gala Concert at the Royal Albert Hall on 6 June, John and Brian agreed to give their time, and they appeared alongside a veritable feast of rock royalty

– Phil Collins, Eric Clapton, Mark Knopfler, Elton John and Joe Cocker – in what was termed a 'supergroup'. Brian says: 'A highlight for me was working with Joe Cocker. His presence seemed to infuse the "scratch band" with an amazing energy. And I was able to play alongside Clapton in "A Little Help From My Friends". A thrill!'

On June 2, Brian's father Harold died. Brian was understandably devastated. He and his dad had been so close and had done so much together, to lose him now was a heart-wrenching blow. The pain he felt was worsened by his personal turmoil. The rift between Brian and his wife had become an unbreachable canyon: his relationship with Anita Dobson was now common knowledge, although they had tried hard to keep it quiet, and he was torn between Anita and his love and devotion to his children. His health was suffering and he went through bouts of deep depression while trying to come to terms with it all and make the best decision for everyone. He finally chose to leave his wife and start a new life with Anita. It was probably the hardest decision he had ever had to make, but making the break and bringing it all out into the open helped to relieve the intense pressure he was under. Once again, the British press had a field day, and the front pages of many of that week's papers carried the story, accompanied by photos of the new couple taken at events they had attended together in the past. Brian was worried about the effect it might have on his children: two were of an age where they knew what was going on, and school friends could be spiteful.

Morris Minor and The Majors, the band John had met on his Virgin flight to Miami, were due to release another single, 'This Is The Chorus', and true to their word, they called upon John to make a guest appearance in the video. John wore a bright blue wig and went unnoticed by most people.

Elsewhere, *The Magic Years* visual anthology had been nominated for many awards, and in June 1988 it earned the award for best

PERSONAL TURMOIL

long-form video of the year worldwide at the International Music and Media Conference – quite the honour.

Meanwhile, Roger was approached by ex-Capital Radio DJ Kenny Everett, now a television celebrity with his own quiz show *Brainstorm*, and asked to appear. He was to be linked to a heart monitor and his heartbeat monitored while the contestants were asked to guess what his heart rate would be after thirty seconds of hard drumming. Roger did his bit and his heart rate was checked again. Luckily for him it wasn't much higher, proving he was quite fit.

On 4 July, The Cross released a fourth single. They chose 'Manipulator', a recently written track and therefore not on the *Shove It* track list. None of the previous singles had gone far in the charts, meaning the videos on which they had lavished so much time and money were never shown, so they thought better of making a video for 'Manipulator'. As it turned out, it was a sensible decision: the single failed to enter the Top 100.

During early 1988 Queen had been approached by Elaine Paige, one of Britain's most popular female recording artists and star of such legendary musicals as *Evita* and *Cats*. Composer Tim Rice suggested to her that she record an album of classic Queen tracks. At first she was sceptical, but after having heard one or two of the band's more melodic ballads she changed her mind. She chose the songs she wanted to sing and had the band's full permission to go ahead. The collection was called, believe it or not, *The Queen Album*.

Thirteen years after it was first released, 'Bohemian Rhapsody' was still a consistent contender in the 'all-time favourite' charts, and it made yet another appearance in September 1988, when BBC Radio One listeners voted it number one single in a nationwide poll. Coming in at a close second was Led Zeppelin's 'Stairway To Heaven', another track that is always somewhere in the top five in these polls but which, strangely enough, has never been released as a single.

In early October, according to *The Sun* newspaper, Brian's

tempestuous relationship with Anita was on the rocks. Apparently there had been a furious row in which Anita had walked out – nothing strange about that; everyone has them. Except that Brian and Anita seemed to be having more of them than most (if you believed the papers, that is). By the next day it was all hunky dory again.

While there may have been difficulties in their personal life, professionally the couple were kept busy. Anita had been asked to appear alongside Adam Faith in a stage musical version of the hit sixties television show *Budgie*. Plans were afoot to make a soundtrack album, and Brian agreed to play guitar on the track 'In One Of My Weaker Moments'.

On 8 October, Freddie and Montserrat appeared at the huge open-air festival La Nit, in Barcelona. The concert was presented on two massive stages erected in front of the famous son et lumière fountain in the Spanish city's Castle Square, arranged by Queen's tour manager, Gerry Stickells. The festival was held to celebrate the start of the four-year Cultural Olympiad, the beginning of which was signified when the Olympic torch and flag arrived in Barcelona from Seoul and the flame was lit. Backed by Barcelona's Opera House orchestra and choir, Freddie and Montserrat performed three tracks from their forthcoming album: 'How Can I Go On?', 'The Golden Boy' and 'Barcelona', accompanied by Mike Moran on piano. All proceeds from the glittering event went to the International Red Cross Association, with the primary aim of helping children suffering in war-torn zones across the world.

The long-awaited album, *Barcelona*, was finally released on 10 October. It was a remarkable mix of opera and pop, emphasis on opera. Freddie had excelled himself vocally, although his voice was occasionally eclipsed by the sheer power of Montserrat's. Montserrat was due in London that day to attend a lunchtime reception at Covent Garden's Royal Opera House for the album launch, and as Freddie wanted her to feel welcome he arranged for a massive billboard on

PERSONAL TURMOIL

the M4 motorway into London to carry a special advertisement for the new album, ensuring the driver knew exactly where it was so he could point it out. The pair met at Freddie's house and were ferried together to the Opera House by limousine, to be greeted by hundreds of ecstatic Queen fans. The press were out in force – after all, this was a free lunch, and with free champagne and wine, too, how could they refuse? It was sad, however, that hardly any of those journalists gave the album a favourable review, and in some cases even went so far as to complain about the sheer extravagance of the launch. They weren't heard complaining as their champagne glasses were refilled for the umpteenth time, though . . .

On the same day as the Barcelona launch, EMI released Queen's *Live In Budapest* video on the relatively new compact disc video system. It combined the best in hi-fi digital stereo with top-quality visuals. Because it was such a new concept, the equipment required to play the discs was horrendously expensive.

October 30 was the date of the annual awards show held by teen-pop magazine *Smash Hits* at London's Royal Albert Hall. Predictably, the nominees were in-vogue young bands or artists, but Queen were represented when a group of their fans turned up with a huge banner that read, 'After 15 albums, 31 hit singles and 663 live shows – Queen are still showing them how it's done!' However the protest was short-lived when Albert Hall stewards removed the banner due to it being a fire risk.

Although Queen failed to score in the *Smash Hits* poll they did well in another. The National Union of Students polled over 22,000 of its undergraduate members on their musical tastes, resulting in 'Bohemian Rhapsody' being voted their all-time favourite song and Queen their all-time favourite live band.

The remainder of 1988 was reasonably quiet: EMI released a set of twelve of the new format 3-inch CD singles but, due to a lack of communication with the band, they were less than perfect. And due to mistakes in the initial remastering of the original tapes, the CDs also contained a slew of errors which, once again, the fans were quick to spot.

November 17 saw the release on EMI Records of the album Brian had produced for Anita, *Talking Of Love*. It was preceded by another single, a cover version of the old Teddy Bears hit 'To Know Him Is To Love Him'. The album featured, by his own admission, some of Brian's finest guitar work.

Although Queen were quiet, Brian found enough work to keep him from boredom. He played guitar for the band Living In A Box on their new single 'Blow The House Down', and also contributed guitar work, at the behest of close friend Tony Iommi, to 'When Death Calls on the Black Sabbath album *Headless Cross*. Not content with that, he then played on the single 'Self', released by all-girl band Fuzzbox. Sometime later he was asked to join rock 'supergroup' Phenomena, featuring, among others, Scott Gorham, Dave Gilmour, Mel Galley and John Wetton. The band was formed to work on a film, and although nothing ever came of that, Phenomena made future albums with a variety of different personnel.

Still more session work came Brian's way in the form of some great guitar work on ex-Frankie Goes To Hollywood vocalist Holly Johnson's single 'Love Train', and vocals for good friend Steve Hackett on the track 'Slot Machine'. Lonnie Donegan was a childhood hero of Brian's, and Brian had previously played with him on an album track. When the skiffle legend asked Brian to write a song for him, he quickly accepted and penned 'Let Your Heart Rule Your Head', which Lonnie intended to include on his new album, assisted on vocals by Brian himself.

In December, Brian attended a concert by rock band Bon Jovi, a great favourite of his, where he was called upon to take the stage, along with Elton John, for the band's encore. Brian had gone along just to watch and wasn't equipped with his faithful Red Special, so declined.

PERSONAL TURMOIL

But the band's guitarist, Richie Sambora, wouldn't be denied his chance to play with the Queen legend and offered him one of his own guitars. Brian, without too much arm-twisting, gave in. It was the only time he could remember playing with another band minus his faithful instrument.

On 4 December 1988, The Cross played a special one-off concert at London's Hammersmith Palais for a Queen fan club Christmas party. They were joined on stage by Brian and John and ex-Manfred Mann vocalist Chris Thompson. It was a small, exclusive concert for fan club members only, and a wonderful Christmas present to them – three-quarters of Queen on stage, together for the first time since Knebworth 1986.

On Boxing Day, BBC Radio One played the Top 100 singles of 1988, in which Queen singles featured throughout, but 'Bohemian Rhapsody' was knocked off its usual number one spot by a young duo called Bros.

CHAPTER 25

THE MIRACLE

WORK ON THE ALBUM BEGUN IN JANUARY WAS NEARING COMPLETION by Christmas. This time the band changed their way of working: they usually wrote individually, each song becoming personal, with the writer insisting on having the final say in the way the song sounded and was recorded. This caused problems and arguments, as each member would want to work on his song more than the others and would fight for his track to be released as a single. This time they decided that every track would be credited 'words and music by Queen', no matter whose was the original idea. The songs they had all started to write as individuals were thrown into the melting pot and picked out and worked on by the whole band. It was difficult at first, as each was reluctant to let his baby go, but they found themselves working more closely than they had in years. When it came to choosing the singles, there was no hassle as royalties were also split four ways. The system worked so well they wondered why on earth they hadn't thought of it years ago.

In January 1989, BBC Radio One held a listeners' poll to determine the best British Queen song. They received over 8,500 phone calls – and the results put 'Bohemian Rhapsody' on top, with 'A Kind Of Magic' second, and 'I Want To Break Free' third.

THE MIRACLE

Meanwhile, Roger had met and got to know members of the eccentric new wave band Sigue Sigue Sputnik, and when they asked him to help them out with a forthcoming single, he agreed. They presented him with a track called 'Dancerama', which they felt needed 'something'. Roger listened to it, agreed that it did and proceeded to remix it.

A sad note in the early part of the year was the death of Denise Morse from leukaemia. Denise fought until the day she died to raise money for the British Bone Marrow Donor Appeal, a charity set up to fund a computer register of bone marrow donors so that those with the disease could be found a suitable donor quickly. Many people died because the right donor couldn't be found fast enough – and Denise's efforts raised several thousand pounds for the appeal. At her funeral 'Who Wants To Live Forever' was played – it was her favourite and the song that kept her going in her last weeks of life. Her story touched Brian, who had written the song, to such an extent that he joined forces with one of the appeal's directors, Malcolm Thomas, and decided to rewrite the song and release a new version in aid of the appeal. His idea was that the track should be sung not by him but by children. He advertised that he was looking for children on the BBC TV programme *Daytime Live*. Tapes flooded in from thousands of young hopefuls, ages ranging from six to sixteen. The task of listening to them fell to Brian and Malcolm, and finally they shortlisted 120, whittled down again to forty-six, half boys, half girls, who were invited to Abbey Road Studios to audition. The studios, engineers and everyone else involved gave their time and effort free of charge in aid of the cause. All the kids were nervous – not only were they at an audition, but many felt intimidated by their surroundings, not having 'seen' a recording studio before – especially such a famous one, although it was their parents who were more excited by the legendary surroundings. The children all performed brilliantly under such circumstances, and then Brian had the hardest task of all

– to choose just two of them. It took about a week for him to settle on Ian Meeson and Belinda Gillett. The song was recorded at Abbey Road, and Roger and John added bass and percussion. It was released by EMI, who were also giving their services free for the charity. Unfortunately, distribution was not well handled, and although the single was advertised by appearances on television and radio, people couldn't buy it in their shops without ordering it, so although it raised a lot of money it didn't make as much as had been hoped.

But raising money was the theme of Roger's exploits on 19 March. He, and many other eminent personalities, converged on Wimbledon Stadium (site of the infamous naked bicycle race) to take part in a charity rock'n'roll banger race, of which all proceeds from the day were to be donated to Nordoff Robbins Music Therapy. Roger didn't win his race but his new personal assistant, 'Big' Martin Groves, did.

All of Queen's album covers in the past had been imaginative, and the new album would be no exception. 'At an "ideas" session we tossed around ways of blending four faces together, to give a visual image of the "organic" working unit we felt we had become,' recalls Brian. Artist Richard Gray, who had worked with Queen previously on the *Kind Of Magic* cover, was briefed with the task. He employed the most advanced computer graphic techniques and started with a head shot of each band member. Then, using a machine called a Quantel Graphic Paintbox, he fed into it the separate photos. When the result emerged the four heads were all blended into one, the four faces dissolving into each other.

The first single from the new album was 'I Want It All' with the B-side non-album track 'Hang On In There'. It was released by EMI on 2 May 1989, the band's thirty-second UK single. The video involved using twelve fifty-foot high Dino light stands, the type usually used to light football stadiums. The director, once again David Mallett, also assembled sixteen Super Trouper spotlights and shot the film in Cinemascope. The single entered the UK chart at number three and was the band's highest chart entry to date. Radio One had organised a charity auction in aid of the Hillsborough Disaster Fund, set up to help the survivors and the families of those killed in the tragic accident at the football stadium, and auctioned a copy of the forthcoming Queen album, which raised £500 unsigned. Brian also recoded a message for a special phone-in prior to the album release, which included snippets from the album.

Freddie's extravagant taste drew him to Switzerland in early May, as he wanted to buy some hand-painted porcelain pieces. The four pieces he bought cost him over £9,000. While he was there, he was invited to a special dinner party held at Frédy Girardet's restaurant in Lausanne, reputedly the 'best restaurant in the world', to be served with fourteen courses – and Frédy Girardet signed Freddie Mercury's menu.

May 22 saw the release of the band's sixteenth album, *The Miracle*. Pre-sales alone ensured it received a platinum award in its first week of release.

Queen hadn't done an interview as a band on television or radio for about ten years – until 29 May. Radio One DJ Mike Reid, a friend of the band, persuaded all of them to gather for an hour-long interrogation. For once during an interview Freddie talked openly about his reluctance to tour again with Queen. His reasons were that they had 'been there and done that' at major venues all over the world, and he wanted to break the 'album, tour, album, tour' routine, and find something different for Queen to do or play. As an aside he commented that he didn't feel he should be running around a stage in a leotard any more. The other members of Queen didn't really agree with him, but they respected his wishes and found other things to occupy them.

After all the years of over-indulgence and excess, Freddie began to realise that life was speeding by and that he wasn't taking the time to relax and enjoy it. He spent more and more time at home in the garden and looking after his six cats. He began keeping Japanese koi carp, which looked like giant goldfish but were worth about a thousand times as much.

The media decided that Freddie must be ill with something if he didn't want to tour. Stories began to circulate and the speculation grew as to what was wrong with him; as far as the press were concerned, he had suddenly contracted every illness from A to Z. They were stories Freddie chose to ignore.

The follow-up single to 'I Want It All' was going to be 'Breakthru'. The band had some great ideas for the video. The song's rhythm suggested trains so they pulled in Hannes Rossacher and Rudi Dolezal and asked them to investigate the feasibility of filming on a moving train. Nothing is impossible – and to make sure it looked realistic, rather than using background films with the band stationary in a studio, the Nene Valley private railway in Cambridgeshire was hired for a two-day shoot. An old steam train was given new front and side plates, renamed temporarily *The Miracle Express* and a decorated flatbed carriage hooked up to it. With the cameras and crew, band and their instruments all in place on the carriage, the train moved along at a cracking pace. The weather, luckily, was glorious on both days, and everyone, band included, enjoyed it – as Brian says, it was 'boys with toys' again.

'Breakthru' was released on 19 June, their thirty-third UK single. ('For a living legend this is shitty,' was *Kerrang!*'s eloquent review.) Roger, when interviewed and asked what he thought of 'Breakthru', said, 'I think it's good. Better by about seven light years than Jason Donovan'. It was getting rather expensive for fans to keep up with single sales now though, as EMI released no fewer than five versions of 'Breakthru': a CD, cassette, vinyl seven-inch and twelve-inch and a shaped picture disc. And, of course, the fans went out and bought all five. It was the in-thing for all bands, it seemed, to release as many different shapes and sizes as possible, although the song remained

THE MIRACLE

the same. Queen again used a non-album track, 'Stealin'', on the B-side.

It seemed also to be the in-thing to make records to help charities: after the devastating earthquake in Armenia rock stars gathered to re-record the old Deep Purple classic 'Smoke On The Water', hoping to raise some much-needed cash to help the survivors. Brian and Roger were asked to play and instantly agreed to help, alongside other stars Bruce Dickinson, David Coverdale, Tony Iommi, Paul Rodgers, Chris Squire and Dave Gilmour.

Freddie was usually the one for extravagant parties, but as Roger turned forty in 1989, he decided to hold one of his own. He sent out invitations to just about everyone he could think of, asking them to join him at a 'schoolboys and schoolgirls' fancy dress party at his house in Surrey, laying on a relay of coaches from central London to ferry guests to the bash and back afterwards. Two huge marquees had been pitched in the enormous gardens of the house, complete with wooden dance floor, stage for two live bands and full disco lights. He had also hired a 'Sky-Tracker', a powerful quadruple spotlight, which was scanning the sky (he'd had to get permission from the Civil Aviation Authority to use it, as planes had to be warned in case they mistook it for landing lights). He had no problem with planes – but local police, and the forces in the next county, had their switchboards overloaded with thousands of calls from worried people, thinking the 'lights in the sky' they could see were unidentified flying objects. People were jumping into their cars and driving to the source of the lights, believing that aliens were landing. It caused chaos as many, still in their nightclothes, parked their cars on the busy main road and made a dash across the carriageway to see if they could get a closer view. The entire affair made front-page news the following day.

August 7 was the release date of Queen's next single, 'Invisible Man'. ('Explores the side of Queen I like least – funky and disco-ey

– and nice stabs of guitar from Brian May don't save it,' wrote *Sounds*.) EMI excelled themselves this time, releasing six versions: a cassette single, CD single, black vinyl seven-inch and twelve-inch plus clear vinyl seven-inch and twelve-inch. Fans, though, did get yet another non-album B-side, 'Hijack My Heart', with Roger on lead vocals. Rudi Dolezal and Hannes Rossacher were drafted in again to make the video.

Hannes and Rudi had also been working on a *Rare Live – a Concert Through Time and Space* for Queen that would depict their live career using rare film footage from their early days through to present day. Released on 21 August, the video was a hugely successful venture, and revealed to many of the band's younger fans how they all looked way back then.

None of Queen had ever been featured in the Madame Tussaud's waxworks museum in London, even though many of their fellow artists had been granted exhibition space. But during early August the museum approached Freddie and asked if he would pose for a model of himself to be made for a special exhibition in Piccadilly's Trocadero Centre. The display would feature the artists who were involved in Live Aid, although only Freddie was asked from Queen. The other stars all sat in person for the artist, but Freddie sent a photo. The entire band, however, were given pride of place in a special video, shown continuously in the exhibition. Brian was invited to critique the exhibition and visited it with television presenter Cathy McGowan. Later they reviewed it (favourably . . .) on TV.

During August and September Brian undertook some promotional work for Queen and for several of the charity projects he had become involved with, including the Armenia single, and another called 'Yes We Can' released under the name Artists United for Nature and featuring Chris Thompson, Joe Cocker and many other well-known singers, proceeds from which went towards saving the rainforests. He visited Greece and Italy and did a lot of work in the UK, for those

The 'Crown' lighting rig, 1977. NEAL PRESTON

The Los Angeles Forum, December 1977. RICHARD CREAMER/MICHAEL OCHS ARCHIVE/GETTY IMAGES

John with Pluto, Disney World, Florida, November 1978.

Roger with green hair, Saarbrücken, 18 August 1979.

Backstage at the Budokan, Tokyo, Japan, 1979. KOH HASEBE/SHINKO MUSIC/GETTY IMAGES

Freddie rehearsing with the Royal Ballet, October 1979. MARK AND COLLEEN HAYWARD/GETTY IMAGES

Appearing on a TV show in Venezuela, September 1981.

With Diego Maradona, Argentina, 1981. NEAL PRESTON

Brian and Anita Dobson, 1990.

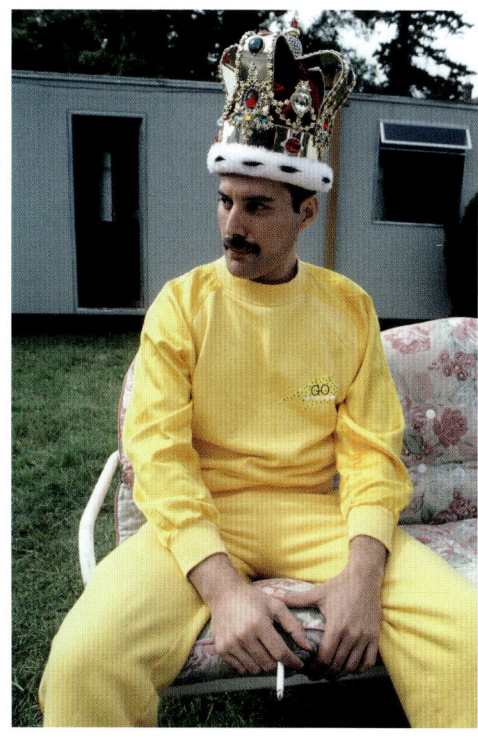

Backstage at Slane Castle, the Magic Tour, 1986.
NEAL PRESTON

Freddie performing at Live Aid, 13 July 1985. GEORGES DE KEERLE/GETTY IMAGES

The band arriving at Knebworth House, 1986. DENIS O'REGAN/GETTY IMAGES

The Cross, backstage in Birmingham, 1988. (Back, L–R) Josh Macrae (drums), Suzie O'List (backing vocals), Roger Taylor (vocals), Clayton Moss (guitar), Peter Noone (bass); (Front, L–R) Gill O'Donovan (backing vocals), Spike Edney (keyboards). JIM JENKINS

John and Extreme's Gary Cherone at the Freddie Mercury Tribute Concert, 1992.
NEAL PRESTON © QUEEN PRODUCTIONS LTD.

The Freddie statue, Lake Geneva, Montreux, Switzerland. ULLSTEINBILD/TOPFOTO

THE MIRACLE

tracks and for the 'Who Wants To Live Forever' single. He also found the time for some rest and relaxation in Los Angeles with Anita. While there, he decided, one morning, to take his son's skateboard for a run. Unfortunately it was more difficult than he thought – he came a cropper, breaking his upper arm. It took six months and much physiotherapy to get it working again. When reminded that he was a grown man and should surely stay away from boys' toys he just shrugged (painfully) and said, 'No chance.'

Brian flew back to the UK to work with actor Gareth Marks, a friend of Anita's who was making his first album and had been portraying Buddy Holly on stage in London in the musical *Buddy*. The track he guested on was called 'Lady of Leisure'.

Roger flew out to Switzerland in late September to work with The Cross on new material. While he had been busy with Queen, The Cross had worked hard together on a lot of new songs and they wanted to spend time committing them to tape. Roger was surprised by how much material the band had gathered while he had been otherwise occupied – almost a whole album's worth.

John, meanwhile, went to Biarritz, a place he and his wife liked so much they had bought a holiday apartment there.

'Scandal', the fourth single from *The Miracle*, was released on 9 October. It was a hard-hitting track aimed directly at the world's press, the band's way of getting their own back without being sued. EMI's sales tactic on this one was to release another six versions – this time the normal CD and cassette singles, plus an ordinary seven-inch and a seven-inch in a special picture bag, and an ordinary twelve-inch and a twelve-inch in a special sleeve with the record itself laser-etched with the band's signatures. Their ingenuity knew no bounds as far as selling as many as possible of the same single was concerned, but again, fans were given a non-album flip side with 'My Life Has Been Saved'. Rudi and Hannes once again took on video duties, filming at Pinewood Studios.

On 21 November Brian was invited to London's Hammersmith Odeon to play with legendary rock'n'roller Jerry Lee Lewis. The show had been planned for some two weeks previously, but Lewis, who was a notoriously unreliable character, failed to show up for rehearsals, so it had to be cancelled. But on this particular night all went well, and the show was filmed for a forthcoming video release.

Towards the end of 1989 there were many 'best of the eighties' programmes on television, one of which was hosted by TV personality Cilia Black. The readers of the *TV Times* and viewers of ITV had been asked to vote for their favourites in several different categories, one of which was band of the eighties. The nominations included Bros, Eurythmics and Erasure, but Queen walked off with the award, all members appearing during the pre-recording of the show to collect it.

The next Queen single, the fifth from *The Miracle*, was to be the title track. Freddie had the idea of using young 'lookalikes' to take the place of the band in the video, and Queen themselves would appear at the end. Auditions were set up at the top children's stage schools in London to find four kids who not only looked a bit like Queen but could perform like them too. It took several weeks to select the four lucky lads out of the thousands that were auditioned, but on the day of the shoot the choice was justified, as they were brilliant. The boy playing Freddie even had the man himself copying him. 'The Miracle' was released on 27 November – and again EMI found six different ways to package it, including a limited edition seven-inch with a hologram cover. The B-side was a great live version of 'Stone Cold Crazy', taken from the Rainbow 1974 concert, and an extra bonus track on the twelve-inch was the wonderful 'My Melancholy Blues', live from Houston in 1977.

In time for the lucrative Christmas market, Picture Music International released a video EP featuring 'I Want It All', 'Breakthru', 'The Invisible Man' and 'Scandal'. It was called *The Miracle Video EP*

THE MIRACLE

but didn't actually include the video for 'The Miracle' as it hadn't been completed in time for inclusion, and PMI wanted to save it, anyway, to include on a proposed *Greatest Flix Two* video for the following year.

The band surprised everyone when in late November they stated they were ready to go back in the studios to start work on the next Queen album. It was quite a shock that they wanted to start work so soon after *The Miracle* was released. But they had been inspired by its worldwide success – it had even sold well in the USA, where Queen's popularity in the last few years had faded somewhat.

Brian, Freddie and John flew out to Mountain Studios in Montreux to start work. Roger was busy with The Cross, completing their album, and flew out to Germany with them to shoot the video for their single 'Power To Love', with Torpedo Twins Rudi and Hannes. The video was a completely over the top affair, featuring large-busted women in tight, low-cut crinolined dresses, men in Charles I-type outfits of short knickerbockers, buckled shoes and long wigs, all indulging in a sumptuous feast – and in each other. In liberal-minded Germany, the video was well received, but in somewhat more prudish Britain it had to be re-edited to clean it up for television. From Germany, Roger flew directly to Montreux to join the rest of Queen.

On 4 December an album entitled *Queen At The Beeb* was released on the Strange Fruit/Band of Joy label, featuring the eight songs Queen had initially recorded back in February and December 1973, as BBC radio sessions. The Strange Fruit company had tracked down the original master tapes of those sessions, and, with the band's full permission, bought them back from the BBC archives and assembled them on an album. It was a great release as far as the fans were concerned as it gave them the opportunity to buy the rare and treasured early Queen without having to resort to badly copied bootlegs.

On 31 December the Cilla Black show *Goodbye To The Eighties*, filmed a few weeks earlier, was shown on television – and it was announced at the same time that Queen's *Greatest Hits* album was the fourth best-selling album of all time, sitting behind Dire Straits' *Brothers In Arms* (1985) and Michael Jackson's *Bad* (1987) and *Thriller* (1982).

Brian's new decade opened in charitable style, with him in the studio on New Year's Day with several other top artists to work on a version of the wonderful 'Sailing', previously recorded by Rod Stewart. The song was to be released under the title of 'Rock Against Repatriation', and all proceeds were to go to aid the Vietnamese boat people, who had settled in Hong Kong but were being forcibly returned to Vietnam.

The Cross were set to release their new single: they had finally signed a record deal with German company Electrola (none of the British record companies seemed prepared to give them a chance, possibly related to the failure of *Shove It* with Virgin). 'Power To Love' came out in Germany on 29 January.

Queen went back into the studios after the Christmas break, full of enthusiasm and new ideas. They decided they would work on the album as a band rather than as individuals: it had all gone so well for *The Miracle*, and anything that ensured harmony had to be a good thing. They flew back from Switzerland in early February. Brian arrived just in time to pop into the Hammersmith Odeon to visit old friends Ian Hunter and Mick Ronson, ex-Mott The Hoople. They were doing a short tour, and Brian joined them on stage to play 'All The Way From Memphis'. Brian said, 'It brought back some great memories. I had seen them perform this song many times with Ariel Bender while we were on tour with them. I particularly remember the night they played it in Memphis. It was a really great feeling, doing it with them after so much had happened to all of us.'

On 18 February it was time again for the annual British

Phonographic Industry Awards ceremony, held at the Dominion Theatre on Tottenham Court Road. At last Queen were recognised: they were presented with an award for their outstanding contribution to British music by BPI chairman Terry Ellis. Hannes and Rudi had edited a special compilation video to be shown at the ceremony, and the band all turned out, in dinner suits, to collect the award. Brian's speech went as follows: 'On behalf of the group, I'd like to say thank you very much to everyone in the industry and, perhaps more importantly, outside the industry who stuck behind us all these years. Because, in doing so, you gave us a lot of freedom to pursue what we loosely call our art to any extent we felt like at the time. And to go out on a lot of strange limbs which seemed very precarious at the time, but we didn't quite fall off. And finally, to get to the point where this happens to us, which is great. And I'd like to say a special thank you to the British Petroleum Industry for giving us this magnificent award in recognition of all the amounts of vinyl which we've recycled over the years. Thank you.'

As they left the stage Roger added, 'Thank you very much' and Freddie gave a gentle wave and a 'Thank you, goodnight'.

After the ceremony most of the celebrity audience went off to a special BPI dinner, except Queen. 1990 was their twentieth anniversary — not *strictly* true if it was taken into account that John only joined in early 1971, but Queen as a name and a band were formed in 1970 so they threw a party to celebrate. They hired The Groucho club in Soho, and invited over 400 guests, tracking down everyone who had ever had anything to do with Queen: ex-roadies, secretaries, photographers, managers, record company bosses and many others. The small club was packed to bursting point, and it was all free all night. A lot of the stars who had attended the BPI awards were also present; they had grown bored of the formal dinner and sneaked off at the first opportunity to join in the Queen fun. To honour the anniversary in his own way, Roger bought girlfriend Debbie Leng an antique platinum and diamond necklace, worth £150,000, which she wore at the party.

Freddie's appearance at the awards show and the party afterwards again sparked off rumours of ill health. At the ceremony he and the other members of the band had been made up for the television lights. But Freddie's make-up only served to make his features seem drawn and gaunt. When a sneaky photographer snapped a shot of him leaving the party in the early hours of the morning (looking the worse for wear after a hard night), which appeared on the front page of a daily paper, people began to get worried.

Freddie said he felt fine, had never felt better, scotching rumours that had begun to spread about his having caught the AIDS virus. It was a statement that helped to relieve the fears of many of his followers. But he added that he still didn't want to tour.

Queen went back into the studios in March 1990 to continue work on their album.

Meanwhile, The Cross released their second album, *Mad, Bad And Dangerous To Know*, on 26 March. The title came from a quote that had been used to describe the eccentric Lord Byron, who had been imprisoned in Chillon Castle in Montreux, near to the studios where most of the album had been recorded.

The Cross had also planned a short tour of Germany. Album sales in the UK had been so low that the record company wouldn't consider paying for the band to tour there, but sales in Germany had been reasonably good. The opening date was 11 May in Hannover. The venues were tiny clubs and theatres, and the audiences, although small, were quite eager. Sales of the album improved in Germany during the tour, but back in the UK it wasn't doing any better, despite the band spending an entire day in Tower Records, on London's Piccadilly, signing copies.

During a break in recording, Brian was approached by theatre director Malcolm Ranson, an avid Queen fan, and artistic director

THE MIRACLE

Jane L'Epine Smith, who was considering a stage production of Shakespeare's *Macbeth*. They wanted to use music by a contemporary composer, feeling that it would make Shakespeare more accessible to younger audiences, and Brian was Malcolm's first choice. Brian took up the challenge readily – it was his first original score for theatre and he was very excited about it.

Sadly, in late July 1990 Roger's father, Michael, died in hospital in Cheltenham, where he had made his home since his divorce from Roger's mother. He had been ill for some time and so his death didn't come as a complete shock. Although he and Roger weren't close, Roger was extremely upset and drove up to Cheltenham for the funeral on 27 July, the day after his forty-first birthday.

During a brief respite from the two projects he was working on, Brian flew up to Nottingham to play guitar on two tracks for a new band, D-Rok. He had got involved with them when he and his son, Jimmy, had been invited to visit the Games Workshop. Jimmy was a computer-game aficionado and the Games Workshop was the biggest manufacturer of fantasy and science fiction games in Europe. The company were branching into the music business, trying to incorporate the heavy metal-type imagery of the games into real life with D-Rok. During his visit, the Games Workshop asked Brian if he would be interested in helping them out with the project, and Brian agreed. The two tracks he had played on, 'Get Out Of My Way' and 'Red Planet Blues', were to feature on the band's forthcoming album, *Oblivion*, which was being released in 1991 on the Games Workshop's own label, Warhammer.

Queen were still in the studios, now Metropolis in London, in July 1990, and the album work was still on schedule for a Christmas release – four tracks had already been finished. The band were taking the recording of this album at an easy pace, which enabled Brian to continue to work on the *Macbeth* music when Queen were idle.

He also dived again into the Hammersmith Odeon, this time to see good friend Tony Iommi and Black Sabbath. He accepted the offer to join them on stage for their encore, much to the delight of the capacity crowd.

In Germany, The Cross released another single from *Mad, Bad And Dangerous To Know*, a track called 'Liar' – not the song of the same name released by Queen many years previously. The B-side, 'In Charge of My Heart', was a song that Roger had written since the album had been recorded, and which had therefore not featured on it.

CHAPTER 26

TWENTY-FIRST CELEBRATIONS

AFTER MUCH DISCUSSION THE BAND FINALLY AGREED ON A TITLE FOR the new album, *Innuendo*. It was taken from a six-and-a-half-minute-long epic track of the same name, one of several they had now completed. In his letter in the fan club magazine Roger said: 'It's the overall best album for years and years . . . the lynchpin track is a sort of heavy-heavy Eastern flavoured bolero-ish epic with a bit of desert-type oasis thrown into the middle . . . not surprisingly it's called "Innuendo!"'

The only problems they were having with the recording and mixing of the album was the absence of a bass player: John was spending much of his time with his family at their apartment in Biarritz, and little of it at the studios. But work progressed, and the album was reaching its final stages.

The Cross released their third single from *Mad, Bad* in November 1990, the beautiful ballad 'Final Destination'. It was, again, only released in Germany, and failed to make any impression on the charts there, even though it featured a live version of Roger's 'Man On Fire' as the B-side.

At the beginning of 1990 Queen had a meeting to discuss their popularity, or lack of it, in the USA. The outcome was the instigation of a search for a new record company to represent them there, and Jim Beach began negotiations with Capitol to buy back the rights to the entire Queen back catalogue. It was all over quickly: Capitol had no objections and were paid handsomely for releasing the rights. It was made known throughout the US music business that Queen were now 'on the market' and looking for a new deal. The carrot dangling in front of the record companies' noses was that back catalogue, never before released on compact disc in America and worth a fortune to whoever could release it. Many companies made offers, including Elektra, the band's original US record company, but the biggest and best came from a brand new company, Hollywood Records.

Hollywood Records were set up by the enormous, multi-million dollar Walt Disney corporation when they decided to branch out into the music industry. Their offer to Queen was rumoured to be in the region of £10 million. They had strong ideas for publicity and promotion, aimed at getting Queen back on the top of the charts and soaring in the popularity stakes. The band and Jim Beach had a good feeling about the company, and contracts were signed in November 1990.

The record company's first task was to find all the original master tapes of the Queen albums and have them completely digitally remastered; they had heard the EMI remasters on CD and were not impressed – they knew they could do so much better, and with no mistakes. The tapes were tracked down from vaults all over the world and shipped to England and the Townhouse studios in Shepherd's Bush, where the work was carried out on the first four albums. Subsequent albums were remastered at Future Disc Systems in Hollywood.

When work on the new album wasn't complete by early November,

TWENTY-FIRST CELEBRATIONS

Queen asked for the release date to be put back to February 1991. EMI were not happy, as the Christmas market was huge and massive sales would be guaranteed. But the band didn't want to rush the album: it was, they considered, one of their best for a long time. By Christmas it was complete, and the band decided that the title track, the six-and-a-half-minute-long 'Innuendo', should be released as the first single in mid-January. Hollywood Records argued that none of the radio stations in the USA would want to play a track that long and, considering the importance of radio play, they requested a different track, 'Headlong', as their single. The band agreed and took over Metropolis Studios for two days to film a video for it.

The idea for the album cover came when Roger found a book by eighteenth-century illustrator Grandville. He showed one particular illustration to the band, a black and white pencil drawing titled *A Juggler of Universes*. They all loved it and called in designer Richard Gray to adapt it for the cover. Richard hand-coloured the drawing and changed it slightly. He also chose several smaller illustrations to use on the back cover. Grandville's drawings were so varied that it was decided to use as many as was necessary to provide cover art for the proposed single releases, too.

To accompany 'Innuendo', they employed the talents of top animator Jerry Hibbert. He was asked to work on a video featuring a variety of characters from Grandville's book. The final video was a fully animated piece that perfectly fit the song.

Just before the release of *Innuendo*, war broke out in the Persian Gulf and Allied Forces were engaged in a monumental air battle. It meant some of the scenes that had been used in the 'Innuendo' video, footage taken during the Second World War, had to be removed and replaced with an innocuous subject – folk dancing.

Meanwhile, Brian had completed his score for the Red & Gold Theatre Company's production of *Macbeth*, and the play opened at the Riverside Theatre in London on 19 November for a five-week run. He attended the theatre almost every night in support of the production – and the music was well received by the press. 'Rather good and unobtrusive', said *The Mail On Sunday*. 'His score creates a feeling of destructive chaos which is reflected on stage', said *The Telegraph*.

On 3 December, Picture Music International released a video of Queen's 1986 Magic Tour gig at Wembley Stadium. Many people in the UK already owned a copy, as it had been televised, but the demand for a Queen live video had been so great (*We Will Rock You* had been reissued and was selling phenomenal amounts) that PMI wanted to cash in on it, and released this one in full digital stereo.

The Cross had only played live in Germany and the Netherlands so far with their *Mad, Bad And Dangerous* album, so the tickets for their one and only UK gig, at a party organised by the Queen fan club at London's Astoria Theatre on 7 December, sold out fast. They played a full set and were joined on stage by Brian for the encore. He played, live for the first time, a track from his own *Star Fleet* album called 'Let Me Out'. He also played the old Queen classic 'Tie Your Mother Down'. It was the first time that song had been performed in many years – and the first time ever with lead vocals shared by Roger and Brian, so none of the audience were bothered when they both forgot the lyrics!

Christmas came and went uneventfully and Freddie's appetite for work grew so keen that he pulled the band back into the recording studios in the first week of January 1991. They flew out to Montreux to record several extra tracks which they could then use as B-sides to singles. But they liked a few of the tracks they were working on so much that they considered them too good for relegation, and decided to include them on their next album.

The single 'Innuendo' was released on 14 January 1991, and sold over 100,000 copies in its first week, guaranteeing its entry into the UK chart at number one, their first since November 1981's 'Under

TWENTY-FIRST CELEBRATIONS

Pressure'. Hollywood Records chose to release 'Headlong' as their first single on 17 January. It was much requested on US rock radio. The album was finally released on 4 February. It shipped over 200,000 in the first week and crashed straight into the UK album chart again in the top position.

Some months previously Brian had been approached by British comedy duo Hale & Pace, who invited him to produce a charity single for Comic Relief. The various hilarious and silly fund-raising events would culminate in one day, Red Nose Day, during which people all over the UK bought plastic red 'clown' noses and wore them in aid of the charity. The Hale & Pace supergroup record was called 'The Stonk', and all proceeds from sales would go to Comic Relief. A star line-up, including David Gilmour, Tony Iommi, Neil Murray and Cozy Powell, converged on Metropolis Studios in late January 1991 to record the track, with Brian producing. (He and Roger also played on it and appeared in the video.) 'The Stonk', which was based on a fictitious dance craze was released on 25 February and after two weeks was stuck firmly at number one in the UK singles chart, raising many thousands of pounds for Comic Relief.

Meanwhile *Innuendo* was having massive success worldwide. The single had dropped quite quickly out of the UK chart, but was climbing steadily elsewhere, reaching the Top 10 all over Europe and even hitting number one in South Africa. The album went to number one in most European countries, and climbed to number thirty in the US *Billboard* Top 200 – a great start for Hollywood Records, who had launched *Innuendo* in the States with a lavish and expensive party on board the *Queen Mary* cruise ship, which had been turned into a hotel (now owned by the Walt Disney Company) and was permanently moored in concrete at Long Beach, California (next door to Howard Hughes's famous plane, the *Spruce Goose*). Brian and Roger were both at the party, and were treated to enormous amounts of food, an endless supply of drinks and a firework show that was the best anyone had ever seen, all exploding to the strains of 'Bohemian Rhapsody'. Freddie and John had declined the invitation; John was tied up with family plans and Freddie had never really been one for record company bashes, preferring instead to stay at home.

For three very cold days in February, Queen and the Torpedo Twins were ensconced in London's Limehouse Studios to film the video for their forthcoming single, a track from *Innuendo* called 'I'm Going Slightly Mad'. The video underlined the title's meaning: Brian was dressed as a penguin and wore four-inch silver-plated fingernails; Roger, at one point, wore a boiling kettle as a hat and rode on a child's tricycle; John pulled faces and had a jester's tricolour hat perched on his head; and Freddie looked ever so slightly insane as Lord Byron. It also featured a man in a gorilla suit and a trio of live penguins, each of whom could only work for half an hour at a time under the hot lights, before they had to be taken outside to cool down in the snow. One of them, known as Cleo, endeared herself to everyone during a shot, when she relieved herself on the black leather settee the band were sitting on!

In February 1991, the Gulf War ended. During the conflict, 'Another One Bites The Dust' had been the most requested record on Gulf Forces radio, and after it was all over 'We Are The Champions' took its spot. Hollywood Records even released (unknown to the band) a special very limited edition CD to the Armed Forces – a mixture of George Bush's 'Victory' speech and 'We Are The Champions'.

'I'm Going Slightly Mad' was released in the UK on 4 March. A bonus track, 'Lost Opportunity', featuring Brian on lead vocals, was included on the twelve-inch and CD formats of the single. The following day, Hollywood Records in the USA released the first flight of remastered compact discs and cassettes, which also featured several remixes as bonus tracks.

The Cross went into Real World Studios in Box, near Bath, in March 1991 to begin recording their third album. Roger spent as

TWENTY-FIRST CELEBRATIONS

Come aboard the **QUEEN MARY**

with

HOLLYWOOD
records

for the launch of

INNUENDO

the new release from

Q U E E N

the champions of entertainment

SATURDAY, FEB. 2, 1991

7:30 - 11:30 p.m.

The Queen Mary Grand Salon
Long Beach Harbor

Party begins at 7:30 p.m.

"Innuendo" show at 9:00 p.m.
in Grand Salon

Special surprise event at 10:00 p.m.

Queen Fireworks show at 10:30 p.m.
on upper deck

R.S.V.P. by January 28
to Hollywood Records at
818/560-7298

much time with them as he could, but girlfriend Debbie was expecting their baby imminently and he wanted to be nearby to London. On 8 March, Debbie and Roger became the proud parents of a son, Rufus Tiger. The Cross switched from Box to the Roundhouse studios in north London to finish the album, and its release was planned for the autumn.

In early April, *Record Collector* magazine, a publication devoted entirely to collectables within the music world, announced that Queen were the second most collectable artists in history, behind The Beatles.

On 13 May 1991, EMI released 'Headlong', the band's thirty-ninth single and another track from *Innuendo*. Again, the single featured a bonus track, 'Mad The Swine'. The song had been written by Freddie and recorded by Queen in 1972 for inclusion on their first album, but they hadn't liked the way the mix sounded, and there wasn't really room for it on the album, so it was dropped. When the album was finished, 'Mad The Swine' was dumped into the vault with all the other material, and there it remained, until research into the band's master tapes and recorded work revealed it. The band retrieved it, dusted it off, made a few minor adjustments to its quality and sound, and unveiled it as the special bonus track. Their fans, particularly those from 'way back', loved it, and it caused even more of a reaction from them than the A-side, which climbed to number fourteen in the UK singles chart.

In early May, Queen flew out to Switzerland for routine work on material for their next album, working on three or four songs. Then, starting in late May 1991, Brian undertook a strenuous 'radio tour' of North America and Canada, to promote both Queen and his own solo album. He took along his guitar, and actually 'plugged in' to the radio consoles and played live to the listening public. During the tour he met hundreds of Queen fans, some of whom travelled from far afield to meet him, and talked to hundreds more on phone-ins. His reception was phenomenal and served to remind him that Queen were still alive and appreciated in North America, even though it had appeared their popularity had dwindled. Many of the people he spoke with had remained loyal followers right from the early days, and yet more were those who had rediscovered the band, proving that Hollywood Records' promise to rekindle much of the celebrity that the band had enjoyed a number of years previously had not been empty. Brian flew back to the UK, tired but elated and somewhat rejuvenated by his experience. He went on to Switzerland alone to do some intensive work on his long-awaited solo album. He had so successfully plugged it during his American radio tour that fans there were eagerly awaiting its debut, giving Brian the impetus to complete it.

On 30 May, while Brian was away in the USA, the other members of Queen went into a small film studio in west London with Rudi Dolezal to shoot a 'lip sync' or mime section for inclusion in a video being partially animated by the Walt Disney Company, the first time Disney had animated a music video. The video was to accompany the second commercial single release by Hollywood Records, a ballad from *Innuendo* called 'Days Of Our Lives'. Brian was filmed alone when he returned and reunited with the rest of Queen during the editing process.

Next up, Hollywood commissioned a special documentary for US television, entitled *Days Of Our Lives*, which would chart the band's career. Editing was done by Hannes Rossacher and Rudi Dolezal using footage from the wealth of interviews, live footage and promos available to them. Hollywood wanted a presenter that would appeal to the heavier rock-oriented audiences, and so approached Guns N' Roses lead singer, Axl Rose. Axl, a self-confessed Queen fan of long standing, was happy to oblige, and wrote his own script for the documentary, which was shown across America.

On 8 August, The Cross released, in Germany only, a single taken from their new album, a track called 'New Dark Ages', filming the accompanying monochrome video with director Paul Voss. Their album, *Blue Rock*, was released in Germany on 9 September, and they played a headlining gig in Helsinki on 3 October, before joining British rock band Magnum as support for a major German tour.

In early August, Brian was asked to guest on the English comedian and folk singer Richard Digance's television show to be broadcast on 17 August, and did so, airing an instrumental track, 'Last Horizons', which would feature on his forthcoming solo album.

In September 1991, the City of Chicago, Illinois, held its annual American Film and Video Festival. The 'Innuendo' video was awarded first prize in the category for creative excellence in the arts, and the amusing 'I'm Going Slightly Mad' video was third in the culture and performing arts category.

October 14 saw the UK release of Queen's fortieth single, 'The Show Must Go On', with their first ever single, 'Keep Yourself Alive', on the B-side. It was released in standard seven-inch and twelve-inch formats, and as two CD singles; one was made available in a small cardboard box as a collector's edition, while a cassette single version was released some weeks later. It climbed to number sixteen in the UK charts and *Top Of The Pops* scored an exclusive when they 'premiered' the video for the single – a compilation of the best of Queen, edited by the Torpedo Twins – four days prior to its release.

During the early part of August, Tribute Productions approached Brian with a proposition. They were organising a huge guitar festival to take place in Seville, Spain, in October, as part of the Expo' 92 celebrations. The plan was to feature many different guitar styles and persuade the best guitarists in their field to play live. Brian was asked to be musical director for the rock night, which meant forming a basic backing band and selecting some of the great guitarists to perform.

After sleepless nights and a million phone calls, on 19 October 1991, Brian took to the stage in Seville with a backing band consisting of Cozy Powell and Steve Ferrone on drums, Rick Wakeman and

TWENTY-FIRST CELEBRATIONS

Mike Moran on keyboards, and Neil Murray and Nathan East on bass. The featured guitarists – alongside Brian, of course – were Nuno Bettencourt, a young American from the American rock band Extreme, Joe Walsh, ex of the Eagles, Steve Vai and Joe Satriani. Guest vocalists were Extreme's Gary Cherone and Paul Rodgers, originally with Free, then later Bad Company. Their fifty-minute set was received ecstatically by the packed crowd, while the event was filmed and recorded to be broadcast on radio and television at a later date.

On 28 October 1991, EMI simultaneously released Queen's *Greatest Hits Two*, the album, *Greatest Flix Two*, the video, and *Greatest Pix Two*, the book. They also released a specially packaged boxed set of *Greatest Flix One* and *Two*, called *A Box Of Flix:* they had remastered the sound to the original *Flix* video, and added four rare bonus videos taken from Queen's earliest days. The week after their release, *Hits Two* entered the UK album chart at number one, and *Flix Two* did the same in the video chart, with *A Box Of Flix* a close second.

Earlier in the year, Brian had been approached by an advertising agency to pen a tune for a series of new Ford television advertisements, and as it was a new avenue for him, he agreed. The campaign began in July, using his song 'Driven By You'. Before it became widely known that Brian was involved, the advertising agency, the Queen office and the television company were all inundated by people asking about the track, assuming that it must be a 'Queen rip-off'. When the truth emerged, demand for copies of that jingle became so high that Brian decided to release it as a single and began promotional work and photo sessions for a planned 25 November release.

CHAPTER 27

SO SAD IT ENDS

OVER THE PREVIOUS MONTHS, FREDDIE HAD BEEN GIVEN NO PEACE by the world's press as they congregated on his doorstep and hounded his every move; speculation was rife that he was seriously ill, not laid to rest by his gaunt, haggard appearance when he did surface during those months. The newshounds were not going to miss it should the rumours prove well-founded.

On 23 November, the rumours were brought into the open by Freddie himself, who issued a statement to the hordes gathered at his door, and the world's press in general, which read:

> *Following the enormous conjecture in the press over the last two weeks, I wish to confirm that I have tested HIV positive and have AIDS. I felt it correct to keep this information private to protect the privacy of those around me. However, the time has come for my friends and fans around the world to know the truth, and I hope that everyone will join with me in the fight against this terrible disease.*

The following day Freddie's admission was front-page news all over the world. But the ink was barely dry on the tabloids before an even bigger story broke. At 7 p.m. the next day, on Sunday 24 November

SO SAD IT ENDS

1991, Freddie's fight was over. He had died of AIDS-related bronchial pneumonia. Everyone was devastated. Only those closest to Freddie had been aware of his illness until his statement, and even for them his death was sudden and painfully shocking. The shock waves of his death were felt worldwide, and tributes and messages flooded into his office and to his house. John, Brian and Roger were shattered: they had lost their closest friend. They issued the following statement:

We have lost the greatest and most beloved member of our family. We feel overwhelming grief that he has gone, sadness that he should be cut down at the height of his creativity, but above all great pride in the courageous way that he lived and died. It has been a privilege for us to have shared such magical times. As soon as we are able, we would like to celebrate his life in the style to which he was accustomed.

In the two days before Freddie's funeral, flowers arrived by the truck-load, vans arriving every few minutes to his house and the Queen office. Floral tributes ranged from a single red rose to enormous wreaths and baskets – by Tuesday night there were enough flowers to cover Freddie's huge front lawn in a double layer. Many fans had gathered outside the house and on that cold Tuesday night, Freddie's staff, Phoebe, Joe and Terry, opened the gates to allow the fans a view of the flowers, all laid out under the Christmas tree.

Freddie's cremation was held on 27 November at the West London Crematorium. It was a private affair and few were invited – his family and a handful of close friends, including Elton John and Dave Clarke. It took four hearses for the flowers alone. In a poignant moment as guests waited to enter the crematorium, a single black cat walked across the tarmac, in front of the guests and assembled hoard of photographers . . .

The service was conducted in the Zoroastrian faith, a Parsee religion, of which Freddie's elderly parents were both strict observers.

Among the music played was a piece Freddie had always adored, the fourth act aria for soprano, as featured in Verdi's opera *Il Trovatore*, performed by Montserrat Caballé.

The tabloids were, in the main, kind about Freddie after his death and most ran several pages in tribute to his enormous talent. BBC Radio One devoted entire programmes to him, as did the BBC television stations and most of the independents. It seemed as if the world was in mourning – but, even then, some members of the gutter press were not happy to let him rest in peace. One or two British and foreign papers tried to instigate the backlash by printing scurrilous and often inaccurate stories about Freddie's 'gay lifestyle' and, in their words, his 'degenerate' way of life. They were stories with no foundation, and those involved soon found that people in general, and fans in particular, wanted nothing to do with such trash. The backlash was vitriolic, then, but short-lived.

Rumours then began to circulate as to how long Freddie had known he had AIDS, some saying he should have made his brave announcement earlier. Only Freddie, and possibly two of his closest friends, Mary Austin and Jim Hutton, knew for how long he had been HIV positive, and for how long he'd had AIDS. For seven years before his death, Freddie had, in his own words 'lived like a nun'. He had been in one faithful and close relationship since 1985, with Jim Hutton, but he had kept it well hidden from the prying eyes of Fleet Street's hacks, knowing full well that they would have ripped him and it apart. The truth of the length of his illness died with him. But looking back on his final months, he showed amazing courage in the face of such a frightening disease: we now know that he made his final video, 'Days Of Our Lives', in great pain. He was hardly able to stand but insisted on getting through it, and he did so, with his usual humour and cheerfulness.

It has also since come to light that he recorded the album *The Miracle* not knowing if he was going to be around to make another,

SO SAD IT ENDS

and that after its completion he insisted on going back into the studios almost immediately to work on the next one. The result was the powerful *Innuendo*. His vocals on that album were so strong that they belied serious illness, leading fans to feel confident that the rumours they were hearing and reading about his ill health were unfounded.

Brian wrote the following for inclusion in a special fan club tribute magazine, mailed out just before Christmas:

As you by now know, Freddie was fighting the terrible AIDS disease for many years, and for much of the time even we didn't know. For Freddie, his art and his friends were everything – he poured himself with huge vigour into both. He was determined that no hint of frailty should mar his music, or our music, or make life difficult for his friends. By refusing to concede anything to the illness, his amazing strength and courage enabled him to continue at full strength in making albums, videos, etc., even though it cost him more and more in private pain. He never in our hearing complained about his lot, and never let despondency creep into his work, his voice seemed to get miraculously better and better. And he died without ever losing control.

Freddie never wanted sympathy, he wanted exactly what the fans gave him – belief, support and the endorsement of that strangely winding road to excellence that we, Queen, have tried to follow. You gave him support in being the outstandingly free spirit that he was and is. Freddie, his music, his dazzling creative energy – those are for ever.

Freddie's last wishes were straightforward: he wanted money to be donated in his name to the leading AIDS charity, the Terrence Higgins Trust. The three remaining members of Queen and their manager, Jim Beach, decided a fitting epitaph was to reissue his classic magnum opus, 'Bohemian Rhapsody', coupled as a double A-side with the poignant 'Days Of Our Lives', and donate all royalties to the Trust. EMI agreed, and gave their own share of the royalties. The single was pressed and released in a week, the fastest EMI have ever turned out a single. It sold over 100,000 copies in its first week of release, entering the UK chart at number one, and remained there for five consecutive weeks.

Even after such a tragedy Queen were still setting precedents, with 'Bohemian Rhapsody' being the first ever single in the UK to be re-released and reach number one again. During its first release it sold 1.3 million copies; second time around it sold 1.1 million, making it Britain's second top-selling single only three weeks after its release (the top-selling single being Bryan Adams' '(Everything I Do) I Do It For You'). It was also the first time a band had had two singles and two albums go straight to number one in the same year. 'Bohemian Rhapsody' was number one over Christmas, the first time a record has been number one twice over the festive season. *Greatest Hits Two* was the third top-selling album of 1991 and *Greatest Hits One* the twenty-fifth. In December, Queen had no fewer than ten albums in the UK Top 100, a feat never before achieved by any recording artist. To follow all that, their *Greatest Hits One* album was certified as going eleven times platinum, making it the bestselling album ever in the UK. They also dominated the video charts, with *Flix Two* at number one for weeks, *Box Of Flix* number two, and *Live at Wembley*, *Rare Live*, *We Will Rock You* and *Flix One* all in the chart at the same time.

Amid all this, Brian's first solo single in his own right, 'Driven By You', had been released, on schedule, on 25 November. In the week before Freddie died, when everyone knew that he was seriously ill and might not live much longer, Brian had wanted to pull the single release, not wanting to seem callous in putting it out in such circumstances. He expressed his concern to Jim Beach, who in turn mentioned it to Freddie during one of his frequent visits. Freddie's comment was typical, even in his own pain, when he said, 'Tell him he must release it – what better publicity could you have?'

Release it he did, and it was a huge success, reaching number six in the UK single chart. But its success cannot be attributed just to Freddie's death; indeed, it could have got swamped in the rush of Queen records. It was, in fact, a great track that appealed not only to Queen fans, but rock fans generally. It reached number one in *Kerrang!*'s rock chart, with Brian admitting to being surprised by its success.

Christmas 1991 was a sad time for those close to Freddie and thousands of fans all over the world. The festive spirit was missing. Brian and John flew out to Los Angeles with their families on holiday, and Roger disappeared to Mauritius. They needed time for peace and reflection, and it gave them all a chance to take stock of their lives and contemplate a future without their charismatic lead singer.

CHAPTER 28

TRIBUTE

THE FOLLOWING YEAR, FREDDIE'S UNTIMELY DEATH WAS STILL ON everyone's mind. On 6 February 1992 Hollywood Records released 'Bohemian Rhapsody' as a double A-side with 'The Show Must Go On'. All proceeds from the sale of the single were donated to the Magic Johnson Aids Foundation in the USA.

On 12 February, the British Phonographic Industry held the annual Brit Awards at London's Hammersmith Odeon, where 'These Are The Days Of Our Lives' was voted best British single. Freddie was posthumously awarded the outstanding contribution to music special award, which was collected by the three remaining members of Queen.

Also on that day, at the same ceremony, plans were announced for a huge concert to be held in Freddie's memory, with the aim of raising AIDS awareness and a vast amount of money for a variety of charities and AIDS research. The chosen venue was London's Wembley Stadium; the date, Easter Monday, 20 April 1992.

Tickets for the event went on sale the day after the Brit Awards, and sold out in a staggering three hours – some feat considering, beyond the three members of Queen, no other act had yet been booked to play.

Organisation for the event began on 17 February, when Gerry

TRIBUTE

Race to see Queen

QUEEN fans snapped up all 72,000 tickets for the Freddie Mercury memorial Aids concert in just six hours.

Telephone lines were jammed when the Wembley Stadium box office opened at 9am yesterday.

Elton John is likely to join U2 and Guns N' Roses on April 20 in the biggest rock event since Live Aid.

Queen drummer Roger Taylor said: "Thanks to everyone for the reflection of feeling for Freddie. We're lost for words"

Proceeds from the concert, only announced at the Brit Awards on Wednesday, will go to Aids charities.

Stickells moved his team into the band's offices in Pembridge Road. Roger – who was the main driving force for staging the show, contacted most of the artists. There was no shortage of people offering their services 'for Freddie'.

Many weeks were spent booking crews, designing the stage and lighting rig, and organising the catering, dressing rooms and equipment. As artists were booked, rehearsal schedules had to be arranged. Transport for so many acts was a nightmare, and dates and times were changed again and again. The atmosphere in the office – a small place not built for being host to such vast amounts of people – was fraught and frantic. Several thousand tickets had been reserved for fan club members and it took weeks to allocate them all and post them out. Tickets had also been set aside for the friends and families of those taking part – and each artist's list of guests grew daily.

The concert was to be televised live by BBC Two and broadcast in stereo by Radio One; it would also be beamed live all over the world. Satellite links had to be arranged, television stations prepared and radio networks set up to take the sound and vision.

Rehearsals for Queen began on 27 March, in a studio in Shepherd's

Bush, west London. The band spent the first week or so brushing up on their older hits, and then getting used to playing their newer material. It was a sad and somewhat apprehensive time for all of them. Playing that material without Freddie was heartbreaking – and the thought of being on that Wembley stage without him was even harder to bear. But they felt they were doing the right thing, not only for Freddie but also for the fans, who all felt the need to say goodbye in some way – and not least for themselves, their own way of letting him go.

After two weeks, rehearsals moved to Bray Studios in Berkshire, home of the great Hammer House of Horror films and many episodes of TV puppet show *Thunderbirds*. The names of those taking part in the concert read like a *Who's Who* of rock music: David Bowie, Guns N' Roses, Metallica, Extreme, Def Leppard, Annie Lennox, Seal, Lisa Stansfield, Elton John, George Michael, Robert Plant, Roger Daltry, Liza Minnelli, Paul Young, Zucherro, Bob Geldof, Tony Iommi, Mick Ronson, Ian Hunter, The London Gospel Community Choir, Spike Edney, Josh Macrae, Chris Thompson, Maggie Ryder and Miriam Stockley. All the artists made great efforts to be available at Bray for rehearsals as, for most of them, it was the first time they had ever sung Queen's music. The studios were buzzing for the few weeks before the concert, and there was no evidence of any of those infamous egos: everyone was pulling together for the common cause.

On Wednesday 15 April, after the greyhound racing had finished, the crews moved into Wembley Stadium and began the long, hard task of building the stage. It was to be a vast edifice, bigger even than the 1986 'Magic Tour' stage that Queen had used. A forty-foot-high Phoenix was to embellish the top of the stage, with two slightly smaller birds either side, hanging over the huge screens.

Meanwhile, the annual Ivor Novello awards were held on 15 April at London's prestigious Grosvenor House Hotel. Brian and Roger attended and collected the award for the bestselling British A-side for

TRIBUTE

'These Are The Days Of Our Lives', and Brian was also presented with the award for best theme from a TV/radio commercial for 'Driven By You'. Brian and Roger then handed a cheque to the Terence Higgins Trust for more than £1 million, the proceeds from the sales of 'Bohemian Rhapsody' and 'Days'.

On Saturday the 18th, building was halted at Wembley as the London Monarchs American football team had a match planned, giving their fans a preview of the half-built stage. Work continued through the night and was going strong next morning as the acts began to arrive for their final soundcheck before the Monday show.

The weather in previous days had been unsettled, and everyone prayed for a good day; weather insurance, in case the concert had to be cancelled should the weather prove too bad, was far too expensive even to consider. But Easter Monday dawned bright and dry, and stayed that way throughout the day.

The crowds had begun to arrive on Sunday, many equipped with sleeping bags to spend the night at the front of the queue. By 10 a.m. on Monday, Wembley was heaving, and the gates weren't due to open until 4 p.m. Backstage, all was reasonably calm, considering the sheer size of the event and the amount of people taking part. Artists arrived in good time and spent the pre-concert hours chatting with friends or drinking in the specially constructed Hard Rock Cafe bar. The atmosphere in that bar was one of suppressed excitement, but there was a tinge of sadness to it all, that the person who had inspired so much and so many wasn't there to witness such an event.

Finally, the gates to The Freddie Mercury Tribute Concert for AIDS Awareness opened at 4 p.m. and the fans poured into the stadium, swarming over the special plastic covering protecting the hallowed turf of Wembley, to head for the stage and the positions they would have to maintain for around six hours. As they streamed in, the multitude of outlets selling merchandise began to sell out. At the end of that day the record for merchandise sales at Wembley had been broken. A free red banner was issued with each glossy printed programme, bearing the words 'Freddie Mercury – AIDS Awareness'. Each person had also been handed a red ribbon as they entered the stadium, to be worn as a symbol of their support for victims of AIDS, their families and all those working in the fight against the disease.

By 6 p.m., as Brian, Roger and John took the stage to open the show with a brief message, the stadium was a sea of red banners. Roger's heartfelt comment, that today, everyone could cry as much as they wanted to, was taken literally by the majority of those present.

The first act on stage after Queen was Metallica, followed by Extreme (playing a Queen medley during their set), Guns N' Roses, and Def Leppard. U2 were shown on video from their previous night's US concert. The atmosphere was one of electric excitement and

TRIBUTE

celebration, but there was a tangible sadness, felt all the more as the three remaining members of Queen took to the stage again halfway through to play their hits. A succession of great artists appeared to sing their hearts out and to speak their feelings, not just about Freddie but about AIDS and its devastating effects. Elizabeth Taylor made a guest appearance with a poignant speech, and although one or two in the audience tried to heckle her, the majority listened to what she had to say and cheered loudly after she had finished. The concert then switched to Johannesburg, and local South African band Mango Groove. It was the first ever concert satellite link between South Africa and the UK.

More stars did their best to hit Freddie's high notes (most had to have the song key changed to make it) and after his set, David Bowie dropped to one knee to recite the Lord's Prayer for 'everyone who knows anyone who has AIDS'. Most of the crowd bowed their heads and joined in with him. Finally Brian, emotional and close to tears, introduced Liza Minnelli. She sang a rendition of 'We Are The Champions' that would have done Freddie proud, and was joined on stage by the entire line-up for a rousing and emotional finale.

The audience, though, were really the stars of that day. They knew every Queen song and every note. They sang at full volume throughout the entire show, they cried and they laughed. It was their day to celebrate and say goodbye to their hero – but also it was hoped that they went home knowing more about the risks of HIV and AIDS, and how to avoid them.

The concert was broadcast to seventy-six countries around the world, with estimated viewing figures for the UK at 6.3 million, and a billion worldwide. A week after the event, *Greatest Hits One* re-entered the UK album charts at number sixteen, and *Greatest Hits Two* climbed back up to number six. Meanwhile, profits from the concert were used to set up The Mercury Phoenix Trust, an AIDS charity which has been active ever since.

Thanks to the effects of the Fox TV broadcast of the tribute concert and also the hit 1992 film *Wayne's World*, starring Mike Myers and Dana Carvey as two long-haired metal-loving best friends who headbanged to the song in a now legendary scene, 'Bohemian Rhapsody' sat at number two in the US *Billboard* singles chart, and the US version of *Greatest Hits*, released under the name *Classic Queen,* climbed to number four in the album chart, achieving a platinum award.

In early June 1992, Brian was working in the recording studio in his country house in Surrey (a room that was once the snooker room) recording tracks for his long-awaited solo album, due for release later in the year. Roger was jetting off to the hot beaches of Bermuda, after which he had plans for another album of solo (as opposed to Cross) material, while John was looking forward to a family holiday in Los Angeles. Musically, he had no immediate plans. As a unit, the three members of Queen were in discussions about the possible re-release of Freddie's solo material, with several tracks remixed by Queen. Freddie and Montserrat's collaboration single of 'Barcelona' was already due for re-issue, as the theme to the Summer Olympic Games.

On 26 May 1992, EMI released *Live At Wembley '86*, a full-length, unedited version of Queen's 1986 Magic Tour concert from Wembley Stadium on double CD, double album and double cassette. In the UK, it entered the charts at number two. It was also released the following week on Hollywood Records in the USA and on EMI/Toshiba in Japan.

Released on the same day in the UK only was the specially packaged collection *Box Of Tricks*. It included a CD/cassette called *The 12" Collection*, which featured special twelve-inch mixes of many of the band's hits – plus a video of 'Live At The Rainbow', the earliest filmed Queen concert, from their triumphant 1974 UK winter tour. Along with a pictorial book, T-shirt, badge, patch and wall poster depicting the band's worldwide single and album covers, it was all neatly packaged in a hinge-lidded presentation case.

TRIBUTE

In early summer 1992, Peter 'Phoebe' Freestone, Freddie's personal assistant and close friend, decided to organise a special tribute to Freddie and his love of opera. On 28 June a bow-tie dinner evening with a performance by the European Chamber Opera Company of Verdi's *Il Trovatore* was held at Whitehall's Banqueting House, with Montserrat Caballé as guest of honour. A further week-long run of the opera was held at the Bloomsbury Theatre, which Brian attended on 4 July.

Elton John had embarked on a massive worldwide tour, dubbed The One Tour, at the beginning of 1992. He featured 'The Show Must Go On' in the set, which he always dedicated to Freddie. On 18 June, he was joined on stage at Wembley Stadium by Brian for the song.

On 20 July 1992, Brian finally completed his long-awaited first solo album *Back To The Light*. It was the culmination of work that had begun way back in 1988; however there was still no firm release date.

In the summer of 1992, the city of Barcelona finally became host to the Summer Olympics. Fans across the world thought Freddie and Montserrat's 'Barcelona' the perfect theme tune for the event, but sadly the Olympic Committee decided against the idea. However, in the UK, the BBC chose the track as their main signature tune for all TV and radio coverage. To capitalise on such publicity, Polydor Records decided to re-release the single in the UK on 27 July. The song peaked in the UK chart at number two – missing out on the top spot to German Eurodance band Snap!'s 'Rhythm Is A Dancer'.

On 30 July, Roger and The Cross appeared at the Gosport Festival, held in a big top in the town's Walpole Park. It wasn't Roger's only appearance at the time, as he also joined Shakin' Stevens in the studio to play on the track 'Radio', for Shaky's *The Epic Years* album – and later appeared in the video for the song, much to the amusement of Queen fans everywhere.

Due to the popularity of the 'Barcelona' single release, Polydor decided to re-issue the album of the same name on 10 August. The sleeve notes were changed to bring events up to date since Freddie's death. The album charted at number fifteen in the UK charts, ten places higher than the original release.

On 24 August, Brian released the second solo single from *Back To The Light*, the poignant ballad 'Too Much Love Will Kill You', which he had performed at the Freddie Mercury Tribute Concert. Many people assumed that the song was about Freddie, but in fact it reflected Brian's pain at the breakdown of his marriage – the song was originally written for his solo album, and Queen and Freddie subsequently recorded a new version for *The Miracle*, although, due to contractual reasons, it didn't make it on to the album. Brian chose to release two CD formats of the track, one of which came in a card case that looked like a pill. The single charted at number five in the UK, number two in Belgium and reached the top slot in the Netherlands.

BBC Radio One often ran polls to determine the public's tastes in popular music, and on 31 August they published a Top 100 Singles poll that featured Queen no less than five times – more than any other artist, including The Beatles, who only managed four placings. 'Bohemian Rhapsody' did, of course, claim the top slot.

The Torpedo Twins, Hannes Rossacher and Rudi Dolezal, were still actively making videos for the band, and in late August they began work on two projects, *Freddie Mercury – The Video* and *The Magic Years* part four, although the latter was never completed and remains unreleased to date. Throughout September they were tasked with making no less than five videos – for 'One Year Of Love', 'Stone Cold Crazy', 'Keep Yourself Alive', 'Seven Seas Of Rhye' and 'Good Old-Fashioned Loverboy', made in preparation for inclusion on video releases in the USA.

Roger and Brian flew out to Los Angeles on 8 September to attend the MTV awards ceremony at the UCLA Pauley Pavilion. Before the event they met up with legendary LA Lakers basketball player Earvin 'Magic' Johnson. In 1991, Johnson retired abruptly after announcing that he was HIV positive, and so became an advocate for HIV/AIDS prevention and safe sex. Brian and Roger handed over a cheque for $300,000 to the Magic Johnson Foundation, raised by sales of 'Bohemian Rhapsody' in the USA.

The MTV awards took place on 10 September, hosted by *Wayne's World* star Dana Carvey. Movie stars Halle Berry and Jean-Claude Van Damme presented Brian and Roger with the award for best video from a film for 'Bohemian Rhapsody', which featured in *Wayne's World*. In turn, Brian and Roger presented the Michael Jackson Video Vanguard award to Guns N' Roses lead singer Axl Rose.

Hollywood Records had previously released 'their' version of Queen's hits, entitled *Classic Queen*, back in March, which had charted at number four in the USA and number one in Canada – where it spent sixteen weeks on the chart and achieved a five-times platinum award. On 15 September, they also released a US version of Queen's *Greatest Hits*, which peaked at eleven in the US charts but, yet again, it reached number one in Canada and earned a platinum award within two weeks of release.

At the end of September 1992, Brian embarked on a tour in Europe to promote 'Too Much Love Will Kill You' and reveal details about the upcoming release of the album. He appeared on Veronica TV in the Netherlands to perform the single, and later the same day was a special guest at a UNICEF music auction gala in Amsterdam. He performed the track there too, and donated a guitar he had played on Queen's 'Crazy Little Thing Called Love' to their auction. The guitar raised 7,500 guilders (approximately 3,500 euros).

Pavarotti & Friends, which took place at the Park Novi Sad in Modena on 27 September, was the first of what was to become a series of benefit concerts hosted by Italian operatic tenor Luciano Pavarotti in his hometown. Brian was a special guest, along with Sting,

Bob Geldof and Mike Oldfield. Brian performed 'Too Much Love Will Kill You' and joined the ensemble for the finale of 'La Donna È Mobile.' The show was broadcast live by BBC Radio Two and filmed for Italian TV. A CD of the show was also released by Decca Records.

Brian's first solo album, *Back To The Light*, was finally released on 28 September to critical acclaim. It entered the UK Gallop chart at number six but hit the top spot in the metal charts. Brian added a poignant message to the sleeve notes for the album:

Dear folks,

This is an album of songs, and the man who finished making it today is very different from the man who started it five years ago. So this is not a set of ideas put down at one moment, nor is it the story of my life; it is merely a collection of attempts made at various times to make sense of life's journey. Thus you won't find much in here about how fab it is to be a rock star in Queen; but you may find, in contrast, glimpses of someone quite small and insecure. I know him well.

Music is joy to me and living in it is sometimes the only safe place to be. Much of what is recorded here is for fun, escapism, music for its own sake, and although I mean what I say, take it all with a small pinch of salt.

In my mind, this album was always called Back To The Light. At its beginning I felt no real hope of finding the light; now it glimmers dimly, encouragingly, but always intermittently in the hall of mirrors around me. I suppose if we ever knew exactly where the light was coming from, getting there would be easy . . .

Brian decided to tour with the album, and so put together a touring band. He was joined by drummer Cozy Powell, with whom he had

TRIBUTE

forged a firm friendship after the two collaborated on tracks for both Brian's album and Cozy's LP, *The Drums Are Back*, earlier in the year. He also recruited Neil Murray (Whitesnake and Black Sabbath) on bass, Spike Edney on keyboards, and session guitarist Mike Casswell. Backing singers – Chris Thompson (Manfred Mann) and two top session vocalists, Maggie Ryder and Miriam Stockley – completed the line-up.

Queen fans in the USA had only ever had one video release, with *Live At Wembley*, but Hollywood Records rectified this when they released both *Classic Queen* and *Greatest Hits* as compilation videos on the same day, 13 October. Both releases featured the 'new' videos that the Torpedo Twins had made earlier in the year.

Elsewhere, the remaining members of Queen attended the British Music Industry (BMI) annual dinner at London's Dorchester Hotel on 14 October, where they were presented with an award as the writers of the music for rapper Vanilla Ice's hit hip hop track 'Ice Ice Baby', which heavily sampled the bassline of 'Under Pressure'. The band were also presented with a cheque for $450,000 (almost £325,000), raised by sales of Hard Rock Cafe T-shirts featuring the *Innuendo* album artwork, which they gratefully accepted on behalf of The Mercury Phoenix Trust.

On 1 November 1992, Brian flew out to Buenos Aires, and arrived just five hours ahead of performing his first solo concert. The rest of The Brian May Band were already there, and had rehearsed in Brian's absence.

Their first performance was an unannounced headline gig at the city's New York City Disco. Still, over a thousand avid fans turned up.

The following day they supported Joe Cocker and The B–52's at the Pista Atlética Del Estadio Nacional in Santiago, Chile, in front of an audience of 6,000. Technically, however, the show was a nightmare. Because of power surges in the Chilean electricity supply, Brian's guitar kept fading in and out throughout the concert. He was forced to abandon his famous guitar solo after just one minute, and the keyboards were also having problems. However, the band kept playing right to the end, and were rewarded with a great reception from the crowd.

November 5 saw them play the Estadio Centenario in Montevideo, Uruguay, where they once again supported Joe Cocker, and this time Brazilian rock band Os Paralamas do Sucesso, in front of 20,000 people. To top that, the next day they performed to a whopping 30,000 people at the massive Vélez Sarsfield football stadium in Buenos Aires, where Queen had conquered South America in 1981. The concert was also broadcast live across Argentina. There was not a dry eye in the place as Brian led the crowd in a tribute to Freddie as they sang 'Love Of My Life.'

Brian decided that while in South America he would film a promo video for the 'Back To The Light' single, and he took over the Imperator Club in Rio De Janeiro on 9 November. The film was shot during the day, and that evening the band played the club and were filmed for a forthcoming TV special to be shown at Christmas on Brazilian television. In the edit for his video, Brian used shots from the live concert. Jim Beach, in an article for the fan club magazine, said of the show: '3,500 people crammed into the Imperator for that final gig, and the next morning the band left for London, knowing that they really had achieved something, and could now confidently play anywhere in the world.'

'Back To The Light' was released on 9 November in the UK, going on to reach number nineteen in the singles chart. The CD was to be released in two parts: Part One was a double box, and included 'Star Fleet' and 'Let Me Out', both taken from the Starfleet Project 'mini album'; Part Two was in a cardboard single CD cover and featured tracks 'Nothin' But Blue' and 'Blues Breaker'. The idea was to simply put both CDs in the first double cover, but of course fans wanted to keep them separate.

Parlophone Records released *The Freddie Mercury Album* on 17 November, a compilation album of Freddie's solo work, including tracks that had been re-mixed by various producers, such as Nile Rodgers and Jon Nevinson. It achieved chart success, hitting number four. But opinions from Freddie's fans were mixed. Many said they preferred the original mixes, as Freddie had intended them to sound, and weren't keen on the 'up tempo' dance style the album now had. The following week, a single was taken from the album, 'In My Defence', which made the Top Ten. In the States, Hollywood Records released 'The Great Pretender' as a single on the same day.

On 19 November, the Torpedo Twins hosted a star-studded party in the Walfisch, a restaurant in Vienna. Brian and Roger attended and performed four songs: Pink Floyd's 'Money', with Roger on drums and backing vocals and Brian on guitar; 'Twist & Shout', with Campino from German punk rock band Die Toten Hosen and Nina Hagen on vocals, Roger on drums and Brian on guitar; and Little Richard's 'Lucille', with Nina Hagen on vocals, Roger on drums and Brian on guitar, and 'Long Tall Sally', with Klaus Meine from heavy metal band Scorpions on vocals, Roger on drums and Brian on guitar.

23 November saw the UK video release of *The Freddie Mercury Tribute Concert*. The double video was re-edited by Dave Mallett, and featured almost all of the artists who had taken part in the historic concert.

Hollywood Records released the Freddie album – titled *The Great Pretender* – on 24 November. It's track listing differed slightly from that of the European release, and included a rock mix of 'My Love Is Dangerous'.

Meanwhile, John was still keeping his distance from all things Queen – he effectively retired after Freddie's death. But his family life was still going strong, and on 5 December 1992, his fourth son (and fifth child) Luke was born.

Although The Cross were effectively no longer a band, they decided

TRIBUTE

to play a concert on 21 December at London's Marquee Club, organised by the Queen fan club. The show sold out so fast that a second show was added the following day. The shows, billed as 'The Cross Christmas Cracker', featured several surprise guests over the two nights: Roger Daltrey on the first night, and, during the encore on the second night, Brian May and Tim Staffell both joined the band on stage – marking the first time the former members of Smile had performed together since 1970.

CHAPTER 29

MOVING ON

ON 2 FEBRUARY 1993 *BACK TO THE LIGHT* WAS RELEASED ON HOLLYWOOD Records in the USA. The US release included a bonus track of a remixed 'Driven By You', which Hollywood released as a single on 14 February.

On the same day in the UK, The Left-Handed Marriage released *Crazy Chain*, a limited edition CD accessible by mail order only. It featured the tracks that Brian had played on way back in 1967 for Bill Richards – 'Appointment', 'She Was Once My Friend' and 'I Need Time'.

Elsewhere, *Wayne's World* was still collecting awards – this time a Brit award for best soundtrack. It was announced by Roger Taylor from the awards ceremony at London's Alexandra Palace on 16 February.

Meanwhile, Brian had made some changes to the line-up of The Brian May Band, as he felt that the original line-up didn't quite gel as a band. He brought in guitarist Jamie Moses, a friend of Spike Edney, to replace Mike Casswell, while New Yorker Catherine Porter and Shelley Preston (of Bucks Fizz fame) took over on backing vocals. The band were now ready to go on tour.

On 23 February 1993, they opened at the Frank Erwin Centre in Austin, Texas as special guests of Guns N' Roses. However, later shows

MOVING ON

were either cancelled or postponed, due to difficulties with singer Axl Rose.

Instead, Brian's promoter organised several headline gigs for the band, to fill in the gaps. The first was at the Roxy theatre in Atlanta, Georgia. They also played Brian's first headline gig in Canada, at the Copps Coliseum in Hamilton, Ontario.

At the show at Boston Gardens, the band were joined on stage by Gary Cherone and Nuno Bettencourt from Extreme for 'Tie Your Mother Down'. As the track ended, Gary dropped to his knees in front of Brian and performed the famous 'we're not worthy' bow from *Wayne's World*.

Queen received more sad news on 28 February. Their good friend and, for a time, assistant manager Pete Brown had passed away.

A couple of months later, The Brian May Band were special guests on *The Tonight Show With Jay Leno*, from Burbank's NBC studios. They performed 'Back To The Light' and were joined by Guns N' Roses' guitarist Slash for 'Tie Your Mother Down'. Jamie Moses said: 'The highlight of the Jay Leno show for me was Slash lighting up a cigarette during rehearsals and being told by a panicky floor manager that it was strictly forbidden to smoke on set. He reluctantly put it out. When we came to do the show, we started the intro to 'Tie Your Mother Down' and Slash was just to my left, behind a curtain. I saw him take out a cigarette and with a cheeky smile light it and come bounding onto the set. The floor manager put his hands to his forehead and shook his head in despair!'

After the performance, Slash invited the band to join *his* band as guests on their forthcoming European tour during the summer. Of course they all said yes!

The final headlining gig of the tour was at the Palace Theatre in Los Angeles. While in the city, the band filmed the video for their upcoming single 'Resurrection', at Raleigh Studios. The film, directed by Eric Zimmerman, featured flames and even a volcanic eruption.

Brian also found the time to record the track 'New Damage' with Seattle rock band Soundgarden, which later featured on the 1994 album *Alternative NRG*, a charity release in aid of Greenpeace. The entire album was recorded on solar-power equipment and featured a number of mainstream groups, including R.E.M., U2, James and UB40.

On 19 April, EMI also released a charity record in the UK, *Five Live*, an EP featuring Queen, George Michael and Lisa Stansfield. It featured five tracks: 'Somebody To Love' (taken from The Freddie Mercury Tribute Concert), 'Papa Was A Rolling Stone', 'Killer', 'These Are The Days Of Our Lives' and 'Calling You'. The EP entered the UK charts at number one on 25 April and all proceeds from the release were donated to The Mercury Phoenix Trust. A US release on Hollywood Records followed on the 20th, while in Japan the EP became a reduced-length LP with the inclusion of bonus track 'Dear Friends', recorded in 1974 and originally appearing on the band's Sheer Heart Attack album.

Meanwhile, during February, Roger had started work on solo recordings in his home studio, Cosford Mill, with his now regular producer/engineer and ex-Cross member, Josh Macrae. He flew out to Los Angeles in April to record with Japanese musician Yoshiki at One On One studios. Singer-songwriter, composer and producer Yoshiki, best known as the leader of top rock band X Japan, for which he is drummer, pianist and main songwriter, worked with Roger on two songs, 'Foreign Sand' and 'Final Destination'.

At the end of February, Queen decided to sell Mountain Studios, and it was bought by producer and engineer David Richards, who had worked extensively with Queen. Roger himself bought many of the instruments and some of the studio equipment.

The Queen fan club was still going strong, as was proven by the record attendance at the eighth annual UK convention, this time held in Ainsdale, near Southport, Merseyside. This year, for the first time, a special video message was recorded by Mary Austin, sitting in the conservatory of Garden Lodge:

> *You know your loyalty to Freddie remains tremendous. With the terrible stigma associated with AIDS, you have shone through. You didn't turn away, you saw the man beyond the disease, loved him through it, despite it and beyond it. By your continued loyalty to Freddie, you help lift the spirits of others, also affected.*
>
> *Without doubt, he would be very proud; you know how he felt about you, he told you often enough and you know he meant every word. Keep it going, he needs you as much now as he ever did.*
>
> *On a more personal note, I would like to thank you for the support you have given me over the past eighteen months. It would have been an extremely lonely road for me without it. Thank you!*

In early May, Brian was approached by the producers of a new television series, *Frank Stubbs Promotes*, starring Timothy Spall as an events promoter and manager. They asked Brian to write and record some music for the series. Brian recorded several short tracks, thematically linked to the title character and collectively titled 'Hard Business'. The collection was eventually recorded as a single track, 'Business', and would feature on Brian's next solo album.

The Brian May Band started their European tour as guests to Guns N' Roses on 22 May, when they opened the show at the Hayarkon Park in Tel Aviv, Israel. Although this was a Guns N' Roses support tour, two of the shows – 30 May in Hannover and 31 in Nuremberg – were supporting Elton John. The band's first headline UK concert was 4 June at the Edinburgh Playhouse Theatre.

Brian released his fourth solo single, 'Resurrection', on 7 June, taken from the album *Back To The Light*. It also featured a bonus track of 'Too Much Love Will Kill You', recorded live in Los Angeles back in April, and charted at number thirty-two. The same day saw the release of a special gold CD of *Back To The Light*, limited to 10,000 copies and released to commemorate the band's UK tour.

On 15 June, the same day The Brian May Band played Brixton Academy, London's Capital Radio held 'May Day', an entire day dedicated to the man himself. At the gig that night, according to Jamie Moses, 'A hundred or so inflatable bananas fell in a sweaty lump from the ceiling of the Brixton Academy during the intro of 'Hammer To Fall'. It was at that point we realised the crew couldn't find the inflatable *hammers* that were supposed to have gracefully floated down onto the crowd.'

The concert that night was filmed for a future release, and after the final show, at the Bournemouth Windsor Hall, the band headed out to Rotterdam for the European leg of the tour, which opened on 21 June at the Ahoy Sportspaleis.

Meanwhile, a remixed version of 'Living On My Own' by Belgian dance producers No More Brothers, was released, accompanied by a video from the Torpedo Twins. It was Freddie's tenth solo single released in the UK, and it entered the chart at number five, eventually climbing to the top slot on 8 August, the first such time a member of Queen had reached the number one slot with a solo release.

The Cross played one final show on 29 June, at the Gosport Festival in Hampshire supported by The Rhino Men. Sadly, the gig marked the band's last, although the members continued to appear individually or occasionally as an almost complete band, at a variety of fan club events and parties. At the end of August, Roger was once again ensconced in his home studio at Cosford Mill, continuing work on his solo material.

On 12 September, Brian played his first ever gig in Switzerland with The Brian May Band, at the Winterthur Musikfestwochen on the Steinberggasse. The open-air show featured, among others, Foreigner, Hazel O'Connor and Texas.

Meanwhile, John Deacon came out of his retirement briefly to

MOVING ON

perform with Roger at the Ruins concert, at Cowdray Park in West Sussex. Brian was away on his solo tours at the time. The event was organised to raise money for the King Edward VII Hospital in Midhurst and was attended by around a thousand people, all dressed in their finest evening wear. Pink Floyd, Genesis and Eric Clapton were also on the bill. Along with Roger and John, the band consisted of Jason Falloon on guitar, Josh Macrae on drums and Adrian Milne on keyboards. Roger sang on 'A Kind Of Magic', 'I Want To Break Free', 'We Will Rock You', 'Radio Ga Ga' and 'These Are The Days Of Our Lives'. Paul Young, of Mike and The Mechanics, joined them on stage for 'Another One Bites The Dust'. Then Roger joined Genesis on drums for 'Turn It On Again', 'Hold On My Heart', 'I Can't Dance' and 'Invisible Touch'. Then, Pink Floyd were joined by Mike Rutherford on bass, and Paul Young on vocals, followed by a set by Eric Clapton – before everyone came back out as 'The Ruins Band' to jam to 'Gimme Some Lovin' and 'Ain't That Peculiar'.

On 25 September, Brian appeared on French television show *Taratata* to perform 'Driven By You' and 'We Will Rock You' with French rock band Pow Wow.

While Brian was still touring, towards the end of September, Roger and John went into Metropolis studios in West London to start sorting through and working on the tapes they had started recording with Freddie at Mountain Studios back in early 1991. In a letter in the fan club magazine of Autumn 1993, Roger, writing on behalf of himself and John, said: 'After two weeks we have assembled the basic material and worked on some of it. It is sounding magnificent; the work is going swimmingly; most of the material will be a wonderful epitaph to Freddie and the work he did with us at the close of his brave life. We feel that after this length of time it is fitting to properly close some chapters and get on with the process of living and "doing".'

Meanwhile, Guild Guitars had previously made only red copies of

Brian's Red Special, but due to popular demand they decided to start producing a green one too. They limited the production to just 2,000 pieces, and informed collectors and fans alike that their 'new design' featured a more accurate remake of Brian's original tremolo and custom-made Seymour pickups. Needless to say, the instrument sold out of that limited run rather quickly.

Next on the list for The Brian May Band was a flight to Montreal, Canada, on 1 October, in preparation for the band's North American tour, which opened at the Montreal Metropolis three days later. On 12 October, Brian was invited to place his hands in concrete for the Royal Oak Walk Of Fame in Detroit – and that evening played the Royal Oak Theatre in the city. After the gig that night the band all went ten pin bowling – a risky sport for guitarists, since broken fingers can end careers. However, the evening went off without a hitch and Jamie Moses was the outright winner, while Spike Edney earned the nickname 'Gutterballs Edney'.

On the band's arrival in Texas, State Governor Ann Richards declared 'Keep Yourself Alive Day' throughout the entire state in honour of Queen, and fans celebrated with a two-day 'Keep Yourself Alive' convention in Dallas.

While in the States, Brian was invited to attend the American Society Of Composers, Authors and Publishers (ASCAP) awards dinner, where he accepted an award on behalf of Freddie and Queen for 'Bohemian Rhapsody', which was the most played record in the USA in 1993. At the end of October, he was busy working on his forthcoming live album, which had been recorded at the Brixton Academy earlier in the year.

When Freddie was a small boy he collected stamps, a collection his father had kept safe. On 17 December, the collection was put up for sale at Sotheby's auction house in London, where it sold for £3,200, twice the expected price, with proceeds donated to The Mercury Phoenix Trust. The buyers were in fact the Royal Mail – the collection was to be shown at the London Postal Museum and would also become part of a touring exhibition.

The Brian May Band's final tour date took place at the Pavilhão Desportivo da Boavista in Porto, Portugal, on 18 December. During 'Hammer To Fall', the crew and technicians all imitated Brian by miming playing guitars, while backing singers Catherine and Shelley threw sparkling confetti over the guitarist and sang 'Merry Christmas' to him. The encore saw the band perform '39' and 'White Christmas' to a very appreciative crowd.

CHAPTER 30

MADE IN HEAVEN

THE EARLY PART OF 1994 SAW BRIAN WORKING ON SOLO MATERIAL, but also joining Roger and John in the studios to work on the Freddie tapes.

Brian simultaneously released *Live At Brixton Academy* on CD double album, cassette and video on 7 February on Parlophone. *Live At Brixton Academy* would be the only release by The Brian May Band as a collective.

On 9 February, Brian joined Paul Rodgers and Company on stage at the London Forum to perform on three songs, 'Bad Company', 'All Right Now' and 'Going Down To The Crossroads'. It may well have been at this show that the seeds for Paul joining Queen were sown . . .

Parlophone Records decided to release a 'promotional' compilation album on 12 February. Called *The Master Sampler*, it included tracks 'Liar', 'Funny How Love Is', 'In The Lap Of The Gods . . . Revisited', 'Lily Of The Valley', 'I'm In Love With My Car', '39', 'You Take My Breath Away', 'Spread Your Wings', 'Mustapha', 'Get Down Make Love (live)', 'Dragon Attack', 'The Hero', 'Staying Power' and 'Keep Passing The Open Windows'.

Brian attended the fourteenth Brit Awards ceremony at London's

Alexandra Palace on 14 February. The event was hosted by Elton John and Ru Paul, and Brian performed live with Bon Jovi and the winner of the best British female solo artist award, Dina Carroll, on the Bon Jovi track 'I'll Sleep When I'm Dead'.

On 29 April, Roger joined a host of guests, including Def Leppard, Ian Hunter and Steve Harley, to perform at the Mick Ronson Memorial Concert, hosted one year after the Spiders From Mars musician died of liver cancer. Roger performed 'A Kind Of Magic' and played drums with Steve Harley on '(Make Me Smile) Come Up And See Me'.

Roger's seventh solo single, 'Nazis 1994', was released on 3 May. The single was not allowed to be advertised, nor indeed played on British national radio, while TV stations refused to show the video or footage of Roger singing the track, and many record stores would not stock it through fear of reprisals from neo-Nazi groups. The radio stations' excuse for not playing the song was 'We steer clear of anything with a political or openly controversial nature'. Sadly, the same attitude applied throughout most of Europe. The track received good airplay in the Netherlands and Belgium, however, even though it was not sold in the Netherlands.

Despite all of that, the single charted at number twenty-two in the UK – making it Roger's most successful single to date, largely, no doubt, due to all the publicity Roger did for the track, discussing the song and censorship.

Next on Roger's list was a trip to Japan, to appear at the 'Great Music Experience' at the Todaiji Buddhist Temple in Nara – the world's largest wooden building – for three nights from 20 May. He first played drums with Toshinori Kondo and Tomoyasu Hotei, before taking to the front of the stage to perform 'Foreign Sand' with Yoshiki on drums and piano. Yoshiki had been filmed earlier in the day drumming to the track, and that footage was seamlessly included in the live broadcast, making it seem as though he were in two places at once.

Roger then went on to play drums with Bon Jovi for two songs – 'Bed Of Roses' and 'Wanted Dead Or Alive' – before the all-star finale with the Bob Dylan song 'I Shall Be Released'. The concert was broadcast live on Japanese television, and many other countries carried footage at a later date. 'Foreign Sand' by Roger and Yoshiki was also released as a single in Japan on 22 May and entered the Japanese chart at number thirteen.

On 25 May, Freddie was posthumously awarded an Ivor Novello award for international hit of the year with 'Living On My Own'. Other recipients that year included Gary Barlow, of Take That fame, and Bono.

Brian attended the *Kerrang!* Great British Heavy Metal Music Awards on 13 June at the London Intercontinental Hotel – to present his good friends Def Leppard with the award for best British band. On 26 June, London's Wembley Arena was the host venue for the Gibson 'Night Of 100 Guitars' event. A host of stars took part, including Paul Rodgers, Thunder, Jimmy Barnes, Robert Palmer and Albert Lee. Brian, along with Andy Fraser (of Free) and Slash, performed on two songs with Paul Rodgers singing – 'All Right Now' and 'Crossroads'. The latter also featured heavy metal guitarist Zakk Wylde.

Brian appeared with Paul Rodgers again at the Montreux Festival on 6 July, held at the Auditorium Stravinski. He played on six songs, and the show was filmed for a later release.

Elsewhere, The Roger Taylor Band, featuring Mike Crossley, Josh Macrae, Jason Falloon and Stuart Bradley, made their first appearance together on 28 July at Gosport's Walpole Park.

Amid all the action, John, Brian and Roger were still spending time together to work on the Queen tapes. Brian wrote in the Queen fan club magazine:

I've shelved any thoughts of solo work, and it's been my turn to delve into those last Queen tracks which we started with Freddie nearly three years ago. Of course the remaining new material is very precious stuff, and in my mind the most important consideration is that this final collection must be worthy of the name Queen, so I've been delving very deep. I'm now very excited about how it's turning out, but only when I am sure that Freddie is coming across in his full glory, in the way he would wish, will I begin to feel happy. Anyway, you can be sure that John, Roger and I will have put in the maximum amount of loving care (and usual arguments!) by the time this thing hits the shops!

On 3 September, Brian flew to Maarweg Studios in Cologne to record a duet with Jennifer Rush, as she was recording his song 'Who Wants to Live Forever' for her new album *Out Of My Hands*.

Two days later, Roger's long-awaited solo album, *Happiness?*, was finally released by Parlophone. It entered the UK charts at number twenty-two – Roger's highest solo chart position yet. Roger wrote and produced all the album's tracks – except those featuring Yoshiki, and one – a song called 'Dear Mr Murdoch' – caused some controversy. The lyrics were a tirade against media mogul Rupert Murdoch, whose *Sun* newspaper had hounded Freddie in his final days. In his autumn fan club letter, Roger said: 'I hope that you enjoy the *Happiness?* album. I suppose it's quite personal – but I think it sort of relates to everybody. I can't honestly say the radio and TV etc. have given it any help at all really – maybe that's what you get for just speaking your mind! Onwards – and "up theirs"!'

To celebrate the release, Roger was invited to host a signing session at the huge HMV flagship store on London's Oxford Street on 6 September. Fans began queuing in the early hours of the morning to ensure they got to see the man himself, the queue eventually stretching right up busy Oxford Street. Roger was very pleasantly surprised that so many fans had managed to make it at what was rather short notice. He showed his appreciation by signing everything presented to him, posing for photographs and staying in the store until the last person in that vast queue had their album signed – almost three hours later!

Happiness was released in Japan on 7 September, and featured an extra track, 'Final Destination', with Yoshiki. However, the controversial track 'Dear Mr Murdoch' was removed from this release.

To capitalise on the success of the album, on 15 September Roger and his band played a hastily arranged one-off gig at London's Shepherds Bush Empire, which sold out even at short notice. Brian went along to offer his support, standing in the wings during the show.

The next single from the album, 'Foreign Sand' with Yoshiki, was released on 19 September, and the CD included both the single and album versions of the song, Roger's 'You Had To Be There' and a bonus track 'Final Destination', also with Yoshiki. Also released was a blue seven-inch vinyl and a twelve-inch picture disc. The single entered the UK chart at number twenty-six.

Roger and the band flew out to Japan on 23 September to prepare for their tour there, and Roger's first solo date in Japan, on 26 September at the Sun Plaza Hall in Tokyo. The concert booked for 29 September at the Kokusai Koryu Centre in Osaka had to be cancelled when a typhoon was forecast and the city was closed down as a precaution. Roger was holed up on the twenty-second floor of his hotel fearing the worst . . . but reported that it was nothing more than a high wind.

On 10 October, Roger became a father again when he and Deborah Leng welcomed their second child, a little girl called Tiger Lily.

In Europe, EMI Records arranged a 'showcase gig' for Roger and his band on 14 October at Presswork, in Cologne for fans and the press. The gig was also filmed for German television. The band then went on to do another 'one-off' show in the City Square in Milan on 24 October.

On 15 November, the first ever National UK Street Collection took place in London, on behalf of The Mercury Phoenix Trust. The brainchild of Queen fan Maureen Barclay, it saw Queen fans uniting with collection buckets and tins to raise funds for the trust. It became an annual event and has raised many thousands of pounds for the Trust over the years.

Meanwhile, Roger's 'Happiness' tour kicked off in the UK at London's Shepherds Bush Empire on 19 November, supported by British rockers Colour Of Noise.

On 21 November, Roger's next single was released – the album's title track 'Happiness' backed with 'Ride The Wild Wind', recorded live at the Shepherd's Bush concert in September. Also released was a seven-inch green vinyl and a twelve-inch picture disc, which included more tracks recorded live at the same concert – namely 'Dear Mr Murdoch', 'Everybody Hurts' and 'Old Friends'. The single charted at number thirty-two.

Roger and the band broke off from the UK tour on 1 December, to guest at the Concertoitalia at Forum Assago. The special World AIDS Day concert featured many top Italian artists, including Renato Zero, Roberto Vecchioni and Rossana Casale among others.

They returned to the UK the next day to resume the tour, in Roger's childhood hometown of Truro at the City Hall. Many of his old childhood and school friends showed up in support at his 'homecoming' gig.

In mid-December, Brian was approached by BBC Radio to provide music for a special radio version of the Marvel superhero story *Spider Man*. The story, entitled *The Amazing Spiderman*, was broadcast daily on Radio One in short episodes between 16 January and 17 March. Brian provided the theme music as well as the incidental music for the series.

On 17 December, the Queen fan club held its annual 'Christmas Extravaganza' at London's Shepherd's Bush Empire. The show featured the Spike Edney All Star Band, and special guest was one 'T. E. Conway', aka Brian May. Dressed in full teddy boy outfit and wig, he performed 'Only Make Believe' and 'Tie Your Mother Down'. Even after the show, many of the audience expressed their disappointment that Brian wasn't there . . . as some hadn't realised Twitty Conway was the man himself!

Roger flew out to Italy on 15 January 1995 for a nine-date tour in the country. The tour opened at the Monfalcone Hippodrome on 16 January. While there, he also appeared on the *Maurizio Castana Show*, performing 'Happiness'. The band also played one date on the island of Malta, Roger's first ever gig there, on the 24th.

Parlophone Records released Brian's *Spiderman* track on 27 January in the UK, under the name of 'MC Spy-D & Friends' – the friends being producer Dirk Maggs and the cast of the radio show. 'The Amazing Spiderman' was the A-side, with 'The Amazing Spiderman (sad bit)' the B-side. Also released on the same day was a CD single and a twelve-inch picture disc, and, on 13 March, a soundtrack album.

At the end of February, Brian also worked on the soundtrack album for *The Rocky Horror Picture Show*. He recorded 'Hot Patootie (Whatever Happened To Saturday Night)' at Abbey Road Studios with Spike Edney, Andy Hamilton and Steve Hamilton. Backing vocals on the track were provided by Madeline Bell, Gareth Marx, Shelley Preston, Anita Dobson and Brian's own daughter Emily May. The track featured on the 'cast' album release on Jay Records. The press release at the time said: 'New freshness was brought by major stars such as Christopher Lee as the Narrator and Brian May as Eddie. Brian May has brought his own unique rock treatment to a stunning performance which is possibly the only chance the world will ever get to hear one of its major rock stars in this role.'

He also went into the studios at about the same time to work with Andrew Lloyd Webber and Jim Steinman on the track 'A Kiss Is A Terrible Thing To Waste', for the stage musical *Whistle Down The*

Wind. The song was performed by Meatloaf for the soundtrack album of the musical, which was released in 1998.

Yet more recording took place at around this time, with Eddie Kramer on the album *A Tribute To Jimi Hendrix*. Brian recorded the song 'One Rainy Wish', which also featured both Neil Murray and Cozy Powell.

The Queen fan club held their tenth annual UK convention over the weekend of 5–7 May. To celebrate the anniversary, a special purple edition of 'Bohemian Rhapsody' was produced – limited to just 2,000 hand-numbered copies. All attendees at the event were able to buy a copy for just £5, with all proceeds donated to The Mercury Phoenix Trust.

Apart from his work on the Queen tapes, John Deacon had been happy in his retirement. However, on 1 July, he was persuaded to appear with the Spike Edney All Stars at London's Shepherds Bush Empire, at a gig to raise money for The Mercury Phoenix Trust. He agreed to appear as his son, Michael, and his band Baker were playing in support. John performed on three songs with the SAS Band – 'My Girl', '634-5789' and 'Crazy Little Thing Called Love'. John was incredibly nervous before the show, and left almost as soon as it was over, ever the reluctant rock star.

Work on the Freddie tapes was still forging ahead, and on 3 July Brian's letter for the fan club magazine spoke about the task: 'A very intense time for us here in Queenland! As I write we only have a few weeks to deliver all the finished mixed tracks, and all the artwork, if we are to meet the deadline for a Christmas onslaught! It feels a bit like the old days, but of course we're all very different in our ways now.'

He continued, 'For me, I can't believe that most of the last eighteen months or so of my life have gone into this – "what, just for a few four-minute songs?!!!" Well, they're pretty precious songs, and I keep remembering this is really the last chance I'll ever have to work with Freddie's wonderful voice.'

In late August, the band joined forces with the British Film Institute by providing £500,000 in funding to young British film directors. They were tasked with making short films to accompany the tracks on the band's forthcoming album. The idea was not only to provide new films for the tracks, as the band were unsure about whether or not they wanted to make videos themselves, but also to showcase the talents of those directors.

Brian and Roger flew out to Dublin on 12 September, to attend an EMI conference. Rupert Perry, the head of EMI Music, presented them with an award for sales totalling more than 23 million copies of their two *Greatest Hits* albums.

The title for the new album had finally been decided – it was to be *Made In Heaven*. Roger wrote in the fan club magazine about finishing the work that had consumed them all for so long – he said: 'The time has come to put to bed this last studio album from Queen, a difficult child indeed!

'"Made In Heaven" was a long process of thought, effort and care. In content of songs, emotion and above all, in power and quality of performance from Freddie, the work is strong indeed. Boy, could that one sing!'

EMI/Parlophone hosted a special evening at Blenheim Palace, in Oxfordshire, on 20 September, to premiere the *Made In Heaven* album to the industry and assembled journalists. There was also a 'playback party' held on the same evening at the Townhouse Studios – but the band failed to attend.

On 1 October, EMI/Toshiba in Japan released a special promotional CD for personnel only. Called *The Greatest History – Show Must Go On*, the CD featured tracks from an array of Queen albums: 'Heaven For Everyone', 'Keep Yourself Alive', 'Killer Queen', 'Bohemian Rhapsody', 'Somebody To Love', 'Teo Torriatte (Let Us Cling Together)', 'We Will Rock You', 'We Are The Champions', 'Crazy Little Thing Called Love', 'Another One Bites The Dust', 'Under

Pressure', 'Radio Ga Ga', 'I Want To Break Free (single mix)', 'A Kind Of Magic', 'I Want It All (single version)', 'Innuendo' and 'The Show Must Go On'.

There was some anger and annoyance in the EMI camp when London's Capital Radio played the band's new single – 'Heaven For Everyone' – on 6 October, three days before it was due to be launched to radio stations and on jukeboxes across the UK. An enquiry was held to find out how the station managed to get a copy in advance – but sadly to no avail, and the culprit was never found.

The single was released to the public on 23 October, on Parlophone Records. The Roger-penned single reached number two in the UK, Top 10 in many European countries, and number one in Hungary and Poland.

The Queen fan club held a 'Made In Heaven' launch party for fans on 29 October at the Hammersmith Odeon. It was also the premiere for the video documentary, *Champions Of The World*. Roger made a short appearance to thank the fans for their loyalty and to say he hoped they enjoyed the album, before heading on to the airport to fly off on holiday. Fans were able to get a free 'I Heard It First' T-shirt and goody bag, and also to celebrate the fact that 'I Want It All' had charted at number three in the UK – as the chart compilers informed the organisers of the event that same night.

Made In Heaven was released on 6 November as a limited edition ivory vinyl as well as the more usual black. The vinyl copies of the album contained a set of three black and white gatefold posters, which represented the band members' favourite photo of themselves with Freddie. The CD release came with two 'bonus tracks' – the four-second 'Yeah' and lengthy twenty-two-minute outro 'Track 13'.

Released on the same day was the two-hour-long home video *Champions Of The World*, by DoRo. The video chronicled the history behind the Queen phenomenon, and included a lot of previously unseen footage and new interviews. And believe it or not, that day marked the day the band finally launched their own 'official' presence on the internet, at queenonline.com.

On 7 November, the album was released by Hollywood Records in the USA and by EMI/Toshiba in Japan.

Elsewhere, Parlophone and the band had been working for some time on a release of the band's entire back catalogue – all twenty studio albums – entitled *Ultimate Queen – The Box Set*. The collection was presented in a deluxe wall-mounted presentation case, with a clear glass front in which you could display the CD of your choice, and which included a Freddie Mercury hologram. Upon opening, all twenty CDs were displayed inside, plus a sixteen-page colour booklet.

Meanwhile, Brian began work on a new song called 'Cyborg', which was to be used for the computer game *Rise Of The Robots*. He also went into Arsis Studios in Surrey to work on 'F.B.I.', which was to be featured on *Twang!* – a tribute album to The Shadows. Arsis was owned by Francis Rossi of Status Quo and built above the garage at his home, and while there Brian played on a track for Quo's forthcoming album, *Raining In My Heart*.

On 17 November, Brian attended a gig at the Royal Albert Hall to see one of his heroes – Hank Marvin – in concert.

Another of Brian's big heroes was Lonnie Donegan, and Brian had written a song for him, which they worked on together. But sadly Lonnie's proposed new album never materialised, and the track – 'Let Your Heart Rule Your Head' – would go on to feature on a Brian solo album.

On World AIDS Day, 1 December 1995, the band donated all the royalties earned by *Made In Heaven* in a twenty-four-hour period to AIDS charities.

CHAPTER 31

ONWARDS

EARLY JANUARY 1996 SAW *MADE IN HEAVEN* **ACHIEVE A TRIPLE PLATINUM** award in the UK, after it sold over 900,000 copies.

On 5 February, the Status Quo album *Don't Stop* was released, featuring Brian on the track 'Raining In My Heart.' A video had been filmed for the track previously, live at London's Brixton Academy, during Quo's first ever fan club convention.

Brian and Roger both attended the 1996 Brit Awards ceremony on 19 February. Roger presented the first Freddie Mercury Award for Charitable Work to War Child, the makers of the album *HELP*. The album was released to raise funds for the War Child charity, which provided aid to war-stricken areas, such as Bosnia and Herzegovina. All the songs were recorded in a single day and featured top British artists including Paul McCartney, Paul Weller, Radiohead, Blur, Oasis and Manic Street Preachers. The album hit number one in the UK compilation chart. It would have reached the top spot on the UK albums chart, too, had compilers accepted it as a single-artist album (despite producers' attempts to circumvent the rules by listing all contributors under the one-off 'supergroup' name 'War Child').

Queen's forty-fourth single, the Brian-penned and digitally

remastered 'Too Much Love Will Kill You', was released on 26 February. It reached number five on the UK singles chart, number two in Belgium and topped the charts in the Netherlands.

The band's twenty-sixth single release in Japan was the reworked Queen version of Freddie's 'I Was Born To Love You', on 28 February. It was an exclusive Japanese release because the song was used in a TV ad for Kirin Ichiban Shibori – one of the bestselling liquors in the country, produced by the Kirin Brewery. The single became the band's first Japanese chart entry since 'Teo Torriate' in 1977.

At the end of February Brian was working in his home studio at Allerton Hill on the track 'All The Way From Memphis' for the Mott The Hoople album *Moth Poet Hotel*. He played guitar, keyboards and provided lead vocals.

On 4 March, Parlophone released a pink vinyl single of 'Too Much Love Will Kill You'. That same day the band's track 'You Don't Fool Me' was released as a single in Europe – and eventually no fewer than sixteen different remixes of the track were released around the world:

A promotional CD, *The Ultimate Collection*, was released in Japan on 18 March, featuring the tracks 'Heaven For Everyone', 'I Was Born To Love You', 'Radio Ga Ga (Extended Version)', 'One Vision', 'A Winter's Tale', 'Made In Heaven', 'Thank God It's Christmas', 'The Great Pretender (Malouf Mix)', 'My Life Has Been Saved', 'Too Much Love Will Kill You', 'We Will Rock You', 'We Are The Champions', 'I Was Born To Love You', 'Heaven For Everyone' and 'The Show Must Go On'. The CD was created to highlight the depth of the band's extraordinary back catalogue, and to promote *Made In Heaven* and the *Champions Of The World* video in Japan. Almost instantly it became a collector's item and, completists still regard it as one of the rarest Queen CDs.

On 19 March, Brian and Roger flew out to Warsaw to collect a Fryderyk award (the Polish equivalent of the US Grammy or the UK's Brit), for best foreign album for *Made In Heaven*.

Roger also attended the Italian Music Awards in Milan, held by music magazine *Musica*, to accept, on behalf of Queen, the award for best international group and best international album, again for *Made In Heaven*.

Around this time, Brian was approached to work on two songs for *The Adventures Of Pinocchio* movie soundtrack. The 1996 fantasy family film was directed by Steve Barron and based on the 1883 novel by Carlo Collodi. Brian wrote and recorded two songs, 'Il Colosso' and 'What Are We Made Of', at his Allerton Hill studio. Both tracks featured vocals by Brian and Norwegian soprano Sissel Kyrkjebø (simply known as Sissel). The album was eventually released on 25 July.

Another project that Brian worked on was a song called 'Reaching Out' by Rock Therapy – a one-off project for the charity Nordoff Robbins Music Therapy. Rock Therapy consisted of Brian and Stones drummer Charlie Watts, with guest vocalists including Paul Rodgers, Sam Brown, Andy Fairweather Low and Lulu.

In April, Roger and Jim Beach made the trip to Kolkata, as The Mercury Phoenix Trust had joined forces with charity Heart To Heart International for an $11 million medical airlift to India. Concerned with the need to raise awareness of AIDS in India, the MPT donated $1 million, specifically targeted at Mother Theresa's AIDS work. Mother Theresa and the Missionaries Of Charity had established the Asha Deen AIDS home in Mumbai, with plans to build a second in Kolkata. Roger accompanied the airlift in a fact-finding capacity and to witness firsthand the work of Mother Theresa. He was deeply moved by what he saw there, and greatly impressed with the ongoing work of the missionaries.

Meanwhile, the Queen fan club held their eleventh weekend convention at Pontins Ainsdale, Merseyside. Among the highlights of the weekend was the private premiere of *Made In Heaven – The Films*, a series of BFI films specially made to accompany the *Made In Heaven* album. The films were given their first public premiere at the Cannes Film Festival on 9 May – with Roger and Brian in attendance on the night of the 14th.

On 17 June, Parlophone released the band's forty-fifth single in the UK – 'Let Me Live'. The track was initially recorded with Rod Stewart and was meant to be included on *The Works*, but due to copyright issues related to some of the lyrics (said to resemble 'Piece Of My Heart', a song that had chart success in the USA in 1968 for Big Brother and The Holding Company, featuring Janis Joplin on vocals), it didn't make the cut at that time. It was subsequently reworked for *Made In Heaven*. Of the track, Brian commented in his fan club magazine letter: 'This track started as a rather rudimentary scrap which was hanging around in the vaults, with very little in the way of Freddie vocals. (Big secret – there IS a tape of us knocking the idea round with Mr Rod Stewart and pals, dating from the Middle Ages!)'

The single charted at number nine in the UK, although it is rumoured that BBC Radio One decided to ban it from their playlists – or it could simply have been it just didn't fit their current playlist format at the time, as the video appeared on *Top Of The Pops* that week.

Two CDs were released at the same time – *The Hits CD*, which featured the single plus remastered tracks 'Fat Bottomed Girls', 'Bicycle Race' and 'Don't Stop Me Now', and *The Rarities CD*, with the single and remastered tracks 'My Fairy King', 'Doing All Right' and 'Liar.' These were all taken from the *Queen At The Beeb* album release. It was also released as a seven-inch picture disc.

Hollywood Records released the band's forty-third single in the USA on 18 June – the track 'Heaven For Everyone' backed with 'Soul Brother'.

Then, in the summer of 1996, Brian started work on what was to become a long project – bringing the work of Victorian photographer

ONWARDS

T. R. Williams to life in the twentieth century. Brian had always had a strong fascination with stereo photography, and Williams was a pioneer in the field of stereography and producing 'daguerreotypes' – the first stereo photographs. Brian made it his mission to scour the world and track down as many of William's original works as possible. In his fan club letter, he said of the project: 'A strangely different avenue, yes – but if this all comes to fruition perhaps his work will excite the world once again. This guy was the great "Rock Star" of his age!'

Roger and Brian attended the annual *Kerrang!* awards on 8 July, to receive a special contribution to music award, whereupon they were inaugurated into the *Kerrang!* Hall Of Fame 1996. At the same ceremony, Bon Jovi received the award for best band in the world.

The Rock Therapy single that Brian had been part of, 'Reaching Out', was eventually released on 15 July. Sadly, it failed to make the Top 100, charting no higher than 126.

On 28 August, both Brian and Roger attended the Venice Film Festival in Lido Island, for a showing of *Made In Heaven – The Films*. At the event they met Robert De Niro, who told them his daughter was a massive Queen fan. He also asked them if they had ever thought of making a Queen musical . . .

In early September, *The Guinness Book of World Records* announced that Queen were the only act ever to have two separate and different 'Greatest Hits' albums sell more than 2 million copies each. They also reported that Queen had sold over 6 million albums in the UK to date.

Queen's forty-sixth UK single, and the final release from *Made In Heaven*, was released on 18 November. 'You Don't Fool Me' came in standard CD format, but a plethora of remixes were also released across the world on maxi CD and twelve-inch vinyl. The single entered the UK chart at number seventeen.

The 'Freddie Mercury Photo Exhibition', sponsored by EMI Music and in aid of The Mercury Phoenix Trust, opened at the Royal Albert Hall in London on 22 November, running until 11 December. The launch party on the 22nd was attended by Brian and Roger, Freddie's parents Bomi and Jer Bulsara, his sister Kashmira and her children, plus many other distinguished guests. The exhibition featured 120 photos, showing Freddie from three months old until the last photos, taken at the video shoot for 'Days Of Our Lives'. There were also many rare and unique photos from Freddie's early days in Zanzibar and India.

On 25 November, Virgin Radio celebrated a 'Queen Day' between 7 a.m. and 7 p.m., with random callers to the station choosing their favourite track from *Made In Heaven*. The tracks to select from were 'Mother Love', 'You Don't Fool Me', 'A Winter's Tale', 'It's A Beautiful Day', 'Heaven For Everyone' and 'I Was Born To Love You.' Special twelve-inch singles were pressed and gifted to many lucky callers, all signed by Roger and Brian, copies of which have since, obviously, become very collectable.

Over the years since Freddie's death, plans had been made for a statue to commemorate him. Much time was spent approaching almost every London borough to host the statue, but none were prepared to put aside a site, for various reasons. Eventually, it was decided that the statue would be permanently sited in the beautiful town of Montreux, in Switzerland – overlooking Lake Geneva and the mountains, as had been depicted on the *Made In Heaven* album cover. Jim Beach said of the decision: 'Montreux had a very special part in Freddie's life. He spent a lot of his last years there as well as writing and recording his final song there. It is also very central for European fans.'

On 26 November 1996, Roger, Brian and members of Freddie's family attended a ceremony to unveil the three-metre-high bronze statue, designed and created by Czech sculptor Irena Sedlecká. The piece was unveiled by Montserrat Caballé, with speeches by Brian and the Lord Mayor of Montreux. At the base of the statue a plaque was placed, with the words, penned by Brian: 'Freddie Mercury – Lover of Life, Singer of Songs'.

Roger flew out to Mumbai to attend the Indian Music Awards ceremony on 30 November. He was presenting the first ever Freddie Mercury Award for Musical Excellence to top Indian pop singer Alisha Chinai. He said in his speech: 'What better place to present this first ever award named after him, than in the city of his childhood.' He went on to perform the Led Zeppelin song 'Rock And Roll' with Robert Plant and Jimmy Page.

Towards the end of the year, Brian decided he had recorded so many other artists' songs and played on so many of their albums, it would be a good idea to put together a covers album featuring tracks by artists who had influenced him. The album would be called *Heroes*.

The end of an era came on 30 November, when Queen finally closed their production office in Pembridge Road, in London's Notting Hill Gate. After Freddie died it was decided it was no longer necessary to have a single hub for the organisation: Jim Beach was already operating out of his offices in the mountains outside Montreux, and both Roger and Brian had developed offices at their respective homes in Surrey. John didn't feel it was necessary for him to have his own office, and so his affairs were dealt with by the band's accountant, Peter Chant, from his office in Berkshire.

It is also at this point that this book ends. Many people, probably including the band themselves, thought that Queen would end when Freddie died. The remaining members of the band have so far proven everyone wrong in that respect. *Made In Heaven* was a great success, and Brian and Roger continue to produce solo material and perform live.

The next chapter in the life of Queen was already in full swing as this book was being updated and revised. It began when they were joined by Paul Rodgers and became Queen + and has gone from strength to strength with Queen + Adam Lambert. It includes huge tours, more solo work, re-released albums, collaborations and much more – but it is going to take a whole new book to document that!

Watch this space . . .

ACKNOWLEDGEMENTS

Special thanks must go to all of those listed below – without many of them the first publication of this book would not have been possible, and the second would have been more difficult! Sadly some of them are no longer with us... RIP to all of those we have lost.

Mary Austin, Louie Austin, Sally Avery-Frost, David Barraclough, Mike Bersin, Jim Beach, Matilda Beach, Lucy Beevor, Doug Bogie, Greg Brooks, Sara Bricusse, Chris Chesney, John Deacon, Emma Donaghue, Pete Edmonds, Wendy Edmonds, Spike Edney, Ronnie Fowler, Peter 'Phoebe' Freestone, John Garnham, Imogen Gordon Clark, Richard Gray, Geoff Higgins, Sharon Herbert, Sue Johnstone, Ruth Keating, Dave Lloyd, Brian May, Alan Mair, Greg Morton, Jamie Moses, Helen McConnell, Barry Mitchell, Bruce Murray, Denise Ousdine, Ricky Penrose, Douglas Puddifoot, Zandra Rhodes, Tim Staffell, Micky 'Miffer' Smith, Peter Smith, David Stock, Roger Taylor, Dominique Taylor, Chris 'Crystal' Taylor, Richard Thompson, Ken Testi, Frank Tunney, John 'Tupp' Taylor, Rupert White.

RIP – taken too soon...

QUEEN - AS IT BEGAN

Bomi & Jer Bulsara, Pete Brown, Lilian Deacon, Dave Dilloway, Joe Fanelli, Fred Gunn, Mike Grose,

Winifred Hitchens (nee Taylor), Jim Hutton, Dolly Jenkins, Pat Johnstone, Ruth May, Freddie Mercury, Val Moss, Jack Nelson, Norman Sheffield, Gerry Stickells.

And our thanks also to:

www.queenonline.com
www.brianmay.com
www.kernowbeat.co.uk
www.queenconcerts.com
www.queenpedia.com
www.prestonpictures.com
www.denis.uk
www.queenincornwall.blogspot.com

The Official International Queen Fan Club
P.O.Box 141
West Horsley
Surrey
KT24 9AJ
01483 281995
www.queenworld.com

INDEX

1984 (band) 7–11, 12–14
'39' 137–8

Abbey, Pete 32
A Box Of Flix 329
A Day At The Races 140, 141–2
Aerosmith 111–12
Ahwai, Robert 261, 274
Airrace 207
A Kind Of Magic 259, 263–4
'A Kind Of Magic' 260–1, 273, 304
'All The Way From Memphis' 314, 372
Andrews, Bernie 86, 96
A Night At The Opera 130, 132, 134, 139
'Another One Bites The Dust' 180–1, 183–4, 204, 324
Anthony, Dee 81
Anthony, John 32, 61, 73, 78, 84–5
Appleton, Mike 91
Arden, Don 122, 127
Art (band) 69
Artists United for Nature 310–11
Aspel, Michael 149
Austin, Louie 75–6, 77
Austin, Mary 33, 77, 84, 140, 251, 293–4, 332, 355

'Back Chat' 210, 211
Back To The Light 343, 346, 352, 356
'Back To The Light' 349–50
Bad News 274, 285–6, 289
Baker, Roy Thomas 78, 84–5, 114, 135, 160
Bangles, The 265

Barcelona 284–5, 300–1, 344
'Barcelona' 282–3, 285, 290–1, 342, 343
Barclay, Maureen 365
Barron, Steve 373
Bart, Pete 'Pedro' 67
Bates, Simon 252
Battersby, Neil 23–4
Bawden, Pete 22, 34
Beach, Jim: film interests 220; Freddie, memorials 333, 376; legacy management 157, 201, 320, 373, 377; Live Aid 251–2; management deals; 119, 127–8, 150, 222, 320; Mountain Studios 167; Roger's jail release 219; solo projects, involvement 282, 297, 349; tours 185, 191–2, 196–7, 223; 239
Beat Unlimited 19
Beck, Ronnie 85
Bell, Madeline 366
Bersin, Mike 43, 45, 50, 76
Betancourt, Rómulo 196–7
Bettencourt, Nuno 329, 353
Beyrand, Dominique 138, 140, 157, 171–2, 177, 217, 228, 263, 293–4
'Bicycle Race' 161–2
Biggles (soundtrack) 261
Black, Cilla 312, 313–14
Black Sabbath 302, 317–18
'Blag' 53
Bloom, Amanda 165
Bloom, George 233
Blue Rock 328
'Blues Breaker' 224, 350
'Body Language' 205, 206

Bogie, Doug 63–4
'Bohemian Rhapsody': 129–30, 131, 132, 133–4, 142, 149, 170, 172, 289, 299, 301, 304, 333–44, 336, 339, 342, 344, 345, 358, 36
Bonham, Jason 207, 254
Bon Jovi 302–3, 361, 362
Bowie, David 196, 202, 338, 341
Bow Wow Wow 206–7
Box Of Flix 334
Box Of Tricks 342–3
Bradley, Stuart 362
Brainsby, Tony 93, 115, 119, 163–4
Branche, Derrick 39
Branson, Richard 137, 291
'Breakthru' 308–9
Brian May Band, The 346–50, 352–4, 355–6, 358, 359
Brokenshire, Roger 20–1
Brown, Errol 260
Brown, Les 24–5
Brown, Pete 128, 134, 151, 157, 353
Browne, Tom 157
Bubblingover Boys 17
Bullen, Nigel 66–7
Bulsara, Bomi 37, 40–1, 132, 376
Bulsara, Farrokh *see* Mercury, Freddie
Bulsara, Jer 37, 38, 40–2, 132, 376
Bulsara, Kashmira 37, 40–1, 376
Burbridge, Derek 147
Bush, Mel 118
'Business' 355

Caballé, Carlos 282
Caballé, Montserrat 220, 282–5, 290–1, 296–7, 300–1, 343, 376–7
Cable, Robin 82, 88–9
'Calling All Girls' 210, 212
Calvar, Geoff 31
Campino 350
Capalbo, Alfredo 185–6
Capital Radio 246, 369
Capitol Records 222, 224, 227, 260, 276, 320
Carey, Peter Gill 24
Carveth, Oscar 20
Casswell, Mike 348
Castledine, Clive 66–7
Cater, Don 70
Chambers, Martin 216
Champions Of The World (film) 369–70, 372
Chant, Peter 157–8, 377
Charles, Jeanette 115
Cheap Trick 142

Chen, Philip 218
Cherone, Gary 329, 353
Chesney, Chris 52, 53
Chester, Ronald 68
Childs, Malcolm 7
Chinai, Alisha 377
Clapton, Eric 224, 298, 357
Clarke, Dave 257, 331
Classic Queen 342, 345
Classic Queen (video) 348
Cocker, Joe 298, 310, 348–9
Cockney Rebel 103, 104
Collins, Phil 245, 248, 298
Colour Of Noise 365
Cousin Jacks, The 18–19
'Cowboys And Indians' 290
Craaft 269
Crallen, Henry 241
Craven, Jim 20, 21
Crazy Chain 352
'Crazy Little Thing Called Love' 173, 174, 177, 184, 212, 282, 344
Croker, David 86
Crossley, Mike 362
'Cyborg' 370

Daltrey, Roger 247, 338, 351
Dane, Derek 172
Daniel, Geoff 21, 24
Dann, James 107
Dare, Jo 259
Davies, Mary 28
Days Of Our Lives (documentary) 327
Deacon, Arthur Henry 65–6
Deacon, John Richard: Bad News collaboration 289; birth and childhood 65–6; charity events/records 297–8, 306, 357, 367; early bands 66–9, 70; education 65, 66, 68; fan club concert 303; fatherhood 126, 158, 170, 226, 350–1; haircut shock 162; homes owned 140, 205, 311; music commitment 107; Porsche incident 245; Queen, audition and early gigs 70–3, 79; sabbatical 342, 350; solo collaborations 216–17, 255, 260, 261, 274, 291, 298; studio partnership 241; synthesizers, use of 179–80; tennis friends 216, 224; tour injury 154, 156; university studies 69, 72, 83; Veronica Tetzlaff, relationship and marriage 72, 120, 140, 216, 271–2; work pressures 271–2; *The Works* promotion 229
Deacon, Laura 170
Deacon, Lillian Molly 65, 132
Deacon, Michael 158, 367

INDEX

Deacon, Robert 126
Deacon, Veronica (née Tetzlaff) 72, 120, 126, 140, 158, 170, 226, 271–2, 351
'Dead On Time' 161, 164
'Dear Mr Murdoch' 363
'Death On Two Legs' 130, 144
Dee, Kiki 139
Def Leppard 338, 340, 361, 362
De Laurentiis, Dino 167
Delsner, Ron 112
De Niro, Robert 375
De Vallance, Dennis 162, 173
Dilloway, Dave 4, 6–9, 10, 11–13
Dobson, Anita 263, 264–5, 275, 277, 287, 290, 298, 299–300, 302, 311, 366
'Doin' Alright' (also 'Doing All Right') 32, 86, 374
Dolezal, Rudi 256–7, 262, 292, 308, 310, 311, 313, 315, 324, 327, 328, 344, 350, 356
Donegan, Lonnie 147, 302, 370
'Don't Stop Me Now' 165–6
Dowding, Dave 18–19
'Dragon Attack' 204
'Driven By You' 329, 334–5, 339, 352
D-Rok 317
Dudley, Michael 19, 20

Eagling, Wayne 172
'Earth' 32
East, Nathan 329
Edmunds, Pete 12, 26, 33, 59, 61, 116
Edmunds, Wendy 60, 61
Edney, Spike 236, 247, 288, 338, 348, 358, 366, 367
Elektra Records: deals 87, 127, 214, 218, 222; significant releases 94, 95, 180–1, 206
EMI: CDs, reproduction errors 275, 301–2; event sponsorship 140, 239–40, 244, 305–6, 345, 375–6; Feldman takeover 127; Freddie, memorial release 333–4; Norman Sheffield's libel threat 130; promotional work 91, 92, 103–4, 105, 143, 158, 195, 368; Queen contracts 81, 85–7, 128, 157–8, 206, 218; Queen's achievements 278–81
EMI Toshiba 218, 368–9
Emmanuel, David and Elizabeth 257
E'pine Smith, Jane 316–17
Etchells, John 166
Evans, Rik 24
Everett, Kenny 126, 129, 131, 140, 141, 177, 299
'Exercises In Free Love' 282, 283
Extreme 338, 340

Fairweather Low, Andy 138
Falloon, Jason 357, 362
Fanelli, Joe 262, 272, 275, 331
Farnell, Christine 70
'Fat Bottomed Girls' 161–2
'F.B.I.' 370
Featherstone, Roy 85–6, 106
Feldman 115, 127
Feldman, Hazel 235
Ferrone, Steve 328
'FEWA' 53
'Final Destination' 319, 354, 364
Fish 265, 267
Fisher, Matthew 23
Fisher, Morgan 207, 210–11
Five Live EP 354
'Flash' 181, 182
Flash Gordon (soundtrack) 167, 170, 177, 181, 182–3
Fletcher, Tony 220
'Flick Of The Wrist' 115
'Foreign Sand' 354, 361, 362, 364
Foster, Nigel 42
Fountainhead 265
Fowler, Ronnie 103–4, 106
Fox 129
Fraser, Andy 362
Freas, Frank Kelly 147, 149, 153
Freddie Mercury Award 377
Freddie Mercury Photo Exhibition 375–6
Freddie Mercury – The Video 344
Freddie Mercury Tribute Concert 1992 336–41, 350
Freeman, Alan 165
Freestone, Peter 172–3, 220, 272, 282–3, 331, 343
Frew, Richard 67
'Friends Will Be Friends' 263, 265
Fryer, Fritz 33
Fun In Space 194–5
'Future Management' 194

Gallop, Jeremy 52, 53
Garnham, John 4, 7–9
Geldof, Bob 247, 254, 338, 346
Genesis 357
Gerulaitis, Vitas 216, 224
'Get Down Make Love' 150
Gettin Smile 212–13
Gillett, Belinda 306
Gilmour, David 323
Girardet, Frédy 307
Globo Television 243, 245
'God Save The Queen' 106

383

'Goin' Back' 88
Goldsmith, Harvey 251–2, 263, 266–7, 269
'Good Old-Fashioned Lover Boy' 144, 145, 344
Gorham, Scott 216
Goulds, Terry 12
Gowers, Bruce 93, 131, 136, 141, 142
Grandville 321
Grant, Brian 210, 212
Grant, Peter 127
Gratzer, Alan 218
Gray, Richard 306, 321
Great Day 99
Greatest Flix 201, 202, 278, 334
Greatest Flix II 329, 334
Greatest Hits 202–3, 278, 314, 334, 341
Greatest Hits II 329, 334, 341
Greatest Hits (video) 348
Greatest Pix 202
Greatest Pix II 329
'Great King Rat' 76, 96
Griffin, Jeff 150
Grob, Alex 167
Grose, Johnny 20–2
Grose, Mike 21–2, 34–5, 55, 57, 59–60
Groves, Martin 306
Guild Guitars 233–4, 357–8
Gunn, Jacky 261
Guns N' Roses 338, 340, 353, 355

Hackett, Steve 302
Hadley, Tony 248
Hagen, Nina 350
Hale & Pace 323
Halford, Rob 174
Hall, Eric 90, 95
Hamilton, Andy & Steve 366
'Hammer To Fall' 236, 237
Hammerton, Pete 6–7
Happiness? 363–4
'Happiness' 365
Harley, Steve 104, 361
Harris, Bob 139, 148
Harris, John 27, 52, 59, 64, 109, 158
Head East 142
'Headlong' 321, 323, 326
Heart 209, 210
'Heart Full Of Soul' 67
'Heaven For Everyone' 290, 296, 369, 374
Heavy Pettin 219
Hectics, The 39
Henderson, Brian 11
Hendrix, Jimi 13, 42, 61, 134

Hibbett, Jerry 321
Higgins, Geoff 43, 46, 48
Highlander (soundtrack) 256, 259, 263
Hillage, Steve 139
Hirschmann, Bob 95, 98
Hodges, Mike 181, 206
Holly, Buddy 3
Hollywood Records 320, 323–4, 327, 336, 345, 348, 350, 352, 354
Holsten, Jack 87
Honda, Minako 264–5, 274
Horide, Rosemary 95–6, 97, 110
Hotei, Tomoyasu 361
Hot Space 204, 207–8
Howell, Eddie 126
Humpy Bong 35
Hunter, Ian 135, 314, 338, 361
Hurrell, George 227
Hutton, Jim 247, 251, 272, 332

Ibex 43, 45–50
'I Can Hear Music' 82, 88
'I'm Going Slightly Mad' 324, 328
'I'm In Love With My Car' 153
Immortals, The 261
'In My Defence' 350
Innuendo 313, 319, 320–1, 323, 332–3
'Innuendo' 321, 322–3, 328
'Invisible Man' 309–10
Iommi, Tony 302, 317–18, 323, 338
Irani, Farrang 39
Irving, John 220
'Is This The World We Created' 228, 253, 256, 258
'It's A Hard Life' 235–6
'It's Late' 150, 159
'I Wanna Testify' 147
'I Want It All' 306–7
'I Want To Break Free' 228–9, 229–30, 304
'I Was Born To Love You' 247–8

Jackson, Michael 218
'Jailhouse Rock' 34, 45, 53, 163
Jazz 160–1, 164–5
'Jealousy' 168
Jenkins, Jim 166
'Jesus' 76
Joan Jett and The Blackhearts 209
John, Elton 147, 150, 249, 253, 255, 298, 302, 331, 338, 343, 355
Johnny Quale and The Reaction 20–1
Johnson, Earvin 'Magic' 345
Johnson, Holly 302

384

INDEX

Johnstone, Pat 35, 98, 137
Johnstone, Sue 35, 98, 137

Kansas 113, 121, 212
'Keep Passing The Open Windows' 223
'Keep Yourself Alive' 76, 86, 90, 91, 92, 95, 328, 344
Kelsey, Peter 32
Khalaf, Trip 199
'Killer Queen' 115, 120, 125, 126
Kirke, Simon 216
Kliebenst, Jogen 165–6
Knopfler, Mark 298
Kondo, Toshinori 361
Kramer, Eddie 367
Kyrkjebø, Sissel 373

Lamb, Chris 187
Lambert, Adam 378
Lambert, Christopher 260
'Las Palabras de Amor' 208, 210
Lazero, Marcus 186
Left-Handed Marriage, The 9–10, 11–12
Leng, Debbie 290, 293–4, 315–16, 326, 364
Lennon, John 183
'Let Me Live' 374
'Let Me Out' 218, 224, 322, 349
'Let's Get Crazy' 195
'Let Your Heart Rule Your Head' 370
Lewis, Jerry Lee 312
'Liar' 76, 84, 86, 92, 102–3
'Liar' (The Cross) 318
Lion Promotions 158
Live Aid 247, 251–2, 253–4
Live At Brixton Academy 360
Live At Wembley '86 (album) 342
Live At Wembley (video) 273–4, 322, 334
Live In Budapest (film) 268–9, 276, 277, 285, 292, 301
Live In Milton Keynes (film) 209, 213–14
Live In Rio (video) 245, 250, 273
Live Killers 166, 169–70
Live Magic (album) 276
Living In A Box 302
'Living On My Own' 252, 255, 356, 362
Lloyd Webber, Andrew 366–7
'Long Away' 145, 146
'Lost Horizons' 328
'Lost Opportunity' 324
'Love Kills' 237
Lovell, Bernard, Sir 14–15
'Love Me Like There's No Tomorrow' 257

'Love Of My Life' 153, 170, 189, 192
'Lover' 53
Lowe, Jacques 202
Lowe, Nick 33
Lurex, Larry 88–9
Lynyrd Skynyrd 118

Mack, Rheinhardt 170, 219, 226
Macrae, Josh 288, 338, 354, 357, 362
Mad, Bad And Dangerous To Know 316
'Made In Heaven' 252
Made In Heaven 357, 362–3, 367, 368, 369–70, 371, 372–3
Made In Heaven – The Films 368, 373–4, 375
'Mad The Swine' 326
Mafilm 268–9, 277
Maggs, Dirk 366
Magnum 259, 328
Mahogany Rush 121
Mair, Alan 77, 82–3, 105
Mallett, David 202, 225, 228, 236, 247, 252, 272–3, 278, 291, 306, 350
Mandell, Fred 210, 217–18
Manfred Mann 138
Man Friday & Jive Junior 216
Mango Groove 341
'Manipulator' 299
'Man On Fire' 232
Mansfield, Mike 90–1
Maradona, Diego 190
Mardin, Arif 204
Marillion 265, 267
Marks, Gareth 311
Marmalade 140
Marx, Gareth 366
Marx, Groucho 141, 142–3
May, Brian Harold: 1984 (band) 7–11, 12–14; alternative career paths 93–4; Anita Dobson, relationship 263, 275, 277, 287, 298, 299–300, 311; astronomy, interest in 2, 9, 10; audience contact 173–4; awards 339; *Back To The Light* project 334–5, 343, 345; Bad News collaborations 274, 285–6, 289; birth and childhood 1–4; Boston's Queen Day 211; The Brian May Band 346–50, 352–4, 355–6, 358, 359, 360; Capital Radio DJ slot 246; Capitol Records deal 222; charity events/records 297–8, 305–6, 309, 310–11, 314, 323, 345, 354, 373; Christine Mullen, relationship and marriage 27, 136, 274–5, 277, 298; covers album 377; Diego Maradona swap 190; education 1, 3–4, 6, 9; Expo'92 guitar festival 328–9; fan club concerts

385

303, 365–6; fatherhood 160, 195, 277; father's death 298; flat sharing 45–7; Freddie's statue 376–7; *Gettin Smile* release 212–13; guest artist, gigs 302–3, 312, 314, 317–18, 322, 328, 343, 345, 346, 350, 351, 353, 357, 360–1, 362; guest artist, records 82, 88–9, 147, 217–18, 228, 231, 281, 290, 300, 311, 317, 354, 363, 367, 370, 371, 372; Guild Guitars deal 233–4; guitar tutor 224–5, 245–6, 250; hepatitis scare 112–13, 114; homes owned 140, 205; Imperial College studies 10, 14–15, 26–7, 72, 85, 94; *Innuendo* party 323–4, 325; Japanese fans 124; Joe Perry friendship 112; Left-Handed Marriage 11–12, 352; *Macbeth* score 316–17, 321–2; Milton Keynes Bowl show 209; Mott The Hoople tour 98; MTV Awards 345; Munich's significance 204; musical influences 2–3, 147; musical talent, early 1–2, 3–4; production collaborations 219, 264–5, 274, 302; promotional work 74, 326–7; Queen, early formations and gigs 57, 59–64; record deal search 78; Red Special guitar 4–6, 93, 217, 233–4; Rock In Rio, fan party 244–5; skateboard accident 311; Smile era 25–36; songwriting rules 76–7; soundtrack projects 355, 365, 366–7, 373; Soweto visit 239; Sparks offer 128–9; stage costumes/make-up 87–8, 105, 131–2; stage preparation 112; Star Fleet Project 218, 222, 223–4; summer jobs 7; Sun City controversies 235, 239, 240; teenage role model 113–14; 'Tie Your Mother Down' intro 144; tourism 248; tribute to Freddie 333; T. R. Williams project 374–5

May, Christine (née Mullen) 27, 136, 140, 160, 195, 217, 248, 277, 298
May, Emily Ruth 277, 366
May, Harold 1–2, 10, 132, 154, 298
May, James 160, 317
May, Louisa 195
May, Ruth 1, 27, 96, 98, 132, 154
McCartney, Paul 175, 176
McConnell, Helen 27, 45, 63, 88
McConnell, Pat 27, 45, 63
McEnroe, John 216, 224
Meatloaf 281, 367
Meeson, Ian 306
Meine, Klaus 350
Mercury, Freddie: AIDS, personal battle 330, 332–3; awards 126; birth 37; birthday celebrations 161, 196, 237, 255, 289–90; 'Bohemian Rhapsody' meaning 129–30; 'Break Free' video 228, 229–30; chandelier swinging 160; charity performances 300; childhood 37–40; commemorative statue 376–7; Darth Vader stunt 181–2; death and funeral 330–2; diva behaviour 88, 109; drugs, non-use 46; Ealing College studies 42, 43; education 37, 38–9, 40; fame, belief in 78, 111; Fashion Aid 257; flat sharing 45–7, 53; helicopter flight fears 209; homes owned 140, 177, 213, 272; Ibex 43, 45–50; Ibiza 92 Festival 285; illness rumours 308, 316, 330; illustrator career 53–4; image change 178, 180; Ivor Novello Awards 126, 133, 362; Japanese collection 125, 136, 154, 186–7, 275; Jim Hutton, relationship 247, 251, 272; 'Keep On Smiling' tape 283–4; Kenny Everett, friendship 124–5, 129, 131, 141, 177; Kensington Market stall 44–5, 57–8, 61, 77, 82–3, 105; Madame Tussaud's model 310; Mary Austin, relationship 77, 84, 140, 251; Montserrat Caballé collaborations 282–5, 290–1, 296–7, 300–1; *Mr Bad Guy* 226, 231, 249; Munich, second home 204, 231–2, 241, 251; musical beginnings 39; name origin 59; opera lover 219–20; photo exhibition of life 375–6; promotional skills 58; Queen, early formations and gigs 55, 57–64; Queen's logo 83; Radio 1 interview 252; Rob Halford challenge 174; Royal Ballet performance 172–3; shopping, love of 154, 187–8, 213, 275, 307; Smile, involvement with 29–30, 33, 42; solo collaborations 82, 88–9, 160, 215–16, 218, 237, 259, 290; solo singles 247–8, 252, 255, 257, 277–8, 356; songwriting rules, Queen 76–7; Sour Milk Sea 34, 52; stage costumes/make-up 48, 60, 87–8, 114, 131, 139, 144, 154, 159, 174, 182, 264; stage persona 57; stamps auction 358–9; summer jobs 41; throat and voice problems 121–2, 143, 238–9; *Time* musical 257, 261–2, 296; tour reluctance 307, 316; tribute concerts 336–41, 343; UK, move to 40–1; 'Under Pressure' session 196; vanity, acts of 106, 134; *Video EP* 269; *Vogue* photo 230–1; wedding witness 293–4; Wreckage 50–2

Mercury Phoenix Trust 341–2, 348, 354, 358, 365, 367, 373, 375–6
Metallica 338, 340
Metropolis (soundtrack) 215–16, 225
Michael, George 338, 354
Miller, Frankie 138
Milne, Adrian 357
Milne, Paul 52
Minnelli, Liza 153, 338, 341
Mitchell, Barry 60, 63
MobileVision 203
'Modern Times Rock And Roll' 96

INDEX

Moore-Eade, Robin 272
Moore, Keith 157
Moran, Mike 282, 283, 284, 300, 329
Morera, Enzo 196, 197
Moroder, Giorgio 215–16, 237
Morris, Jo 35
Morris Minor and The Majors 291, 298
Morse, Denise 305
Moses, Jamie 352, 353, 356, 358
Moss, Clayton 288
Mott The Hoople 94–6, 98, 111–12, 113, 314, 372
Mr Bad Guy 226, 231, 249
Mr Big 131
Mulcahy, Russell 256, 259, 260
Mullen, Christine *see* May, Christine
Murray, Bruce 39
Murray, Neil 323, 329, 348, 367
Musicians' Union 240–1
'Mustapha' 168
'My Country' 195
'My Fairy King' 86
'My Love Is Dangerous' 350
'My Melancholy Blues' 150, 312

Nail, Jimmy 246
Nash, Robin 103
'Nazis 1994' 361
'Need Your Loving Tonight' 182
Nelson, Jack 80–1, 83–4, 85, 86, 87, 95, 102, 104–5, 121, 126
'New Dark Ages' 327–8
News Of The World 147, 149–50
No More Brothers 356
Noone, Peter 288
'Nothin' But Blue 349–50
'Now I'm Here' 119, 120, 134, 176
Numan, Gary 205, 220
Nutz 106, 109, 110–11

Ogden, Roger 'Splodge' 66
'Ogre Battle' 96
'One Vision' 256–7
'One Year Of Love' 344
Opposition/New Opposition, The 66–9
Osbourne, Jeffrey 217
Os Paralamas do Sucesso 349
Others, The 7

Page, Jimmy 274, 377
Paige, Elaine 299
'Pain Is So Close To Pleasure' 272
Parfitt, Rick 216, 219

Parliaments, The 147
Pascoe, Jack 20–1
Pastorius, Jaco 135
Pavarotti, Luciano 220, 345–6
Peel, John 31, 90, 92
Penrose, Ricky 22
Perez, Liza 13
Perry, Joe 112
Perry, Rupert 368
Petersen, Colin 35
Pickard, Therese 137
Pink Floyd 27, 357
Plant, Robert 220, 296, 338, 377
'Play The Game' 178
PMI releases 282, 312–13, 322
'Polar Bear' 31
Pope, Tim 232, 235
Porter, Catherine 352, 359
Powell, Cozy 323, 328, 346, 367
'Power To Love' 313, 314
Pow Wow 357
Prenter, Paul 151, 199, 213
Presley, Elvis 212
Preston, Shelley 352, 359, 366
'Princes Of The Universe' 260
'Procession' 94
Puddifoot, Doug 89–90

Queen 81–2, 84–5, 89–90, 92
Queen II 93, 102, 107, 108–9, 111, 115
Queen: 10cc support 99, 100; 20th Anniversary party 315–16; aftershow parties 108, 135, 144, 145, 154, 156, 163–4, 166, 175, 210, 211, 213, 267–8, 271; album cover designs 89–90, 147, 149, 164, 202, 227, 306, 321; audience contact 173–4; Australian tours/festivals 99, 101–2, 136, 248–9; awards, film and video 246, 273, 292, 298–9, 328, 345, 352; awards, music 128, 139, 149, 157, 159–60, 183–4, 232–3, 284, 312, 314–15, 336, 338–9, 348, 358, 368, 372–3, 375; Canadian shows 203, 210; Capitol Records deal 222, 320; charity performances/events 140, 176, 205, 253–4, 266–7, 297–8, 307, 370; charity recordings 239–40, 256, 258, 333–4, 339, 345, 354; collectable artist 296, 326; Cornish Tour 1971 73–4, 75; De Lane Lea Studio recordings 74–7; drugs, non-interest 133; early formations and gigs 55, 57–64; Elektra Records contract 127, 214, 218; EMI contracts 85–7, 128, 157–8, 206, 218; EMI's achievements advertisement 278–81; EP release 144; European festivals 171, 226–7; European tours/shows 95, 118–19, 144,

158–9, 165–6, 174, 181–2, 183, 206–7, 236, 238, 263, 264, 265–6, 268–9; fan's antics 117, 124–5, 135; *Flash Gordon* soundtrack 167, 170, 177, 181, 182–3; Freddie's death and funeral 330–2; Freddie's Tribute Concert 1992 336–41; Golden Rose Festival 231, 262; Groucho Marx meeting 142–3; *Highlander* soundtrack 256, 259; Hollywood Records deal 320; Hyde Park 1976 138–9; Imperial College gig 95–6, 97; Japan, tours and fanbase 109, 124–5, 135–6, 143, 167–8, 186, 212–13, 250, 372; *Jazz* pre-launch party 163–4; John Deacon's inclusion 70–3; John Lennon's death 183; Kempton Park races 140; Knebworth Park concert 269–71; Kutlawamong School patrons 239–40; lighting rigs 99–100, 116, 145, 152, 158, 162–3, 179, 206, 236, 264; Live Aid 247, 251–2, 253–4; logo design 83; management deals secured/severed 80–1, 126, 128, 133, 150–1; management restructure 157–8, 377; Mexico tour problems 198–200; Mike Reid interview 307; Mott The Hoople support tours 96–8, 111–13; Mountain Studios, owners 167, 354; Munich's significance 204; music press poll success 99, 102, 125, 133, 183–4; music press relations 98–9, 110, 118, 119; music press reviews *see* individual albums/singles; name origins 55, 56; New Zealand tour 247, 248; Peel Session 92; popularity polls 159, 299, 301, 345; pre-fame gigs 74, 77–8; private plane 152, 212; promotions, band controlled 93, 157–8; Queen Day event 376; radio broadcasts 86, 92, 94, 96, 126, 133, 141, 150, 157, 273–4; record deal search 78–9; Rock In Rio festival 243–5; solo artist collaborations 135, 205; songwriting rules 76–7, 304; South American tours 185–6, 187–93, 196–8; stage costumes/make-up 87–8, 105, 131–2, 174, 237; Sun City, concerts and controversies 235, 238–41, 258; synthesizers, use of 179–80; television broadcasts 91, 103–4, 119, 132, 133, 145, 182, 210, 212, 220, 237, 273–4, 312; touring pressures 271–2; tourism 136, 153, 159, 164, 186–7, 191, 248–9; UK, one-off shows 137–9; UK tours 106, 107–11, 116–18, 131, 132–3, 145, 159–60, 174–6, 182, 208–10, 236–7, 262–3, 266–8; unofficial publications 201; US tours 120–3, 134–5, 142, 152–5, 162–4, 165, 179, 180–1, 211, 212; Vatican gig idea 227; video single/EPs 273, 282, 312–13; Wimbledon concert rejected 169; World Record achievements 375
Queen + 377–8

Queen At The Beeb 313, 374
Queen At The Rainbow (film) 118, 135
Queen Fan Club: Brian's Freddie tribute 333; The Cross gigs 292, 322, 351; inception 98; Mary Austin's tribute 355; personnel change 136–7, 165, 261; special events 165, 303, 365–6, 369; video shoots 147–8, 225, 228, 291; weekend conventions 261, 285, 354–5, 367, 373–4
Queen – The Magic Years (film) 292, 298–9

'Radio Ga Ga' 225–6, 228
Ralphs, Mick 216
Rana, Victor 39
Ranson, Malcolm 316–17
Rare Live (video) 310, 334
Rarities CD 374
Rea, Chris 265
Reactions/Reaction, The 21–4
Reid, John 127–8, 129, 139, 150–1, 156, 249
Reid, Mike 220, 307
Reid, Terry 177
Reizner, Lou 32
'Resurrection' 354, 355–6
Rhodes, Zandra 105
Rice, Tim 299
Richard, Cliff 257, 262, 296
Richards, Bill 7, 9–10, 352
Richards, David 167, 246, 255, 259, 287, 354
Richardson, Peter 285–6
Richardson, Tony 220
'Ride The Wild Wind' 365
Robertson, Alan 174
Rock In Rio festival 243–5
Rock Therapy 373
Rodgers, Paul 329, 360, 362, 378
Roger Taylor Band, The 362, 364–5, 366
Ronson, Mick 314, 338, 361
Rose, Axl 327, 345, 353
Rose, Howard 134
Rossacher, Hannes 256–7, 292, 308, 310, 311, 313, 315, 324, 327, 328, 344, 350, 356
Rossi, Francis 370
Rota, Jose 185, 187–8, 191, 198
Royal Choral Society 205
Royal Philharmonic Orchestra 205
Rudge, Peter 127
Rush, Jennifer 363
Ryder, Maggie 338, 348

Sambora, Richie 303
Sanger, John 7–9

INDEX

Satriani, Joe 329
Savage, John 69
'Save Me' 174, 175, 176–7
'Scandal' 311
Screaming Lord Sutch 23
Sedlecká, Irena 376–7
'See What A Fool I've Been' 105
'Seven Seas Of Rhye' 103–5, 106, 113, 265
Sex Pistols 143
Seymour, Jane 257
Sharkey, Feargal 246
Sheer Heart Attack 114–15, 117, 120
'Sheer Heart Attack' 149
Sheffield, Barry 79–80
Sheffield, Norman 78, 79–80, 91, 95, 109, 119, 120, 122, 130
Sheraton-Smith, Tony 79
Shilling, Gertrude 175
Shirley, Edwin 119, 271
Shove It 294
Siddell, Dave 74–5
Sideway Look 246
Sigue Sigue Sputnik 305
Slash 353, 362
'Sleeping On The Sidewalk' 149
Smile 25–6, 27–35, 45, 212–13
Smith, Chris 31
Smith, Mel 195
Smith, Mick 'Miffer' 43, 45–6, 47–8, 50–1
Snell, John 20
Snowdon, Earl of 202
'Somebody To Love' 140, 141
'Son And Daughter' 90, 92, 96
'Soul Brother' 202, 374
Soundgarden 354
Sour Milk Sea 34, 52
Sparks 128–9
Spector, Phil 82
'Spread Your Wings' 150, 158
Squirer, Billy 205, 210, 231, 259
Staffell, Tim 7–9, 13, 15, 25–6, 28, 31, 32–4, 35, 42, 45, 48–9, 351
Stansfield, Lisa 338, 354
'Star Fleet' 223, 349
Star Fleet Project 218, 222, 223–4
Status Quo 253, 370, 371
'Staying Power' 204
Steinman, Jim 366–7
'Step On Me' 31, 32
Stevens, Shakin' 343–4
Stewart, Al 94
Stewart, Rod 154, 244

Stickells, Gerry 134, 139, 151, 152, 173–4, 175–6, 185, 191–2, 198, 199–200, 223, 243, 256, 300, 336–7
Stockley, Miriam 338, 348
Stoddart, Peter 70
'Stone Cold Crazy' 59, 312, 344
Stone, Mike 84
Straight Eight 181
Straker, Peter 160, 161, 278
Strange Frontier 216–17, 231, 232, 233
'Strange Frontier' 233
Strange Fruit label 313
Supercharge 139
Swimmer, Saul 203

Taylor, Chris (Crystal) 216, 219, 229, 294
Taylor, Clare 16, 20
Taylor, Elizabeth 341
Taylor, Felix Luther 177, 225
Taylor, Gavin 267, 273
Taylor, John 'Tupp' 43, 46–7, 50–1
Taylor, Michael 16, 19, 154, 317
Taylor, Roger Meddows: album cover designs 145, 147, 164; birth 16; birthday celebrations 160, 309; 'Breakthru' review 308; charity events/records 306, 309, 323, 357, 361, 365, 371; Cornish Tour 1971 73–4; Debbie Leng, relationship 290, 293–4, 315–16, 326, 364; degree courses 24, 73, 83; Dominique Beyrand, relationship 138, 140, 157, 171–2, 177, 217, 263, 293–4; early bands 18–24; education 16, 17, 24; fast cars and boats 171–2, 219, 220, 289; fatherhood 177, 263, 326, 364; father's death 317; flat sharing 45–7, 61; *Fun In Space* 180, 194–5; *Gettin Smile* release 212–13; guest artist, gigs 350, 361–2; guest artist, records 82, 88–9, 94, 129, 205, 212, 255, 343–4; hair bleach mishap 171; *Happiness?* 363–4; homes owned 84, 140–1, 205; home studio 140–1, 354; *Innuendo* party 323–4, 325; Kensington Market stall 44–5, 57–8, 61, 77; Monaco arrest 219; Mother Theresa 373; Mott The Hoople 111; MTV Awards 345; musical beginnings 17–19; production collaborations 177, 195, 246, 246–7, 254–5, 259, 305; promo videos 230, 232, 233, 278; Queen, early formations and gigs 57–64; radio broadcasts 299; record deal search 78; Rock School judge 261; The Roger Taylor Band 362, 364–5, 366; skiing 216; skinheads incident 48–9; Smile era 25–36; solo singles 143, 147, 232, 354, 361; sound experiments 109–10; *Strange Frontier* 216–17, 231, 232, 233; television broadcasts

220; tourism 213, 229; tour rehearsal 115–16; 'Under Pressure' session 196; *The Works* promotion 229; *see also* The Cross
Taylor, Rory 263
Taylor, Rufus Tiger 326
Taylor, Tiger Lily 364
Taylor, Winifred 16, 18, 19–20, 28, 73, 132, 154
Teardrop Explodes 209
'Tenement Funster' 144
'Teo Torriatte' 143, 167–8
Terence Higgins Trust 296, 333
Testi, Ken 43, 47, 49, 61, 78, 99
Tetzlaff, Veronica *see* Deacon, Veronica
'Thank God It's Christmas' 241
The Cross: albums 290, 294, 311, 316, 324, 326, 328; band formation 287–9; Electrola deal 314; fan club concerts 303, 322, 351; promotion 291–2; singles 293, 299, 313, 318, 319, 327–8; tours/shows 294–6, 297, 316, 328, 343, 356
The First Ten Years (book) 201
The Freddie Mercury Album 350
The Game 170, 179–80, 183–4, 204, 223
The Greatest History (promo CD) 368–9
The Great Pretender 350
'The Great Pretender' 277–8, 282, 350
The Hits CD 374
The Hotel New Hampshire 220–1, 223
'The Man From Manhattan' 126
The Master Sampler 360
The Miracle 304, 306, 307
'The Miracle' 312
The Miracle Video EP 312–13
'The Night Comes Down' 76
Theresa, Mother 373
'These Are The Days Of Our Lives' 327, 332, 333, 336, 339
'The Show Must Go On' 328, 336
The Works 222–3, 225, 227–8, 232, 242
The Works Video EP 238, 241, 246
Thin Lizzy 142
Thomas, Dave 84, 121
Thomas, Malcolm 305–6
Thompson, Chris 228, 303, 310, 338, 348
Thompson, Richard 7, 10, 13, 30, 47, 48, 49, 50, 52
'Tie Your Mother Down' 138, 142, 144, 322, 353
Todorow, Camy 255
'Too Much Love Will Kill You' 345, 355–6, 370–1

Townshend, Pete 104
Tremeloes, The 140
Trident: Queen deal 78–80, 81–2, 83–5, 90–3; withdrawal 119–20, 122–3, 125, 126–7, 150
Tyne Tees Television 209, 267
Tyrannosaurus Rex 14, 22, 28
Tyrell, Rob 52

Ultimate Collection 372
Ultimate Queen – The Box Set 370
'Under Pressure' 196, 202, 207, 212

Vai, Steve 329
Vance, Hilary 177
Van Halen, Eddie 217–18
Verson, Wally 181–2
Viola, General 190
Voss, Paul 328

Wakeman, Rick 328
Wallace, Eugene 129
Walsh, Steve 329
War Child 371
Wayne's World 342, 345, 352
'We Are The Champions' 147–9, 156, 324
'We Will Rock You' 148, 149, 150, 153, 156, 171
We Will Rock You (film) 203–4, 217, 219, 237–8
'White Queen' 144, 160
'Who Wants To Live Forever' 272–3, 305
Williams, Boris 52
Williams, David 68–9
Williams, T. R. 374–5
Wreckage 50–2

Yeadon, Terry 28, 31, 74
Yes 30, 64
Yoshiki 354, 361, 362, 364
'You Don't Fool Me' 372, 375
'You Had To Be There' 364
Young, Paul 357
Young, Richard 66–9
'You're My Best Friend' 136
'You Take My Breath Away' 138

Zakatek, Lenny 261
Zimmerman, Eric 354
Z'zi Labor 269